Comparative criticism

15

The Communities of Europe

Comparative criticism

An annual journal

The Communities of Europe

15

Edited by

E. S. SHAFFER

READER IN COMPARATIVE LITERATURE
SCHOOL OF MODERN LANGUAGES AND EUROPEAN HISTORY
UNIVERSITY OF EAST ANGLIA

 **CAMBRIDGE**
UNIVERSITY PRESS

CAMBRIDGE UNIVERSITY PRESS
Cambridge, New York, Melbourne, Madrid, Cape Town, Singapore,
São Paulo, Delhi, Dubai, Tokyo, Mexico City

Cambridge University Press
The Edinburgh Building, Cambridge CB2 8RU, UK

Published in the United States of America by Cambridge University Press, New York

www.cambridge.org
Information on this title: www.cambridge.org/9780521443517

© Cambridge University Press 1993

First published 1993

A catalogue record for this publication is available from the British Library

ISBN 978-0-521-44351-7 Hardback

CONTENTS

ILLUSTRATIONS

CONTRIBUTORS

HAZARD ADAMS is Byron W. and Alice L. Lockwood Professor of Humanities in the University of Washington at Seattle and Professor of English at the University of California at Irvine. His two most recent works are *The Book of Yeats's Poems* (1991) and *Antithetical Essays in Literary Criticism and Liberal Education* (1991), both from the University Press of Florida. He is working on *The Book of Yeats's Vision*.

SUSAN BASSNETT is Professor of Comparative Literature and Head of the Centre for British and Comparative Cultural Studies at the University of Warwick. She has translated widely from Spanish and Italian, and has written on translation studies, theatre studies, women's writing, and Latin American literature. Her next book, forthcoming 1993 from Blackwell, is *Comparative Literature in the 1990s*.

YVES BONNEFOY was born in Tours in 1923. He is generally considered to be one of the greatest living French poets. He was awarded the Prix Montaigne in 1980, the Grand Prix de Poésie from the Académie Française in 1981, the Prix Goncourt in 1987, and the Bennett Award (USA) in 1988. His poetic career spans nearly four decades, from his earliest volume, *Du mouvement et de l'immobilité de Douve* (1953) to his sixth and most recent, *Début et fin de la neige* (1991). Author of numerous books and essays on poetics and art history as well as translations into French of Shakespeare and Yeats, Bonnefoy has held the Chair of Comparative Studies in Poetics at the Collège de France since 1982.

MALCOLM BOWIE is Marshal Foch Professor of French Literature at the University of Oxford and Fellow of All Souls College. He is the author of studies of modern French poetry and fiction, and of the recent *Lacan* (Fontana, 1991). His *Psychoanalysis and the Future of Theory* is forthcoming from Blackwell.

ix

INGA-STINA EWBANK is Professor of English at the University of Leeds.
She has written widely on English Renaissance drama and
Scandinavian literature, and has translated plays by Strindberg and
Ibsen for performance by the RSC, the National Theatre and the
Peter Hall Company. She is completing *The Word in the Theatre*,
which compares Strindberg's and Ibsen's use of language with
Shakespeare's, and is also writing a book on Strindberg and the
Intimate Theatre.

JOHN FELSTINER is the author of *The Lies of Art: Max Beerbohm's Parody
and Caricature* and *Translating Neruda: The Way to Macchu Picchu*
(Stanford University Press, 1980). He has written on Paul Celan for
numerous journals and his new book *Paul Celan and the Strain of
Jewishness* will be published by Yale University Press. He is Professor
of English at Stanford University.

HAROLD FISCH is Emeritus Professor of English at Bar-Ilan University
in Israel. He is the author of *Jerusalem and Albion* (Routledge,
1964), and more recently *A Remembered Future: A Study in Literary
Mythology* (1984) and *Poetry with a Purpose: Biblical Poetics and
Interpretation* (1988), both published by Indiana University Press. He
is currently working on a study of biblical patterns in the novel and
a comparative study of *King Lear*, *Samson Agonistes* and Blake's
Milton from the angle of biblical hermeneutics.

DOUWE FOKKEMA is Professor of Comparative Literature and Director of
the Research Institute for History of Culture, Utrecht University.
Apart from publications on Chinese literature, semiotics, modernism
and postmodernism, he wrote, together with Elrud Ibsch, *Theories of
Literature in the Twentieth Century* (1977), *Modernist Conjectures: A
Mainstream in European Literature* (1988) and *Literatuurwetenschap
en cultuuroverdracht* (1992). His present research is concerned with
cultural participation and innovation of cultural conventions.

ARMIN PAUL FRANK is Professor of English (North American Literature)
at Göttingen, and founding director of Sonderforschungsbereich 309,
a nationally funded centre for comparative research in literary
translation. He is co-editor of *Göttinger Beiträge zur Internationalen
Übersetzungsforschung* (Berlin: Erich Schmidt Verlag). He has
recently edited, with Ulrich Mölk, *Frühe Formen mehrperspektivischen
Erzählens von der Edda bis Flaubert: Ein Problemaufriss* (Berlin:
Schmidt, 1991). The present paper is taken from a book of
American–British literary comparisons, in preparation under the
working title 'Transatlantic Deviating Responses'.

HENRY GIFFORD is Emeritus Professor of English at the University of Bristol. His publications include *Pasternak: A Critical Study* (Cambridge University Press, 1977; reissued in 1991 by Bristol Classical Press), and *Poetry in a Divided World* (1986; text of the Clark Lectures for 1985).

GARY HANDWERK is Associate Professor of English and Comparative Literature at the University of Washington, Seattle. Author of *Irony and Ethics in Narrative* (Yale University Press, 1985), he has published articles on Joyce, Beckett, Meredith, Friedrich Schlegal and Godwin. He is presently at work on a critical study of Romantic ideas of historicity and narrative.

MALCOLM V. JONES is Professor of Slavonic Studies at the University of Nottingham. He has published extensively on Dostoevsky, and his most recent book is *Dostoevsky after Bakhtin* (Cambridge University Press, 1990). A recent article on Bakhtin and the Gospels will appear in *Mikhail Bakhtin and the Study of Culture*, edited by Anna Tavis and due to be published by E. M. Sharpe in 1994. He is presently interested in Russian critical theory and religious thought.

MARZELL KAY was born in 1927 in Vienna and emigrated with his family to Britain in September 1938 following the German annexation. He studied at Birmingham and now lives in Israel. He has written on Jewish relations with the nations of the desert and the frontier of Palestine in the Hellenistic and Roman eras, and on the relation between the Italian occupation authorities and the Jews of Vichy and occupied France. He is active in the Israel Translators' Association and the Fédération Internationale des Traducteurs, Paris.

RICHARD KING is Associate Professor of Chinese at the University of Victoria in British Columbia. He is the author of several articles on contemporary Chinese fiction, especially by women, and has recently completed a volume of translations from the work of the Shanghai writer, Zhu Lin. Current projects include a study of rhetoric, melodrama and fiction in the Cultural Revolution and a translation of Gu Hua's gulag novel, *The Scholars' Garden*.

YITZHAK OREN is the pen name of Itshak Nadel. Nadel was born in Siberia to Russian-Jewish parents in 1917, grew up mainly in China, and moved to Palestine in 1936 to read literature, history and philosophy at the Hebrew University of Jerusalem. Since the 1940s he has been a major figure in Hebrew literary life, with contributions to the literary press and periodicals, and translations of major Russian literary works into Hebrew, as well as his own original works. Work

available in English includes *The Imaginary Number: Short Stories*
(Berkeley, CA: Benmir Press, 1986). He was awarded the Israeli
Prime Minister's Prize for literature in 1978 and the Newman Prize
for Literature in 1989.

JONATHAN O. PEASE is Associate Professor of Chinese at Portland State
University in Oregon. Recently he has been working on Chinese
classical poetry, particularly that of the Northern Sung and Five
Dynasties. Work in progress includes a book-length study of Wang
An-shih's later poems, and a bilingual anthology of Chinese poetry.
Wang An-kuo's Jade Rewards and Millet Dream is forthcoming from
the American Oriental Society.

J. M. RITCHIE is Emeritus Professor of German at the University of
Aberdeen, and Director for the Research Centre for Germans and
Austrians in Exile in Great Britain at King's College, Aberdeen. He
is the author of *German Literature under National Socialism*
(Beckenham: Croom Helm, 1983), is presently the holder of a
Leverhulme fellowship, and is working on an extensive study of exile
in Great Britain.

LISA SAPINKOPF's translations of Bonnefoy and other authors have
appeared in nearly fifty journals in the United States, Canada and
Britain. She has collaborated with Bonnefoy, whom she met while an
undergraduate at the University of California at Santa Cruz. She has
recently published her translation of his most recent volume,
Beginning and End of Snow (QRL Poetry Series, 1992) and *Clay and
Star – Contemporary Bulgarian Poets* (Milkweed Editions, 1992). She
has won the American Translators Association Prize, the Fernando
Pessoa Portuguese Translation Prize, the Quarterly Review of
Literature Poetry Prize, the Columbia Translation Center Award and
the Robert Fitzgerald Translation Prize.

LIU SOLA was born in China in 1955, and came to England in 1988. She
is well known in China for the popular and controversial stories she
wrote there between 1985 and 1988. Her novel *Chaos and All That*
(*Hundun jia li-ger-leng*), from which the two translated excerpts in
this volume are taken, was published by Breakthrough Press of Hong
Kong in 1991.

ACKNOWLEDGEMENTS

We wish to thank the Strahov Library in Prague for permission to reproduce the 'Symbolic Map of Europe as a Virgin'. Grateful thanks also to Friends of Hereford Cathedral for permission to reprint an illustration of a section of the Mappa Mundi; to the *Independent on Sunday* for permission to reproduce a section of their map 'The New Europe 1992'; to the National Gallery of Scotland for permission to reproduce Tiepolo's *The Finding of Moses*; to Faber and Faber Ltd for permission to reprint an illustration from Charles Rosen's *The Classical Style* (1971).

Acknowledgement is made to Deutsche Verlags-Anstalt GmbH for permission to publish translations of poems in Paul Celan's *Mohn und Gedächtnis* (1952) and *Von Schwelle zu Schwelle* (1955); to S. Fischer Verlag GmbH for permission to publish translations of poems in Paul Celan's *Sprachgitter* (1959) and *Die Niemandsrose* (1963); and to Suhrkamp Verlag for permission to publish translations of poems in Paul Celan's *Atemwende* (1967), *Fadensonnen* (1968) and *Zeitgehöft* (1976).

We wish to thank Editorial Losada of Argentina for permission to publish translations of poems from Pablo Neruda's *Obras Completas*.

We are grateful to Liu Sola for permission to publish translations of excerpts from her novel *Hundun jia li-ger-leng* (*Chaos and All That*); to Yitzhak Oren for permission to publish the translation from the Hebrew of 'Andartat ha-Tehiya' ('A monument to a new life'), first published in Tel Aviv by *Keshet*, 15 (1962); and to Yves Bonnefoy, who has kindly granted permission to publish translations of poems from *Ce qui fut sans lumière*.

We should also like to thank Ms Wu Yeen-mei, at the East Asia Library, University of Washington, for her help in obtaining the illustration for Wang Ling's *I Dreamed of Locusts*. Thanks also to Eva Kushner at Victoria University, Toronto and Shawn Winsor at the Northrop Frye Centre in Toronto for providing us with a photograph of Northrop Frye.

A Symbolic Map of Europe as a Virgin

Comparative Criticism 15, pp. xv–xxiv. Copyright © 1993 Cambridge University Press

EDITOR'S INTRODUCTION

Comparative Literature in Britain and Europe

In volume 1 of this journal, published in 1979, we considered the history of the discipline of Comparative Literature in this country and its state at the time the journal was inaugurated. The picture then was one of a subject that had long existed and been represented by distinguished practitioners in this country, yet one which had only recently, since the founding of the 'new universities' in 1963 in the wake of the Robbins Report calling for university expansion and modernization, begun to take on institutional presence. Its historical existence was amply proven, and even the name itself had long been in evidence. Matthew Arnold spoke of the 'comparative literatures' in 1848, declaring that attention to them over the previous half century showed 'that England is in a certain sense far behind the continent'. The first book entitled *Comparative Literature* was published by H. M. Posnett in 1886 in 'The International Scientific Series', devoted to post-Darwinian developments in all the sciences, of which comparative literature aspired to be one, employing the 'historical method' described by J. S. Mill in his *Logic*. (For an account of the probing early work on the method of comparative literature, see my Introduction to volume 2 (1980), 'The "Scientific" Pretensions of Comparative Literature').

But the organization of comparative literature in Britain in institutional terms – the establishment of degree programmes, chairs, departments, and journals – had lagged behind Europe and North America. (See 'Comparative Literature in Britain: organization', in *Yearbook of General and Comparative Literature*, 30 (1982).) Chairs had been established in Europe from 1871, and in North America from the first decade of the twentieth century. Without these appurtenances and material proofs the subject seemed shadowy. The first appointment in this country was that of Dr Glyn Tegai Hughes as Lecturer in Comparative Literary Studies in Manchester in 1953, with the support of the distinguished medievalist and Professor of French, Eugène Vinaver. In 1963 a number of degree courses and departments had sprung into being in a climate of enthusiasm for a more open university system, including a wider range of subjects and fresh interdisciplinary pursuits. At Essex University, a Department of Literature was formed within a School of Comparative Studies, with Donald Davie as Professor of Literature. Sussex University and the University of East Anglia formed Schools of European Studies and English and American Studies; at East Anglia, J. W. McFarlane was appointed Professor of European Literature; at Sussex, A. K. Thorlby was appointed as the first Professor of Comparative Literature in 1967. The home 'fields' of these appointees were diverse: in the case of Hughes and Thorlby, German Romanticism; in the case of Davie, English contemporary American, and Russian, poetry; in the case of McFarlane, Norwegian and drama (he was the translator of Ibsen's plays for the Oxford Ibsen). At the time of writing the introduction to volume 1 there were three professors of Comparative Literature, one at Sussex, two at East Anglia. The only undergraduate course leading to a B.A. in Comparative Literature was offered at East Anglia, where one or two modern foreign languages were studied to Honours level in conjunction with English and comparative literature; the Universities of Essex, Sussex, Warwick (with its Department of English and Comparative Literature), and York (with its Department of English and Related Literatures) had undergraduate programmes with strong comparative elements, although with less language work.

At post-graduate level, which was often considered most appropriate for comparative work, there were M.A.s in Comparative Literature at East Anglia, Manchester, and Sussex; at Essex, there were M.A.s in Literary Translation and in the Sociology of Literature; at Warwick, a Graduate School of Comparative Literature. At Oxford there was a B.Phil. in General and Comparative Literature.

If now we raise our heads above the parapet to survey what has happened to our subject in the years since volume 1, we may do so with some trepidation. There has been a major crisis in the universities, and the years since 1981 have been siege years. Small departments or subject areas in interdisciplinary subjects have come under particular fire. The 'cuts' have caused widespread retrenchment and many 'voluntary' redundancies, as well as considerable administrative regrouping. The ratcheting down of funding has been inescapable, and continued throughout the government's U-turn in the mid-eighties from a policy of reduction in size of student intake to a sudden demand for an increase in student numbers, with still less funding. The two Research

Assessments that have taken place on a national scale have addressed themselves to returns on research from a pre-established list of subject areas; comparative literature has never figured in the list of subjects assessed. Reporting under other heads in part reflects the fear of institutions to appear to have any but large, traditional subject groupings with professorial or (in the jargon of the eighties) 'managerial' heads. The returns of comparatists have been included in other units' returns, under the headings of the individual language departments or of European Studies. Comparative Literature in general was forced – or chose – to parade under other banners.

Given these parlous circumstances, we may be surprised less by what has been lost than by how much remains, and how much has been added.

At the undergraduate level, most of the comparative literature courses just named remain. At East Anglia, despite administrative reshuffles and redeployments, and the loss of one of the chairs, the degree programme is still intact, and has been joined by a joint degree in Comparative Literature and Philosophy (reflecting the strength of literature and philosophy combinations in several institutions), and in Literature and Art History, which shares its first-semester course with Comparative Literature. At Essex, an undergraduate Minor in Translation is now offered. At Glasgow, a first-year course has been devised that is largely comparative in nature, including classics in translation and an interesting selection of non-canonical texts.

At the post-graduate level, the M.A. in Comparative Literature at UEA, founded in 1974, remains (joined from 1993 by an M.A. in Translation Studies, and both strengthened by the presence of the British Centre for Translation Studies); at Essex the M.A. in Literature Translation remains and the M.A. in Sociology of Literature is now the M.A. in Cross-Cultural Studies); and at Warwick, the Graduate School of Comparative Literature has become the Graduate School of Comparative Literature and British Cultural Studies, with a professorial head, Susan Bassnett. There have been considerable alterations, some through 'natural wastage' (as the unhappy phrase has it), some through political interventions: the M.A. at Manchester and that at Sussex have been discontinued, the latter through the retirement of A. K. Thorlby. At Manchester the Department of Comparative Literary Studies was disestablished in 1988, and members of it moved into the French Department. Given the pioneering role of the University of Manchester in the establishment of comparative literary studies in Britain, the loss of the Department of Comparative Literature Studies and most of its undergraduate offerings, as well as of the M.A., is especially saddening; but one active member remains, Penny Brown, with strong interests in Spanish and women's studies, although now administratively under the aegis of French Department. Two new M.A. programmes have been established, in contemporary poetry and in fiction, with a stress on creative writing; some teaching in the European novel remains. At Oxford, the B.Phil. in General and Comparative Literature disappeared when all B.Phil. degrees were abolished in favour of the more familiar M.Phil.; there is now an M.Phil. in European Literature.

If some have been lost, new and enterprising post-graduate degrees have been founded: the M.Sc. in Comparative Literature at Edinburgh in 1982, based on the excellent range of modern languages (strengthened by a new Scandinavian Department, after the closure of several Scandinavian Departments in other parts of the country); and the further development of Comparative Literature at Kent at post-graduate level with strong links to communications and image studies. (See the account by Bernard Sharratt in *Comparative Criticism* 11, 'Communications and image studies: notes after Raymond Williams'.) At Queen Mary and Westfield College in London an M.A. in European Studies was set up; Malcolm Bowie, Professor of French, set up the Institute of Romance Studies in parallel with the long-established Institute of Germanic Studies, but with a programme more adventurously comparative and interdisciplinary than its name indicates. Bowie moved to Oxford as Marshal Foch Professor of French in 1992, but the M.A. and the Institute continue.

In surveying this scene after fifteen years, thirteen of them under severe financial and political pressure, we can take some satisfaction in the fact that despite losses that we feel keenly, on balance comparative literary studies are alive and well in Britain, and even in some respects strengthened. The crisis led to a good deal of drawing in of horns, but also to innovation under pressure, and to the adoption, sometimes in rapid succession, of new courses and practices that may have taken much longer to be tested and to establish themselves in normal times.

Interdisciplinary courses in the visual arts, film, and media studies have become more common. Cultural studies have been an area of growth. In the United States, where much emphasis has been placed on 'political correctness', cultural studies have often acted to curtail or call into question traditional comparative literary studies, which are sometimes regarded as dominated by a 'canon' of 'great names' largely white, European, and male; in Britain cultural studies have for the most part proved an ally and a means of survival. This may be because awareness and conscious study of ethnic and other minority cultures was long overdue. There can be little doubt either that the growing awareness of the European Community in this country has improved the position of a wide range of courses related to area studies and to broader cultural and social programmes, including languages, in many combinations.

The very recent abolition of the binary system in higher education, that is, the divide between universities on the one hand and polytechnics and colleges of higher and further education on the other, and the wholesale promotion of polytechnics to university status, cannot yet be assessed in its effect on comparative literature. There will clearly be a great deal of activity, some of it certainly in the subject areas we have named that are congenial to polytechnics but that have shown themselves generally popular options in the universities in recent years. There are some signs that comparative literature will be seen as one way forward in these new universities, as it was in the new universities of the 1960s.

One heading under which comparative literature is flourishing is that of 'Eng. Lit.' understood in a vastly expanded way. English is now a 'World Language', and knows no bounds. Comparatists must always welcome their subject being taken up by others who earlier resisted it, even while then having to struggle to maintain it as an institutional division known as 'Comparative Literature'. The more generally acceptable its aims, methods and perspectives become, the more unwilling others are to acknowledge it as a separate discipline. Comparatists are accustomed to this process, and view it with some irony. But it is a familiar phenomenon in intellectual and institutional history and an important mode of survival, indeed of expansion.

If we have survived these years, there is no cause for complacency. The position of the university sector has worsened in crucial ways: in funding and salaries, in the independence of research, and in all the processes, now much curtailed, that used to be known as academic freedom. (See my introduction to volume 11 (1989), 'The Future of the Disciplines', and Wolf Lepenies' essay in that volume, with its keen insights into the intense difficulties of maintaining 'academic freedom' in universities subject to political and economic control.) Yet the events of this period may have the salutary effect of reminding us that our belief that we possessed and enjoyed academic freedom was in many ways an illusion, and that like all freedoms it is an ideal that requires constant struggle to assert and defend. Within this situation it is not only for 'comparative literature' that we are concerned but the humanities as a whole, whose position has slipped so far below that of the sciences. Nor is it enough to defend the humanities as against the sciences. The sciences themselves have been cut to the bone, threatening Britain's international role in scientific research, and eroding the industrial base. Any report at this juncture on any one subject or discipline is merely an 'interim report', and all of them are in need of our constant support.

During this difficult period in Britain the British Comparative Literature Association, founded in 1975 at the first Conference on Comparative Literature to be held in Britain, at the University of East Anglia, Norwich, has maintained the discipline as best it could, through a series of congresses and workshops, translation competitions, and publications. *Comparative Criticism* has attempted create and maintain an international profile for the subject as practised in Britain. A second journal and newsletter, *New Comparison*, has attempted to give houseroom to members.

Since Britain joined the International Comparative Literature Association in 1977, the ICLA has continued to add to the number of national associations and individual members affiliated to it. New national associations have set up their own journals; we have noted the associations and journals in Switzerland, Italy, Portugal, and in Chinese-speaking areas. Reviews of successive volumes of the *Comparative History of European Literature*, including Stephen Bann's review of the volumes on *The Avant-garde* (in our volume 7), and Gary Handwerk's of *Romantic Irony* (in the present volume). The ICLA Committee on Literary Theory has been particularly active since its founding in 1986, holding annual colloquia since 1988. These activities represent international cooperation, often fraught with difficulties and real disagreements about the nature and methods of literary history, which continued to permit representation of the countries of Eastern Europe through the Cold War period that ended in 1989.

Our contributors in this volume remind us further that 'the communities of Europe' which must make up the 'European Community' are constantly regrouping and redefining themselves, often in extreme conditions of war, exploration, exile and emigration, and in less extreme forms of dissension and disunity. Henry Gifford (one of the *doyens* of our subject in this country, and the author of *Comparative Literature*, which addressed itself crucially to the nature of modernist poetry) writes on the rôle of writers in culture. J. M. Ritchie describes the effects on twentieth-century European writers of displacement from their communities and alienation from their languages. Susan Bassnett considers the shifting boundaries of Europe, the fables that still lurk at its fringes – 'here be monsters' – even in the educated imagination. The interaction of European culture with the non-European is explored in Armin Paul Frank's depiction of dialogue between Europe and North America. Malcolm Bowie takes us deeper into the problems of the relations between the disciplines, in this case, psychoanalysis and the visual arts, suggesting some new possibilities, and Harold Fisch takes us into the complexities of interpretation itself as a mode of community. Hazard Adams, the distinguished American critic, remembers the impact of Northrop Frye, a member of the Board of this journal whose death we mourn, on his own and subsequent generations of humanists. Douwe Fokkema scrutinizes recent discussions of the 'canon'. Educational systems and particular disciplines within them – and their journals – can be no exception to, indeed should present a central model for, the need to rethink and reform, to carry out continuing internal reviews, not merely to respond to external pressures.

Part II, 'Literature, Translation, and Performance', is in this volume given over to the winning entries in the British Comparative Literature Translation competition of 1991, which was divided into several sections. For this year, in honour of the European Community, prizes were offered for translations from any languages used in the Community. Specialist readers and judges selected the fine contribution by John Felstiner, his translations from the Spanish of Pablo Neruda – a Latin American poet, but writing in Spanish, a language of the EC; all manuscripts were anonymous, so we were pleasantly surprised to discover that the winner of the first prize was a translator already well known for his work. Second prize went to Lisa Sapinkopf for her versions of Yves Bonnefoy, certainly one of the finest poets (and translators from the English) in the European Community. A number of further commendations were made; and several of these contributions will appear in later volumes. In the entries for the Special Prizes, there were a gratifying number of outstanding translations. In Chinese, Richard King's powerful and resourceful rendering of Liu Sola's politically and linguistically challenging novel *Chaos and all that* about the harrowing recruitment of children during the Cultural Revolution won the first prize, with Jonathan Pease's rendering of a classic Chinese poetic text by Wang Ling as second prize. In the category of Hebrew, Yiddish, or writing in any language on a Jewish theme, the range was startlingly wide, from the Hebrew classics to the modern Hebrew of the first prize-winner, Marzell Kay, the translator of the well-known Israeli writer Yitzhak Oren, and the great German-Jewish poet Paul Celan, writing in German, translated by John Felstiner, who won second prize in this category. No prizes were awarded this year in the categories of Swedish or of Persian.

We are grateful to the generous donors of the Special Prizes: the K. P. Tin Foundation, Hong Kong; the Spiro Institute, London, who have established this prize in honour of Hannah and Jacob Lieberman; the Anglo-Swedish Literary Foundation and the Swedish Embassy, London; and the Foundation for Iranian Studies.

The results of the 1992 Translation Competition will be published in volume 16. The next Translation Competition, for which the deadline for entries is 15 December 1993, will again be an open competition, not confined to EC languages. The following Special Prizes will also be available: for translation from the Swedish; from the Persian; and from Hebrew, Yiddish, or from any language on a Jewish theme. The prizes in each case will be £350 for first prize, £150 for second prize, and will carry with them as before publication in *Comparative Criticism*. Commended entries may be published. Prize-winners and other entrants may qualify for bursaries at the British Centre for Literary Translation at the University of East Anglia to support specific translation projects.

Inquiries and requests for entry forms for the next BCLA Translation Competition (*deadline* 15 December 1993: please note change of deadline) should be directed to Dr Nicholas Crowe, St John's College, Oxford University, Oxford OX1 3JP. The judges of the competition are: Edwin Morgan, the well-known Scottish poet; Daniel Weissbort, poet, translator, and editor of *Poetry in Translation*; Arthur Terry, translator from the Catalan, and formerly director of the M.A. in Literary Translation at the University of Essex; Peter France, Professor of French at Edinburgh University, and noted translator from French, Russian, and Chuvash; and Elinor Shaffer, *ex officio* as editor of *Comparative Criticism*.

The BCLA was host to the International Comparative Literature Association Literary Theory Colloquium, on the topic of 'The Third Culture: Literature and Science', held at the Institute of Romance Studies at London University 13–17 April 1993; this was the sixth annual Literary Theory Colloquium, and will be published by DeGruyter as a volume in the series 'European Culture'.

The BCLA held a conference at the University of Essex on 2–3 July

1993 on 'Word in Time': on Poetry, Narrative, Translation, in honour of Arthur Terry, retiring president of the Association and Professor in the Department of Literature, specializing in Hispanic literature.

The next triennial Congress of the International Comparative Literature Association will be held at Edmonton, Alberta, Canada in August 1994.

There is a call for papers for a Special Issue on 'Postcolonial Literatures' of the *Canadian Review of Comparative Literature*, eds. Steven Tötösy and Sneja Gunew, the Research Institute for Comparative Literature, University of Alberta, Edmonton, Alberta, Canada T6G 2E6.

Submissions of articles, translations, and original writing in English for volumes 17, 18 and 19 are welcome. The theme of volume 16 will be 'Revolutions and censorship'; we shall be concerned with writing affected by censorship whether official or accidental, and with responses to it such as self-censorship and conversion, whether forced or voluntary, imprisonment and displacement by exile or death. Joyce's famous phrase enjoining 'silence, cunning and exile' on the writer who would be the conscience of his race has had to be the watchword of many writers in our times. This theme has been broached in earlier volumes, for example, in Lesley Milne's examination of the censored and uncensored versions of Bulgakov in volume 14, and in this volume in Malcolm V. Jones's review of the gradual reconstruction of Mikhail Bakhtin's work from the effective obscurity of his inner exile in Russia; but it proved too large and challenging to contain merely as an aspect of 'The Communities of Europe'. J. D. Adler, Professor of German at Queen Mary and Westfield College, London, will be collaborating editor.

The theme of volume 18 will be 'Walter Pater and the culture of the *fin-de-siècle*'; we are glad to welcome back as collaborating editor Stephen Bann, Professor of Cultural History at the University of Kent, who collaborated on previous volumes, 3 and 11. This volume marks a new departure, as we have not hitherto included the name of any individual in our title; but it seems highly appropriate, as we approach the millennium, to engage with the figure who perhaps more than any other embodies the notion of the English *fin-de-siècle* of the last century. A conference will be held round this topic at Kent in July 1994.

Volume 19 will be on the topic of 'Literary devolution: writing now in Scotland, Ireland, Wales, and England'. It will be in conjunction with the Triennial Congress of the British Comparative Literature

Association, to be held in Edinburgh in July 1995, which will make an occasion for regional voices to be heard. For this volume we would welcome original writing in any language or dialect now or ever in use in Great Britain. Current translations from past or present writing are also welcome. We hope to have an extensive selection of current writing, as well as essays dealing with the historical and contemporary significance of 'devolution' in the arts.

Guidelines for contributors are available on request, containing information on house style, illustrations, permissions, and copyright. The annual deadline for submission of manuscripts (two copies) is 1 March of the year preceding publication. All correspondence should be addressed to the Editor, *Comparative Criticism*, Cambridge University Press, The Edinburgh Building, Shaftesbury Road, Cambridge CB2 2RU.

E. S. Shaffer

PART I
The communities of Europe

Comparative Criticism 15, pp. 3–18. Copyright © 1993 Cambridge University Press

On recognition and renewal

HENRY GIFFORD

In all the moral confusion of Europe in the twentieth century its greatest poets may turn out to have been the surest guides. This might seem a singularly old-fashioned statement. Matthew Arnold believed that poetry would become for humanity 'an ever surer and surer stay',[1] and the idea evokes a now faded image – the high-minded reader subjecting to intelligent perusal the works of the poet-sages ancient and modern. 'The eternal note of sadness...Sophocles long ago / Heard it on the Aegean...' This dignifies our disquiet, and 'Dover Beach', from which the lines come, is one of Arnold's successes in poetry. Yet they bear out what Eliot said about his being 'academic poetry in the best sense; the best fruit which can issue from the promise shown by the prize-poem'.[2] Such modern poets as I shall discuss would never have qualified for the facile triumph of a prize-poem. They had to educate their readers out of that 'educated' taste on which the latter prided themselves. I am not contending that the poet is primarily a teacher. If in any sense he ministers to our spiritual or moral sickness, that is only because he obeys the injunction, 'Physician, heal thyself.'

What then is the ground for asserting that the poetry of a few men and women has been of such central importance to the age beginning in the second decade of this century? Europe some eighty years ago saw itself as the guardian of civilization, the world's natural presiding genius. Nothing could be more poignant than Henry James's letter to another novelist, Rhoda Broughton, on 10 August 1914, six days into the First World War:

Black and hideous to me is the tragedy that gathers, and I'm sick beyond cure to have lived on to see it. You and I, the ornaments of our generation, should have been spared this wreck of our belief that through the long years we had seen civilization grow and the worst become impossible. The tide that bore us along was then all the while moving to *this* as its grand Niagara...It seems to me to *undo* everything, everything that was ours, in the most horrible retroactive way...[3]

'Ornaments of our generation' – the innocent vanity sounds rather absurd to a time that has swept its own mantelpiece bare. The full cadences of his letter bespeak a bygone leisure and calm – even though James had before this confessed to 'a sense of disaster'. The worst is now possible, everywhere. Cavafy only a year later published a strangely prophetic poem to be confirmed by the new order of things, which indeed was merely a very old one restored. The Theodotus of its title was the time-server who brought to Julius Caesar the head of his opponent Pompey on a bloodstained dish. It ends with a warning:

> And don't feel complacently that in your life
> circumscribed, ordered and prosaic
> such spectacular and dreadful things do not exist.
> Perhaps at this very time into a neighbour's
> well-regulated house there enters –
> invisible, insubstantial – Theodotus
> bearing just such a ghastly head.[4]

George Seferis commented on this poem: 'Horror is not the exclusive privilege of Caesar, or of the poet.' The ghastly head is 'the symbol of everyday horror in our own ordered life'.[5] Fifty years after Cavafy's poem he wrote one of his own that reflects the savage civil war in Greece, when it had been cleared of the Nazis:

> Who was it heard at noon
> the dagger being whetted on the stone?
> What horseman came
> with tinder and torch?
> Everybody washes his hands
> and refreshes them.
> And who disembowelled
> the woman, the infant and the house?
> No one is guilty, not a trace.
> Who went away
> with clatter of hooves on the paving stones?
> They have expunged their eyes, blind.
> No witnesses remain for anything.[6]

In that poem is recorded the final degradation of the age we live in, and it is happening in Europe. Was it to this that the tide had been moving, through all the confident and vainglorious years of the European past?

Recognition and renewal sum up the particular duties of the poet in Europe, now and always. He has at his disposal the long memory of the European consciousness, surely unique in the history of civilizations. There is in our own history an element of rare good fortune, at least on the spiritual and cultural plane. Europe would seem to have been destined for unity in diversity. The three main language groups of the continent – Romance, Germanic and Slavonic – share the same origins and are permeable by one another. Europe's boundaries are roughly coextensive with those of Christendom before the fall of Constantinople, and all through the Western half of the continent, until the late seventeenth century, Latin was current as the language in which literate men could freely move in a common intellectual realm. The Eastern Church did not impose Greek on the liturgy in its provinces, as Latin had been imposed in the Roman obedience. Thus the Russians failed to participate in the Renaissance, and so too did the Greeks, although it was refugee scholars from Byzantium who started the process. Eliot wrote in 1951: 'We are all, so far as we inherit the civilisation of Europe, still citizens of the Roman empire...'[7] This view was rightly challenged by Seferis. Nonetheless, from Eliot he learned to appreciate Dante as 'a teacher, a master of the craft' who remained that for him throughout his life.[8]

By the beginning of this century the poets of Western and Eastern Europe had come virtually to share the same culture. As Czeslaw Milosz has written, young men like himself, from the so-called 'blank spots on the map', flocked to Paris, marvelling at 'the perfect stability and the continuity of the life in *la ville lumière*'. Later he would have to acknowledge

There is no capital of the world, neither here nor anywhere else...[9]

The lights of Paris went out in 1940. All that we have today, as Auden put it in his poem 'September 1, 1939', are those scattered 'ironic points of light' that 'flash out wherever the Just / Exchange their messages'. His identification of the Just (spelt with a capital letter) may sound a trifle complacent, and to be ironic is not the whole of a poet's witness. More important perhaps, and more closely bearing on the role of the poet, is the exchanging of messages. The breakdown of civilized life in Europe, should that eventually come, would not destroy this communication between 'the Just', if we may interpret that term as meaning the best poetic minds of the age.

But how can one be sure of this? Almost the only certainty in these times is that all predictions about the shape of things to come are untrustworthy. Yet there seems no reason for despair when it is possible to show that in the very recent past, and under conditions all but intolerable, such communication had still not been suppressed. Osip Mandelstam, whom the Russian poet of today nearest to him in sympathies, Joseph Brodsky, has called 'the child of civilisation',[10] is here the exemplary case. It is not a matter only of his convictions, as a European with responsibilities towards all that Europe means, but what greatly enhances his achievement is that he was compelled to act on the central stage of our time. The twentieth century has been described in various ways. This has been a time, according to one view, in which Europeans, without realizing it, have thought in German, under the spell of Nietzsche or Marx, of Freud or Jung, or finally perhaps of Kafka. Alternatively, we may have shared with the rest of the world the stresses of adapting to the American century. But the inescapable fact is that for seventy-five years Europe has been hypnotized by events in Russia. The vast territories of what chose to be called the Soviet Union – though it was a union only by fiat, and the Soviets had no real say in its government – served as the proving ground of tendencies which had been building up in Europe ever more formidably since the Enlightenment. Russia was not the expected theatre for their demonstration in practice. Nor could Mandelstam have foreseen his own part as a main witness and judge of these events. But poetry has always been nourished by the unforeseen. In that way it is undoubtedly true to life.

Had he not perished in a concentration camp, probably at the end of 1938, Mandelstam would have been a prime target for Stalin's campaign of the late 1940s against 'cosmopolitanism'. He is a poet of extraordinarily wide culture, even among the Russian poets, his contemporaries. Mandelstam had the good fortune to attend the Tenishev School in Petersburg, almost certainly the best then in Russia. This gave him a good classical background, though knowledge of Greek came to him later as a personal discovery. He studied Old French at Heidelberg, and at the Sorbonne more briefly; his verse renderings of fragments from the twelfth century *Vie d'Alexis*, for example, are faithful to the medieval spirit; his earliest essay was a penetrating study of Villon. Later he would become as much devoted to Dante as any twentieth-century poet, including Eliot. Mandelstam indeed felt it was necessary for him to reject the allures of Tasso and Ariosto. Their mellifluous tones delighted him, but he was afraid that to follow them would compromise his integrity as a Russian poet.

The Acmeist movement, headed by Nikolay Gumilyov, Akhmatova's first husband, in which Akhmatova herself and Mandelstam were the outstanding participants, remained entirely a Petersburg school. Architecture, not music, was the analogue it sought for poetry, and the architecture of the city, the work mainly of Italian masters, set it apart from the limitless Russian hinterland. Mandelstam's first book of poetry was entitled *Stone*, and three of its most characteristic poems are sonnets that describe buildings: Hagia Sophia, Notre Dame, and the Admiralty in Petersburg. The geographical spread is representative of his interests. He delights in the craftsman's skill that fashioned these buildings, but though they will outlive the generations he does not see them as monuments. An essay of this time (1913), 'The Morning of Acmeism', defines the architecture of Notre Dame as 'a festival of physiology', Dionysiac in its revelling. Mandelstam values the Middle Ages because, along with their rationality and mysticism, they reveal 'a sense of the world as a living equilibrium'.[11] The classical poetry of the Acmeists, and of Mandelstam in particular, does not deal in monuments. He has nothing in common with Hérédia, he is not like Gautier a worker in 'marble, onyx, enamel', though Gautier was an acclaimed master of the Acmeists. The essential quality of Mandelstam's imagination is the daring behind the regular forms, the inner dynamism that he admired above all in Dante.

So far I have been able to avoid reference to one of Mandelstam's most famous pronouncements. He had been asked, before an audience some time in the earlier 1930s, what may have been intended as a hostile question, how to define Acmeism, and he promptly said: 'Nostalgia for world culture.'[12] The reason for being shy of this phrase is that the word 'nostalgia' today carries heavier overtones than it probably did for Mandelstam. Nostalgia by now has become the English disease, or disability. It seeks to preserve the forms of the past, the great houses that few can afford to live in, the ceremonial masking a void. But restoration is not the same as renewal, and this brings us to Mandelstam's understanding of recognition. We shall see that when he spoke of a nostalgia for world culture, he did not imply that poetry should cease to be forward-looking. He would have agreed with Eliot that it must 'urge the mind to aftersight and foresight'.

In the Petrograd of 1921, the hungriest year, Mandelstam was not alone in believing that 'at last we have gained an inward freedom, a real inward gaiety'. The material privations seemed to have made possible a life of the spirit, a metamorphosis in which the word became flesh, and mere bread – a joy and a mystery. That ideal soon vanished over the horizon. But the essay expressing it, 'The Word and Culture', has nothing illusory at the centre. Here Mandelstam expounds an idea to which he would remain constant. This he defines in a memorable image:

'Poetry is a plough turning up time so that time's deepest layers, its black earth, come out on top.' His was one of those epochs, he contended, in which humanity is not satisfied with the present day. The deep layers of time appeal to it as strongly as virgin soil does to the ploughman. And he makes a further pronouncement: 'Revolution in art leads inevitably to classicism.'[13]

This is not an ironic prediction of the triumphs of Soviet architecture, the heavy and inert classical style that no totalitarian regime can do without. Mandelstam, we might have guessed from his essay 'The Morning of Acmeism', being interested only in the 'dormant forces' of architecture – as revealed in the structure whether of a poem or a building – could not understand classicism as other than revolutionary. Later he would decry any attempt to seek in Dante's *Commedia* a monument from the past. 'Time for Dante', he objected, 'is the content of history understood as a single synchronic action.' This made Dante our contemporary and inexhaustibly new.[14]

Mandelstam's paradoxical claim in 'The Word and Culture' is that in 1921 the old world, seemingly lost beyond recall, was actually more alive than it had ever been. He quotes from his poem 'Tristia,[15] a line that would be virtually the device on his shield in all future campaigns:

> And sweet to us is only the moment of recognition.

The poem not only takes its name from Ovid's cycle lamenting his banishment from Rome, but recognizes the situation of Ovid as one that will be re-enacted in the twentieth century:

> Who can tell from the word 'parting'
> What separation lies before us?

It has all happened before, and repetition is the law of life.

But the corollary of this demands that the act of repetition should bring renewal, making the past utterance more urgently ours. Mandelstam cannot be content with the historical Ovid, Pushkin or Catullus. He needs to have them 'afresh'. And he is haunted by a line from Catullus, 'Let us hasten to the renowned cities of Asia' – *ad claras Asiae volemus urbes*. It belongs to a poem set in the spring, the season of renewal, and it 'torments and troubles' Mandelstam, he says, as no 'Futurist riddle' ever did.[16] Significantly, the two following lines speak of a mind trembling with desire to go wandering, and of feet which eagerness makes stronger. The 'silver trumpet', as he calls it, of Latin verse like Catullus' had never been heard in Russian. It must be; and his own 'Tristia' does miraculously catch the authentic note.

Mandelstam is very much a representative poet of the age, in his situation and in the profound sense he entertains of European tradition. When I say representative I am thinking principally of his peers, the leading national poets in other countries who more than ever before turned to the immense range of European poetry, past and present, to sustain their own efforts. It is interesting that like Eliot and Seferis he should have approached that tradition with something of the anxiety felt by the dispossessed. He doubtless exaggerated a little when he asserted that his Jewish father spoke no real language but, if Mandelstam is to be believed, 'the ornate and contorted speech of an autodidact', at home neither in German nor in Russian. His mother, also Jewish, prided herself on the bookish jargon of the Russian intelligentsia which she had carefully acquired.[17] As a small boy in imperial Petersburg, inspired by its military and civic splendours, Mandelstam saw that it held no place for him.[18] Eliot was not dispossessed in that absolute fashion, but like Ezra Pound he had emigrated to Europe in search of a finer civilization, consoling himself with the belief that 'the consummation of an American' was 'to become...a European – something no born European, no person of any European nationality, can become'.[19] Seferis had been born outside Europe, though in an ancient Greek community, that of Smyrna, lost to him forever when it fell to the Turks in 1922. He would always regret the crowding of Greek culture into one small mainland territory, when it had once spread, in Cavafy's words about its language, 'as far as Bactria and to the Indians'. In exile with the Greek government during the Second World War, he was driven to meditate on the meaning of Hellenism and the prospects of its survival. Hellenism naturally was central to the idea he had formed of European culture.

Poetry, in spite of notable successes won in the twentieth century, has been hard pressed on many sides. For that reason, if no other, its best practitioners have become Europeans in the truest sense. They have collaborated in a single endeavour with the keenest mutual recognition. It might be argued that this has always been so. The Latin poets were adept and untiring pupils of their Greek predecessors; Chaucer measured his strength against the courtly poets of France and turned later to Dante and to Boccaccio as a story-teller, while Dante's own choice of Virgil as his guide and mentor in the first two canticles of the *Commedia* exemplifies the spirit of European poetry at its most vital, in the endless task of assimilation and the discovery of new strengths. It is also true that the same tides of fashion, both in sensibility and form, have flooded every corner of European poetry from one age to the next.

However, what seems to be specific to ours is the international status, during their lifetime, of major poets. This may have been anticipated by Goethe, the prophet of *Weltliteratur*, but, a conscious Olympian, he presided from his unchallenged eminence. He had no need to form alliances, or to do more than bow graciously to a rising star like Byron, whose personality dazzled him, but about whom Goethe said 'The moment he reflects, he is a child.'[20] In our own century, and this becomes more true the nearer we are to its end, the poet is compelled to seek out others who share his vision. This I have called European, though it might be more accurately defined as international.

Eliot maintained that 'European culture has an area, but no definite frontiers: and you cannot build Chinese walls.'[21] One salient feature of our intellectual history is that ever since the time of the Greeks the frontiers have been open. Europeans are receptive learners, and the forces that have shaped their civilization came from afar. Consider the beginnings of the Greek experiment. It started in Ionia, on the western fringe of Asia Minor. Here Homer is said to have been born (Seferis' own city of Smyrna has claims to be reckoned the place); the first stirrings of philosophical thought established the Ionian school, the Seven Wise Men headed by Thales of Miletus; the first historian of Greece, Herodotus, came from Halicarnassus. Seferis was enthralled by the spectacle of Hellenic enlightenment spreading from the age of Alexander the Great, and he acknowledges, like Cavafy, that the civilization founded by the Greek diaspora was the work both of Hellenes and non-Hellenes. Thus from the start European culture owed much to foreign peoples bordering the Eastern Mediterranean, to Egyptians, to Hittites, and many others; as it later would to Hebrew religious thought. Finally, having received so much from beyond, 500 years ago Europe began to overflow into the New World. It would spread its main languages, those of the colonizers, Spanish, Portuguese, English, French, Dutch, not only through the Americas but all over Asia, Africa and the Pacific. The result has been the Western civilization of modern times that the rest of humanity is unable to resist, no matter how ruinous some of its effects have proved to be.

So the extent of this 'area' of European culture, both in time and space, is very large, and its character highly diversified. If we look back to the situation just before the First World War, in those astonishing four or five years during which the arts throughout Europe were seized with the spirit of innovation, one thing stands out clearly. The movement was, within the whole of Europe and to some degree in the

Americas, practically simultaneous and therefore international. This
may have been Europe's last major contribution to world culture. It is
certainly remarkable for its achievement in poetry, then and in the
period that carried on the initial impulse until the aftermath of the
Second World War and our present decline.

Here it is appropriate once more to invoke Mandelstam. In 1922 (a
year incidentally that saw many seminal works appearing throughout
Europe) he published a much longer essay than 'The Word and
Culture', in which he dealt with an issue of concern to many twentieth-
century poets. 'On the Nature of the Word' is a far-ranging and
profound disquisition on the relation not only of a literature, but a
nation's survival in the spirit, to the language. Like Bergson he is
interested above all in 'the inner connection of phenomena'. His was a
mind, as he explains, that sought 'unity and connection', and in his view
the Russian language is 'not only a door into history, but history itself'.
It seemed to him that 'the falling dumb of two or three generations
would bring Russia to historical death'. He defined nihilism as
'excommunication from the word'.[22]

Is it extravagant to maintain that excommunication from the word
constitutes the darkest of all menaces in the world today? Mandelstam
went on to protest that the fire which devours philology – a cherishing
of the word – 'is ulcerating the body of Europe...laying waste for
culture the soil' it has already scorched.[23] To recognize this peril in
1922, before the wholesale debasement of language by the totalitarian
regimes in Europe, was perhaps not difficult, but only a poet could have
had the insight to gauge its magnitude. The centrality of this vision is
what now needs to be shown.

Mandelstam accused Russian Futurism of displaying 'a lack of faith
in language which is simultaneously a fast runner and a tortoise'.[24]
When reviewing the literary scene in Moscow at this time, he said that
poetry always needs 'the twofold truth of invention and memory'. This
he thought Pasternak alone among the Muscovites had achieved.[25]
Language as a fast runner has been recognized by Joseph Brodsky:
discussing the poetry of Marina Tsvetaeva he claims that the language
can urge a poet into regions not attainable otherwise, and beyond the
reach of spiritual or psychological concentration in itself. This
precipitancy is due to the speed with which a poet's ear outpaces both
imagination and experience.[26] Language at the service of poetry makes
its own connections, enlarging consciousness, and validating what might
otherwise have appeared inconceivable. However, it is the second

aspect, that of language as tortoise, which counts possibly even more. One might put it thus: in poetry the tortoise makes feasible the victory of the hare, or better, when the hare arrives at the winning post of new discovery, we perceive that it was really a winged tortoise.

Recalling Mandelstam on the backward reach of poetry, a plough that turns up the deep layers of time, we are not likely to underestimate the resources of memory. He says in 'On the Nature of the Word' that 'the Russian language, exactly like the Russian national character, has been formed by endless admixtures, crossings, graftings and foreign influences'.[27] That holds too for other major languages of Europe, and pre-eminently for English. Eliot (who was not really much interested in either Russian literature or its language) once explained to a German audience what it was that made English in his opinion 'the most remarkable medium for the poet to play with'. He considered it to be (and perhaps rightly) 'the richest language for poetry' because it has been made up from such 'a variety of elements'. There is, he points out, 'the Germanic foundation', 'a considerable Scandinavian element', 'the Norman French element', followed by 'a succession of French influences', and with the sixteenth and early seventeenth centuries 'a great increase of new words coined from the Latin'. These facts are well known, but it is useful to be reminded, in the same paragraph of his lecture, that a Celtic element has its place too. And that leads Eliot to note the various rhythms that these languages have contributed to English poetry. 'Even today', he added, the English language can be refreshed 'from its several centres: apart from the vocabulary, poems by Englishmen, Welshmen, Scots and Irishmen, all written in English, continue to show differences in their Music'.[28] These words were spoken in 1946. Half a century later we are more conscious of the pressures upon English from communities throughout the world.

Thus poetic language echoes with ancestral voices, sometimes all but lost, at others emerging with a sudden clarity. This is not to suggest that history goes in cycles, but rather that with each new situation the language enables a poet to place it in the context of earlier experience and judgement. Eliot has stated that 'only at certain moments... a word can be made to insinuate the whole history of a language and a civilisation'. The process is made possible by 'an allusiveness which is in the nature of words, and which is equally the concern of every kind of poet'.[29] Here he may seem to emphasize rather too much the poet's deliberate choice: for him the critical activity was something in composition that must be seen as crucial. It is in the nature of poetry that the successful word does actually insinuate itself. A passage in *Doctor Zhivago* relates how Yury worked when the poetic fit came upon him. At a given moment 'the relation of forces in creativity was turned on its head'. Now the primacy went not to the poet but to the language which like a mighty stream bore him along. Pasternak maintains that the poet's next move is decided for him by the actual state of world poetry and thinking at a given time.[30] We could interpret this as meaning that continuity has been restored; and continuity is another name for the renewal which gives a poet his unique authority.

In one of his most celebrated poems, 'Church Going', Philip Larkin tells how, on entering an undistinguished church as a sightseer, he feels impelled in spite of himself to an act of 'awkward reverence', the removal of his cycle clips. It puzzles him that this 'accoutred frowsty barn' should have such an effect, and he foresees a time when every church might stand useless and derelict. Yet even then someone will 'forever be surprising / A hunger in himself to be more serious', and will tend there through the 'suburb scrub', because 'A serious house on serious earth it is.'[31]

The experience recorded in that poem may be summed up as 'a halt in the wilderness'. Brodsky wrote a poem so entitled in 1965, about the Greek church in Leningrad, demolished to make way for a concert hall.[32] From the window of the house of a Tatar family living near by, he watches the bulldozer at work in the churchyard. Late that evening he sat amid the ruins of the apse:

> Through spaces in the altar shone the night.
> And I – where now the altar had been holed –
> looked upon tramcars as they speeded by,
> upon a string of street-lamps burning wanly,
> and what you generally don't meet in church
> now I could look at through the church's prism.

Only the dogs will retain a memory of the churchyard fence against which they once lifted their legs:

> That is what we call 'doglike devotion'.
> If this it was that brought me now to serious
> talk of the relay race of generations,
> I believe only in the relay race.
> To be precise, in those who know the smell.

He recognizes that the few Greeks remaining in Leningrad have failed to carry their cross. It had been their duty to reap a harvest of souls;

their field was overgrown; the plough had been abandoned. Which, he asks, is the more remote from us – the Orthodox faith or Hellenism?

> What are we near to? What lies just ahead?

You notice that this poem about a church, now tottering to its ruin, has inspired 'serious talk'. The poem concludes:

> Does there await us now a different era?
> And if so, then what duty do we share?
> What shall we have to bring as sacrifice?

Mandelstam's essay 'On the Nature of the Word' claimed for Acmeism that it had been 'not merely a literary but also a social phenomenon in Russian history. Together with it there was brought to birth in Russian poetry a moral force.'[33] As for Brodsky himself, I have already mentioned his strong affinities with Mandelstam. It was from Mandelstam's close friend and ally, Anna Akhmatova, that he learned principally a moral attitude. She had been quick to perceive that his kind of poetry would be very different in its procedures from her own. But rightly in his selection of essays, *Less Than One*, he places the tribute to Akhmatova immediately after the opening autobiographical sketch. 'She was', he pronounces, 'essentially a poet of human ties...' 'Cherished, strained, severed', these are shown by her 'first through the prism of the individual heart, then through the prism of history, such as it was'.[34]

The church's prism, the prism of the individual heart, the prism of history – they are all brought to a single focus in poetic language. That is what makes it far from unreasonable to claim that here is the steadiest light on our dilemmas in the threatened chaos of a civilization under increasing strain. Anna Akhmatova's crowning achievement was to speak not as in her youth introspectively with the voice of a highly conscious woman in love, and for the most part unhappy love, but rather on behalf of her hundred million compatriots bewildered by their sufferings. Great poetry, of the kind written not by Akhmatova alone in her generation, enables the reader to understand the perplexities of the time. They are exposed in a truly historical perspective, that of the recorded moral experience of humanity. More specifically, for the concerns that have prompted the calling of this conference, such poetry draws upon the treasury of Europe.

On one occasion Eliot and Seferis met in the very modest office assigned to Eliot by Faber and Faber. (Seferis always marvelled at Eliot's humility.)[35] The conversation turned to the idea of his at last making a pilgrimage to Greece. Eliot ventured the opinion that this would be like going to find your mother. Seferis' reply, as Eliot must have recognized, to judge by the startled attention with which he looked at him, was obviously a very personal one. 'It would be', he said, 'like going to confront yourself.'[36] Just a year later he visited Cyprus for the first time, and the experience bore out the truth of his words. In a note to the collection of poems he dedicated to the people of Cyprus in 1955 he says: 'It was the revelation of a people and moreover it was the experience of a human drama which...measures and judges our humanity.'[37] Coming to this island, which had lived under so many foreign dominations while yet remaining true to itself, he was reminded of the Smyrna he had known in his boyhood. He found in Cyprus familiar customs, and a vibrant Greek language, its dialect not far removed from that once spoken in Smyrna. This was the more heartening because, only three years before, wandering in the lost Ionian lands he had felt utter despair. It seemed to him the very moment when all was sinking into the earth. 'The Greek language, churches, houses, inherited gestures. Two or three generations more and they will all have been extinguished.'[38]

There are times when any of us may share his sense of desolation. Seferis, however, was able to overcome the nightmare which had made him accept *The Waste Land* as the authentic voice of his own generation throughout Europe by taking comfort from the robust and open speech of the unlettered peasant General Makriyannis, a leader of the nineteenth-century liberation of Greece, and also by turning like Odysseus to communicate with the spirits of the more ancient dead. When the living had failed him, Homer and Aeschylus were still at his side. And there was a further support. 'For many centuries', he could assert, 'the only genuine poet of our Race has been the anonymous and illiterate people'.[39] It is fifty years since he wrote the words. Today everywhere 'the anonymous and illiterate people' are an endangered species. There is no chance of discovering another Cyprus in Europe. If there were, it would soon be overrun by tourism.

'Because civilisations are finite', Brodsky has written, 'in the life of each of them comes a moment when centres cease to hold.' And what keeps them from disintegration 'is not legions but languages'.[40] His example of how it is 'men from the provinces, the outskirts' that do 'the job of holding' is the West Indian poet Derek Walcott. He claims for Walcott, as he would for himself, that a host of other poets, from at least half a dozen national cultures, are 'the cells in his bloodstream', since 'poetry is the essence of world culture'.[41] This term, as Brodsky uses it, does not imply the domination, or worse the elimination, of other cultures. Rather it means that in poetry we can find the past and present, the near and the seemingly remote, still in touch, 'the complete consort dancing together'. Eliot was referring to the words of a successful poem but his image can be extended to the throng of allusions that come together when the language itself directs the poet's activity. It can achieve harmony in disorder, the meeting of opposites in mutual recognition.

When the century was still new, and the October revolution, five years after the seizure of power, had still to be properly understood, Mandelstam proposed a mission that today sounds ironic in the extreme. He saw the nineteenth century as a bringer of catastrophe; with the First World War as its outcome, he could well be right. Those emerging from the ruin he likened to survivors 'cast by the will of destiny upon a new historical continent'. Their task must be 'to europeanise and humanise the twentieth century', and endue it with what he called 'teleological warmth'.[42] Our political failure does not falsify the promise of European poetry, that it will continue to keep fresh and regenerate the forces that have made it so broadly resonant and, as Mandelstam believed, inexhaustible. Here is a water table which cannot be drained dry as long as the language survives. Seferis prescribed for the writing of a poem,

> Nourish it with the soil and the rock you have.
> For the rest –
> Dig in the same place to find it.[43]

NOTES

Translations, whether in prose or verse, unless otherwise indicated, are my own.

  1 Matthew Arnold, 'The Study of Poetry', *Essays in Criticism, Second Series* (London, 1888), p. 1.
  2 T. S. Eliot, *The Use of Poetry and the Use of Criticism* (London, 1954), p. 105.
  3 Henry James, *Selected Letters*, edited with an introduction by Leon Edel (London, 1956), p. 251.
  4 C. P. Cavafy, *Poiimata 1897–1933*, edited by G. P. Savidis, sixth edition (Athens, 1989), p. 25. Translated by Edmund Keeley and Philip Sherrard in *Collected Poems* (Princeton, 1975), and by Memas Kolaitis in *Collected Poems*, vol. II (New York, 1988).
  5 Giorgos Seferis, *Dokimes*, vol. I (1936–47) (Athens, 1981), pp. 436, 334.
  6 Giorgos Seferis, *Poiimata*, edited by G. P. Savidis, fourteenth edition (Athens, 1982), 'Epi skinis' v, p. 289. Translated by Keeley and Sherrard as 'On Stage', *Collected Poems*, p. 409.

7 T. S. Eliot, 'Virgil and the Christian World', *On Poetry and Poets* (London, 1957), p. 130.

8 Seferis, 'Sta 700 Chronia tou Dante', *Dokimes*, Vol. II (1948–71) (Athens, 1981), p. 249. Translated by Peter Thompson as 'To 700 Years of Dante', *P.N. Review*, 45 (1985), 29–35.

9 Czeslaw Milosz, *The Witness of Poetry* (Cambridge, Mass., 1983), pp. 7–9.

10 The title of Brodsky's essay on Mandelstam in *Less than One: Selected Essays* (London, 1986).

11 Osip Mandel'shtam, 'Utro akmeizma', *Sobranie sochinenii*, edited by G. P. Struve and B. A. Filippov, vol. II, second edition (New York, 1971), pp. 323, 325. Translated as 'The Morning of Acmeism' by Sidney Monas, in *Osip Mandelstam: Selected Essays* (Austin and London, 1977), pp. 130, 132, and by Jane Garey Harris in *Mandelstam: The Complete Critical Prose and Letters* (Michigan, 1979), pp. 63, 65.

12 Nadezhda Mandelstam, *Hope Against Hope: A Memoir*, translated by Max Hayward (London, 1971), p. 246.

13 Mandelstam, 'Slovo i kul'tura', *Sobr. soch.*, vol. II, pp. 223, 224, 227. Both Monas and Garey Harris have translated this essay as 'The Word and Culture' in the works cited in note 11.

14 'Razgovor o Dante', *Sobr. soch.*, vol. II, p. 389. Translated as 'Conversation about Dante', by Clarence Brown and Robert Hughes in the Monas selection, and also by Garey Harris. The passage occurs in section v of Mandelstam's essay.

15 O. Mandel'shtam, *Stikhotvoreniia*, edited by N. I. Khardzhiev (Leningrad, 1979), pp. 110–12. Translated by Bernard Meares in Osip Mandelstam, *50 Poems* (New York, 1977) and by James Greene in Osip Mandelstam, *Poems*, second edition (London, 1980).

16 Mandelstam, *Sobr. soch.*, vol. II, p. 224.

17 'Chaos iudeyskii', *ibid.*, pp. 66–7.

18 'Rebiacheskii imperalizm', *ibid.*, p. 52. This piece and the one cited above belong to his autobiography, *Shum vremeni*, translated as *The Noise of Time* by Clarence Brown in *The Prose of Osip Mandelstam* (Princeton, 1965).

19 T. S. Eliot, 'On Henry James: In Memory', *The Question of Henry James*, edited by F. W. Dupee (London, 1947), p. 124.

20 Matthew Arnold, 'Byron', *Essays in Criticism: Second Series*, p. 185.

21 Eliot, *Notes towards the Definition of Culture* (London, 1962), p. 62.

22 Mandelstam, 'O prirode slova', *Sobr. soch.*, vol. II, pp. 242, 247–8. Translated as 'About the Nature of the Word' by Monas and 'On the Nature of the Word' by Garey Harris; see note 11.

23 *Sobr. soch.*, vol. II, p. 250.

24 *Ibid.* p. 247.

25 'Literaturnaia Moskva', *ibid.*, pp. 328, 330. Translated as 'Literary Moscow' by both Monas and Garey Harris.

26 In his preface to Marina Tsvetaeva, *Stikhotvoreniia i poemy*, vol. I (New York, 1980), p. [43]. Translated by Barry Rubin as 'Footnote to a Poem' in *Less Than One* (see pp. 202–3).

27 *Sobr. soch.*, vol. II, p. 245 ('O prirode slova').

28 *Notes towards the Definition of Culture*, pp. 110–11.

29 *On Poetry and Poets*, p. 33.

30 *Doctor Zhivago*, XIV, viii.

31 Philip Larkin, 'Church Going', *Collected Poems*, edited with an introduction by Anthony Thwaite (London, 1988), pp. 97–8.

32 'Ostanovka v pustyne', in his verse collection of that name (New York, 1970), pp. 166–8.

33 *Sobr soch.*, vol. II, p. 258.

34 'The Keening Muse', *Less Than One*, p. 52.

35 'Gramma s'enan xeno philo', *Dokimes*, vol. II, p. 23. Translated as 'Letter to a Foreign Friend', by Rex Warner and Th. D. Frangopoulos in George Seferis, *On the Greek Style* (London, 1967). See p. 180.

36 *Meres*, vol. VI (Athens, 1986), p. 53.

37 *Poiimata*, p. 335.

38 *Meres*, vol. V (Athens, 1977), p. 204. Translated by Athan Anagnostopoulos, as George Seferis: *A Poet's Journal. Days of 1945–1951* (Cambridge, Mass., 1974), p. 171.

39 *Dokimes*, vol. I, p. 217.

40 'The Sound of the Tide', *Less Than One*, p. 164.

41 *Ibid.*, p. 169.

42 'Deviatnadtsatyi vek'', *Sobr. soch.*, vol. II, p. 283. Translated as 'The Nineteenth Century' by both Monas and Garey Harris; see note 11.

43 'Therino iliostasi', *Poiimata*, viii, p. 299. Translated by Keeley and Sherrard, 'Summer Solstice', viii, p. 421.

Comparative Criticism 15, pp. 19–33. Copyright © 1993 Cambridge University Press

European literary exiles

J. M. RITCHIE

Exile has always been with us. In the Ancient World banishment from the homeland to some distant place far from the beloved capital city, far from one's native language, was considered one of the worst punishments which could be imposed. But while it was common enough and Ovid was certainly not the only figure in the classical world to suffer such a fate, it was still an individual fate.[1] In the modern world exile seems to have become the norm, a mass fate rather than an individual one. It has become easy to think of exile as a feature, say, of Nazi Germany or Soviet Russia, or, moving further away from Europe, a characteristic of South America.[2] Everybody will have his or her own examples. Looking back over French literary history Jean Améry points to Voltaire, who was in exile for a time, and Victor Hugo too.[3] Further afield Hermann Bang had to leave Denmark because of his homoerotic tendencies and wrote most of his works in an exile of a kind, though with this last example some of the difficulties of the term already became apparent, for exile is not the same as emigration, especially not self-imposed exile. Henry Miller, whom Jean Améry also quotes, was not in any political danger when he exiled himself, nor was he being pursued by the courts of law. Kurt Tucholsky was in voluntary Swedish and French exile long before the Nazis came to power, making real exile essential, were he to stay alive. James Joyce became a European wanderer long before it became the literary thing to be.

I am, of course, limiting myself to literary exile and therefore this takes no full account of the transfer from the individual experience of the conscious intellectual to the mass experience of thousands of others. In Britain alone, for example, there must have been some 60–70,000 exiles from the German-speaking lands after 1933 and before 1945.[4] Only a few hundred of these were artists, intellectuals or writers and only a handful of these numbers bore names which would be recognized by the general public. So a distinction has to be made not only between the reason for exile in the first place – were such people politically undesirable in the eyes of the new Nazi Germany, were they communists, socialists or even royalists, were they persecuted and pursued for reasons of race, for example simply because they were Jews, or were there other reasons which made life in the homeland an impossibility after 1933? The further distinction already indicated is that between the famous and the less than famous, those who had already made a name for themselves in the literary world and those whose literary careers had hardly begun. One thinks, for example, of the experience of Walter Kerr, who had been the most famous theatre critic of the Weimar Republic, a man whose wit and word-power were feared and admired throughout the German-speaking world. Forced into exile he could at first feel at home in France, whose language and culture he had long had at his fingertips. Compelled to leave France he reluctantly made for England, a country whose language he did not know and in whose culture he could never feel at home. Deprived of the living theatre which had been the focus of his literary activities for so long and deprived of the language of which he had been such a master, he faded into obscurity. His daughter, Judith Kerr, writing in English, became the noted member of the family.

There are more examples of famous writers who faltered and faded when deprived of their roots in their language and culture than there are examples of those who positively gained from the exposure to a foreign language and culture. As a contrasting example Jean Améry quotes the brothers Mann, Thomas and Heinrich. Heinrich, the older of the two, had made a name for himself as a writer before Thomas. Heinrich was already known for his novels critical of the Prussian excesses of the Wilhelmine Empire, and he was to become better known through the film version of *The Blue Angel* with Marlene Dietrich and Emil Jannings. What was more important, he was to become a true democrat and opponent of emerging fascism while Thomas was still toying with dangerously nationalistic anti-republican sentiments. Like Kerr, Heinrich felt at home in his first phase of exile in France, and like Kerr he too felt uprooted when forced to flee yet again. He never felt at home, nor was he ever a success, in exile in North America. Thomas Mann, by contrast, was very reluctant to leave Nazi Germany and had to be persuaded to do so by his children Klaus and Erika. He first followed in Heinrich's footsteps and accepted Czech citizenship, as a passport is the exile's most precious possession, and proceeded to the United States, where he grew ever greater in literary stature and took over the role which by rights should have been that of his brother, namely as the representative of the other, better, Germany, and the voice of reason for democracy against National Socialism. Thomas Mann in exile was able to operate at the highest level, consorting with the President of the United States and the most influential opinion-makers in the land, while his brother was almost ignored and had to live on handouts. There were others in exile in America who were almost equally successful, at least in financial terms – Lion Feuchtwanger, Franz Werfel, with the *Song of Bernadette*, and Erich Maria Remarque, who had become wealthy since the world-wide acclaim given to *All Quiet on the Western Front*; but it was Thomas Mann who was invited to the White House.

For some, fame of such an international kind only came later. Brecht, for example, as a notorious Marxist, had been one of the first to go into exile. Unlike many of his fellow followers of the Communist creed, he did not settle in the Soviet Union – most of those who did never survived the purges and show-trials[5] – but after various moves, for example, through Scandinavia, he too landed in America, where despite his most intense efforts he never found the Broadway success he longed for. There is no doubt, however, of the influence exile had on him and the influence he was to have both on his host countries and on the rest of the world. What made exile a creative experience for him and a less than creative experience for Heinrich Mann and for so many others?

Failure in exile could and did lead to depression and despair of the deepest kind. Not surprisingly there are many cases of suicide in exile. Jean Améry reminds his readers of the case of Ernst Toller, the brilliant dramatist of the Expressionist generation, who had been an inspiring revolutionary in the Weimar Republic; who had survived imprisonment to become an even greater writer and literary leader. In exile from National Socialism he had become an international figure, speaking at rallies, organizing support for republican Spain. How great then was the dismay when he suddenly committed suicide in a New York hotel room. Was it because of the psychological strain, was it because of the apparent invincibility of the German army, which was marching through Europe? Whatever the reason exile proved not an individual fate, but one which for too many of the best ended in suicide. The list of exiles from Nazi Germany who took their own lives is long: Ernst Toller, Stefan Zweig, Friedrich Hasenclever, Walter Benjamin, and many more.

I shall have to return to the matter of suicide in exile because it is such a dominant feature, but first I shall turn to the question of language. Exile means loss of the homeland and loss of the language, loss of the roots in the language which any author has from birth, loss of the living stream of the language in which the author lives, loss of the public for the author's work; in fact it is only too easy to see the whole question of language and exile in terms of loss. The author is restricted to the written language, runs the risk of contamination from the language of the host country; the French are not the only nation to fear anglicisms, to see the purity of the classical idiom tarnished by the incursion of barbarisms from the other tongue. But, of course, it is possible to see things differently. The German language has not been the same since its unwieldy sentences benefited from the pithiness of modern English or modern American style. Brecht naturally introduced gangster idioms into his German when he was presenting Adolf Hitler as an American hoodlum, but his language shows Anglicisms and Americanisms in other works and not to any disadvantage. If alienation is his intention, then he can alienate by exploiting the possibilities of the exotic other language. I cite Brecht particularly because I see him as an example of one on whom exile, however unpleasant and undesirable, did have fruitful effects.

But language considered from every aspect was always a problem. Thomas Mann learned to give some of his famous addresses in English, a very Germanic, accented English. Brecht could read American gangster novels, but his wife Helene Weigel did the shopping. Both Thomas Mann and Bertolt Brecht wrote German and relied on translators. Franz Werfel, Lion Feuchtwanger and Stefan Zweig had world-wide success with their plays and novels written in exile, but they had to rely on translators. The same fate awaits the exile to this day, and especially the noted exile. The exiled writer has no choice. If he is to survive in the country of exile he has to be translated and no literal word-for-word translation will do. Brecht's life in exile shows a frantic search for the translator who will successfully translate his plays into the other theatrical culture, not merely into the other idiom. At the time he failed, but in the end he succeeded: Brecht has become a world-wide success in translation. Franz Werfel's comedy *Jacobowsky and the Colonel* was almost the only play to be successful in English at the time, because it was put into the capable hands of Sam Behrmann who transformed the very German original into a totally American play, a hit, with Werfel fighting every inch of the way against every change which was being inflicted on his precious German.[6] Poets, of course, had particular problems.

The fundamental exile issue therefore was that of language, but, of course, the writer did have a choice. He could and can choose between translation and abandoning the native language and moving over entirely into the language of the host country. Poets, as I have mentioned, have special problems. Joseph Brodsky, who has been a citizen of the United States since 1977 of course writes in Russian, and it was for his poetry that he was awarded the Nobel Prize for Literature in 1987.[7] Recently, and to the alarm of some critics, he has started to write poetry in English. The best example of a refusal to change is Erich Fried, who arrived in England from Vienna when still in his teens and when asked what he was going to become replied – a German poet.[8] He remained in exile for the rest of his life and lived in London, and although he did return to Austria and Germany after 1945 he never settled there. He learned enough English to translate Shakespeare beautifully and there is no doubt that his verse has been influenced by extensive reading of English poetry, but his fame came because of his German poetry written in England but not in English. Of the other exiles from National Socialism the Austrians proved more flexible as language-changers than the Germans, and the journalists more flexible than the men or women of letters. Elias Canetti, the Nobel Prize-winner who, like Erich Fried, was to spend many years in exile in England, had perhaps changed language often enough. Born in Rutschuk, Bulgaria, of Ladino-speaking Jewish parents, he learned English very early, but then changed to Swiss German before the Viennese German of Karl Kraus made its lasting imprint upon him. To him too fame came late, especially for his remarkable memoirs written in German while living in England. Earlier than Canetti, the German-writing Hungarian Arthur Koestler had settled in England after escaping almost certain death in Franco's Spain. He immediately changed to English and had remarkable success in that language. There is no need for the reminder that Koestler too committed suicide.

According to Jean Améry, Thomas Mann was especially aware of the effect exile could have on the language of the writer and quotes him confessing that he found himself saying to his wife: 'es bekommt wärmer' – the classic example usually occurring in the apocryphal tale of the exile in the restaurant who calls, 'waiter when do I become a sausage'. Thomas Mann then went on to hope that he would never write anything like that. Brecht does it deliberately, for comic and alienating effect, but when a writer does change language there is a great temptation for the ordinary reader and certainly the critic to look for signs of non-native language. Conrad and Nabokov are famous for English which is almost too good, too rich in lexical range, delighting too much in grammatical complexities. Certainly with one of the Austrian exiles, Robert Neumann, who did perform the language-switch, critics who read him realized that while he was capable of writing readable English it was English such as no English author had ever written before.[9] Sometimes an exiled author had to change language more than once. Then it becomes possible, as in the case of Ernst Erich Noth, to pursue the author as he changed from German to French and then from French to American English before going back into German again.[10] It is rare for an author to be completely integrated into the language and culture of the country of exile. But what of the author who tries, for instance, to become 100 per cent American? One thinks, for example, of the Polish writer Jerzy Kosinski. He not only personally experienced the Holocaust, which claimed all but two members of his family, he also lost the power of speech completely. To lose and regain speech must be an incredibly traumatic experience. To lose one's literary language and gain another must be equally traumatic, yet this is what he did. He managed to get out of Poland and make his way to America, where he graduated from the 'university of life' by working as a truck-driver, a parking-lot attendant, a cinema projectionist, a driver for a night-club entrepreneur and so on. He also enrolled as a Ph.D. candidate at Columbia University and obtained a Ford Foundation Fellowship. Two years later he wrote *The Future is Ours, Comrade*, a collection of essays about collective behaviour in a Communist society. An instant best-seller, it was serialized by *The Saturday Evening Post* and condensed by *Reader's Digest*. This book attracted the attention of Mary Weir, the widow of a steel magnate. Some two years later they were married. Thereafter Jerzy Kosinski lived a life at the top of the social tree with a private jet, luxury homes and apartments, polo horses and skiing lodges. He also published one best-seller after another and won one literary prize after another. He taught English at Wesleyan, Princeton and Yale universities. But can one tell that one is reading a Pole writing American? Well, he did not change his name. Jerzy Kosinski is a very Polish name and in his most famous novel *The Painted Bird* he seems to be telling the story of his own life – the story of a dark-haired, olive-skinned boy, escaping the Holocaust, the story of a boy perhaps Jew or gypsy (this is never precisely specified) who wanders alone from one Slav village to another, who experiences incredible brutality and cruelty, but, and this is perhaps the most important point, who survives. Clearly too the opposite is the case. The dark-skinned boy, like the painted bird of the title, will not survive, will never be able to integrate, to be accepted:

The painted bird circled from one end of the flock to the other, vainly trying to convince its kin that it was one of them. But dazzled by its brilliant colors, they flew around unconvinced...We saw soon afterwards how one bird after another would peel off in a fierce attack. Shortly the many-hued bird lost its place in the sky and dropped to the ground.[11]

Jerzy Kosinski himself never became completely integrated into the American way of life. His physical powers began to fail before his mental powers. When he felt he could no longer ski or play polo at the highest level he committed suicide by placing a plastic bag over his head. Another suicide in exile.

What of the language he wrote? What of his English? In the postscript to his novel *Being There*, which became a truly remarkable success even before the Peter Sellers film version, one critic is quoted as saying that Kosinski wrote his novels sparsely, as though they cost a thousand dollars a word, and a misplaced or misused locution would cost him his life.[12] *Being There* is extremely sparse: Kosinski was a language perfectionist who rewrote every page many times and took up to three years over a short novel. Such care could also describe the difficulty of writing in a foreign language. It also evoked the notorious reaction from the *Village Voice*, which claimed that Jerzy Kosinski was not the author of his own novels: the classic suspicious response towards the exile, especially the successful exile. One encounters the same response towards the most famous exile of them all, Ben Traven, many of whose critics and readers refuse to accept that novels generally available in English could have been written by a German anarchist, living in Mexico City, writing about the South American jungle. How could a German write *The Treasure of Sierra Madre*?[13] How could a Pole write *Being There*?

While the *Village Voice* could claim in 1982 that Kosinski did not write his own books, whether on grounds of flaws in style or in content, there is no doubt that an exiled writer like Kosinski felt he had to prove not only that he had adjusted to the host culture, but also that he had successfully assimilated the host culture. Hence, for example, other critics have claimed that Kosinski's book *The Hermit of 69th Street* was his reply to the *Village Voice* accusation, in that it was a vast book 'riddled with literary quotes and footnotes'. Kosinski called it an auto-fiction rather than autobiography, though the main character, Kosky, is clearly himself. 'If you take the sin out of Kosinski you get Kosky', the author himself is quoted as saying. Kosinski is also a writer in whose writings sex, like violence, is not only a recurring theme, it is almost his most dominant theme, and Kosinski accepted this:

Sex is important to my characters and in my own life. Sex is a life force, a procreative force and a creative force.[14]

I must admit that I find the sex in Kosinski's novel not only exaggerated (though well written) but also quite ridiculous, though this may be due to my own limited range of experience. But both elements, the parade of literary knowledge and the focus on sex are, for me, reminiscent of other modern writers. The best example in this context is another exile, a Czech, who over the years has had enormous international success, namely Milan Kundera. In Prague, the younger Kundera was famous for his many love affairs, of which he made no secret. Sex was certainly important for him. Since 1975, however, he has lived in exile in Paris; since 1981 he has been French. If sex was the first impulse in his adult life, literature has been the second, and for years now he has led the literary life, like Kafka, his Prague predecessor on whom he seems to model himself. Indeed, the Mexican novelist Carlos Fuentes has described him as 'the second K.'. Somehow, like Kosinski, he manages to fuse the two themes of sex and the apocalypse, sex and the Stalinist, totalitarian state, into one significant exile image of the modern world as we experience it. As he expressed it himself in a discussion he had with Philip Roth, quoted as an afterword to *The Book of Laughter and Forgetting*:

I have the feeling that a scene of physical love generates an extremely sharp light, which suddenly reveals the essence of characters and sums up their life situation. Hugo makes love to Tamina while she is desperately trying to think about lost vacations with her dead husband. The erotic scene is the focus where all the themes of the story converge and where its deepest secrets are located.[15]

This sharp light was at its sharpest in *The Incredible Lightness of Being*, a book which enjoyed acclaim from all quarters, as one critic put it 'all the way from *Le Monde* to *Newsweek*; not since Hemingway's *The Old Man and the Sea* has a work of narrative prose enjoyed such unanimous welcome'.[16] Kundera continues to write and, like one who has written an essay on *The Art of the Novel*, or like Kosinski, who had lectured to large audiences on the novel, he writes in a knowing, postmodern manner. Like Kosinski, Kundera likes to show his literary awareness by quoting. So at the end of part 3 of *The Book of Laughter and Forgetting* he tells the reader in a footnote: 'Quotations are from the following works: Annie Leclerc *Parole de femme* 1976; Paul Eluard *Le Visage de la paix* 1951; and Eugene Ionesco *Le Rhinocéros* 1959.' Not surprisingly

Milan Kundera's latest novel *Immortality* is also redolent with literature, and especially full of Goethe. Like Kosinski, Kundera 'hones and polishes, searches for the mot juste'.[17] According to his English translator, Peter Kussi, because he strives for universal comprehension Kundera in effect writes for translators; an important motive for his terse, lucid style is to make *their* job easier. As Kussi confirms, Kundera believes that a contemporary author must transcend parochial boundaries. He fully shares the concept of *Weltliteratur*, formulated in 1827 by Goethe:

National literature does not mean very much in the present age; the epoch of world literature is at hand and everyone must now exert himself to hasten its approach.[18]

When Goethe wrote these words about world literature he had no idea that he was coining what was to become, for some, a definition of comparative literature; of course, he had equally no idea that by the second half of the twentieth century the greater part of literature in the world would be produced in exile.

The number of countries in which people are persecuted for religious, political or other reasons has been steadily rising. According to a count carried out by Amnesty International in 1986 the number of guilty countries then was around 122. By the year 1992 this number will have risen again. Those of us who are lucky enough to live in countries which receive, rather than expel, must consider ourselves extremely fortunate. According to Horst Bienek, whose essays on this subject have been published under the title *Language and Exile – the Gradual Stifling of Screams*, we shall be judged by how we respond to those in exile among us.[19] Once upon a time thousands left Franco's Spain for exile in faraway South America: Argentina became the host country for many refugees from Europe.[20] Fifty years later the exodus goes the other way – from Chile, Argentina, Uruguay, from any of these countries with quasi-fascist dictatorships the exiles scatter to form a new diaspora. Is it easier for Spanish-speaking South American writers to survive in exile in post-Franco Spain or will they be better received in Paris? When the military junta collapsed in Argentina should the exiles have immediately returned from Europe? In answer to this question I have to say that my knowledge of Germany and German literature makes me familiar with both possibilities. After 1933 it was possible for German writers to go into exile, either into German-speaking Austria, or into that other haven of German culture, Czechoslovakia. After the takeover of Czechoslovakia and the Anschluss with Austria, France, Switzerland, Belgium, the

Netherlands, Sweden, the Soviet Union, Mexico, Brazil, Turkey, Palestine, Australia and New Zealand became countries of exile. Vast surveys have had to be devoted to German and Austrian literary figures in North America alone. How does one measure the influence of these waves of exiles on the host countries?

In similar studies devoted not to literature but to scientific transfer, statistical methods are employed, citation indices are used, numbers of Nobel Prize-winners are counted in a profit-and-loss manner; but comparative literature of late has become chary of measuring influence. Nevertheless, in arts others than literature it is sometimes easier to identify the impact which the arrival of exiles can have on the host culture, an impact similar to that of the sudden arrival of hitherto unknown technological, industrial or scientific know-how such as European refugees from National Socialism were capable of bringing to the rest of the world. Opera in England, for instance, was in a very bad way until it was revitalized by Busch and Ebert, who staged Mozart in German at Glyndebourne.[21] Here a clear before-and-after effect is present. Opera before exile – opera after exile.

Similarly, the arrival of Rudolf Laban in England from Germany had a clearly measurable effect on dance culture. Laban's influence radiated out to reach almost every aspect of life in Britain, from ballet and movement to the factories in which the lives of the workers were made not only easier, but also more productive, when Laban's theories of movement were put into practice. Even now, many British colleges of education seem to train teachers in Laban movement.[22] Similarly it is possible to claim that art history did not exist in England before the arrival in London of the Warburg Institute from Hamburg and thereafter the arrival in exile of scholars like Ernst Gombrich. Names which spring to mind are Wittgenstein and Freud, who brought with them from Austria not merely their own individual greatness, their own personal thoughts or idiosyncrasies, but whole Viennese schools of thought and a foreign culture for grafting on to the host culture. So is one justified in talking about influence?

Although at the very beginning of the National Socialist regime there were examples of Germans going into exile in German-speaking countries, the main effect of the regime was to force the unwanted further afield. For a long time it was not possible for Germans to write in German for Germans. With the end of the Nazi regime and the subsequent division of Germany into two, we do, however, have a more recent example of Germans being forced out of one part of Germany into another, Germans being forced into exile, thereby losing their homeland, but not losing their language, retaining the means of expression, but no longer writing for those who could understand what they had to say. The history of recent German literature is not a wholly divided history recording the literature of the German Democratic Republic separate from and for a while not equal to the literature produced in the free West, in the Federal Republic, Austria and Switzerland, it also has to take account of those from the East who moved West or even, if examples can be found, of those who chose to move from West to East – though if there is an element of free choice they would not be exiles.

I must raise one further general point – the matter not of forced emigration, but the possibility, should it arise, of *remigration*, going back to the homeland. Exile has been compared with a serious illness, which affects the mind as well as the body, leaving the mind sometimes, as we have seen, in a state of depression and despair, close even to suicide.[23] Too often, for the exile, the years pass and the possibility of return fades. Even if and when the ban is lifted and return is a possibility, the exile is estranged from everything he once held dear, home has become foreign, he and she no longer belong. The image can be extended, and has been extended to make the exile the key figure of the modern age, a *Jean sans Terre*, as if this represented some kind of psychological existential state. Yet the result in real, individual cases is far too harrowing to allow for generalizations of this kind – Jerzy Kosinski was on the point of going back to Poland in triumph when he committed suicide.

Cseslaw Milosz left Poland in 1951. Born in 1911 in Lithuania, in 1949 he was an official in the Polish Embassy in Paris when he turned his back on the Communist regime and ended up in America, where from 1960 onwards he taught Slav literature at Berkeley. His return to Poland thirty years later was a triumphant one, for the man the world had forgotten had won the Nobel Prize for literature. (Are there really so many Nobel Prize-winners in exile?) Photographs from the period show Milosz standing alongside Lech Walesa, wearing a Solidarnoscé badge and being received by the Polish pope.[24] Milosz could go back, but for others return was and still remains difficult. Now that the Berlin Wall has come down will the banished exiles return to the East? At least they now belong to one united country, so there is no passport problem. But will Kundera leave Paris, now that he is a French citizen enjoying international success? Will he be tempted by the change of regime in

Czechoslovakia? Will there be an exodus of the South Americans from Paris and from Spain if and when the Argentine example is followed and other Latin American countries have democratic elections? For Germans, Austrians and Czechs after the collapse of National Socialism the problem of return, remigration after emigration was, if anything, more complicated.[25] For some the grounds for exile had been political, for others there had been reasons of race or religion. If Jewish they may have had less desire or inclination to return to a land which had brought about not only their own banishment but the destruction and death of their families. For others again the question of return may have been a matter of age or circumstance. If they had left Germany or Austria or Czechoslovakia at an early age, had married and had a family abroad, they might have felt less willing to uproot themselves. Yet in general the pull was strong and many did return; but for many the disappointment was great; antisemitism was still prevalent, especially in Austria, and later the Waldheim affair confirmed people's worst suspicions: remigration was to prove harder in some respects than emigration. Of course, experiences were different for those who chose to return to East or West Germany. Many who returned to what was to become the Federal Republic failed to find the regard they had enjoyed before; other authors who had not gone into exile had taken their place; inner emigrants, so called, were favoured over real emigrants; there were still Nazis or neo-Nazis around in surprisingly high places. Experience in the East, in the German Democratic Republic, was different. Those who returned tended to be life-long left-wingers; they were acclaimed, given professorships and preference; at least one became an ambassador. Brecht came back from America and was given his own theatre and his own ensemble to put on his plays. Becher came back from Russia (one of the comparatively few survivors of the purges) and became Minister for Culture; but inevitably there were difficulties for those who failed to toe the party line. The most ironic case is that of Stefan Heym who returned from America, where he had enjoyed success as a novelist after switching language to English. He was not allowed to publish his novels in the East and had them published in the West to much official censure. When the Wall came down this remarkably active man, who had been attacked in America for his critique of capitalism and censured in the German Democratic Republic for his outspokenness, found himself as the insider being interviewed constantly to explain the world-wide failure of real socialism. If the collapse of socialism in the German Democratic Republic came as a shock to many, including experts who had been studying the regime from the outside for years, how much greater was the shock over the collapse of the Communist regime in Soviet Russia.

Here yet again, writ large, we have the exile's dilemma – to return to the homeland or not to return? Would Solzhenitsyn go back? According to recent reports Natalia Solzhenitsyn arrived in Moscow in May 1992 after eighteen years of exile. She had come to buy a house and prepare for Alexander to come back to live in the motherland. There were no government officials to meet Mrs Solzhenitsyn, but there was a reception by a committee of authors with flowers. According to reports Mrs Solzhenitsyn said: 'I have lived for this moment through all these years.' She brought with her Yermolai, the all-American son, who last saw Russia when he was three.

We have to go back thirty years or so for the first impact of the Solzhenitsyn voice, when Khrushchev's brief period of liberalization allowed publication of *One Day in the Life of Ivan Denisovich*. Inside Russia his later books were banned and by 1974, when he was finally exiled, and by then a Nobel Prize-winner, the thaw was over. In exile Solzhenitsyn has been active and vocal, promoting a return to Russia's authoritarian, nationalist and orthodox Christian values. No doubt such views will be welcomed by many. There is also no doubt that such views will be rejected by many more. Alexander Solzhenitsyn, now 72 and resident for a long period on a 50-acre estate in Cavendish, Vermont, may, like many other exiles, find that the return from exile will present as much heartbreak and despair as the original exile. The restoration of a greater Russia of the kind he would have liked to see, which would include the Ukraine, Byelorussia and parts of Kazakhstan, is now presumably beyond the bounds of possibility.

I conclude with some brief general thoughts and questions on the problem of exile and comparative literature. Is there such a thing as exile literature? Is this restricted to literature produced in exile or is it even literature *about* exile? As far as the latter question is concerned, in my own experience, while literature produced in exile is often about exile, this is by no means the only theme of exile literature. Hence as far as 'theme' is concerned, I would not anticipate endless investigations into the 'theme of exile in...' On the other hand there can be no doubt that the experience of exile does have an influence on the writer, resulting perhaps in nostalgia, a return to childhood, paradise lost, certainly a return to history, in the form of historical novels and plays. This does not necessarily mean an escape from the horrors of the present, but rather a search for parallels which help reveal the significance of contemporary events. One thinks, for example, of Heinrich Mann's vast historical novel *Henri Quatre*, in which, as Broermann has shown, points of comparison are obvious but never forced.[26] As far as the impact which the experience of exile may have on the author is concerned, this may manifest itself, as we have seen, in the author's language, both positively and negatively; the influence may also be revealed in the genre selected. It is well known that German literature was more successful in the narrative form of the novella than in the form of the novel or the short story. Yet after the Second World War the novella seemed to die for a time and to be replaced by the short story. Can this be put down in part to exile exposure to the form, as well as to the simple fact of English and American cultural and military domination? And if one accepts the pressure of influence at all, does the presence of exiles have an influence on the host country? Can literature go out and conquer the world (even from a position of weakness which exile represents) in the same way, say, as German science or Japanese industrial knowhow can conquer the world? Why was Kosinski so successful in America or Kundera in France? How could so many writers in exile become Nobel Prize-winners? There are plenty of questions for comparative literature to tackle if and when it confronts the problem of exile.

NOTES

1 *Ovid: Sorrows of an Exile* (Tristia). Translated by A. D. Melville, with an introduction and notes by E. J. Kennedy (Oxford, Clarendon Press, 1992).

2 H.-B. Mueller, ed., *Latin America and the Literature of Exile. A Comparative View of the 20th Century European Refugee Writers in the New World* (Heidelberg, 1983).

3 Jean Améry, 'Vom immerwährenden Schriftsteller-Exil', in *Autoren im Exil*, edited by Karl Corino (Frankfurt am Main, 1981), pp. 254–64.

4 Weiner Röder, *Die deutschen sozialistischen Exilgruppen in Grossbritannien 1940–1945* (Hanover, 1968), p. 23.

5 David Pike, *German Writers in Soviet Exile, 1933–1945* (Chapel Hill, 1982).

6 J. M. Ritchie, 'The Many Faces of Jacobowsky', in *Franz Werfel: An Austrian Writer Reassessed*, edited by Lothar Huber (Oxford, 1989), pp. 193–210.

7 Valentina Polukhina, *Joseph Brodsky: a Poet for Our Time* (Cambridge University Press, 1989).

8 Erich Fried, 'Der Flüchtling und die Furcht vor der Heimkehr', in *Autoren im Exil*, pp. 265–76.

9 Sylvia Patsch, *Österreichische Schriftsteller im Exil in Grossbritannien: ein Kapitel vergessene österreichische Literatur: Romane, Autobiographien, Tatsachenberichte auf englisch und deutsch* (Vienna, 1985).

10 Eric Robertson, 'The French Exile of René Schickele and Ernst Erich Noth', *German Life and Letters*, 45 (1992), 244–8.

11 Jerzy Kosinski, *The Painted Bird* (Boston, 1978), p. 50.

12 Quoted from the postscript 'On Kosinski', to *Being There* (London, 1989), p. 111.

13 Karl S. Guthke, *B. Traven. The Life Behind the Legends* (New York, 1987).

14 Kosinski quotations are from an interview with Pearl Sheffy Gefen three days before Kosinski committed suicide in New York; reprinted in *Weekend Guardian*, 25–26 May 1991, 10–11 and 33.

15 Quoted from 'Afterword: A Talk with the Author by Philip Roth', in Milan Kundera, *The Book of Laughter and Forgetting* (London, 1987), p. 236.

16 Jürgen Serke, 'Milan Kundera. Ein unaufhaltsamer Fall', p. 107. Quoted from *ibid.*, in Jürgen Serke, *Das neue Exil. Die Verbannten Dichter* (Frankfurt am Main, 1985), p. 85.

17 Quotations and comments from Peter Kussi on translating Milan Kundera, winner of the Independent Award for Foreign Fiction, in *The Independent*, 22 June 1991, 28.

18 Quoted from Peter Kussi's essay, *ibid.*, in which Kundera's commitment to *Weltliteratur* is doubly stressed.

19 Horst Bienek, *Das allmähliche Ersticken von Schreien*, Sprache und Exil heute (Munich, 1987).

20 See *Bolitin de Literatura Comparada*, special issue: 'La Argentina en la literatura de exilo'. Año XI–XII Universidad Nacional de Cuyo Mendoza – R Argentina, 1986–7.

21 Erik Levi, 'Carl Ebert, Glyndebourne and the Regeneration of British Opera', in *Theatre and Film in Exile. German Artists in Britain, 1933–1945*, edited by Günter Berghaus (Oxford, 1989), pp. 179–88.

22 Valerie Preston-Dunlop, 'Rudolf Laban and Kurt Joos in Exile: Their Relationship and Diverse Influence on Dance in Britain' in *ibid.*, pp. 167–78.

23 Hilde Spiel, 'Das Haus der Sprache', in *Die Zerbrochene Feder, Schriftsteller im Exil*, edited by Ota Filip and Egon Larsen with Günter W. Lorenz (Stuttgart, 1984), p. 11.

24 See 'Cseslaw Milosz, Ein Polnisches Wunder', in Jürgen Serke, *Das neue Exil*, pp. 185–207.

25 See, for example, *Eine schwierige Heimkehr. Österreichische Literatur im Exil 1938–1945*, edited by Johann Holzner, Sigurd Paul Scheichl and Wolfgang Wiesmüller (Innsbruck, 1991).

26 Bruce M. Broermann, *The German Historical Novel in Exile after 1933. Calliope contra Clio* (Pennsylvania State University Press, 1986), p. 59. In addition to *Henri Quatre* Broermann analyses historical novels by Wolfgang Cordan, Bruno Frank, Robert Neumann, Edgar Maass, Lion Feuchtwanger, Alfred Döblin, Joseph Roth, Thomas Mann and Herman Broch.

Comparative Criticism 15, pp. 35–56. Cambridge University Press 1993

At the edges of the world: drawing new maps

SUSAN BASSNETT

On Saturday 21 September 1583 Dr John Dee, mathematician, philosopher, map-maker and astrologer to Queen Elizabeth I, left England accompanied by his assistant Edward Kelley and their families to travel to Cracow in Poland. They took ship from Gravesend and, as detailed in *A True and Faithful Relation of what passed for many Yeares between Dr John Dee ... and Some Spirits*[1] followed a circuitous path via Amsterdam, up the Zuider Zee to Harlingen and then in a series of small boats crossing short stretches of water until they came to Embden on 17 October. Communicating with spirits at different places where they rested, they proceeded on to Bremen, and thence across to Lübeck, finally reaching Stettin on Christmas Day. It had taken them three months, travelling through a remarkable range of places, by boat and overland, but it then took them only four days to travel more than 200 miles down to Posen, despite the rigours of winter. Eventually, on 13 March 1584 the travellers reached their destination. Dee notes where they lodged in Cracow, and furthermore:

Master Edward Kelley came to us on Fryday in the Easter week by the new Gregorian Kalender, being the 27th day of March by the old Kalender, but the sixth day of April by the new Kalender, Easter Day being the first day of April in Poland, by the new Gregorian institution.

Dee took great care to record both the old style of dates and the new once he had arrived in Poland, for although the Gregorian calendar was very recent, it had been adopted throughout Catholic Europe, and scholars from protestant countries, although refusing to accept such a papist reform (the Gregorian calender was not accepted in England until 1752) were nevertheless extremely interested. Dee had written an

---

* This paper is based on a lecture given at the British Comparative Literature Association Triennial Congress held at the University of Warwick, July 1992.

unpublished discourse to the Queen inviting her to 'peruse and consider as concerning the needful Reformation of the Vulgar Kalendar for the civil yeres and daies accompting or veryfying, according to the time truly spent'[2] in February 1583, and the question of calendar reform was clearly an important factor in his travels across Northern Europe and subsequent sojourn in Cracow, Prague and Trebon in Southern Bohemia.

Dee's interest in calendar reform marks a shift in his scientific work that appears to coincide with his meeting with Edward Kelley, who served as his medium in the summoning of spirits, and his departure from England and central Europe. In the 1570s a great deal of Dee's time had been spent on map-making, advising such travellers as Martin Frobisher who was seeking a north-western passage to Cathay and Sir Francis Drake who sailed around the world in the years between 1577 and 1580. Dee had previously, in the 1550s, advised on the early voyages to try and find a north-east passage to Cathay and published his *General and Rare Memorials pertayning to the Perfect arts of Navigation* in 1577. Peter French, Dee's biographer, noting that the two central sections of this work are missing, possibly because they contained politically sensitive material, points out that Dee was preoccupied with the establishment of an 'incomparable British Empire'.[3] Dee was a product of the great age of voyages of discovery, the moment when map-making became a science rather than an art, when the map became an instrument of hegemony, the means by which whole civilisations could be conquered, millions of slaves traded across oceans and whole patterns of social relations altered irrevocably. As Mary Hamer says, map-making signifies a process of massive change:

the very activities of measuring, ordering, regulating and standardizing, the production of accuracy that is the prerequisite of scale mapping, involve a rigorous shaping of the material world that is at odds with and alien to the forms in which the material world has it prior existence.[4]

But Dee moved away from map-making, shifted his focus to the problem of measuring time and dates and turned his attention to making contact with the anti-material world of the spirits, a shift that has troubled generations of scholars unable to reconcile mathematics, map-making and magic in the manner of Dee's contemporaries. Not that all his contemporaries were able to effect such a reconciliation either: John Foxe, for example, referred to him as 'the great Conjurer' and 'a Caller of Divils',[5] terms of abuse that provoked Dee so much he demanded a public retraction.

Considering the life of John Dee through the lenses of twentieth-century consciousness, we may well share Peter French's sentiments when he asks: what *can* one make of a man like John Dee? He is either a figure who has been taken very seriously indeed, as Frances Yates did,[6] or dismissed as a charlatan, as one of a number of shadowy philosopher-magus figures whose paths crossed occasionally in central Europe at the end of the sixteenth century. My own interest in him, however, and the reason for mentioning him in this context, comes not from any desire to demonstrate anything particularly startling, but rather to introduce the crucial issue of explicit and implicit knowledge.

Let me explain. I am currently preparing an edition of the poetry of Elizabeth Weston (1582–1612), an Englishwoman who lived and wrote in Prague, and who was hailed as the tenth Muse, famed throughout Europe for her learning, her linguistic skills and her ability to write Latin poetry. Her works give an account of her life: born in England, taken at an early age to Bohemia, brought up by a beloved step-father and her mother, after the death of her noble father, one John Weston. Biographical accounts are fairly consistent; they detail her life as traceable through the slim volumes of her verses: the *Poemata*, published in 1602 and the *Parthenicon*, probably published in 1606/7.[7] The inscription on her tomb in the cloisters of St Thomas in Prague describes her as

> Nobilitate patriae praeclara Britannia
> Seculi nostri Sulpitiae
> Cui nomen dant litterae illibati
> Minervae floris
> Suadae decoris
> Musarum delicii
> Foeminarum exempli.

A noble Englishwoman, writing startling personal poetry, heavily cross-referenced with Ovid's *Tristia*, for just as he had ended his days in exile on the Black Sea, so Westonia claims to be exiled from her native land.

But this reading of her life, carefully constructed in the pages of her poetry, is at variance with an alternative reading that emerges from some poems published separately, and from the linking of two other biographies, that of John Dee and Edward Kelley, his much-maligned assistant. Kelley, the man for whom no biographer or scholar that I have ever read can utter a positive word, was none other than Elizabeth Weston's beloved step-father, and the answer to how she came to be in

Prague in the first place can be found by looking at the journey to central Europe undertaken by Dee and Kelley and their families in 1583. The account of the journey that we have traces the summoning of spirits in different places; there is a concealed account that can only be speculatively constructed, which would trace the story of Jane Dee and Johanna Kelley and their children, present throughout and yet absent almost entirely from Dee's journal entries of that period.

The texts left to us by Dee, by Kelley himself (there are letters and two treatises on the Philosopher's Stone together with the *Theatre of Terrestrial Astronomy*) and by Elizabeth Weston are all concerned in different ways with mapping, with detailing precise information, with recording the results of experiments, the coming and going of visitors, the exact time of meetings and of departures, the point of origin, the source of a family name. In their different ways, they are all concerned with public declarations of 'truth' and when that truth was questioned, they responded immediately. Dee demanded that Foxe retract his 'conjurer' insult thirteen years after it had first appeared in print; Kelley wrote to Burghleigh proclaiming his honest intentions of returning to England to manufacture gold for Elizabeth's campaign against Spain. The British Library edition of *Parthenicon* has a hand-written address to the reader inside the front cover by Elizabeth Weston, complaining about editorial distortion of her work:

Everything you see here printed, Reader, in this small book, under my name, I do not deny I wrote. But yet there is a reason why this publication troubles me. You see, the poems are flung together, randomly joined to the early ones I wrote as a young bride while printing errors swarm like ants (and I fear cruel spite will put the blame on me). A so-called friend who does not have the right has filled my pages with his own ideas. Poets of worth, whose names I am glad to see he has combined with most unwelcome things. He has left out my best poems, and you'll note my words are mixed with other people's verse. Can you, I ask, call this Westonia's book, you who have given Westonia so little room? You should have risked your reputation on an unspoiled book, worthy of fame instead of linking your great works of art with a woman's feeble verse and helpless rhymes. Though I shall not deter you, let the reader read all with an open mind and unbiased taste. There will be time, if Fate permits it so for Westonia's pages to be filled with rhymes by her.[8]

To explore the works of Elizabeth Weston and by implication Dee and Kelley is to enter a different psychic world, one where the boundaries between objectively verifiable data and subjectively constructed reality are drawn so differently that we cannot comprehend the criteria they used. Stephen Greenblatt, Umberto Eco, Michel Foucault and countless others have all reminded us time and again of the shifts of perception taking place in the late sixteenth century in Europe, the period when, according to Foucault, 'thought ceases to move in the element of resemblance'.[9] The very term 'Renaissance', overtly and visibly a term of growth, change and the new carries within it a covert story of the death of a previous world. Foucault suggests that the death of the age of resemblance leaves nothing behind but games:

And it was also in the nature of things that the knowledge of the sixteenth century should leave behind it the distorted memory of a muddled and disorderly body of learning in which all the things in the world could be linked indiscriminately to men's experiences, traditions, and credulities. From then on, the noble, rigorous, and restrictive figures of similitude were to be forgotten. And the signs that designated them were to be thought of as the fantasies and charms of a knowledge that had not yet attained the age of reason.[10]

The change in the ordering of explicit and implicit knowledge that took place in the sixteenth and early seventeenth centuries is impossible to map. The best we can do is to intuit it, through the texts we have at our disposal. So Westonia's complaint about editorial distortion has to be set against her own explicit attempt to conceal her paternity (her father was a clerk from Chipping Norton in Oxfordshire, her mother a local girl from the same village) and against her (fictitious) insistence on a noble past, while Dee's precise recordings of dates and times has to be set against the apparently random information he chose to include in his Diary and the notes on communications with the spirits. Such contradictions reveal the fallacy of attempting to read another age, another culture on the same terms as we endeavour to read the one we consider to be our own.

This is a good time for practitioners of 'comparative literature' or 'comparative studies' or 'comparatistics' or however we choose to describe what we do. We have moved on a very long way in the last twenty years or so, away from the sterile debates about the nature of comparing, the problems of boundaries and distinctions and definitions. Now we are able to celebrate the playful in the text, the absence of final solutions, the concept of *difference* – and we don't even have to call ourselves postmodernists in order to do so. We are perhaps in a better position to look at periods of great transition, such as the Renaissance, than at any time this century, for there is greater flexibility in literary study now and the notion of the definitive reading has quietly been laid to rest, freeing us to build bridges and establish connections between our own and other worlds.

When I first started teaching comparative literature at the University

of Warwick, I began by trying to determine the parameters of the
activity of comparing. Some of those parameters were imposed upon
me: comparative literary study had to take place across language
boundaries, for a start. A French author could be compared to a
German, but a comparison between an English and a United States
author could not be defined as 'true' comparative literature because of
the common language. The question of cultural diversity never seemed
to arise, and it was hardly surprising that finally my students revolted
against such constraints and switched their allegiance to the newly
developed field of Translation Studies, where questions of linguistic
diversity are subsumed in an examination of the processes of intercultural
transfer of texts. Now, in the light of significant developments such as
Translation Studies, feminist criticism and post-colonial theory
especially, we can rethink the significance of 'comparing' literatures.

Foucault declares that there 'exist two forms of comparison and only
two': the comparison of measurement, which 'analyses into units in
order to establish relations of equality and inequality', and that of order,
'which establishes the simplest elements and arranges differences'.[11] It
seems to me that comparative literary study in the past has been overly
concerned with the first type of comparison, and has only latterly moved
towards the second. And one of the most significant developments of the
new-style comparative literary study involves a change in our readings
of accounts of journeys, of the tales told by travellers of their experiences
of other cultures, of the information they include and exclude, the
explicit and the implicit. Which brings me back to Dee, Kelley and the
small Elizabeth Weston travelling by boat and on horseback for six
months across northern Europe en route from London to Cracow.

With Dee's account in one hand, and a European atlas in the other,
I traced the stages of their journey through what is now the Netherlands,
Germany, the former GDR and Poland. Then I asked the elementary
question of why they followed that route, and so looked in Muir's
Historical Atlas (pages 38 and 39), which gives a colour-coded picture
of the political boundaries in effect in Western and Central Europe
between 1555 and 1648, with a small inset map, also colour-coded, of
Religions of Central Europe at the same time. Dee and his party had
carefully steered a course through Calvinist and Lutheran territories,
avoiding Catholic-dominated territories, making their way down from
the Baltic coast into central Europe along a carefully selected route that
would ensure they lodged in friendly territory until they reached their
destination. Europe to Dee must have been a mental construct mapped

along religious boundaries, with criteria of accessibility that were unique to his age.

Also unique to his age, but coming from a very different starting-point, is a map of Europe held in the Strahov Library in Prague, which is a symbolic representation of Europa as a virgin, dated 1592 (see the frontispiece to this volume). The virgin's head, wearing a crown, is Hispania, her shoulders Gallia, and her left arm curves round the Dutch coast, bending at the elbow into Dania, and her fingers grip a slender rod which cuts off Norvegia and Svetia. Her right arm stretches down through Italia, and the orb she holds is Sicilia. The collar around her neck is the Montes Piranei, the curve of her neckline contains Gallia, her breasts are Germania and Swevia, with a glowing golden heart that is Bohemia. Her long gown stretches out through Polonia as far as Moscovia on the left-hand side, and down through Albania and Graecia to the Pelopponesus on the right. A great artery runs down her body, through the cities of Vienna, Buda and Alba Graeca into a delta at the hem of her skirt. Parallel to this artery runs a decorative border of mountains, from Illiricum to Constantinopolis. The entire gown from collar to hem is coloured green, making the uncoloured patches of the southernmost tip of Norvegia and Svetia, along with the northernmost part of Mauritania and the easterly part of Asia Minor, stand out palely in comparison. Most significantly the uncoloured islands of Anglia and Hibernia float just beside her left ear, disproportionately large in relation to the rest of the map. The defeat of the Spanish Armada four years earlier in 1588 had effectively ended the emperor's ambitions of annexing the islands, but the sheer size of these uncoloured land masses floating so tantalizingly close to the virgin's crown suggest that they remain an object of desire. This vision of Europe, which reflects the imperial concept of a continent united under the crown of imperial Spain is a map of Europe that Dee fearfully avoided as he plotted his course through safe Lutheran and Calvinist lands, out of the emperor's range.

The unknown map-marker who produced that text may have been working on it at the same time that Fynes Moryson, a student of Peterhouse, Cambridge, as he describes himself in his opening sentence, set off on his journey round Europe that was published as *His ten Yeeres travels thorow Twelve Dominions*. The first of these journeys, in 1591, followed a similar route to that of Dee's party, but contains considerably more detail of what happened along the way. Fynes Moryson, appropriately for a student, is obsessively concerned with how much things cost, and recounts little anecdotes abut people and places. I quote here his first account of Prague, which gives some indication of the tone of his writing:

So as Prage consists of three Citiies, all compressed with wals, yet is nothing lesse than strong, and except the stinch of the streetes drive back the Turkes, or they meete them in open field, there is small hope in the fortifications thereof. The streets are filthy, there be divers large market places, the building of some houses is of free stone, but for the most part are of timber and clay and are built with little beauty or Art, the walles being all of whole trees as they come out of the wood, the which with the bark are laid so rudely, as they may on both sides be seen. Molda in the winter useth to be so frozen, as it beareth carts, and the ice thereof being cut in great peeces, is laid up in cellers for the Emperour and Princes to mingle with their wine in summer, which me thinkes can neither be savoury nor healthfull, since neither the heat of the clime, nor the strength of the Bohemian wines (being small and sharp) require any such cooling.[12]

With subsequent journeys, Fynes Moryson became increasingly confident, giving lengthy accounts of what people wore, the food they ate, their courtship and marriage practices, punishments and countless other details. He also begins to address the reader directly and to offer advice to other travellers, assuming a far more authoritative role than the enthusiastic undergraduate voice of the first itinerary. And with greater authority comes another more cautionary note:

a traveller must sometimes hide his money, change his habit, dissemble his Country and fairly conceal his Religion...[13]

More cynically, he warns against the foolishness of being caught in the wrong place with the wrong religious credentials, and advises travellers to hold their tongues:

Let them stay at home who are so zealous, as they will pull the Hostia or the Sacrament out of the Priest's hand. They should do better to avoid the adoring thereof, by slipping out of the way, or restraining their curious walkes, for inordinate desire of Martyrdome is not approvable.

Fynes Moryson and Dee both travelled across the body of Europa, but their accounts are different in tone, context and, if I may be permitted to use the word, intent. Dee records the spirit encounters, with the geographical data incidental, whilst Fynes Moryson records a random collection of anecdotes, experiences, vignettes and images. Reading his Itineraries we lose track of where he is, and although he tells us that it took him two and a half days to each Augsburg from Nuremberg and his horse cost him 2 dollars, his concern is not with the spatial at all. Dee's account of his journey is conditioned by his experience as a map-maker, Fynes Moryson is out on a kind of quest, wandering through the world in search of adventures. Significantly, he notes the size and strength of fortifications in the cities he visits, because a constant subtext in his writing is the fear of attack by the Turks. Most important of all, however, is the narrative persona, for whilst Dee's narrative is presented as a series of notes and jottings, Fynes Moryson's is a carefully crafted whole, with a dominant I speaker who leads the reader with him along the roads of Europe, pausing occasionally to preach, to patronize and to give advice to those he deems more inexperienced.

The debates on translation that have raged on down the centuries have frequently concerned the visibility or lack of it of the translator. Is the translator a transparent channel, a kind of glass tube through which the SL text is miraculously transformed in its passage into the target language, or is the translator herself an element in that process of transformation? Similar questions have begun to be asked about map-makers, questions that challenge the supposed objectivity of a map and ask what the map might be for, what it might be seeking to represent. Post-colonial theory has called into question the organization of geographical space, inviting us to consider the prioritizing of the starting-point, the cultural base of the map-maker. So European Renaissance cartographers prioritize Europe, just as Piri Reis (*c.* 1470–1554), the great Turkish mariner and author of the *Kitab-i-Bariye*, gave priority to the Muslim Mediterranean world.

The map-maker, the translator and the travel writer are not innocent producers of texts. The works they create are part of a process of manipulation that shapes and conditions our attitudes to other cultures while purporting to be something else. Map-makers produce texts that can be used in very specific ways, translators intervene in the interlingual transfer with every word they choose, travel writers constantly position themselves in relation to their point of origin in a culture and the context they are describing.

In 1992, the *Independent* published a map of the new Europe to assist its readers in orienting themselves with the collapse of the communist regimes in the East. The opening of borders immediately called into question the very terminology that had been in place for decades. Finally it could be recognized that Vienna is, in geographical terms, much further to the east than Prague, a city formerly designated as part of Eastern Europe. The language of East and West, borrowed from geography, had come to acquire a political significance, just as the language of North and South does in Ireland (the most northerly geographical point in Ireland is in the South, and Willie Docherty's captioned photograph entitled *The Other Side* states that 'West is South' and 'East is North', an apparent conundrum that is completely comprehensible to anyone familiar with the situation in Northern Ireland.[14]

The *Independent* map offers a new enlarged version of Europe. This Europe does not stop at the Black Sea, the point generally regarded as the most easterly boundary in the twentieth century. Previous boundaries had been many and varied, depending on political as well as linguistic criteria. In 1834 Alexander Kinglake, author of *Eothen or Traces of Travel Brought Home from the East*, noted:

I had come, as it were, to the end of this wheel-going Europe, and now my eyes would see the Splendour and Havoc of the East.[15]

He had reached Belgrade.

Suddenly, Europe has stretched, changed direction, moved thousands of miles into what was once Asia. What are we meant to read into this revision of geographical, ethnic, religious and political boundaries? That because the former Soviet Union was classified as a European state, now that it has ceased to exist are its component parts *de facto* parts of Europe too? (Though not all the component parts, by any means.) That the map-makers see the conferral of European status as a positive attribute? That EEC states are looking hungrily towards the natural resources said to lie beneath the soil of what were once termed Central Asian states? That we should all now wipe out centuries of conditioning that saw Islam, as Edward Said puts it, as symbolic of 'terror, devastation, the demonic, hordes of hated barbarians'?[16]

Besides, the anonymous *Independent* map-maker was so concerned with looking out to the Caspian Sea that he or she cut Iceland off altogether. The small, Scandinavian island up in the North Atlantic has suddenly, like Atlantis, vanished without trace. Could such an omission have anything to do with the end of the Cold War, one may ask, and the abrupt demise of Iceland's importance as a strategic base for the monitoring of Soviet military action? The omission was not remedied in the enlarged version of the map which followed the first one. One stroke of the pen added Azerbaijan and subtracted Iceland from what is now a Europe that stretches across a continent and a half. Only the southern part of Norway, Sweden and Finland appear. The whole bias of the map is away from Northern Europe towards those areas that were once part of the Roman Empire: Bithynia and Pontus, Cappadocia, Armenia,

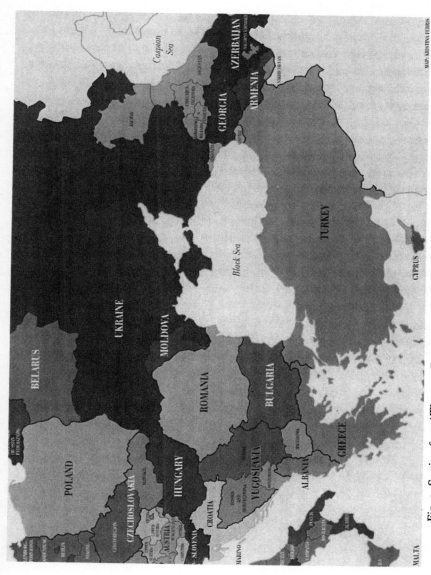

Fig. 1. Section from 'The new Europe 1992', a map provided by the *Independent* newspaper.

Colchis and the Caucasus. The rise and fall of the Ottoman Empire is wiped away with this cartographical manipulation.

In Fynes Moryson's Europe, the fear was of encroachment by the Turks, and during the reign of Suleiman the Magnificent (1520–66) the Ottoman Empire had extended down as far as the Persian Gulf and northwards through what is now part of the Ukraine, north-westwards through part of Hungary, Croatia and Slovenia. Unable to capture Vienna in 1529, there was to be a second Turkish siege of the city as late as 1689, and in the latter half of the seventeenth century the Ottoman Empire claimed a large part of what is now southern Poland, territories in the Caucasus, Cyprus and Crete. Fynes Moryson's anxiety was based on concrete evidence; the Ottoman military machine was highly efficient, the annexation of lands systematic and thorough.

So if we want to try and imagine how Dee or Moryson constructed a mental map of the world, we have to think of (1) a Europe divided and mapped out according to religious frontiers; (2) a Europe, Catholic and Protestant alike, looking nervously eastwards scanning the horizon, like the soldiers at the outpost in Dino Buzzati's wonderful novel, *Il deserto dei Tartari*, for possible signs of movement that could signify attack; and (3) a Europe reaching greedily out across the Atlantic, seizing the opportunity, as scholars such as Peter Hulme and Sabina Sharkey have pointed out, to penetrate and fertilize virgin lands elsewhere.[17]

It is now accepted that the discourse of the great age of colonialization makes extensive use of gender metaphors. 'Oh my America', says John Donne of his Mistress's naked body, 'my new found land'. And a growing body of scholarship suggests that this figurative language extends a long way back, through medieval Europe into Roman times. Outside the boundaries of what a culture deemed to be 'civilization', all kinds of terrors lurked, and those terrors were frequently depicted in terms of sexual difference. New territories could therefore be described as 'virgin' lands; the notion of a rich Orient was linked to eroticism and lasciviousness – 'the beds i' the East are soft', says Shakespeare's Antony (II. 3.50); and fantasizing about the sexual habits of other cultures led (as it still does in a great deal of contemporary travel writing) to unsubstantiated generalizations of the kind proclaimed by Tacitus when he announced:

Thus it is that the German women live in a chastity that is impregnable, uncorrupted by the temptations of public shows or the excitements of banquets. Clandestine love affairs are unknown to men and women alike... The young men are slow to mate, and their powers, therefore, are never exhausted.[18]

Tacitus is here describing the barbarians of the Northern forests, but from the perspective of a writer who argues that his own society has degenerated, while the Germans are still relatively unspoiled. Hence it was essential to present the Germans in idealized terms, in order for the corruption of the Roman world to be more sharply exposed. Significantly, Tacitus was reread during the Reformation from a quite different perspective again: his account of the chastity of German women and the inherent nobility of German men could be read as an example of the purity of the Protestant heritage in contrast with the excessive sensuality of Rome. Later still, as Ernest Renan suggested, the distinction made by Tacitus between North and South, between Germans and Romans, was used in the struggle against Napoleon.[19] And, of course, Madame de Staël enshrined that binary opposition of North and South in *De l'Allemagne*.

In the age of imperial expansion in the nineteenth century, the split between North and South widened yet again. With the Ottoman Empire crumbling, the threat from the East diminished, and the tone of many writers introducing the East to fellow Europeans was distinctly patronising and pejorative. Moreover, the tendency to describe alternative cultures in sexually figurative language took on another dimension. E. W. Lane, translator of the *Arabian Nights* (his version appeared in 1840) announced with the confidence reminiscent of Tacitus' assertions about the chaste Germans that:

the women of Egypt have the character of being the most licentious in their feelings of all females who lay any claim to be considered as members of a civilised nation... What liberty they have, many of them, it is said abuse; and most of them are not considered safe unless under lock and key... some of the stories of the intrigues of women in The Thousand and One Nights present faithful pictures of occurrences not infrequent in the modern metropolis of Egypt.[20]

Faithful pictures: the discourse of faithfulness that has so dogged Translation Studies and from which we are finally beginning to emerge is also a dominant discourse in travel writing. Travellers have pretensions towards faithfulness, insisting that we believe their accounts simply because they have been there and we have not. So Lane can assure us with confidence that Egyptian women are the worst in the world, whilst his contemporary Richard Burton provides us with the important information that tallow candles were forbidden in harems and 'bananas when detected were cut into four so as to be useless'.[21] The line between pornography and travel writing is pretty finely drawn in certain cases.

Rana Kabbani and a range of other scholars drawing upon feminist methodologies have started to examine the way in which European travellers eroticize the Orient and transform it into the locus of their own sexual fantasies.[22] This is another whole new dimension of Comparative Literary Studies and an important one, for as we learn how cultures construct other cultures, how the explicit and the implicit are woven together, so we also learn about the manipulative processes that underlie such self-proclaimed 'objective' or 'faithful' depictions of reality.

I want now to turn to the two poles of the *Independent* map: the vanished island of Iceland in the North Atlantic and the huge expanding Turkic realms in Asia. It says a great deal about how we structure our world that we have come to want our maps to be constructed along latitudinal and longitudinal lines, which leads inevitably to oppositions at different edges. A glance at alternative mapping conventions, such as the Mappa Mundi (*c*. 1290), shows what happens to a mental concept of the world when such linear conventions are not used: the top of the world is not the North but the East, where the sun (God) rises in glory and the centre of the earth, as Dante tells us, is in Jerusalem. With these conventions in place, the world is drawn quite differently. (Note, however, that the designer of the Mappa Mundi did not forget to include the island of Ultima Thule, generally held to be Iceland, and the Orkneys and Faroes as well.) The oceans flow round the rim of the circular world, not as an expanse of uncharted water but as a gently encircling band.

The presence of dog-headed beings, bat-eared humans, mermaids and griffins has long since been dismissed by more 'rational, scientific' ages. Today, we want accuracy from our maps, we want to believe in the truth of maps, the lack of bias of map-makers. I suggest that the *Independent* map shows up the fallacy of that belief in objectivity, for in our acceptance of mapping conventions of whatever period, we consign our belief into the hands of the map-maker, just as when we read a translation we want to trust the good faith of the translator. And, as I have said before, the activities of map-making, translating and writing about one's travels are never totally innocent activities.

Claudio Magris's book on the Danube (*Danubio*, 1986) explores the history of the binary opposition of North and South in European cultural history through a journey down the Danube, the river that flows out of the heart of Europe towards the East. Starting with the source of the Danube, which is also virtually the same as that of the Rhine, he

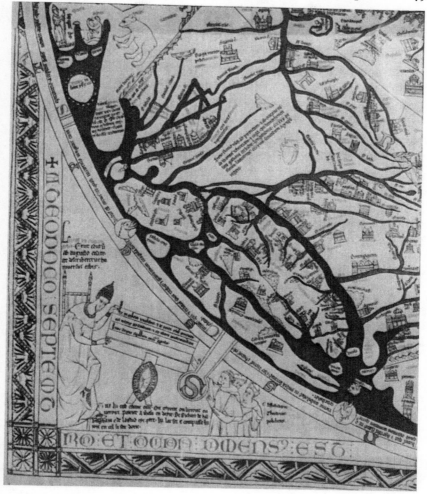

Fig. 2. Section of the Mappa Mundi, *c*. 1290.

looks in both directions, contrasting the symbolic significance of the two great rivers:

> Ever since the *Song of the Nibelungs* the Rhine and the Danube have confronted and challenged each other. The Rhine is Siegfried, symbol of Germanic virtue and purity, the loyalty of the Nibelungs, chivalric heroism, dauntless love of the destiny of the Germanic soul. The Danube is Pannonia, the kingdom of Attila, the eastern Asiatic tide which at the end of the *Song of the Nibelungs* overwhelms Germanic values: when the

Burgundians cross it on their way to the treacherous Hunnish court, their fate – a
Germanic fate – is sealed.[23]

The Song of the Nibelungs, which most contemporary Europeans know
only through Wagner, is part of the body of Germanic epic poetry that
reached its highest point in the Norse sagas of medieval Iceland.
Significantly, and very significantly indeed if we consider the marginal
position of Iceland today in topographical terms and in terms of
European cultural history, the great Norse sagas remained outside the
mainstream of medieval Europe. The sagas are the great European
absent texts, a central part of contemporary Icelandic culture but largely
unknown   anywhere else. Had they been known, they might have
changed the history of European literary production. Because they are
relatively unknown, they offer instead the fascination of what might
have been, texts that are to Iceland what the works of Hesiod and
Homer are to Greece, as the foreword by Paul Taylor to his and
W. H. Auden's *Norse Poems* attests.[24]

   In 1871 William Morris made his first journey to Iceland, and the
journals of his travels in 1871 and again in 1873 give an account of his
attempts to engage with the unknown. After his return from the second
journey he writes:

The journey has deepened the impression I had of Iceland and increased my love for
it. The glorious simplicity of the terrible and tragic, but beautiful land, with its well-
remembered stories of brave men, killed all querulous feeling in me, and has made all
the dear faces of wife and children and love and friends dearer than ever to me. I feel
as if a definite space of my life had passed away now that I have seen Iceland for the
last time... it was no ideal whim that drew me there, but a true instinct for what I
needed.[25]

Morris's Icelandic journals are curious texts. He gives meticulous details
of where he went, together with maps, but they are quite remarkably
unemotional. The impression on reading them is of a conscious attempt
at self-restraint, and one passage will suffice as an example of what I
mean:

we all drove together up a steepish hillside on the top of which lay a comfortable looking
stead and a church bigger than usual, which was Ingialdsholl, the scene of the (fictitious)
Viglundar saga. The folk were abed when we came, but they all tumbled out in the
greatest good-temper when we knocked them up: then as the night was now well on,
and gotten windy too, we asked leave to sleep in the church, in which all things were
soon arranged while I sat by the kitchen fire to make cocoa and milk hot, all the
household assisting... so to bed on the tombstones of Icelanders dead a hundred and
fifty years, within the screen much and prettily carved: the stones were hard, and there

was a goodish draught through the church floor, but all that made little difference to me five minutes after I had settled my blankets.

His daughter, who edited the journals, provides an explanatory footnote to this episode by his companion Eirikr Magnusson:

here Morris omits mentioning an incident unique in his journey. When he was 'settled in his blankets', he offered to tell us the Saga of Biorn the Champion of the men of Hitdale. The offer was accepted readily enough; and he told the whole saga in abridgement with remarkably few slips, winding up with the old rhyme:

> And here the saga comes to an end:
> May all who heard, to the good God wend

and the audience was still awake when he finished![26]

We look in vain for anything other than pedantically recorded details of landscape, food and accommodation. Yet the Icelandic journeys changed Morris as a writer. In 1876 he published his versions of *The Story of Sigurd the Volsung and the Fall of the Nibelungs*, and a reading of his novels shows the way in which he transformed the Icelandic landscape into the setting for his fantasy-world fiction. Morris is an example of what I would call the idealistic traveller, the utopian socialist aesthete who had already created an Iceland of the imagination that he went in homage to visit. Iceland was part of Morris's dream of a common Northern inheritance, offering a model of democratic society and artistic richness.

In contrast, W. H. Auden's and Louis MacNeice's *Letters from Iceland* (1937) show the consequences on holding up an imaginary Iceland as emblematic of Northern purity and idealism.

Great excitement here because Goering's brother and a party are expected this evening. Rosenberg is coming too. The Nazis have a theory that Iceland is the cradle of Germanic culture. Well, if they want a community like that of the sagas they are welcome to it. I love the sagas, but what a rotten society they describe, a society with only the gangster virtues.[27]

Louis MacNeice's' *Eclogue from Iceland* draws a picture of a society in decline, sold out by international capitalism:

> Us too they sold
> The women and the men with many sheep.
> Graft and aggression, legal prevarication
> drove out the best of us...
> And through the sweat and blood of thralls and hacks,
> Cheating the poor men of their share of drift
> the whale on Kaldbak in the starving winter.

And so today at Grimsby men whose lives
Are warped in Atlantic trawlers load and unload
The shining tons of fish to keep the lords
Of the Market happy with cigars and cars.[28]

For Morris and for Auden Iceland was inspirational. Both translated
Norse poetry, both saw in the early model of democracy a socialist ideal,
both saw similarities between their vision of Iceland and ancient Greece.
Their Icelands were male societies, and on some level they play at being
Vikings themselves, distanced from home and family, and though
Auden is more playful than Morris (his *Letters to Lord Byron* are very
funny) they are both part of the same game. Auden is at pains to
dissociate himself from the Nazi view of Iceland as a place of racial
purity, the repository of Aryan civilization, but nevertheless both the
views of Iceland and its history come from the same source: from
readings of Tacitus.

Travellers to Iceland stress the remoteness of the place, the virtues of
human courage in surviving the harsh climatic conditions, the power of
the great unknown texts of European cultural history. Generalizing, we
can say that there is a tendency to perceive Iceland as a model of a
fictitious Germanic past, and travellers such as Morris and Auden
approached it with reverence. Grey, strong, terrible, bitter cold, solemn
– these adjectives recur through Morris's journals, and despite the
greater levity of Auden's and McNeice's *Letters from Iceland*, the same
tone prevails:

So we have come   In that island never found
As trippers North   Visions blossom from the ground
Have minds no match   No conversions like St Paul,
For this land's girth   No great happenings at all.

If the volcanic ruggedness of Iceland is seen as symbolic of the virtues
of restraint and self-discipline, the beauties of Turkey and especially of
Instanbul are repeatedly seen in terms of sensuality. Travellers' tales of
sexual encounters with veiled ladies abound. Here is Alexander
Kinglake's story of one such meeting in the streets of Constantinople:

Of her very self you see nothing, except the dark, luminous eyes that stare against your
face, and the tip of the painted fingers depending like rosebuds from out of the blank
bastions of the fortress. She turns and turns again, and carefully glances around her on
all sides, to see that she is safe from the eyes of Musselmans, and then suddenly
withdrawing the yashmak, she shines upon your heart and soul with all the pomp and
might of her beauty. And this, it is not the light, changeful grace that leaves you to doubt
whether you have fallen in love with a body, or only a soul; it is the beauty that dwells

secure in the perfectness of hard, downright outlines, and in the flow of generous colour. There is fire, though, too – high courage, and fire enough in the untamed mind, or spirit, or whatever it is which derives the breath of pride through these scarcely parted lips.[29]

There is a postscript to Kinglake's tale – the lady touches him and cries 'There is a present of the plague for you', which he explains is a common Turkish joke against Christians. It is an odd story, which combines elements of voyeurism and sexual fantasy (the mysterious veiled lady exposing herself to a passing European) but without a sexual finale, and stylistically it stands out from the surrounding narrative, being written in the present tense and the whole sequence starting with the tentative phrase 'And perhaps as you make your difficult way through a steep and narrow alley...'. It also contrasts sharply with Kinglake's insistence on writing honestly ('my excuse for the book is its truth').

An earlier visitor to Turkey also insisted that she was telling the truth about the society she encountered. Lady Mary Wortley Montagu's Turkish letters describe the social customs, dress and conversations of aristocratic Turkish women she met during her stay in Constantinople. Lady Mary's *Letters* are interesting in that she is concerned with dispelling fantasies about Ottoman sexual customs, as demonstrated by the letter of 10 March 1718 to her sister, describing a meeting with the favourite wife of the late Emperor Mustapha:

I did not omit this opportunity of learning all that I possibly could of the Seraglio, which is so entirely unknown amongst us. She assured me that the story of the Sultan's throwing a handkerchief is altogether fabulous.[30]

The reference here is to a story by Paul Rycaut, recounted in his *Present State of the Ottoman Empire* (1668) who claims that 'the Damsels being ranged in order by the Mother of the Maids, he (the Sultan) throws his handkerchief to her, where his eye and fantasy best directs, it being a token of her election to his bed'.[31] Lady Mary cuts through the pornographic fantasies of the lascivious life of ladies of the seraglio: she continually seeks to draw parallels between the Turkish court and the courts of London and Vienna. One of her longest accounts tells the story of the Spanish noblewoman to whom, as she delicately puts it, 'the same accident happened to her that happened to the fair Lucretia so many yeares before her, but she was too good a Christian to kill herself as that heathenish Roman did'.[32] Instead, the Spanish lady refuses the ransom money and the liberty offered by her Turkish lover, having 'very discretely weighed the different treatment she was likely to find in her

native country'. Balancing the fact that her Spanish relatives would
'certainly confine her a nunnery for the rest of her days', whilst her
'Infidel lover was very handsome, very tender, fond of her and lavished
at her feet all Turkish magnificence' the Lady chooses a Moslem
husband and rejects the offer of freedom from her Christian relations.
The story is told with considerable glee, and Lady Mary obviously
celebrates the unorthodox decision of the Spanish woman to choose her
own way in life. In many respects Lady Mary's letters are a refreshing
change from the conventions of voyeuristic 'truth-telling' and celebrate
the rights of women to assert themselves, besides rejoicing in the
opportunity to contradict male stereotypes of the Orient. It would be far
too simplistic to describe Lady Mary as a feminist, and yet there are
ways in which her letters prefigure some of the concerns of feminism
later in the eighteenth century. Likewise, Julia Pardoe's *The City of the
Sultan and Domestic Manners of the Turks* (1837) and *The Beauties of the
Bosphorus* (1839) show an author concerned with rebutting the growing
volume of pornographic travel writing that offered 'expert' insights into
the sexual mores of the Orient.

When I look at the *Independent* map of the new Europe of the 1990s,
I cannot help but recall the shifts in the map of Europe across the
centuries and what those shifts have signified. The desire to appropriate
areas that are commonly described as 'weak', 'undeveloped', 'marginal'
(and, though not explicitly stated, but sharing the same vocabulary,
'feminine') in unclaimed areas of the world around the Black Sea and
the Caucasus has led the map-maker to boldly assert the boundaries of
Europe right into Asia (though interestingly in 1985 Eric Newby, the
well-known travel writer, endeavoured to divide Asia into Near, Middle
and Far, according to idiosyncratic criteria.[33] Likewise, a certain
uneasiness with the Germanic past and contemporary political
expediency has resulted in the elimination of Iceland altogether. I
suggest that the polarization of East and West, North and South, as
strong as it ever has been for more than 2,000 years, is also now to be
looked at in terms of genderized language and the emerging history
of colonial exploitation. Map-making, travelling, translating are not
transparent, they are very definitely located activities, with points of
origin, points of departure and destinations. The great development in
Comparative Literary Studies is that such questions are now on our
agenda; the time has come not only for us to compare accounts, but to
question the premises on which those accounts were written in the first
place. We, too, are in the process of moving from simply mapping to

the far more sophisticated science of balancing different systems of calculating times and dates. John Dee, by moving from commercial cartography to conversations with entities from another dimension was, in his own way, our precursor.

NOTES

1 *A True and Faithful Relation of what passed for many Yeares between Dr John Dee, a Mathematician of Great Fame in Q. Elizabeth and K. James their Reigns, and Some Spirits: Tending (had it succeeded) To a general Alteration of most States and Kingdomes in the World... with Preface by Meric Casaubon*, printed by D. Maxwell for T. Garthwaite (London, 1659).

2 Charlotte Fell Smith, *John Dee: 1527–1608* (London, 1909), p. 133.

3 Peter French, *John Dee. The World of an Elizabethan Magus* (London, Routledge and Kegan Paul, 1972), p. 180.

4 Mary Hamer, 'Putting Ireland on the Map', *Textual Practice*, 3, no. 2 (Summer 1989), pp. 184–202.

5 Peter French, *John Dee*, p. 8.

6 Frances Yates, *The Rosicrucian Enlightenment* (London, Routledge and Kegan Paul, 1972).

7 See Susan Bassnett, 'Elizabethan Jane Weston: The Hidden Roots of Poetry', in *Prag am 1600* (Frankfurt am Main, 1988), pp. 239–51; Susan Bassnett, 'Revising a Biography: A New Interpretation of the Life of Elizabeth Jane West, Based on Her Autobiographical Poem on the Occasion of the Death of her Mother', *Cahiers Elisabèthains*, no. 37 (April 1990), pp. 1–8.

8 My translation.

9 Michael Foucault, *The Order of Things* (London, 1970), p. 51.

10 *Ibid.*, p. 51.

11 *Ibid.*, p. 53.

12 Fynes Moryson, *An Itinerary containing his ten yeeres travell thorow twelve dominions* (London, 1617), p. 29.

13 *Ibid.*, p. 415.

14 Willie Docherty, 'The Other Side' (Waterside, Derry 1988), *Unknown Depths*, Belfast: Ffotogallery 1991.

15 Alexander Kinglake, *Eothen, or Traces of Travel Brought Home from the East* (pub. 1844) (Oxford University Press, 1982), p.7.

16 Edward Said, *Orientalism* (London, 1978), p. 59.

17 See Peter Hulme, *Colonial Encounters* (London, 1986); Sabina Sharkey, 'Ireland and the Iconography of Rape: Colonisation, Constraint and Gender', University of North London, Occasional Papers Series, no. 4, September 1992.

18 Tacitus, *Germania*, trans. H. Mattingly (Harmondsworth, 1948), p. 116.

19 See Ernest Renan, 'What is a Nation?' (lecture originally given at the Sorbonne, March 1882) in Homi K. Bhabha, ed., *Nation and Narration* (London, 1990), pp. 8–23.

20 E. W. Lane, *Manners and Customs of the Modern Egyptians* (London, 1836), p. 296.

21 Richard Burton, *The Book of the Thousand Nights and a Night* (London, 1885–8), 17 vols., vol. I, pp. 234–5.

22 Rana Kabbani, *Europe's Myths of Orient* (London, 1986).

23 Claudio Magris, *Danube*, trans. Patrick Creagh (London, 1990), p. 29.

24 W. H. Auden and Paul B. Taylor, *Norse Poems* (London, 1981).

25 William Morris, *Journals of Travel in Iceland, The Collected Works of William Morris*, vol. VIII (New York, 1966), pp. xxxiii–xxxiv.

26 *Ibid.*, p. 139 and p. 239.

27 W. H. Auden and Louis MacNeice, *Letters from Iceland* (London, 1937), p. 119.

28 *Ibid.*, pp. 128–9.

29 Kinglake, *Eothen*, pp. 36–7.

30 *The Complete Letters of Lady Mary Wortley Montagu*, ed. Robert Halsband, vol. I, 1708–20 (Oxford, 1965), p. 383.

31 Paul Rycaut, *The Present State of the Ottoman Empire* (1668), p. 39.

32 Mary Worley Montagu, *Complete Letters*, vol. I, p. 408.

33 Eric Newby, *A Book of Travellers' Tales* (London, 1985).

Comparative Criticism 15, pp. 57–79. Cambridge University Press 1993

Transatlantic responses: strategies in the making of a New World literature

ARMIN PAUL FRANK

Der Amerikaner, der den Kolumbus zuerst entdeckte, machte eine böse Entdeckung.
(Georg Christoph Lichtenberg)

The subject of this paper is, quite frankly, a discovery I did not set out to make.[1] Perhaps 1992 is a year when scholars are permitted to indulge in the Columbus syndrome. Or, again, the hallmark of genuine scholarship may well be that the researcher follows facts, as interpreted, into areas beyond those circumscribed by the assumptions that underlie the act(s) of interpretation. However this may be, my starting-point was the view, based on disciplinary study, that the historiography of American literature suffers from not being comparative enough, and the impression, based on less thorough reading, that literary comparatists, to their loss, do not take things American sufficiently into account. This is why I posed as my problem an instance of inner-English comparative criticism, namely the relationship between British and American literature, not as we may be seeing it today, but as it was seen and, in a sense, invented, by the participants.[2] And being a philologist by methodological persuasion, I focused, as my starting-point, on a single text. I should probably add that I think of philology as the discipline which studies a culture in and through its language and literature, or languages and literatures, as the case may be, with the philologist employing as a favored method what Ezra Pound, with a different emphasis, called "the method of Luminous Detail": namely the identification and exegesis of those texts which shed (surprising) light on the contexts in which they have their historical place.[3]

A luminous detail for the relationship of British and American literature and culture in the eighteenth century is George Berkeley's occasional poem "America or the Muse's Refuge: A Prophecy" (1726), better known in its revised version, "On the Prospect of Planting Arts and Learning in America" (1752).[4] I propose, *first*, to elucidate the

second version historically by indicating how the various kinds of
translatio Berkeley drew upon are combined to form the gist or core of
a cultural morphology that connects America with Europe; I intend,
second, to approach this connection from a contemporary perspective in
terms of the empire–colony dichotomy and to indicate three principles
which writers resident in the thirteen North American colonies and in
the later United States of America employed in order to achieve literary
"independence"; and I should, *third*, like to conclude by touching on
the question of generalization: did writers in other colonies and post-
colonial nations employ similar strategies? Were similar strategies
employed in other cultural situations?

I

"America or the Muse's Refuge" was written at the time when Berkeley
was certain that Parliament and King would underwrite "a very noble
endowment" for his plan to establish a "College or Seminary" on the
Bermudas, designed to train "the Youth of our *English* Plantations...for
the Ministry" and to bring up "the Children of savage *Americans*" to
become "Missionaries for spreading the Gospel among...their own
Blood and Language."[5] Since the poem is harsh both on royalty and
education ("Truth and Sense" are said to have been supplanted by
"The Pedantry of Courts and Schools"),[6] it was clearly unpolitic to
write such verses. Even so, Berkeley sent them, thinly disguised as "a
poem wrote by a friend of mine with a view to the [Bermuda] scheme,"
to one of his aristocratic and political friends, enjoining him to "suffer
no copy to be taken of it."[7] Whether or not we should read the verses
as the inside story ("the spirit")[8] of the Bermuda project or not, it is
clear that this occasional but nodal poem expresses an emerging attitude
of "Europe-weariness," written as it was at a time when many began to
be fascinated with monuments of decline and fall; when almost everyone
on his grand tour sat down to muse on the ruins of the Colosseum; and
when one who had done so went home to trace, in his truly monumental
study, the long-drawn-out decline and fall of the Roman Empire.
Indeed, the first volume of Gibbon's history could not have appeared in
a more alarming year, for the British Empire: in 1776, when a major
chunk, the North American colonies, was breaking away.

When Berkeley published the revised version more than thirty years
after his project had failed, it now stood on its own. He pointed to
America in lines such as

> In happy Climes the Seat of Innocence,
> Where Nature guides and Virtue rules,
>
> ...
>
> There shall be sung another golden Age,
> The rise of Empire and of Arts;

and he was quite outspoken about the contrast:

> Not such as *Europe* breeds in her decay;
> Such as she bred when fresh and young.

The last stanza is the one that is normally quoted:

> Westward the Course of Empire takes its Way;
> The four first Acts already past,
> A fifth shall close the Drama with the Day;
> Time's noblest Offspring is the last.
> (Berkeley, *Works*, vol. VII, 373)

The elements of this poem are a number of quite conventional *translationes*, of movements sweeping across the Near East and Europe, East to West, mainly; some of the combinations, such as *empire* with *arts*, are equally conventional.[9] The luminous quality which the poem possesses consists in its overall composition, in the combination of various *translationes* that forms a timely cultural morphology, gathered, as it were, at the jumping-off point.

As for *empire*, it is customary to distinguish several *translationes*: a legal construct designed to justify the coronation of a Franconian king known as Charlemagne at Aachen, in 800, as Emperor of Rome; the corresponding formula *translatio imperii a Graecis ad Francos* devised in the eleventh century as a rationale of the emerging Holy Roman Empire, in its full designation, *Das Heilige Römische Reich Deutscher Nation*.[10] There is a Protestant version whose proponents quarreled with the Franconian *translatio* because the Popes had had their hands in it. In this sense, the Reformation was seen as a *translatio ad Teutonicos*, from corrupt, Babylonish Rome to the faithful Germanic nations to the North and Northwest. The evidence compiled by Samuel Kliger indicates that this view was shared, in the eighteenth century, by Northern Germans and Britons alike, as well it might, seeing that in 1714 the House of Stuart – with Charles II and James II leaning towards Catholicism, France, and absolutism – was finally supplanted, on the throne of England, by the House of Hanover – Protestant, German, and quick to abrogate several royal prerogatives to the Whig leaders.[11] This gave rise to a sense of a special German–British kinship, one upshot being the establishment of something like a British–German *régime* (in the cultural sense given to the term by Anthony Pym[12]) resulting in a special cultural exchange and in political cooperation, which eventually put an end to France-dominated neoclassicism and, later, to Napoleonic imperialism.

If I see it correctly, the most ambitious and far-reaching idea of *translatio* employed in Berkeley's verses is the conjunction of the westward course of empire with the five acts of world history regarded as *theatrum mundi*. The background is the so-called "Danielic *translatio*" (also known as "the four kingdoms" or "the four monarchies," Dan. 2.31–45), allegorically interpreted as God's plan to have world dominance shift four times from nation to neighboring nation. The four world powers of the past were variously identified, but always included Rome. Berkeley here joined many authors in looking across the Atlantic for the fifth and final one, as yet in the future.[13] The particularly ambitious part is his combination of the various *translationes* – of whatever is present of them in the poem – with a cyclical idea of history (sometimes known as stadialism) that was prevalent in eighteenth-century Britain and America among philosophers and artists.[14] According to this view, a dominating culture is subject to the law of cyclical change in four or five states, or stages (variously identified): The *savage* (hunting and fishing) is normally supplanted by the flowering of civilization in the *pastoral* state (herding and farming), when "nature guides and virtue rules," and this, in turn, is followed by the *trade empire*, whose height of power is, at the same time, the height of moral and physical decay, so that the *destruction* of the empire at the hands of barbarians is practically inevitable.[15] Sometimes, as in Thomas Cole's monumental cycle of allegorical paintings, a fifth state is added, *desolation*, when Nature as vegetative force overgrows the ruins, thus providing a scene precisely for those Romantic musings, however different they might be, at the Colosseum and at Lord Holland's Seat where "mimic desolation covers all."[16] What makes for the *cultural morphology* that informs Berkeley's verses is the combination of this cultural stadialism with the four Danielic empires so that what emerges is an image of the wheel of a cultural *fortuna* rolling, in four stately revolutions, basically from East to West, from Babylon to Britain, as it were. As one culture declines and falls, the inception and rise devolves on the designated nation to the West.

It is this last consideration, in view of the fifth and final cycle on North American soil, which introduces the decisive complication.

Though Berkeley does not indicate precisely whom he regards as "Time's noblest offspring," his general depiction of the "savage *Americans*" as "inhuman and barbarous" and standing sorely in need of Christian instruction would seem to imply that he is not among the primitivist admirers of the noble savage but sides with those who saw the colonists, the emigrants from Europe "in her decay," as the agents of "another golden age."[17] But regardless of his opinion – since it is indeed the emigrants who took over America – the *translatio imperii et studii* from the British Empire to North America can only be upheld if we add a completely new kind of *translatio*, a *translatio populi*. This accounts for the decisive difference, compared with the transfer from Persia to Greece, from Greece to Rome, from Rome to one of the modern nations. And to reflect on this difference is to prepare the ground for the to me surprising insights.

II

The Western emigration of Europeans was made possible by what, from a European point of view, is usually – and justly – called the Age of Discoveries. From a more comprehensive perspective, it can just as appropriately be called the age of intercontinental, for the most part transoceanic, encounters between cultures that were, in a sense, superimposed upon the encounters that had been going on all the time on each continent. If I see it correctly, there are three such types of intercontinental encounter: the first is *colonization*, here etymologically understood as the establishing of settlement colonies.[18] Under the prevailing conditions, this amounted to large-scale emigration from many countries for the purpose of occupying and settling the non-European continents (Siberia included), with the concomitant displacement and marginalization (or worse) of the indigenous population, and resulting in poly-ethnic nations made up mostly of immigrants and their descendants. The nature of this new kind of multi-national nation (for which the USA is clearly paradigmatic) is, in several ways, based on an *ethos of difference*: difference in comparison to the nations of origin which the emigrants, for the most part, had, after all, left for good; internal differences between immigrants coming from different nations, each of which was, rightly or wrongly, perceived as ethnically homogeneous; and different speeds of achieving a sense of American identity, depending, in part, on the origin of the recent immigrant and on the culture area in question. Images such as "melting-pot," concepts such as "trans-nationality," but also claims of supremacy and bids for separateness put forward by various ethnic groups characterize life in a post-colonial nation of this type.[19]

The other two types of intercontinental collision can be passed over here: *colonialization*, the setting up of trade colonies, best represented by India, I think, and resulting in a multi-national nation of quite different origin, composition, and cultural profile, and *non-permeation*, with later more or less voluntary and controlled opening to the West, as in the Meiji Period in Japan, the paradigmatic country in this respect.

For the thirteen American colonies to declare political independence in the name of human rights (only two years after the Regulating Act made into law in London had subjected the India Trading Company and the Indian sub-continent to control by the Crown of England) was a performative act that can be pinpointed in the very text: "We, therefore, the Representatives of the United States of America... solemnly publish and declare, that these United Colonies are, and of Right ought to be / Free and Independent States."[20] To gain factual independence was, of course, a different matter. And to be accepted as a subject of international law is, indeed, to achieve independence in the sense of sovereignty. Soon afterwards, during the constitutional debate, linguistic independence was proclaimed by Noah Webster and others, and programs for literary and intellectual independence kept being filed for at least another fifty years, culminating in Emerson's Phi Beta Kappa oration of 1837. All this is psychologically understandable but utterly illogical. Under conditions of colonization, linguistic, literary, cultural independence in the sense of separateness is downright impossible. Colonists start out with precisely the moral, physical, and cultural equipment which their compatriots possess who stayed at home. This situation as well as its consequences is quite different from that of the colonialized indigenous cultures such as India or Cameroon. Anglo-Indian culture is the result, mainly, of the anglicization of a very small part of the indigenous population, with institutional and cultural ramifications which obviously go beyond the 1 percent of English-speaking citizens of contemporary India. Anglo-American culture, by contrast, has come about by grass-roots processes, as it were, of Americanizing British imports, in interaction with some of the other *adstrata*.[21]

What has been called "literary independence," whether of the USA or any other country, "new" or "old," is really a question of having one's literature respected first at home and then abroad. And since the former imperial power accompanied the rise of the transatlantic upstart with such encouraging – shall I say – catcalls as (to quote just one representative opinion from *The British Critic* for 1818), "The Americans have no national literature, and no learned men,"[22] it was to be expected that the American mockingbird would respond with a whole series of countercalls. What one can say from the safe distance of 200 years or so is that American literature, as a literature written by colonists and, later, by citizens of former colonies, is not unrelated to the literature of the – former – imperial center, Britain, nor is it necessarily imitative of it. Neither is such a related but different literature brought about by programs. What counts are the actual literary works and the strategies that went into their making. The American quality, or qualities, of American literature can, I think, be identified – at least during its formative period, which spans at least 150 years, with 1776 as the axis – by studying in detail how American writers responded, in their works, to British models. To be precise: this is the view which I held when I set out to rethink the matter for this paper.[23] I have since come round to the conviction that this is only one of three main strategies by which writers under conditions after colonization define their new national identity, as follows:

First, American writers have responded to British models by inscribing into their own works deviating responses of various kinds and in ways which alienate the respective model, which make it into something foreign.

Second, during a more restricted period of time, American writers have defined their national identity by relating their work to another national model which I would describe as *naheliegend fernliegend*, or covertly overt; for a few decades after 1815 and for an important group of American writers, this new model consisted of Germany and its literature.

Third, beyond these two main relations, the first discriminating, in a way, against the former imperial center, and the second privileging, for a while, another literature as the covertly overt new model, attempts were made to set up something like immediate foreign literary relations, to place American literature into the concert of yet other literatures, avoiding British mediation. The main instruments were translations, and series and anthologies of translations.

At this time, I feel most at home with the strategies of writing deviating responses to British models simply because I have pursued this line of inquiry for several years now, and partly because two studies

along similar lines were recently published.[24] The earliest prominent
case is *The Sot-weed Factor; or, A Voyage to Maryland,* in which
Ebenezer Cook transformed, in deadpan fashion, Samuel Butler's one-
sided Restoration satire on the Puritans into double-edged transatlantic
hudibrastics.[25] To an unwary reader, these adventures of an English
tobacco merchant in colonial America, published in London in 1708,
may appear as just another item in the vogue of hudibrastic
pamphleteering.[26] To the extent that Maryland, in this first-person
narrative, is presented from the point of view and compass of knowledge
of a visitor newly arrived from London, the colonists appear as what
contemporary readers easily recognize as hillbillies: ragged, dirty, lazy,
hard-drinking, swearing, cheating, and worse. In the context of its time,
the poem may well be regarded as an imitation of similar denunciations
of the London rabble in near-contemporaneous verse, for instance by
Edward Ward;[27] it also reflects attitudes then popular in Maryland and
contains allusions to such popular exoticist writings as Aphra Behn's
Oroonoko (1688).[28] But insofar as the author adopted several of the
structural features of Samuel Butler's burlesque romance and anti-
Puritan satire of 1663 and included pointed verbal echoes, it seems
reasonable to regard *The Sot-weed Factor* primarily as a response to the
original *Hudibras.*[29] The methodological model for this approach has
been derived from the study of literary translations: in both instances,
there is a privileged relation, that between the target and the source text
in translation studies, and between response and model in literary
response studies; and in both instances, the "derived texts" contain
phrases from, references to, reminiscences of other texts which have
come in either as elements of the medium or as parts of a technique of
purposeful allusion.[30]

Butler's trend-setting work was easily the most successful of
Restoration poems, going into nine printings in the very year of its
publication, being steadily reprinted until the 1840s, winning its author
a royal pension, being set next to *Paradise Lost* by Samuel Johnson, and
inspiring some 150 poets and versifiers to adopt the mode. Its
distinction has, I think, been neatly characterized by John Sutherland
when he called *Hudibras* a "sort of national monument to tell us what
many Englishmen thought and believed three hundred years ago."[31]
Part of the success formula was Butler's travesty of the basic Quixotic
situation by sending a Presbyterian knight, Sir Hudibras, and his
Separatist squire, Ralpho, on burlesqued chivalric exploits. What seems
to have been at least as attractive to the Restoration audience was

Butler's across-the-board put-down of those who had been in power during the Puritan Commonwealth and the Cromwellian Protectorate. This is why Butler was read as the major literary partisan of King, Canterbury, and the rising commercial middle classes.[32]

Not only did Cook take the travesty one step further, he also transformed it into a more complex work by making the comic hero, the sot-weed factor, over into a first person narrator and, putting him on horseback and giving him an equally anonymous Sancho Panza, Ralpho, taken from the Maryland hillbillies, for companion, sending the two of them on a mock-heroic journey of exploration among the colonists. What makes *The Sot-weed Factor* an American divergent response is the distinctive use Cook made of the main structural difference, in comparison to *Hudibras*: the first-person narrator. The following incident from the opening may be taken as representative: after the dangerous ocean crossing, the ship is now safe at anchor "in *Piscato-way*," a creek and small town on the eastern bank of the Potomac River, some 12 or 15 miles south of what is now Washington, D.C. – the geography is important. The London merchant sets up store; but after having seen his first Americans, he decides to leave everything behind and to go and get a first-hand impression of them. So he crosses the Potomac River, he says, going West:

> I crost unto the other side,
> A River whose impetuous Tide,
> The Savage Borders does divide;
> In such a shining odd invention,
> I scarce can give its due Dimention.
> The *Indians* call this watry Waggon
> *Canoo*, a Vessel none can brag on;
> Cut from the *Popular-Tree*, or *Pine*,
> And fashion'd like a trough for Swine:
> In this most noble Fishing-Boat,
> I boldly put myself a-float;
> Standing Erect, with Legs stretch'd wide,
> We paddled to the other side:
> Where being Landed safe by hap,
> As *Sol* fell into *Thetis* Lap. (lines 56–70)

There is clearly more than one way of reading this. For my purpose, I can disregard everything except the geography and the sot-weed factor's exceptional canoeing technique. Since it may remind a British reader, among other things, of punting on the River Cam, its description may pass his reality censor unnoticed. But anyone familiar with canoeing – as, we may well assume, the colonists were – will recognize something odd. The oddity, I submit, consists of more than what Lemay remarked upon: "When Cook describes the 'merchant stranger' as 'Standing Erect, with Legs stretch'd wide' (line 67) while crossing a river in a canoe, the poet knows that every American reader will scoff at a tenderfoot so ignorant that he does not sit down in a canoe."[33] But whether the sot-weed factor is alone in the canoe or as a member of a group, and regardless of how much syntactical guidance we take from the punctuation, since "Standing Erect" can be taken to modify both "we" and "I," a connoisseur of canoeing will recognize that this is no way of budging a canoe an inch, let alone crossing an impetuous river. And though he says he crossed over, the narrator nevertheless remains on the eastern bank, as confirmed by the description of the setting sun: you can observe *Sol* sink into *Thetis*' lap only when you stand on the eastern side of a body of water; West of the Potomac River, you could see the sun disappear behind some hills – possibly, on a clear day, behind what we now call the Blue Ridge Mountains. But since all the adventures which serve to debunk the Marylanders take place after the narrator said he crossed the river – which, as the text says to a reader knowledgeable about American geography, he could not have – where are we?

We might take the easy way out and read *The Sot-weed Factor* as a muddled imitation of the British model. We might say that the narrator misrepresents or misremembers basic facts – so what else does he misrepresent? Or we might take the text seriously and read it as a calculated, surreptitiously divergent response: not as the one-sided satire that *Hudibras* is but, in basic agreement with Lemay, as double-edged transatlantic hudibrastics, depending, for this effect, on two differently informed audiences, audiences which really existed for the poem: the polite London reader, as ignorant of the hard facts of life in the colonies as his representative, the sot-weed factor, may enjoy having all his prejudices confirmed about the colonial rabble; the colonists, on the other side – of the Atlantic – may share secret laughs at the ignorant citybilly. The hudibrastics backfire. For the informed American reader, the relationship between *us* who share guffaws at the expense of *them* has been inverted in a way which escapes the London reader. I agree with Lemay that *The Sot-weed Factor* is an early instance of "American folk humor culminating in Mark Twain and William Faulkner"[34] – specifically, a variant of the genre of deadpan tales, in which under-handed barbs of ridicule are stuck into the back of the Eastern visitor who dies laughing about the uncouth Westerners. It is a territorially and culturally – not denominationally – separatist poem which alienates the unnoticing British narrator and his London readers as "none of us colonists."

This, you might say, is the sneaky colonial way of making an American work independent of the British model it apparently imitates. A typical post-colonial way of doing the same is plain contradiction. There is, for instance, more than one American poet flatly negating Oliver Goldsmith on many counts of his *Deserted Village*, a poem which holds a position, in late eighteenth-century British literature, very similar to the one *Hudibras* had in the later seventeenth century;[35] there is Poe, flamboyantly surpassing Dickens's "The Drunkard's Death";[36] there is Hawthorne, silently emending Scott's *The Heart of Midlothian*.[37] Occasionally a British writer – George Eliot – returned the compliment, with strikingly illuminating results.[38] If one considers, for instance, that Hawthorne replaced Scott's black-and-white moral evaluation of the fallen woman and her paramour by a truly complex characterization, and that this dualistic morality is precisely what George Eliot put back in again with a vengeance when she rewrote *The Scarlet Letter* in *Adam Bede*, it becomes clear how similar the Scottish historical romance of the 1820s and the English rural realism of the 1850s really are in contradistinction to the subversive fiction of the American Renaissance. One also can recognize that there is something fundamentally wrong about Susan Manning's and Robert Crawford's association of Scotland and America under the heading of provincialism.[39] In my reading, the difficulty with the one study is that the author purposely sidesteps the issue of real literary relations, whereas the other does not take the question of influence much beyond recording similarities. Yet "influence" studies are necessary, though they are illuminating only if one forgets the typical orientation, only if one inverts the idea of literary inflow. To recognize that a second writer has adopted something from an earlier one is only the starting-point. The really interesting question is: what did he make of this borrowing? I'm quite aware that this question is being asked, here and there, in influence studies. Might it not be possible to promote the asking of it by inverting the metaphor, by no longer talking about influence or suggesting that something is flowing down into the later writer's work, and by beginning to talk about literary response, to put the activity where it really is: with the second writer responding to the first? And how, and for what purpose, does he respond?

The best way of answering such questions would be to present detailed case studies; the second best, to summarize the results of one. Oliver Goldsmith's *The Deserted Village*, the popular and critical success of the 1770s, elicited some British and five North American poetic responses, for the most part during the remaining quarter century. Like many European pastorals, *The Deserted Village* is written from a nostalgic point of view. It is, indeed, as a representative commentator, Peter V. Marinelli, put it, based on "the art of the backward glance," so that "Arcadia, from its creation, [is] the product of wistful and melancholy longing. The pastoral poet reverses the process... of history."[40] As in Virgil's first eclogue – which, together with the fourth, had been canonized by Samuel Johnson for the British eighteenth century – Goldsmith's pastoral idyl is praised by a speaker who has just lost it, who has just come to realize that there is no return. The difference is that for Virgil's exile Meliboeus it is a personal loss; the pastoral state as such endures unchanged for others, notably for Tityrus who goes on happily and unthinkingly enjoying it. Whereas in Goldsmith, the idyl itself is totally destroyed, at least as far as the village of Auburn is concerned, and every single one of the victimized villagers has no choice but to look forward to the horrors of an American exile. In this limited sense of victimization, the outcome of *The Deserted Village* is tragic.

Now, on the other hand, all American and Canadian responses (except the two versions of a sequel written by Thomas Coombe, a Loyalist forced to remigrate after independence) present the idyl as something which you can build with your own hands, something which is part of the historical process, an active utopia to be put into practice on North American soil. (In the political and economic life of the USA, literary pastoralism had its counterpart in Jeffersonian agrarianism: various Land Acts and Homestead Acts were passed in order to legalize pastoralism into existence, nationwide.) The Americans among the responders to Goldsmith are quite explicit in correcting the tearful and fearful image of America held by the emigrants from Auburn, suggesting that to build an agricultural idyl in America is a happy ending for the poor exiles. These counter-poems are neither nostalgic nor retrospective nor regressive nor tragic. There is, then, a North American counter-genre to the European pastoral. One might call it the pastoral of the future; or one might feel that doing so is like calling a play with a happy ending a tragedy. Whatever naming strategy one finally opts for, it should not obliterate the extent to which American deviating responses veer away from European norms. To disregard what one might call the transatlantic alienation effect in literature is to underestimate the non-European nature of much of American literature, is to overlook typological possibilities which, as far as I can see, do not have any counterparts in European literature.

With regard to the second strategy that helps to achieve American literary identity, namely to adopt German literature as the covertly overt new model, I must restrict myself, for the most part, to referring to recent research by Kurt Mueller-Vollmer of Stanford.[41] The best, but, in my reading, not the first starting-point are British and American reviews of Madame de Staël's *De l'Allemagne* and of its translation *Germany* which appeared on both sides of the Atlantic in 1813 and 1814. The leading opinion expressed in the *Edinburgh Review* (and reprinted in America in the *Analectic Magazine*) was that the French author showed that it took Germany, a country devoid of any significant literature up until recently, not more than fifty years to develop a national literature, "perhaps the most characteristic possessed by an European nation."[42] And to put America on the literary map now that the USA had won political independence was the great patriotic ambition and duty of American writers. Mueller-Vollmer shows that many of them looked to German literature and culture in order "to derive powerful stimuli for the making of an American cultural and literary identity."[43] For a significant phase in American cultural history and for leading intellectuals, Germany, through Madame de Staël, became a model for American cultural aspirations. Thus, for instance, shortly after her book was so widely publicized, numbers of young Americans began to study at the Northern German Protestant universities which de Staël had recommended. The New England writers who were to promote American literary nationalism in the 1820s, 1830s and 1840s by combining it with an emotional idealism later called "Transcendentalism," learned much, for their specialty, from de Staël's exposition of German speculative metaphysics.

While things German thus became an incentive for American writers in the wider orbit of the Transcendentalists, there are also earlier and independent responses. A case for "American Independence and a German dream" can be made with regard to Washington Irving's *Sketchbook* of 1819. While the English sketches are related to English models, the most American of the sketches, "Rip Van Winkle," drawing, for the most part, on German sources, is basically a somewhat deviating response to a German fairy-tale, contaminated with an ironic

version of the Kyffhäuser saga about the Emperor who founded the
Holy Roman Empire. Accordingly, once Barbarossa emerges from his
long sleep he will renew the Empire and lead Germany to new glories;
when Rip / R.I.P. / Requiescat in Pace / van Winkle emerged from
his, he found America independent – but is this transatlantic Empire in
the making all that glorious?

The third area, the setting up of foreign literary relations
independently from Britain by means of serialized and anthologized
translations, can briefly be exemplified by an open series of translations
initiated by George Ripley, of the Transcendentalist group, in 1838. The
very title, "Specimens of Foreign Standard Literature," suggests the
program of building a national literature by looking abroad. The
objective is to stimulate "our own intellectual independence and
activity." Sole reliance on British literature and British mediation is "to
impoverish ourselves" – this is a polite version of my point one, the
cultural dissociation from Britain. My point three, the establishment of
foreign literary relations, follows immediately: "If our scholars would
improve our literature, they should cultivate an intimacy not only with
that of England but with that of continental Europe."[44] And if one
examines the contents of the fourteen-volume run until the demise of
the series in 1842, the German model is secretly waiting in the wings.[45]
The series opens with two volumes by French philosophers, Cousin,
Jouffroy, and Constant, and volumes V and VI offer more by the same
authors. The remaining ten volumes are devoted to "Germany, the
land of light, the home of thought," as James F. Clarke stylized it in his
introduction to the three theological volumes.[46] And to recognize that
this description echoes a line from the American national anthem,
"Land of the free and home of the brave," is to realize the culturally
exemplary status here ascribed to Germany. Accordingly, the standards
set for American literature, in Germany, are the poetry of Goethe and
Schiller, of Uhland, Körner, Bürger, and twenty others, as well as folk-
songs. In the estimation of Ripley and his collaborators, German
literature deserves to be presented to American readers in the form of
a three-volume history, the one by Wolfgang Menzel.[47] Menzel's
position is not easily characterized in a few words. He was one of the
highly respected German men of letters, especially after he had become
the successful editor, in 1825, of a leading literary journal, the *Literatur-
Blatt* supplement to Cotta's *Morgenblatt für gebildete Stände*.[48] To
recognize that he was a radical nationalist in literary matters, very much
down on Goethe for the way in which the latter, in Menzel's view, had

adulterated German literature by foreign admixtures, is not to say that he was a literary chauvinist. His impressive anthology, *Die Gesänge der Völker: Lyrische Mustersammlung in nationalen Parallelen*, for instance, shows his admiration for the national varieties of expressing the common themes of humanity; his emphasis was on the national purity of the respective expressions.[49] While I will admit that I lack an organ for registering national purity in literature, and while I insist that Goethe's practice and idea of the international constitution of each national literature is truer to the facts as I know them, I can nevertheless appreciate the historical situation in which Menzel wrote and the relation that exists between his kind of literary nationalism and Herder's notion of the unique identity of each national literature and culture, with each playing a complementary part in the composite literary universe.[50] The American translator of Menzel's literary history, C. C. Felton, stressed the intimate relation between national literature and "national character," which Menzel also posited, but took exception to Menzel's criticism of Goethe – almost predictably, because Goethe is the featured poet in Ripley's series.[51]

The three strategies, the anticipated one of alienating British models by inscribing deviating responses into American works, and the two unexpected ones, the adoption of Germany as a new model and the establishing of broader literary relations largely by means of translations, are, in my reading, the essential elements in the history of the making of American literature. I would assume that its formative period can be considered closed when the two privileged relations, the discrimination against British and the favoring of German models, fade into the general hum and buzz of international literary give and take, and when later American authors find earlier American works worthy objects to contend with.

III

By way of a conclusion, I should like at least to touch on the question of generalization: is the American case characteristic of literatures that have come about by colonization, and is it characteristic of these literatures only? The best way to answer the first half is to look at other post-colonization literatures (the situation of post-colonialization literatures is essentially different). Unfortunately, I do not have the wide and thorough comparative reading in any other literature in either America that would allow me to pinpoint relevant strategies. But scholars better equipped in this respect might, I think, profitably begin with a case such as the following where a similar pattern seems to emerge. Studies by Estuardo Núñez and, more recently, by David Sobrevilla indicate that Manuel Gonzales Prada, a radical Peruvian separatist, tried to dissuade his contemporaries of the later nineteenth century from employing, as their model, Spanish national Romanticism, and he translated much German Romantic poetry (notably ballads, because of their objective element) in order to provide a superior model.[52] He does not seem to have had the desired success. In another country, in Argentina, it would seem that a shift from the model of the former imperial power, Spain, to a new model, France, was successful.

While these are not much more than hints and guesses, I have more evidence on the second half of the question of generalization. It would seem that the pattern I have distinguished for the formation of an American national literature also applies, with modifications, to definable situations in other than post-colonization cultures. There are certain pertinent similarities between the situation of the thirteen American colonies and of the German countries in the second part of the eighteenth and in the early nineteenth centuries: just as each of the colonies and former colonies had its own regional profile in terms of population, religion, economics, outlook, etc., so each of the twenty-odd German-speaking kingdoms and principalities of central Europe had its profile, though of much longer historical standing. Regarded as an aggregate, neither territory had a single cultural center. Whereas, by about 1800, the American colonies had achieved political unity and independence – though the process had been neither steady nor unanimous – German political unity was nowhere to be seen, and the Napoleonic wars were about to impose various forms of dependence on the German countries. To take the long view: after the defeat of Austria, the partial abdication of Emperor Franz (I of Austria), in 1806, brought to an end that construct which had given legality to the German nation, namely the Holy Roman Empire.[53] There was thus a political entity, the USA, in search of a literary and cultural identity, and, on the German side, an emerging literature whose importance was about to be recognized abroad, thanks largely to Madame de Staël and her British and American reviewers, and this literature was in search of a political identity.

It is this background that gives significance to an exchange of letters which took place in 1808–9 between the officer in charge of Bavarian schools and universities, Niethammer, a former professor of history at Jena, and Goethe.[54] Niethammer invited Goethe to compile *ein deutsches Volksbuch*, a German national anthology for use in schools and at home. Among the reasons Niethammer gave in an elaborate résumé is that by making German children read and learn the same literary works of value, the unification of Germany might be achieved, if not politically then, at least, in the minds. And whenever Niethammer referred to *teutsche Nationalbildung*, he seems to have had in mind two objectives in one: the literary education of Germans and the formation of a German nation.

This is, in a nutshell, the request – and also, in a sense, the challenge. Goethe responded within ten or twelve days and, later, drew up two outlines; and though for reasons that have not been recorded the project fell through, the emphases which Goethe set do not only have a bearing on my specific historical problem but may be of interest to our own time and to other countries as well.

Goethe was quite emphatic about a point that was absolutely counter to Niethammer's view. The plan to inculcate a sense of national identity through common reading will work only if the reading goes beyond national literature to include a substantial portion of works of international origin:

Keine der neuern Nazionen darf an entschiedene Originalität Anspruch machen, der Deutsche vielleicht am wenigsten, der seine Bildung von aussen erhalten und Gehalt und Form meistens von Fremden gewonnen hat. Das fremde Gut ist unser Eigentum geworden. Völlig eigenes, Angeeignetes durch Behandlung, durch Übersetzung, alles würde aufzunehmen seyn. (*Goethes Werke*, XLII:2, 416)

[None of the modern nations may take pride in originality in any decisive sense of the word, the German perhaps least of all; for it has obtained its institutional and individual culture as well as the content and form of its poetry, for the most part, from abroad. These imports have become our own. The anthology must include texts that are completely our own, texts that have been appropriated through manipulation, through translation.]

And he added – in 1808 – that, since the book was, in part, intended for children, great care must be taken to point to the achievements of other nations. We have here the earliest Goethean reference to an idea he was later to elaborate under the term "world literature" – so often quoted, so often misunderstood. And I am grateful for his insistence on the role played by literary imports in establishing literary identity. It coincides, after all, with my third point about the achievement of national literary identity. There is no paradox in this. Not to recognize what has been appropriated – and in what way – is to misunderstand the nature of a national literature.

The second main idea in Goethe's proposal coincides with my point about the secretly obvious model. In the sketchy form characteristic of the later notes, Goethe explicitly identified the Bible as the model for such an internationally national anthology: "Die höchste Form einer solchen Samml [!] finden wir in der Bibel" (*ibid.* p. 421). And he vindicated the paradigm of Ancient Hebrew poetry precisely by exemplifying his recommendation of pointing to the significance which the achievements of other nations have for one's own: in his outline, he is quite specific in pointing out what, in his view, Hebrew culture owed to Near Eastern and Mediterranean neighbors.

I think I can justify my qualification of the covertly overt model in two ways. At first glance, the Bible as model for German literary identity is, I suppose, far-fetched. On the other hand, in the long process of replacing the preference for the ancients with that for the moderns, and of breaking up the united front of the moderns by national profiles, the decisive breakthrough for the nation as culture-constituting entity (or, to use the later idealistic terminology, as culture-defining subject) originated in the British–German regime and occurred with the focus on Ancient Hebrew poetry. I must compress a long and complex story by saying merely that the crucial work is the influential study *De Sacra Poesi Hebraeorum Praelectiones* which Robert Lowth, an Old Testament scholar at Oxford, published in 1753. The Göttingen orientalist Johann David Michaelis gave it a long and enthusiastic review in the *Göttingischen Anzeigen*, one of the foremost mediating cultural journals of its time. Shortly afterwards, he had the book translated, adding his own commentary. And Johann Gottfried Herder responded to these ideas, not only in his respected *Vom Geist der ebräischen Poesie* (1782–83), but in a number of scattered concise definitions of the nation precisely as culture-defining subject. Seen in this connection, Goethe's choice of the Old Testament as the model for his international anthology for the formation of a cultural Germany takes on precisely that quality of covert overtness which the new model appropriate for this purpose must have.[55]

The actual anthology never materialized. It took another forty years until one of the large numbers of opinionated liberal-democratic writers who are so much part of the literary and political background of nineteenth-century cultural life in the German-speaking countries, Johannes Scherr, published a massive anthology of world poetry, dedicated to the cosmopolitanism of Goethe, and he did so in the year of the unsuccessful national, democratic, and republican revolution of 1848. In so doing, Scherr ushered in the age of world literature in the medium of multilateral translation anthologies.[56]

To continue this line of inquiry into the field of translation anthologies would be an altogether different matter.[57] What remains to be done is to admit that, in the case of Goethe's plan for an international national anthology of poetry, there is no place for point one of my analysis of the American situation, mainly for two reasons: the situation of the German-speaking countries at the beginning of the nineteenth century is not a post-colonization situation – there is no (former) imperial center visible; and by this time, the cultural predominance of France in literary matters has already been overcome – by 1908–09, Goethe had been twice beset by the not unegotistical admiration of Madame de Staël, who regarded him as the distinctive and representative German genius, adding: "no one besides is so remarkable for a peculiar species of imagination which neither Italians, English, nor French have ever attained."[58] Allowing for this difference, I hope to have indicated a pattern of interliterary dynamics, of international literary contacts, relations, transfer, and appropriation that is characteristic of definable cultural situations within and outside the imperialism-colonization context.

NOTES

1 This paper is based on a plenary lecture given at the 1992 BCLA Conference under the title, "Across Europe and Beyond: Thoughts on *translatio imperii, studii, ingenii.*" The topic was inspired by the conference theme and led to unanticipated results. While I want to make a printed paper as methodical as possible, I should yet like to retain something of the sense of discovery that went into the original presentation. The paper is written in a variety of American English.

2 *British*: The moment the term *American*, with its geographical or political reference, is introduced, *English* is reduced from a linguistic (literature written in varieties of English) to a geographical or political application, too (the literature of England). For this reason, and particularly because I deal primarily with two Irish authors and draw on Scottish publications for support, I have opted for the geographically more inclusive term.

3 Cf. Ezra Pound, "I Gather the Limbs of Osiris" (1911), *Selected Prose, 1909–1965*, edited by William Cookson (New York, 1973), p. 21. I am here more interested in the variety Pound called "symptomatic," the other being "donative" (p. 25) and especially prized by Hugh Kenner in *The Pound Era* (London, 1972), esp. pp. 152–53.

4 Cf. *The Works of George Berkeley, Bishop of Cloyne*, edited by A. A. Luce and T. E Jessop, vol. VII (London, 1955), 369–73.

5 Cf. A. A. Luce, *The Life of George Berkeley, Bishop of Cloyne* (London, 1949), p. 108; Berkeley, *Works*, VII, 369, 347.

6 Berkeley, *Works*, VII, 370, 373.

7 *Ibid.*, p. 369; on the intimate relationship between Berkeley and his correspondent, Sir John Percival, cf. Luce, *Life*, pp. 49–50.

8 Cf. Luce, *Life*, p. 96. Luce gives no evidence that the poem played any part in the eventual failure of the Bermuda project (*Life*, pp. 136–52).

9 Cf. Ernst Robert Curtius, *Europäische Literatur und Lateinisches Mittelalter* (Bern, 1948), p. 36.

10 Werner Goez, *Translatio imperii* (Tübingen, 1958), pp. 74, 76, *passim*.

11 Cf. Samuel Kliger, *The Goths in England* (Cambridge, Mass., 1952), pp. 33–34, *passim*; for the characterization of the transition of 1714, cf. G. M. Trevelyan, *A Shortened History of England* (Baltimore, Md., 1959), pp. 380–81.

12 Anthony Pym, "Les notions de 'réseau' et de 'régime' en relations littéraires internationales," *L'Internationalité littéraire*, edited by A. Pym (Calaceite, Spain, 1988).

13 Gustav H. Blanke, "Remarks on the Transit of Ideas: 'America is West,'" *The Transit of Civilization from Europe to America: Essays in Honor of Hans Galinsky*, edited by Winfried Herget *et al.* (Tübingen, 1986), pp. 59–74. For a reading of the first version of the poem in terms of the theme of "nature's course," cf. Hans Galinsky, *Naturae Cursus: Der Weg einer antiken kosmologischen Metapher von der alten in die neue Welt* (Heidelberg, 1968), esp. pp. 98–104, for that of the second, Klaus Lubbers, "'Westward the course of empire': Emerging Identity Patterns in Two Eighteenth-Century Poems," *Literatur im Kontext – Literature in Context: Festschrift für Horst W. Drescher*, edited by Joachim Schwend *et al.* (Frankfurt am Main, 1992), pp. 329–43.

14 On cyclical views of history in Britain and America, cf. Stow Persons, "Cyclical Theory of History in Eighteenth-Century America," *American Quarterly* 6 (1954), 147–63; cf. also John D. Scheffer, "The Idea of Decline in Literature and the Fine Arts in Eighteenth-Century England," *Modern Philology* 34 (1936–7), 155–78.

15 Berkeley saw the "South Sea Bubble" of 1720–1 as the alarming symptom precisely of this moral decline: "It is to be feared the final period of our State approaches" ("An Essay towards preventing the Ruin of Great Britain," *Works*, VI, 84–85).

16 Cole's entire cycle is reproduced in Angus Fletcher, *Allegory: The Theory of a Symbolic Mode* (Ithaca, N.Y., 1964), ill. 16–20; Thomas Gray's poem has been quoted from *The Oxford Anthology of English Literature*, vol. I, edited by J. B. Trapp *et al.* (New York, 1973), 2216.

17 Cf. esp. Berkeley, *Works*, VII, 359.

18 I am not sure whether *settlement colony* is a current English collocation. Following German usage, it is intended to contrast with *trade colony*.

19 Of the various concepts denoted by the term *nation*, I enlist, for my purposes, the one of sovereign statehood, as in "United Nations," and an ethnically based one. Among the historical studies devoted to these matters, I still find the ones by Hans Kohn most instructive; among the more recent inquiries, Benedict Anderson's

Imagined Communities: Reflections on the Origin and Spread of Nationalism, second edition (London, 1991) is particularly rewarding.

20 *Documents of American History*, edited by Henry Steele Commager, ninth edition (Englewood Cliffs, N.J., 1973), vol. I, p. 102.

21 In a recent article, "American Literary Emergence as a Postcolonial Phenomenon," *American Literary History* 4:3 (1992), 411–42, Lawrence Buell purposely blurred this distinction (p. 412). I should not like to argue his approach here and prefer to leave the decision to the reader as to whether his and my findings are contradictory or complementary.

22 Quoted in Robert Weisbuch, *Atlantic Double-cross: American Literature and British Influence in the Age of Emerson* (Chicago, 1986), p. 12.

23 The previous reflections under section II, the following first principle, and the brief outline of aspects of American responses to Goldsmith's *The Deserted Village* have been condensed from a paper, "The Pastoral of the Past and Pastorals of the Future," which I read at the Sevilla Conference of the EAAS in April 1992 and which is being made ready for publication in the Conference proceedings. Points 2 and 3 are the unanticipated new insights.

24 This is, in addition to Weisbuch's *Atlantic Double-cross*, Linden Peach, *British Influence on the Birth of American Literature* (London, 1982). I single these out from a rising number of American–British comparative studies because both, despite the term *influence* in their titles, are reasonably argued *response* studies.

25 There are two versions of Cook's *The Sot-weed Factor* extant. The earlier London version studied here, available in microfilm in the American Culture Series, reel 386, no. 6 (Ann Arbor Microfilms, 1968), is most easily accessible in *The Heath Anthology of American Literature*, edited by Paul Lauter *et al.* (Lexington, Mass., 1990), vol. I, 614–31. Among the several studies, Edward H. Cohen's *Ebenezer Cooke: The Sot-Weed Canon* (Athens, Ga., 1975) is, I think, best for biographical and textual matters, and J. A. Leo Lemay's chapter in his *Men of Letters in Colonial Maryland* (Knoxville, Tenn., 1972), pp. 77–110, for its literary and cultural perspicacity.

26 Cf. Edward Ames Richards, *Hudibras in the Burlesque Tradition*, Columbia University Studies in English and Comparative Literature, vol. CXXVII (New York, 1937), esp. 39–58.

27 Without the narratological modification, cf. *ibid.*, p. 105.

28 Cf. Lemay, *Men of Letters*, pp. 78, 88, *et passim*.

29 The features include a parody of the knight-and-squire situation; the technique of turning key words of a particular sect's creed against its members, which Cook transferred from Butler's invective against Puritans to his attack on cheating Quakers (lines 613–20); and several verbal borrowings (cf. Lemay, *Men of Letters*, pp. 79, 85).

30 For the parallel, cf. Armin Paul Frank, "'Translation as System' and *Übersetzungskultur*: On History and Systems in the Study of Literary Translation," *New Comparison* no. 8 (Autumn 1989), esp. 94–95.

31 John Sutherland, *English Literature and the Late Seventeenth Century*, The Oxford History of English Literature, edited by Bonamy Dobrée and Norman Davis, vol. V (New York, 1969), 157.

32 For a comprehensive characterization of Butler's opinions expressed in other writings, cf. Richards, *Hudibras*, pp. 3–24.

33 Lemay, *Men of Letters*, p. 80.

34 *Ibid.*, p. 87.

35 For a detailed comparative study, cf. my 'Pastoral' (note 23).

36 Cf. my "In der Grosstadt vereinsamt: Von der Ungleichzeitigkeit zeitgleicher Motivik bei Dickens und Poe," in *Motive und Themen in englischsprachiger Literatur als Indikatoren literaturgeschichtlicher Prozesse*, edited by H.-J. Müllenbrock *et al.* (Tübingen, 1990), pp. 183–202.

37 Cf. Peach, *British Influence*, pp. 91–137.

38 Cf. my 'Amerikanische und britische Erzählliteratur im Vergleich: Der Fall Hester gegen Hester," *Anglistentag 1981: Vorträge*, edited by Jörg Hasler (Frankfurt, 1983), pp. 266–80.

39 Cf. Susan Manning, *The Puritan-Provincial Vision: Scottish and American Literature in the Nineteenth Century* (Cambridge, 1990); Robert Crawford, *Devolving English Literature* (Oxford, 1992).

40 Peter V. Marinelli, *Pastoral* (London, 1971), p. 9.

41 Kurt Mueller-Vollmer, "Staël's *Germany* and the beginnings of an American National Literature," in *Germaine de Staël: Closing the Borders*, edited by Madelyn Gutwirth *et al.* (New Brunswick, N.J., 1991), pp. 141–58, 217–22. Cf. also the same author's "Herder and the Formation of an American National Consciousness during the Early Republic," *Herder Today*, edited by Kurt Mueller-Vollmer (Berlin, 1990), pp. 415–30.

42 James Mackintosh, review of *De l'Allemagne, Edinburgh Review* 22 (1813), repr. in *The Reception of Classical German Literature in England, 1760–1860: A Documentary History from Contemporary Periodicals*, edited by John Boening, vol. 1 (New York, 1977), 511.

43 Mueller-Vollmer, "Staël's *Germany*," p. 142.

44 Editor's Preface to "Specimens of Foreign Standard Literature" edited by George Ripley (Boston, 1838), vol. I, xi.

45 Though the USA does not have renown for translation activity, other series, such as the French Classics, with Madame de Staël's *Germany* (cf. below, note 58) in a leading position, serve to balance the picture.

46 Translator's Preface in *ibid.* vol. x, viii. Cf. John Wesley Thomas, *James Freeman Clarke: Apostle of German Culture in America* (Boston, 1949).

47 *Die deutsche Literatur* (Stuttgart, 1828, rev. 1836).

48 Cf. Hartmut Steinicke, *Literaturkritik des Jungen Deutschland* (Berlin, 1982), pp. 22–4; Walter Dietze, *Junges Deutschland und deutsche Klassik* (Berlin, 1957), pp. 21–35.

49 (Leipzig, 1851), pp. iii–vi.

50 For a concise summary (which, however, does not make the necessary distinction between Herder's and Goethe's views), cf. Ernst Merian-Genast, "Voltaire und die Entwicklung der Idee der Weltliteratur," *Romanische Forschungen* 40 (1972), esp. 207–12.

51 *Specimens*, edited by Ripley, vol. VII (1840), esp. ix–xvi.

52 Cf. Estuardo Núñez, *Autores Germanos en el Perú* (Lima, 1953); David Sobrevilla, "Übersetzungen aus der deutschen Literatur in den Gründungsjahren peruanischer

Literatur," *Übersetzen, Verstehen, Brücken bauen*, edited by Armin Paul Frank *et al.* (Berlin, in preparation).

53 Karl Ploetz, *Auszug aus der Geschichte*, 24th revised edition (Bielefeld, 1951), p. 519.

54 *Goethes Werke*, herausgegeben im Auftrage der Grossherzogin Sophie von Sachsen (Weimar), vol. XLII:2 (1907), 397–428.

55 The background for this story – not the story itself – can be synthesized from Lawrence Marsden Price, *The Reception of English Literature in Germany* (Berkeley, Calif., 1932); Horst Oppel, *Englisch-deutsche Literaturbeziehungen*, 2 vols. (Berlin, 1971); Rolf P. Lessenich, *Dichtungsgeschmack und althebräische Bibelpoesie im 18. Jahrhundert* (Köln, 1967); Ernst Merian-Genast, "Voltaire."

56 *Bildersaal der Weltliteratur*, edited by Johannes Scherr, 2 vols. (Stuttgart, 1848); several reissues and expanded editions through 1884–85.

57 See forthcoming proceedings from a symposium held at Göttingen in June 1992 on "Translation Anthologies as Media of International Literary Transfer." The proceedings include papers on countries in Europe, both Americas, and Asia, and are being prepared for publication with Erich Schmidt Verlag, Berlin.

58 For convenience' sake, I quote from the 1814 Murray translation, revised by O. W. Wright, *Germany*, by the Baroness de Staël-Holstein (Boston, 1859), part II, p. 175.

Comparative Criticism 15, pp. 81–102. Cambridge University Press 1993

Comparison between the arts: a psychoanalytic view

MALCOLM BOWIE

Psychoanalysis studies the plasticity or transformability of desire and is itself, as a theoretical doctrine, quite remarkably subject to transformation. This situation is potentially confusing, but potentially fruitful also. It is perhaps especially illuminating for those who concern themselves with the migration of meaning between art forms, and with the often obscure structural kinship that exists between works in different media (between literature and painting, say) or between the different elements of a composite medium (opera, ballet, 'performance', say). In the following pages, I shall offer a preliminary sketch of a possible future style of comparative criticism – one that would take psychoanalysis seriously as a Protean science of transformation in the mental sphere, and then eagerly turn back to art.

I shall begin with a detail from Tiepolo's *The Finding of Moses* (*c.* 1740), which now hangs in the National Gallery of Scotland in Edinburgh (fig. 1). What I have in mind is the diagonal frieze, in the top right of the main group, formed by the young pink face of Pharaoh's daughter, the older grey face of the duenna who attends her, and the skull-like mountain crag that completes the sequence (fig. 2). Titian's magnificent *Three Ages of Man*, which hangs nearby in the gallery, suggests one way in which this detail may be read: Tiepolo, painting some two hundred years after his illustrious Venetian predecessor, has recapitulated the 'three ages' topos, handed it over to the main female actors in his drama and concentrated it into a single descending band of expressive incident. From youth, to age, to death. From light-suffused flesh, to lined and shadowed flesh, to the mineral shell that lies hidden beneath the skin. The twin summits of the mountain form a chiasmus with the uppermost outline of the older woman's hair. Tiepolo has organized things within the main rightwards movement of his narrative design in such a way that this lesser movement, to the right and down,

Fig. 1. G. B. Tiepolo, *The Finding of Moses.*

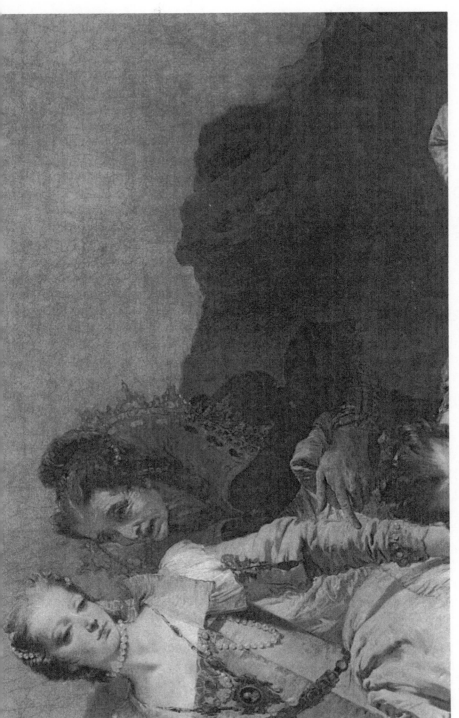

Fig. 2. G. B. Tiepolo, *The Finding of Moses*, detail: Pharaoh's daughter and her duenna.

brings about an energetic transformation of ground into figure. Inert nature is suddenly animated, as it is for Wordsworth in the first Book of *The Prelude*:

> ...a huge Cliff,
> As if with voluntary power instinct,
> Uprear'd its head.

The mountain outcrop, brought to life by the crone's head nearby, becomes a gesturing and grimacing *memento mori*. By an opposite and equally terrible motion the woman is confirmed in her progress towards death. She is prematurely mineralized.

There is exquisite terror in this detail, but nothing very surprising about it at the level of structure. Tiepolo's painting is behaving as we expect considerable works of art to behave – becoming plural, exploiting its motifs by overdetermining them, striving from flatness to a multifarious play of depths and distances. Pharaoh's daughter is involved in another relationship, and here too Tiepolo's irony is delicately reinforced by his manipulation of space: in her aristocratic aloofness she shrinks away from the flushed infant who, sprawling and bawling beneath her, seems ready to tumble backwards through the picture-plane. The princess occupies the place of greatest tension between infancy and death, and the sumptuousness with which she is painted has a tinge of parody. The already theatricalized and nostalgic costume style of Veronese has been turned into another kind of theatre – one that proclaims the lateness of the hour and glories in a knowing and disabused cult of the past.[1] Tiepolo is an ironist and a master of figurality. Hesitation between figure and ground is part of his stock-in-trade. He extracts substance from his ornaments, and ornament from his substances. What can psychoanalysis tell us about an artist like this that cannot already be satisfactorily articulated in formal and art-historical terms? A good deal, I shall be suggesting in a moment. But beforehand I shall set down rapidly some further examples of the ways in which the transformational machinery of an art-work may be exposed to view.

The following are common types of event in the unfolding of musical argument: accompanying figures seized upon and submitted to thematic development; melodies reduced to their rhythmic bare bones; rhythmic patterns extended and elaborated into melody; coloratura embellishments given independent expressive force, as in the Queen of the Night's arias in *The Magic Flute*. We could remind ourselves too of polyphonic writing – Palestrina's, for example – in which all figures have a ground comprising a wealth of other figures, and in which musical structure temporizes between its horizontal and vertical axes, between forward drive and a timeless lingering over its component layers. If we turn from music to poetry with these examples still in mind, certain familiar textual effects may begin to sound 'like music' without being describable in strictly musical terms. Roman Jakobson spoke memorably of the ways in which the axis of selection can become implicated, and as it were gratuitously actualized, in the axis of combination;[2] this meant, in non-technical language, that poetry in its moment-by-moment elaboration had ways of making the reader scan back and forth through the verbal texture of the work, and of supplying him or her with more connections, and a richer sense of choice, than the plain business of making sense required. Donald Davie, in his *Articulate Energy*, describes how syntax can become a species of rhyme;[3] and this mechanism, in his account, is perfectly compatible with the perspectival role that rhyme proper can have in the construing of a poem's syntax.

Examples could be multiplied, indefinitely, from these and the other arts, of a single underlying event-type, whereby certain elements within the overall design of a work change their status and their role before our eyes, or upon the inward ear with which musical or verbal sound is made intelligible. I am not talking about the process whereby simple structures are put to work to generate more complex ones, or kernel ideas are allowed to germinate, ramify and interweave. Nor am I referring to the stimulating constraints that are placed upon this elaboration of little into much by such shared structural dispositions as the sonnet, the fugue or classical variation form. What interests me particularly is the way in which the work of art both maintains and blurs its own hierarchical distinctions, by seeking self-consistency for each of its separate modes or levels and then puncturing this consistency by allowing other modes or levels to interfere. This of course happens so often in those artefacts that we call 'works of art', and so conspicuously, that it has seemed to many commentators to provide art with one of its defining characteristics.

When it comes to understanding what comparison between the arts is and is for, and to imagining what ground-rules it might need to observe in order to become coherent and decently remote from dilettantism, these structural shifts and intrications offer a special benefit: they place comparison under the twin signs of dynamism and complexity. There are two obvious ways of thinking comparatively in these border territories. On the one hand the structural vocabulary and syntax of one art can be put to work upon another; on the other hand, a diplomatic language can be assembled by observing and comparing a wide variety of artistic practices. The latter would be a structural Esperanto of sorts, a lingua franca in which the transactions between, say, poetry and painting, music and drama, or sculpture and narrative could be accurately described and boldly theorized. The second of these options strikes me as much more promising, even if more laborious, than the first. Such an approach avoids the loose metaphorizing of one medium at the hands of another that still bedevils much comparative work of this kind. (I am thinking of the endemic muddle that afflicts discussion of words and music in opera and lieder, and of the enfeebled painterly vocabulary that is still often recycled in the discussion of descriptive prose.) Splendid instances of this diplomatic or transactional critical writing do exist: Carl Dahlhaus's essay on Schoenberg's *Erwartung*, in which the tensions and complementarities between the verbal, motivic and instrumental dimensions of the work are articulated with compelling clarity and nuance;[4] Michael Fried's *Absorption and Theatricality*, on eighteenth-century French painting;[5] Charles Rosen's pages on opera and spoken drama in *The Classical Style*;[6] or David Scott's *Pictorialist Poetics*, on the manifold interactions between poetry and painting in nineteenth-century France.[7] Dahlhaus's work is particularly instructive in our present context, for it concentrates in close-up on the dynamics of a single monodrama and shows how an appropriately 'diplomatic' critical language can specify the disjunctions and indecisions upon which a given work is built quite as successfully as its zones of harmonious structural embedding.

Until now I have been talking about two separate kinds of transformation: on the one hand, those that may be observed inside the individual work and, on the other, those that take place when different arts are brought into alignment and caught up in each other's signifying field. In both cases the theoretical imagination faces the same challenge. What sort of dynamics, or energetics, or kinaesthetics do we need to account fully for the transformational processes themselves and for the expressive intensity that certain of them achieve? I am not at all sure that we need, or can acquire, a single theory to perform this task. It could be that the most convincing results will always be obtained by a prudent hybridization (or an inspired yoking together) of the technical languages available for each structural level considered alone, and that any master-theory of their interplay will sooner rather than later become vacuously self-confirming. With this reservation in mind, I come at last to the possible role of psychoanalysis in comparative discussion of artistic meaning in its various modes. What can this theory – which is in some respects the darling psychodynamic system of the age, at least in the Humanities departments of the West – actually *do* when confronted with the signifying welter that even only moderately complex works of art can unleash?

For the student of literature and the other arts, Freud's theory has at least two native dispositions. On the one hand it is a quest for mental origins, for the first causes by reference to which the individuality of individual minds can be understood and a set of typical life-historical narratives constructed for human beings at large. Working in this register, psychoanalysis has a dourly insistent retrospective tenor. It traces its causal path back from the speech, the dreams, the symptoms and the behavioural oddities of the subject, under observation in the here and now, to the anterior world of traumatic incident which makes the present structure of the subject intelligible. Back psychoanalysis goes – to the primal scene, the primal phantasy, the primal configurations of libido within the triangular paradigm of the family. From this journey back scientific knowledge and therapeutic know-how flow. But, on the other hand, Freud studies the transformational texture of minds in action, the interference patterns between unconscious and conscious mental activity, the volatile but at the same time seemingly highly organized fabric of the individual's desires. This second disposition is often at odds with the first. The processes by which energy is transmitted, and ideational and affective materials are transformed, prove to be so intricately intermeshed, and so elaborate in the causal schemes they imply, that any premature recourse to an originating event, or scene, or psychical lesion can easily seem facile. Those who look to the founding documents of psychoanalysis for guidance on the study of art often find that Freud as a reader of mental text and texture outstrips in hermeneutic skill the neighbouring Freud who was an inveterate excavator of first causes.

Another recurrent tension that is visible throughout the formative decades of the psychoanalytic movement will have a familiar air to scholars of literature, painting and music. How can passion be described? Can it be described at all if it is removed from the articulatory systems by way of which it comes into view? For Freud, the psychoanalytic account of the mind could not be complete without specifying the fundamental propulsive forces that made mental events happen. Much practical analytic work could be done on the separable and recombinable ideas or signifying elements that minds became minds in processing, but it never seemed satisfactory to remain silent about the drives (*Triebe*). Psychoanalysis needed to embrace them not simply because the Darwinian legacy had made them into one of the central scientific preoccupations of the age, but because they were an indispensable aid to empirical observation in the field of psychopathology: in the absence of an energy-source, and distinguishable energy-types, it was not always clear how the contents of the observational field could be differentiated and construed. The unfathomable drives, even in a loose hypothetical configuration, told the scientist what was there to see, and the clinician what was there that needed remedying.

Freud's energy-languages and drive-theories are astonishingly labile. He speaks of libido, wish and drive, of instinctual force, pressure and impulse, of 'cathectic energy' (*Besetzungsenergie*), 'quota of affect' and 'sum of excitation'. Yet how occult these forces remain, even when they seem about to become quantitatively measurable, in comparison with the processes of extension and elaboration that they fuel. When psychoanalysis begins to speak of these processes it abruptly sheds its air of make-believe and returns to the *terra firma* of discrete, serially arranged events. Its process-language is not of course automatically exempt from vagueness, but the terms that comprise it – associative sequence or pathway, displacement, conversion, sublimation, transference or secondary revision, dreamwork or working through – all hold out the promise of causal connection between earlier and later mental states.[8] In skilled hands each of them offers help towards the exact delineation of structure. And, when they are in action together, these terms can map the switches that take place between structural levels, and pinpoint the connections between mental activities previously partitioned off from each other. Looking back towards his ghostly natural forces from the variegated mental interlace that such forces animate, the psychoanalytic theorist is in a position very similar to that of the formal analyst of a sonata or a sonnet or a carving, who pauses to wonder what it is in him that obscurely stirs and seeks furtherance as his attention spreads across the contours and the inner faceting of his chosen work. What animal instinct or neural current or demiurgic energy? Practitioners of both kinds have difficult judgements to make. If they talk too much about hidden powers, the concreteness and complexity of transformational process will begin to ebb away. If they talk too little about those powers, they will be left with a mere box of tricks to study and many pointless exercises in classification and measurement to perform.

There was a time when Freud was thought of by admirers and detractors alike almost exclusively as a seeker after mental origins, and by his detractors among scholars of art and literature as one whose quest for Oedipal origins in particular equipped him poorly for serious aesthetic discussion. But things are now changing fast. Partly under the impact of Lacan's teaching and partly as an effect of the searching intellectual histories of psychoanalysis that have appeared in recent years, Freud's work has become a series of *mises-en-scène* of the desiring intellect. Even in those central doctrinal areas where once a monumental stillness reigned, Freud's thinking has become restless and multiform. Freud reread in this way is more impressive for his wayward dream-analyses, his unfinishable case-histories, his anthropological fantasies and his inventive appropriation of artistic materials than for his tales of mental origins sought and found. The 'new' Freud is a dramatist, a novelist, a fabulist and, above all perhaps, a rhetorician. Long before Lacan translated certain of Freud's terms into rhetorical language proper – before *Verdichtung* (condensation) became metaphor and *Verschiebung* (displacement) became metonymy, for example – those terms, it is now frequently claimed, had been behaving rhetorically of their own accord: thinly disguised as a psychophysicist or a hydraulic engineer, Freud had set about isolating the underlying figures and tropes by which desiring minds pursued their headlong course.[9] His 'process-language', as I have been calling it, offered, then, two quite different benefits: it moved psychoanalytic discussion back towards 'hard' science and towards testable notions of causality, but at the same time it placed an important emphasis on the artful processes of speech itself, by way of which the mental scientist had access to all other modes of connection and transformation within his field of enquiry.

It is at this point that works of art as transformational devices can come into productive alignment with Freud's account of mental process. Before turning to my two main examples, I shall enunciate briefly and dogmatically three basic principles and say a few words about each.

(i) The psychoanalytic account of mental process is combinable with, and to some extent translatable into, the analytic idiom appropriate to each individual art-form. Psychoanalysis is overwhelmingly concerned with the production and transformation of meaning, and is akin, in its search for economy, flexibility and exhaustiveness in the handling of its concepts, to numerous other analytic languages, including those that are seemingly best attuned to the workshop conditions of artistic production, and to the grain and texture of artistic materials.

(ii) Psychoanalysis, while recognizing the egotistical force of the individual's desire – or the grain and texture, as one might say, of personal motives and goals –, is profoundly interpersonal in its theoretical and observational habits. The analytic dialogue is a transactional and transferential affair. It is part of that larger 'web of interlocution', to use Charles Taylor's versatile phrase, in which and by means of which the individual creates, maintains and modulates his or her sense of selfhood.[10] Psychoanalysis pays attention, therefore, not simply to expressive gesture 'on stage' but to the offstage presences in relation to which such gestures make sense, and to the invisible and phantomatic relationships that any human utterance tacitly includes and re-edits.

(iii) The unconscious, which is the offstage presence *par excellence*, the unappeasable spectre at every communicative feast, prevents meaning from reaching fullness, completion, closure, consummation. Meaning is to be had in psychoanalysis only intermittently, as a momentary purchase achieved upon a constant interplay of levels, systems, structures, registers, intensities and investments. Psychoanalysis is a theory of meaning not simply arrived at and grasped but dawning and expiring, still out of sight or already on the wane. The meaning it studies is impure and unsimple, and resides in speech that is haunted by an unsheddable past, drawn forward into a desired future and always chequered and partial.

My first example is taken from Mozart and Da Ponte's *Così fan tutte* (1790), in which musical, verbal and dramatic modes of meaning converge and converse with extraordinary energy and wit.[11] In particular I shall comment on the great climactic duet in which Fiordiligi and Ferrando declare their love: 'Fra gli amplessi'. *Così* is, of course, directly concerned with what is nowadays known as the 'mediatedness' of desire. Throughout the work Mozart and Da Ponte create a range of teasing ambiguities by their ingenious reliteralizing of theatrical metaphor. 'The comedy is delightful', sings Don Alfonso as his plotting begins to take effect in Act I, but desire in performance and as performance is almost all we can know of desire in this mental universe. Everywhere passion is simulated, staged, spied upon and subjected to knowing commentary and discussion. Da Ponte's text supplies a complex geometry of criss-crossing perspectives and a dramatic fabric that is alive with ironic side-lights and reversals.

At the start of the scene in which this duet is to figure, Fiordiligi is preparing to join her lover Guglielmo at the wars and to this end dons one of Ferrando's military uniforms. There is nothing strange about a further disguise at this point in a plot where so much of the action has already been conducted *en travesti*. In hiding, Guglielmo watches Fiordiligi, admires her new resolve and, being a brash imperceptive fellow, sees no hidden warning in her choice of uniform. Da Ponte's stage directions make it plain that Guglielmo and Alfonso are able to listen and watch from an adjoining room as Fiordiligi gradually yields, and as Ferrando's simulated emotion suddenly begins to sound real in the radiant A major setting of 'Volgi a me pietoso il ciglio'. The web of interlocution here is complex indeed: each onlooker has a distinctive view of the scene that unfolds before him and a separate stake in the outcome of events. The characters upon whom they are spying each undergo a change of heart that is musically and textually highlighted as the scene proceeds. The whole drama changes course here. Moreover the present stage action is not only elaborately patterned in itself but eloquently recapitulates earlier events. Among several retrospective references in the score at this point, none is richer in irony than Ferrando's 'Volgi a me', in direct response to which Fiordiligi is lost. Its key and much of its phrasing are those of 'Un'aura amorosa', his song of fidelity in Act I, but the earlier object of his fidelity, Dorabella, is at this very moment being abandoned. The 'reality' of his new love is enforced by a musical reference to an earlier passion that has not been sustained.[12]

   This fulcrum-scene in the opera as a whole has its own pivotal point; the vocal phrase in which Fiordiligi finally tells of her new love is completed not by the voice but wordlessly, by the oboe:

Fordiligi's capitulation, taken from Charles Rosen, *The Classical Style*.

Charles Rosen, in the course of his brilliant analysis of the interaction between music and drama in Mozart's operas, comments on this passage from vocal to instrumental song: 'Fiordiligi's answer – her defeat – is the most exquisite of cadences, in which it is no longer the vocal line that carries the dramatic meaning, but the long-drawn-out and finally resolved phrase of the oboe. The classical realization of the cadence as an articulate dramatic event finds its triumph here.'[13] This cadence has another role too in the music drama. Ever since the sisters' melismatic swooning upon the word 'amore' in their first duet, Mozart has introduced moments of unwilled and unlegislated rapture into the rational argument of the drama. In the soaring climactic phrases of the trio 'Soave sia il vento', and in the duets that launch each of the centrally placed garden scenes, the characters are heard reaching out – beyond their stratagems, their feigning, and their self-deception – towards a region of clear and intense erotic sensation. Each of these moments also sees verbal fretting and point-making being cast aside in favour of sustained, self-delighting vocal sound. The whole procession of these moments is now completed and superseded in the rediscovery of instrumental sound that follows Fiordiligi's 'Crudel, hai vinto'. At last, rapture has been fully incorporated into the plot: the wordless cadence looks forward as well as back and triggers a rapid sequence of stage events.

In this scene, Mozart and Da Ponte have created an erotically saturated theatrical space, but without for a moment offering us a mere Bacchanalian or pansexual vision of desiring humankind. Erotic relationships are differentiated, held apart and kept in tension. The peculiar virtue of a psychoanalytic approach to this sort of dramatic texture is that it allows the space between relationships, and between the different expressive systems that are in play simultaneously, to be surveyed and measured. Discussing the dreamwork, and alluding to Nietzsche, Freud spoke of the continuous 'transvaluation of psychical values' that was to be observed on the inner stage of the dreaming mind (v, 655),[14] but this process was, according to the analysis he had already laid out in *The Interpretation of Dreams*, an extremely well-organized affair. Psychical values changed as ideas or images or verbal signs moved from system to system or from one associative sequence to another. Nothing could be understood of the native logic that the dreamwork possessed until the obdurate separation between these internal organizations – the space between them – had been granted at least as much explanatory weight as the general plasticity and compliance of the mental material. By the time the hearer reaches 'Fra gli amplessi' the associative pathway of Mozart's music has already become a complex self-referring weave and its forward movement has drawn into itself numerous retrospective loops. For instance, the oboe that completes Fiordiligi's cadential phrase has been prominent in the orchestral writing from the beginning of the Andante secion of the overture, where it appears as a solo instrument, and the sublime exchange between oboe and soprano voice has been prefigured in a series of woodwind dialogues that also begins early on in the overture.

At a much simpler level, Da Ponte's text has certain of the same characteristics: it quotes itself, refashions its witticisms and wordplay, and has all the characters drawing attention to the verbal medium in which their destinies are being played out. Psychoanalysis, as I have already noted, confers privilege not upon any one system but upon the space between and upon transforming movements across it. It helps us to map the separate articulations of desire that are present in this scene (and in this opera more generally) and to plot the points of convergence, condensation or crossover between those articulations as they develop over time. 'Fra gli amplessi' is the story of a gradual convergence between the expressive registers of music and text, but one in which equilibrium is no sooner found than lost again, as instrumental sound reasserts its claims as a vehicle of Eros.

Remembering a further, and central, process-notion from the psychoanalytic model, we could say that at this moment the elaborate transferential scenario that Don Alfonso has constructed for the two couples – in which each would undergo an experimentally induced and reversible change of heart – has broken down under pressure from a now fully acknowledged 'real' emotion. This is the scene in which Fiordiligi massively switches *Besetzungsenergie* from baritone to tenor, and in so doing creates a problem for many commentators on the work.

If *Così* is a story of two fine-grained sensibilities seeking each other out, and if 'Fra gli amplessi' is the glorious occasion of their mutual recognition, how can Mozart and Da Ponte even have contemplated a return to the *status quo ante* in the finale of Act II? This anxiety about the ending of the work found its extreme expression in Joseph Kerman's *Opera as Drama* (1956), where the seeming retreat of the four lovers to their original pairings is described as 'in the last analysis improbable and immoral'.[15] This view not only overlooks the role that temperamental differences may play in the kindling of sexual attraction (a sensitive soprano may yearn for a coarse-grained baritone), but under-represents the ambiguity and the ironic guile of the entire work.[16] The psychoanalytic view of desire in transit and in transformation, but flowing always between organizations rather than from one incandescent singularity to the next, is well placed to preserve these qualities of the music drama. Tension and dissonance between the expressive systems of music and text are essential to this work, for they are the very medium in which differences of affective disposition and erotic intensity are shaped and modulated. Mozartian interlocution is endlessly resourceful: it is alive to social as well as personal meanings, to parodic utterances as well as to the plain languages of passion and sentiment, to pretence and performance as well as to unaccountable delight. Psychoanalysis – of a suitably flexible and non-coercive kind – is in its turn alive to the strange co-existences that occur in the interlocutory field. It has to take them seriously in order to remain in touch with its own origins as a science of speech and with the exalted ideal of dialogue upon which its own therapeutic practices are based. In due course, psychoanalysis may even help us to understand the enigmatic emotional dialogue that runs through the whole of Mozart's music, and that Karl Barth caught perfectly in one of his periodic tributes to the composer: 'his music is not effortlessly accessible... This ever-present lightness possesses something very demanding, disturbing, almost provocative, even in the most radiant, most childlike, most joyful movements.'[17]

The dialectical virtuosity of *Così* can be preserved by other than psychoanalytic means, of course. Rosen's account of Mozart opera in *The Classical Style* or Ivan Nagel's in *Autonomy and Mercy* (1988)[18] make only glancing contact with Freudian notions, yet restage the dialectic and the textural variety of the stage works in critical writing of compelling energy and nuance. Not even their skill, however, is able to catch the speed and deftness with which operatic meaning is created, dissolved and reborn in the Mozart–Da Ponte masterpieces. The unconscious beckons at this point, but it would make no psychoanalytic sense to call on the concept in describing meaning that is simply lost or latent for the time being in the development of a complex musical and dramatic argument. Extended musical forms are, after all, arts of memory, ways of regulating the resurgence of past material into the continuous present of a work's unfolding. Such forms also allow the history of an emotion to remain audible even as that emotion seeks a new expressive outlet. They belong, however artfully, to the ordinary temporality of human living. Yet the Freudian unconscious proper does begin to have a special usefulness when past material returns strangely and obliquely to the present musical texture. Or when the argument suddenly skids from one associative pathway to another. Or when remembrance, without warning, gleams out brightly or looms up darkly from within a plot that is tidily working itself out. These are perhaps different incarnations of Barth's 'demanding, disturbing and almost provocative' thing. Meaning is not just making itself heard on cue and according to plan: some portion of it is being actively cancelled, and then, by an unaccountable grace, restored. And always at speed. Psychoanalysis has an eye for such mysteries. Performing the diplomatic role that I outlined earlier, trading between systems with its customary diligence, a psychoanalytic approach takes us forward to the moment when diplomacy breaks down under pressure from an ungovernable *Unheimlichkeit* or an indecipherable joy.

My second example involves, at long last, comparison of the kind that my title promises – between the separate arts of literature and music. However, I have protected myself from the charge of arbitrariness that exercises of this kind often attract by choosing two artists who were contemporaries and who had some knowledge of each other's work; Proust and Fauré.[19]

The role of music in *A la recherche du temps perdu* has been much studied, not least by Proust's narrator within the novel itself, and by Proust in his correspondence. One of the novel's best-known themes is the peculiar potency – affective and structural – of a musical theme, Vinteuil's *petite phrase*. This melodic fragment seems to encapsulate a spectrum of emotional states and to offer, in its recurrence after long intervals of time, an organizing principle for the narrator's projected literary work. Much attention has been paid by critics to those large-scale structural ideas that are called into play by Proust to prevent the central span of his very long book from collapsing under the weight of its copious descriptive detail. Architecture and music in particular have supplied many weight-bearing components of this kind, and have encouraged critics to 'think big' in their surveys of Proust on music. Two composers are especially favoured as reference points. Proust writes at length about Wagner, and the Wagnerian *Leitmotiv* provides at the very least a useful intuitive image of structure emerging from, or being thrust upon, a relentlessly through-composed literary work. Proust writes sparingly about César Franck, but even if he had said nothing at all about that presidential figure in the musical life of late nineteenth-century France, Franck's 'cyclical form' would have offered a similarly useful analogue for the grandiose repetitions and varied restatements around which much of Proust's plot is constructed.[20]

The problem is that commentators have been so willing to follow Proust's lead in celebrating the overall quasi-musical architecture of the novel that they have often overlooked the extraordinary structural density of the Proust paragraph or paragraph-sequence and the quite different musicalizing procedures that such textual 'movements' involve. The case of Fauré is instructive in this respect, although seldom remarked upon. Far from offering a working model for the entire book in the manner of Wagner and Franck, Fauré's compositional technique has been thought relevant to Proust only at the level of the individually eloquent phrases that it manipulates, and a circumstantial question about the composer's role in the novel – 'to what extent did a real Fauré work contribute to the imaginary Vinteuil sonata in which the *petite phrase* is first heard?' – has blocked off potentially more fruitful lines of enquiry. Between the overall pattern of the book and the semantic power of its constituent phrases and sentences, there is of course a multifarious world of textual invention. It is here that Proust displays his day-to-day power of elaboration and here too, I shall be suggesting, that the comparison with Fauré comes into its own.

The following passage from the closing section of *Du côté de chez Swann* has an 'elaborative' energy altogether characteristic of the novel's textual middle-ground. Legrandin has provided the narrator with one verbal portrait of the coast near Balbec, and Swann now draws the same landscape quite differently:

'Je crois bien que je connais Balbec! L'église de Balbec, du xiie et xiiie siècle, encore à moitié romane, est peut-être le plus curieux échantillon du gothique normand, et si singulière, on dirait de l'art persan.' Et ces lieux qui jusque-là ne m'avaient semblé être que de la nature immémoriale, restée contemporaine des grands phénomènes géologiques – et tout aussi en dehors de l'histoire humaine que l'Océan ou la Grande Ourse, avec ces sauvages pêcheurs pour qui, pas plus que pour les baleines, il n'y eut de Moyen age – ç'avait été un grand charme pour moi de les voir tout d'un coup entrés dans la série des siècles, ayant connu l'époque romane, et de savoir que le trèfle gothique était venu nervurer aussi ces rochers sauvages à l'heure voulue, comme ces plantes frêles mais vivaces qui, quand c'est le printemps, étoilent çà et là la neige des pôles. Et si le gothique apportait à ces lieux et à ces hommes une détermination qui leur manquait, eux aussi lui en conféraient une en retour. J'essayais de me représenter comment ces pêcheurs avaient vécu, le timide et insoupçonné essai de rapports sociaux qu'ils avaient tenté là, pendant le Moyen Age, ramassés sur un point des côtes d'Enfer, aux pieds des falaises de la mort; et le gothique me semblait plus vivant maintenant que séparé des villes où je l'avais toujours imaginé jusque-là, je pouvais voir comment, dans un cas particulier, sur des rochers sauvages, il avait germé et fleuri en un fin clocher. On me mena voir des reproductions des plus célèbres statues de Balbec – les apôtres moutonnants et camus, la Vierge du porche, et de joie ma respiration s'arrêtait dans ma poitrine quand je pensais que je pourrais les voir se modeler en relief sur le brouillard éternel et salé. Alors, par les soirs orageux et doux de février, le vent – soufflant dans mon cœur, qu'il ne faisait pas trembler moins fort que la cheminée de ma chambre, le projet d'un voyage à Balbec – mêlait en moi le désir de l'architecture gothique avec celui d'une tempête sur la mer.[21]

What had originally, following Legrandin's description, been fantasized as a realm of pure natural process, uplifting in its exhibition of wild, inhuman force, is now revealed as bearing the proud traces of *homo faber*. What had originally belonged to geological time now takes its place in the procession of the centuries and of their changing artistic styles. The broad argument of the passage sets forth a single main contrast – between nature and culture – and then, in a last climactic sentence, resolves it. There, nature and culture are no longer twin contestants in a struggle for dominion over the material world but 'natural' partners in an endless series of transvaluative exchanges: in the right sort of mind – the narrator's, say – desire can flow freely back and forth between Gothic buildings and the stormy sea.

But the ingenuity and wit of the passage lie in the way this argumentative outcome has already been prefigured in local metaphorical exchanges between the two counterposed themes. The 'cultural' Gothic trefoil colonizes the landscape in the manner of a gradually spreading organism, and becomes a real leaf, a carbon-based, chlorophyll-laden trifolium, in the process. The Gothic style itself hovers above the countryside, seeking its points of attachment, and then, once attached, germinates and flowers. The grand organizing contrast is not really a contrast at all. Art sweeps towards the natural wilderness of the Norman and Breton coasts at yet another untameable natural force.

The Fauré works that I have in mind for comparative purposes are not those that Proust seems especially to have admired – the early songs and piano pieces and the first Violin Sonata, for example – but the late chamber works that were composed in the years just before and just after Proust's completion of his great novel: the Second Piano Quintet, Op. 115 (1919–21), the Piano Trio, Op. 120 (1922–3) and the String Quartet, Op. 121 (1923–4). These works represent the last blossoming of Fauré's contrapuntal skill, and their counterpoint is the vehicle for a searing and seamless expressivity. Violent contrasts are for the most part avoided, as are perfect cadences and the highlighting of sectional breaks in sonata movements. Norman Suckling, in his pioneering study of the composer, spoke of Fauré as often presenting 'his successive themes not as a contrast or a balance, but rather as the complement or the extension of each other'.[22] And Robert Orledge has described in the following terms the two main themes (A and B) on which the first movement of the Piano Trio is built:

Development of A and B in separate paragraphs, either by extension or motivic cross-play, begins immediately after the exposition, and it is always difficult to tell what is theme and what is extension, so continuous is the musical flow. In B, for instance, the repeat of the start on the strings immediately incorporates A_1, which sends the music off in a totally new direction, and Fauré was a past master at fusing apparently incongruous ideas into one continuous thread in his long, organic developments.[23]

What looks like a cult of unity, pursued at the expense of excitement and variety, has prevented these works from enjoying wide popularity, and certain of their detractors have complained that not only the thematic building-blocks out of which movements are made but also the movements themselves are simply too much alike. I should prefer to see these works as exercises in the tantalizing deferral of identity, or in the relocation of difference from the macro-structural level to that of textural detail.

What Proust in his extended paragraph-movements and Fauré in his late chamber style have in common, then, is a liking for near-sameness and for fluent compositional procedures that tend to dissolve the differential devices – whether of plot or of sonata argument – on which their chosen medium familiarly depends. Both are willing to sabotage a large amount of conventional sense-making machinery in order to safeguard the continuity of their tightly interwoven associative sequences. At this point the Freudian account of unconscious mental functioning may again be consulted with profit, although we need to remind ourselves of what is clearly not the case here. If and when the unconscious is thought of as having a useful structure-supplying role in twentieth-century art, the most promising access routes are often thought to be those of automatic writing, stream of consciousness, or the 'free' association of ideas or verbal sounds. Loosen up, let go, be associative, and the unconscious is yours. Proust and Fauré take a markedly different route. By way of elaborate technical calculation they create worlds of pure desire-propelled transformational activity. Working within the exacting secondary processes that belong to their chosen craft, they produce – from afar, as it were – a mimesis or a working model of the primary process itself. Condensation and displacement are reinvented by consciousness and then allowed to contest or override the 'higher' structural principles that are still ostensibly in force. The immediate effect of this upon readers or hearers coming straight from the products of earlier artistic dispensations – those of Balzac or Beethoven, for example – is likely to be that of a sudden uncomfortable dedifferentiation in the mental field. All the landmarks have gone. The expressive idiom is ever-varying yet ever self-identical. The concurrent associative chains that these works trace are presented not as a phased dialogue between clear and distinct points of view, but more as a perpetual lattice or tissue of interconnected motifs.

This is 'processiveness' or 'transformationalism' of a kind which causes no difficulty for psychoanalysis – the unconscious just is, *ex hypothesi*, a transformative system that runs on interminably – but which can create real panic in the sphere of art. How are climax, conclusion and closure to be achieved once the dynamo has been set going? What latecoming alternative principle of structure can be wrested from the dedifferentiated flux in order to bring its ceaseless expressive striving to a fitting end? Proust's narrator in the passage I have quoted ends by talking about desire itself: the motivating force 'behind' his procession of images and conceits is at last shown forth and calls a temporary halt to their production. Fauré proceeds to the final climax of his Allegros simply by intensifying and making louder the seamless contrapuntal exchanges that are the stuff of such movements. In neither case are we entitled to expect a convincing argumentative resolution or a full release of tension. The continuum races on, even as a large conclusive gesture is called upon to silence it.

One safe conclusion that can be drawn from my two main examples, as discussed here, is that any 'diplomatic' critical idiom derived from psychoanalysis is likely to be more appropriate to certain comparative exercises than to others. We could perhaps go further and suggest that psychoanalysis is of particular use in analysing works of art that originate in the same broad cultural context as itself. The crisis of Enlightenment values that echoes throughout Freud's writings is already present in the undecidable contest between rationality and Eros that *Così fan tutte* enacts. More strikingly still, *Le Temps retrouvé* and the second of Fauré's Piano Quintets belong to the same year as *Beyond the Pleasure Principle* and address the same traumatized European bourgeoisie. Even if we grant the psychoanalytic approach its freedom to travel across the centuries and the continents, it is still subject to an important restriction: it illuminates works that have elaborate internal faceting and high levels of transformative and transvaluative activity, and has correspondingly little to say about countless admirable works that do not possess these qualities. It is tempting to forestall further discussion by concluding that psychoanalysis in its entirety is simply a rather recondite form of Romantic irony, and that Freud will always be at his best in the company of his fellow ironists.

The case of Tiepolo, with which I began, is instructive in this respect. When Lacan came to choose an emblematic painting, one that was somehow 'about' the origins of modern subjectivity, he chose *The Ambassadors* by the younger Holbein, and reread its ingenious allegory of knowledge from the viewpoint of the *memento mori*, the anamorphic skull, that hovers over the geometrically patterned pavement at the foot of the painting. Tiepolo's *Finding of Moses* is, for psychoanalysis if not for art history, the same sort of work – one in which the intimate life of the conflicting human drives is opened up to public display. In Tiepolo's painting the lively disorganized limbs of the newly discovered infant are already framed by an overarching intimation of death. Eros and Thanatos have been driven into confrontation, and psychoanalysis is ready armed to explore the space of their conflict.

Even when the limitations of the psychoanalytic approach have been fully rehearsed, however, one of its main virtues remains undimmed: it provides an exacting way of describing or redescribing the interactive components of works of art, and of opening up new channels of communication between art forms. And it can occasionally do this in a way that preserves an important tension between questions of structure and questions of emotional response. In due course we may possess a general 'systems theory' appropriate to artistic experience, but until that day arrives psychoanalysis will have many useful tasks to perform in the realm of comparative criticism.

NOTES

1 The critical literature on this painting is small, and now dominated by Michael Levey's brilliant pages in *Giambattista Tiepolo: his Life and Art* (New Haven and London, 1986), pp. 77–81. Details of the Veronese *Finding of Moses*, now in Dresden, that is likely to have been a source for Tiepolo's work are to be found in Hugh Brigstocke's catalogue *Italian and Spanish Paintings in the National Gallery of Scotland* (Edinburgh, 1978), pp. 142–5. All five of Veronese's versions of the subject are illustrated in *L'Opera completa del Veronese*, edited by Remigio Marini and Guido Piovene (Milan, 1968), p. 119. In none of them is there any equivalent to Tiepolo's frieze.

2 *Language in Literature*, ed. Krystyna Pomorska and Stephen Rudy (Cambridge, Mass. and London, 1987) p. 71.

3 *Articulate Energy. An Inquiry into the Syntax of English Poetry* (London, 1955), p. 91.

4 'Expressive Principle and Orchestral Polyphony in Schoenberg's *Erwartung*', in *Schoenberg and the New Music*, trans. Derrick Puffett and Alfred Clayton (Cambridge University Press, 1987), pp. 149–55. Among outstanding recent contributions to the comparative study of literature and music are Nicolas Ruwet's *Langage, musique, poésie* (Paris, 1972), Steven Paul Scher's collection *Music and Text. Critical Inquiries* (Cambridge University Press, 1992), which contains essays by John Neubauer, Paul Alpers, Marshall Brown, Anthony Newcomb and Lawrence Kramer among others, and the works mentioned in note 11 below.

5 *Absorption and Theatricality. Painting and the Beholder in the Age of Diderot* (Chicago and London, 1980).

6 *The Classical Style. Haydn, Mozart, Beethoven* (London, 1971), pp. 288–325.

7 *Pictorialist Poetics. Poetry and the Visual Arts in Nineteenth-Century France* (Cambridge University Press, 1988).

8 Freud's technical languages are studied in great detail, both historically and in terms of their divergent semantic fields, by J. Laplanche and J.-B. Pontalis in their *The Language of Psycho-Analysis*, trans. Donald Nicholson-Smith (London, 1973).

9 For Lacan's transposition of Freud's *condensation* and *displacement* into rhetorical terms, see *Ecrits* (Paris, 1966), pp. 511ff (160ff in Alan Sheridan's translation, *Ecrits. A Selection* (London and New York, 1977)).

10 See *Sources of the Self. The Making of the Modern Identity* (Cambridge, Mass. and London, 1989), pp. 36ff and p. 525 n. 12.

11 On the theoretical background to this convergence and on the new status of music in the late eighteenth century, see John Neubauer, *The Emancipation of Music from Language. Departure from Mimesis in Eighteenth-Century Aesthetics* (New Haven and London, 1986) and Marian Hobson, *The Object of Art. The Theory of Illusion in Eighteenth-Century France* (Cambridge University Press, 1982).

12 On the self-referential components of Mozart's score, see Daniel Heartz's 'Citation, Reference and Recall in *Così fan tutte*' in *Mozart's Operas* (Berkeley, 1990), pp. 229–53 and, with special reference to 'Fra gli amplessi', Andrew Steptoe's *The Mozart–Da Ponte Operas. The Cultural and Musical Background to 'Le Nozze di Figaro', 'Don Giovanni', and 'Così fan tutte'* (Oxford: Clarendon Press, 1988), pp. 236–42.

13 *The Classical Style*, p. 316.

14 My reference is to the short work *On Dreams* (1901) as it appears in the Standard Edition of Freud's *Complete Psychological Works*, edited by James Strachey (London, 1953–74).

15 *Opera as Drama* (New York, 1956), p. 116.

16 Andrew Steptoe concludes his discussion of 'Fra gli amplessi' with this timely reminder of the work's ambiguity: 'Yet the final enigma is unresolved. Ferrando may be expressing a true passion in the "larghetto", addressing Fiordiligi with genuine ardour. Alternatively, he may be treacherously raising his attack on to a new level of emotional duplicity, spurred on by his own humiliation at the hands of Dorabella... In either case, the structure of the musical score, and the grand

tonal design linking the diverse episodes of the story, have a transcendent dramatic relevance to *Così fan tutte*' (*The Mozart–Da Ponte Operas*, p. 242).

17 Karl Barth, *Wolfgang Amadeus Mozart*, trans. Clarence K. Pratt (Grand Rapids, Mich., 1986), p. 48.

18 *Autonomy and Mercy. Reflections on Mozart's Operas* (Cambridge, Mass. and London, 1991).

19 For a detailed account of their relationship, together with a previously unpublished letter from Proust to Fauré, see Jean-Michel Nectoux, 'Proust et Fauré', *Bulletin de la société des amis de Marcel Proust et des amis de Combray*, no. 21 (1971), 1101–20. Proust also figures in Nectoux's *Gabriel Fauré. A Musical Life*, trans. Roger Nichols (Cambridge University Press, 1991).

20 On the role of music in *A la recherche* there are now a number of excellent studies, including John Cocking, 'Proust and Music', in *Proust. Collected Essays on the Writer and his Art* (Cambridge University Press, 1982), pp. 109–29, and Jean-Jacques Nattiez, *Proust as Musician*, trans. Derrick Puffett (Cambridge University Press, 1989). On music as a 'return to the unanalysed' in Proust, see Edward J. Hughes, *Marcel Proust. A Study in the Quality of Awareness* (Cambridge University Press, 1983), pp. 164–70.

21 *A la recherche du temps perdu*, ed. Jean-Yves Tadié (Paris, 1987), vol. I, 377–78.

'Yes indeed I know Balbec! The church there, built in the twelfth and thirteenth centuries, and still half Romanesque, is perhaps the most curious example to be found of our Norman Gothic, and so singular that one is tempted to describe it as Persian in its inspiration.'

And that region which, until then, had seemed to me to be nothing else than a part of immemorial nature, that had remained contemporaneous with the great phenomena of geology – and as remote from human history as the Ocean itself or the Great Bear, with its wild race of fishermen for whom no more than for their whales had there been any Middle Ages – it had been a great joy to me to see it suddenly take its place in the order of the centuries, with a stored consciousness of the Romanesque epoch, and to know that the Gothic trefoil had come to diversify those wild rocks too at the appointed time, like those frail but hardy plants which in the Polar regions, when spring returns, scatter their stars about the eternal snows. And if Gothic art brought to those places and people an identification which otherwise they lacked, they too conferred one upon it in return. I tried to picture how those fishermen had lived, the timid and undreamt-of experiment in social relations which they had attempted there, clustered upon a promontory of the shores of Hell, at the foot of the cliffs of death; and Gothic art seemed to me a more living thing now that, detached from the towns in which until then I had always imagined it, I could see how, in a particular instance, upon a reef of savage rocks, it had taken root and grown until it flowered in a tapering spire. I was taken to see reproductions of the most famous of the statues at Balbec – the shaggy, snub-nosed Apostles, the Virgin from the porch – and I could scarcely breathe for joy at the thought that I might myself, one day, see them stand out in relief against the eternal briny fog. Thereafter, on delightful, stormy February nights, the wind – breathing into my heart, which it shook no less violently than the chimney of my bedroom, the project of a visit to Balbec – blended in me the desire for Gothic architecture as well as for a storm upon the sea.

22 *Fauré* (London, 1946), p. 109.

23 *Gabriel Fauré* (London, 1983), p. 188.

Comparative Criticism 15, 103–123. Copyright © 1993 Cambridge University Press

Authority and interpretation: Leviathan and the 'covenantal community'

HAROLD FISCH

For Eldad Melamed in gratitude for his wisdom and skill

In the state of "meer Nature" Hobbes tells us "every man has a Right to everything."[1] His egotism is unrestrained; he is guided only by his own fears and vanities. He says with Shakespeare's Troilus in effect that the will is infinite and the desire is boundless, but unlike Troilus he does not add that the act is a slave to limit. He knows no limits, pursuing his own intensities without regard to the rights of others. Here, we may say, is a radical formulation of Renaissance individualism. The self is supreme. And because such a state is intolerable, being no less than the war of every man against every man, it has to be terminated. Articles of peace are agreed upon, and this is done "by Covenant of every man with every man."[2] As the language suggests, this arrangement preserves the principle of free individuality, every man voluntarily agreeing to surrender his rights for the sake of peace. But paradoxically its effect is the total abolition of individual freedom. For the contract or covenant of every man with every man results, as is well known, in the "Generation of the great Leviathan" – a commonwealth ruled over by an absolute monarch whose power over his subjects is total and whose will is supreme, for all have agreed irrevocably "to submit their Wills, every one to his Will, and their Judgments, to his Judgment."[3] This is the root paradox of Hobbes's system of anthropology and political philosophy. Unlimited freedom is matched by unlimited subjection. Parallel to it is the contradiction between the rational decisions which bring the State into existence and the irrational surrender of all decision-making powers by the citizens once it is there.[4]

It is not generally noted that behind this model of the commonwealth there is a prior and even more fundamental paradigm. In the *De Cive* he maintains that language itself and the possibility of communication between men "depends on the compacts and consents of men."[5] And there too such consent is designed to put an end to intolerable chaos, namely, the chaos of conflicting meanings and usages. Not only poetry with its extravagances, but language as such, that of ourselves and others, menaces us with radical disorder. As a result we must seek agreement as to names and their significations, for nothing can be determined concerning "the appellations of things" without such consent. Those who think otherwise take away the use of speech and with it the very basis of social existence. "For he who hath sold a whole field, will say he meant one whole ridge; and will retain the rest as unsold. Nay they take away reason itself; which is nothing else but a searching out of the truth made by such consent."[6]

The control of language by "consents of men" is thus a precondition for any kind of rational inquiry and it is not surprising that Hobbes raises the issue again and casts about for a solution at the outset of *Leviathan*:

Seeing then that *truth* consisteth in the right ordering of names in our affirmations, a man that seeketh precise *truth*, had need to remember what every name he uses stands for; and to place it accordingly; or else he will find himselfe entangled in words, as a bird in lime-twigs; the more he struggles, the more belimed. And therefore in Geometry, (which is the onely Science that it hath pleased God hitherto to bestow on mankind), men begin at settling the significations of their words; which settling of significations, they call *Definitions*; and place them in the beginning of their reckoning.[7]

Language is treacherous, especially metaphorical language; it will take you where you do not want to go. Thus there is always a traitor in the house. At the end of *Leviathan* we still find him saying, "There is nothing I distrust more than my Elocution."[8] Metaphors will creep in it seems no matter how hard you try to eliminate them. Indeed, there is more than one metaphor in the very passage just quoted, with its talk of birdlime and geometry. And what is *Leviathan* itself taken as a whole but one prodigious metaphor drawn from the book of Job where the great sea-monster "seeth every high thing below him: and is King over all the children of pride"?[9] How then is one to bring language under control and thus limit the infinite freedom of utterance granted by nature to every individual speaker?

To achieve this there is need for consent and agreement (a notion reiterated in chapter 31 of *Leviathan* where he affirms that "words have their signification by agreement and constitution of men"[10]) but there is also need for authority. In the above-quoted passage he proposes to give to language the rigor and authority of mathematics – a notion evidently inherited from Bacon.[11] Sharing a confusion common in the seventeenth century, he finds in geometry a mathematical norm as well as a model of inductive reasoning. Geometry, says Hobbes, "is the onely Science that it hath pleased God hitherto to bestow on mankind." His ideal seems to be a mode of discourse based on the principle of computation and aimed in nominalistic fashion at ordering our knowledge of particular individual entities as given in perception.[12] Presumably the philosopher who, like Euclid, settles by rigid definitions the significations of name and terms, functions in the realm of language rather as the sovereign functions in civil society. Such an idea in the seventeenth century did not remain entirely in the realm of theory. The Royal Society in 1665 set up a subcommittee on linguistic reform, aiming in Hobbesian fashion to achieve "a mathematical plainness" and a strict correspondence of words to things in scientific discourse.[13] The project seems to have been abandoned after a couple of years. Had it continued it would have introduced into the area of language the authority of the Royal Society, and indirectly, that of the sovereign himself.

Hobbes's most acute problem is, however, not the fashioning of a philosophical language, important though that is, but the interpretation of texts and in particular – since what he is fashioning is a Christian Commonwealth – the text of the Scriptures. How is that text to be understood and who are its authorized interpreters? Here the danger is not simply that we will write bad philosophy; the failure to find an agreed interpretation for the Word of God threatens the very stability of the Commonwealth, "reduc[ing] all Order, Government, and Society, to the first Chaos of Violence, and Civill warre."[14] Hobbes had seen this happen in England with the proliferation of the Puritan sects during and after the Civil War of 1642–6. If Milton rejoiced that London was the mansion-house of liberty and that now the time seemed to have come when "all the Lord's people are become prophets,"[15] Hobbes was filled with horror. Here was confusion and chaos. His horror at the results of such unbounded freedom of interpretation, is, it may be affirmed, his root experience as a political philosopher. He had witnessed the final catastrophic effects of Protestant biblicism. The open Bible of the reformation rendered in the vernacular and given to every man and woman to interpret had resulted in something like the war of every man against every man. Michael Oakeshott properly relates this to Hobbes's concept of "the meer state of Nature." For if everyone interprets for himself we are back in the state of nature.[16] It may be truer to say that Hobbes's nightmare vision of the state of nature was itself an outgrowth of his prior reaction to the chaos of conflicting interpretations. That was evidently his fundamental paradigm.

This raises the whole question of interpretation. On the one hand it is clear to Hobbes that texts need to be interpreted – they do not interpret themselves. Indeed, without interpretation they can hardly be said to exist – "it is not the dead voice or letter of *the word of God*, which is the canon of Christian doctrine; but a true and genuine determination. For the mind is not governed by Scriptures, unless they be understood."[17] On the other hand, the moment we open up the text for interpretation, a radical instability ensues: why one interpretation and not another and where does the process end? There is no escape from the hermeneutic problem either in regard to the Bible or to any other text. He discusses the nature of the problem and the way it might be resolved in the important passage which follows the sentences just quoted from *De Cive*:

Now that interpreter whose determination hath the honour to be held for *the word of God*, is not every one that translates the Scriptures out of the Hebrew and Greek tongue, to his Latin audience in Latin, to his French in French, and to other nations in their mother tongue; for this is not to interpret. For such is the nature of speech in general, that although it deserve the chief place among those signs whereby we declare our conceptions to others, yet cannot it perform that office alone without the help of many circumstances. For the living voice hath its interpreters present, to wit, time, place, countenance, gesture, the counsel of the speaker, and himself unfolding his own meaning in other words as oft as need is. To recall these aids of interpretation, so much desired in the writings of old time, is neither the part of an ordinary wit, nor yet of the quaintest, without great learning and very much skill in antiquity. It sufficeth not therefore for interpretation of Scriptures, that a man understand the language wherein they speak. Neither is every one an authentic interpreter of Scriptures who writes comments upon them. For men may err; they also either bend them to serve their own ambition; or even resisting, draw them into bondage by their forestallings; whence it will follow, that an erroneous sentence must be held for *the word of God*. But although this might not happen, yet as soon as these commentators are departed, their commentaries will need explications; and in process of time, those explications expositions; those expositions new commentaries, without any end. So as there cannot in any written interpretation whatsoever, be a canon or rule of Christian doctrine, whereby the controversies of religion may be determined. It remains, that there must be some canonical interpreter, whose legitimate office it is to end controversies begun, by explaining the word of God in the judgments themselves; and whose authority therefore must be no less obeyed, than theirs who first recommended the Scripture itself to us for a canon of faith; and that one and the same person be *an interpreter of Scripture*, and *a supreme judge of all manner of doctrines*.[18]

Interpretation thus serves to recall the circumstances of the original utterance – time, place, countenance, gesture, as well as the aids to understanding which the original speaker might have provided through his living presence. This takes us far beyond literal interpretation, the mere understanding of the words, and nearer to something like the reconstruction of a primary event and its adaptation to new times and places. Interpretation, he seems to say, is fluid and uncertain and he stresses the enormous difficulty of attempting to reconstruct the original setting. Perhaps Hobbes would want to say with Rudolf Bultmann that we would do better to ignore the historical background and by interpretation free the text from that setting, demythologize it. But whereas Bultmann, indeed Protestant theology in general, would welcome the unending process of interpretation as a way for each and every person to relive the saving word, the *kerygma*, for himself, Hobbes finds such a prospect appalling. It leads to religious and political anarchy. This is not because he regards a text as fixed and determined *in advance*; on the contrary it is only the interpreter who brings it to life – without him it is "a dead voice or letter." But the exercise of human freedom in interpretation must be curbed. The Bible is too dangerous and too important for that. For the sake of peace and for the sake of determining those controversies which threaten the foundations of the commonwealth, there must be a "canonical interpreter, whose legitimate office it is to end controversies" (*ibid.*). We are back with Hobbes's central paradox.

Elsewhere in *De Cive* and in *Leviathan* we hear more about this "canonical interpreter." He is, it seems, no other than the sovereign, or someone designated by the sovereign for this task.[19] The commonwealth consists of citizens united in one person and only the commonwealth has the power to make laws as well as to interpret texts. Nor are there two governments of law-making authorities. In his Erastian fashion Hobbes sees the Church and the Commonwealth as united in the person of the King. There can be no separation of Church and State such as would create two separate sources of authority in the Commonwealth. That way ruin lies and disorder.

This position taken by Hobbes clearly contradicts the Protestant stress on the individual soul as the arena where religious meaning is discovered, the spirit answering to the spirit in a lonely personal encounter with a text that is full of power and mystery. It is equally opposed to the Catholic standpoint: the Catholic Church tends to insist that only authorized interpretations of the Word are acceptable, but the Church itself is clearly the source and *locus* of such authority. There can be no question of a secular government having any standing in such matters. If this results in tension and conflict between Church and State, so be it. It is part of the necessary duality of Christian existence. We are subject to the temporal city and its rulers, but we also belong prospectively to the City of God; we are pilgrims of eternity. The Church and its duly appointed head, deriving their authority from the founder of Christianity itself, guide us in that pilgrimage. Nor is this just a matter of inherited privilege, of a formal authority. The Church can interpret the laws and mysteries of the faith because those to whom it delegates this task are men of learning whose spiritual gifts enable them to achieve an inward understanding of the Word. Such understanding would evidently be lacking if the authority to determine meaning were to be located ultimately in the person of the civil ruler, the "mortall God" of the Hobbesian commonwealth. Hobbes has, it seems, pushed his doctrine over the brink of absurdity by giving the absolute ruler not merely unlimited political power, but unlimited hermeneutic privileges also.

Hobbes's explicit and several times repeated notion that only the sovereign is authorized to interpret the Bible has evidently proved an embarrassment to readers and critics, for they rarely refer to this aspect of his system. F. C. Hood, who takes Hobbes's concern with Scripture and religion more seriously than most scholars, writes as though the interpretative privileges of the monarch related only to the legal parts of the Bible or at least to those parts which might become the subject of civil law. The monarch's right to legislate in such areas, he suggests, is consistent with seventeenth-century legal doctrine in England and goes back to the Act of Supremacy of 1534.[20] If this were so, there would be nothing irrational about Hobbes's notion. But in fact a close look at his references to the hermeneutic prerogatives of the sovereign shows that he views these as going beyond the matter of law-making on the basis of the Bible.[21] For instance, in chapter 38 he develops his notion of the meaning of "Eternall Life", which he understands as an indefinite continuation of terrestrial existence, such as Adam lost when he sinned, and not a promise of living eternally in heaven. This is part of Hobbes's speculative materialism, supported by his unorthodox reading of the narrative and poetic parts of the Bible, with prooftexts from Genesis, Job, Matthew and other books. It is not easy to see how Hobbes's views or those of his opponents on such a question could be of concern to the sovereign in his capacity as law-maker. It belongs to the region of faith or opinion, and elsewhere Hobbes had excluded the area of opinions and beliefs from State control.[22] And yet twice in this chapter he makes it clear that in his ideal republic, *Leviathan*, such issues as the nature of eternal life would be submitted to the arbitrament of the sovereign ruler. Thus he qualifies his presumption in offering so original an interpretation of this notion with an apologetic gesture of submission to authority:

By which it seemeth to me, (with submission nevertheless both in this, and *in all questions whereof the determination dependeth on the Scriptures, to the interpretation of the Bible authorized by the Commonwealth*, whose subject I am,) that Adam if he had not sinned, had had an Eternall Life on Earth.[23]

Later in the same chapter he has a similarly cautionary remark on the question of the biblical doctrine of "the Kingdom of God." This again Hobbes understands as a terrestrial, not a heavenly, kingdom but it came to an end in the biblical period and will only be resumed at the time of the Second Coming. In the meantime every Christian owes absolute loyalty to the civil government. Hobbes ranges widely over many places of Scripture to prove this remarkable thesis. Here too he says that the debate on this issue can only be determined ultimately "by them, that under God have the Soveraign Power."[24] There is a doubly circular argument here: Scripture grants to human kings absolute power, including the authority to interpret Scripture, but that very interpretation of Scripture is validated by the king exercising the authority to interpret.

This is a paradoxical situation to be sure, but the paradox is more fundamental than that; it belongs to Hobbes's essential hermeneutic posture rather than to the contradictions that emerge when we examine this or that doctrine. As an interpreter, making a free, independent and original examination of the Bible, he is in the main Protestant tradition. Many of his views can be matched among the sectarians. His materialism and mortalism can be matched in Milton's *De Doctrina Christiana*[25] and also among the Levellers and the Anabaptists. Moreover, in his analysis of texts he uses the same logical methods as the Puritans of his century, developing his argument by endless dichotomies and reducing metaphors to bald statements. Like them "Hobbes is a Ramist at heart."[26] Even his rationalizing way of dealing with such mysteries as angels, spirits, and the nature of hell is part of a new, emerging tendency in Protestant exegesis. It can be detected earlier in the century in the writings of William Chillingworth and John Hales and later on among rational theologians such as John Tillotson and Edward Stillingfleet.[27] All this shows Hobbes claiming the Protestant privilege of free inquiry into the open Bible. He even allows himself the right to question the authorship and date of various books of the Old Testament, thus anticipating Spinoza's biblical criticism, that of Richard Simon and others. And yet, starting with this implicit claim to free, independent interpretation and exercising that freedom by devoting no fewer than seventeen chapters of *Leviathan* to biblical exegesis, he proceeds to surrender the right of an independent, critical judgment to the authority of the State. And to compound the paradox, he finds support in the very texts which he so freely interprets for the surrender of the right to interpret them. This is the fundamental *aporia*. Thus he cites the examples of Abraham and Moses who, he says, were in effect kings with the exclusive right to interpret the word of God in their time and place. By means of a typological reading of the relevant places of the Old Testament, these figures become the model for the sovereign in a Christian commonwealth.[28]

Some years ago I suggested that Hobbes is a kind of apostate Jew, his ideas bearing a strange but inverted relation to biblical hebraism; his tendency, like Milton's in his divorce tracts, is to try to bring the teaching of the New Testament into line with Old Testament norms.[29] Thus he understands the second verse of Genesis as referring not to "the Spirit of God" which "moved upon the waters," but "a Wind…which might be called *the Spirit of God*, because it was Gods work."[30] With this in mind he proceeds to demystify the references to spirits in the Old and New Testaments. The "Holy Ghost" in Luke 4: 1 and elsewhere "may be understood, for *Zeal* to doe the work for which hee [i.e. Jesus] was sent…How we came to translate *Spirits*, by the word *Ghosts*, which signifieth nothing, neither in heaven, nor earth, but the Imaginary inhabitants of mans brains, I examine not."[31] In the same way he notes (correctly) that the word for angel in the Old Testament means no more than messenger. Such messengers are either dream images or corporeal figures. And he then proceeds to apply this insight to the New Testament, insisting that to speak of them as "Incorporeall Substance, is to say in effect, there is no Angel nor Spirit at all."[32]

Turning to the biblical conception of Man, he denies on the basis of Job 14: 12 and Ecclesiastes 3: 19 that the soul of man is a "living Creature independent on the body." Hobbes's account of human nature in general, as Ronald Hepburn remarks, "is reminiscent of Old Testament psychology with its unabashed stress on the physical."[33] In effect, Hobbes rejects the Augustinian boundary separating natural from supernatural, the earthly city from the heavenly city, physical from metaphysical, body from soul, and supports this from the evidence of the Old Testament. He replaces a hellenistic dualism with a monism which has no room for immaterial phenomena. We only know of things on this earth; in the Old Testament he tells us (correctly) there is strictly nothing said of heaven or hell, for hell or *Gehinnom* is simply the name of a place in Jerusalem associated with Molech worship. The salvation of the saints in the latter days, like the messianic kingdom for the Jews, will be not in heaven but on earth.[34] In my earlier study, I argued also that Hobbes's idea of covenant and contract, though evidently owing much to contemporary Puritanism, loses its interior, metaphysical character ("the Covenant of Grace") and is grounded instead, as in the Hebrew Bible, in obedience and moral obligation.[35] His model for the obedience due to civil monarchs is that of the relations established between Moses and the Israelites after the covenant-assembly at Mount Sinai.[36]

In all these matters, he has evidently made the Hebrew Bible his norm, finding in it a model more congenial to his temper than the evangelical doctrine which states that "my kingdom is not of this world." Thus he was able to argue that God's kingdom as announced at Sinai (Exodus 19: 6) would be based on the free consent of those governed combined with the absolute authority of the governor (*ibid.* 19: 8, 24: 3). But when Hobbes adopts this paradox into his system, it seems inevitably to give rise to a series of logical contradictions; in the context of the Hebrew Bible it finds its solution in the fact that God is at one and the same time creator and lawgiver. As creator he bestows on Man his privilege of freedom and as lawgiver he imposes on him an imperative burden of obligation. His kingdom is a real kingdom, as authoritarian in its way as Hobbes's Leviathan, but the freedom given to the subjects is likewise a real freedom and, unlike that which Hobbes's *anthropoi* enjoy in the state of nature, it is not forfeited when they swear obedience to their sovereign. This paradox of freedom and authority is at the heart of the hebraic system. In the experience of the Covenant it is the fruitful tension between the two which gives meaning to the dialogue between God and Man. It becomes a real dialogue between a morally free agent and an omnipotent divine sovereignty. There is no such dialogue between Hobbes's "mortall God" and the civil society over which he rules. The mystery of this paradox has been lost in Hobbes's severe "mathematical" demonstrations.

And of course the poetry of the paradox is lost also. Man in the Old Testament is, as Hobbes recognized, a creature formed out of the dust, living and dying, and returning to the dust from which he came. But he is nevertheless made "in the image of God." Our destiny is on this earth not in heaven, but then the earth itself is "full of His glory" (Isaiah 6:3). The word for "glory" in this passage (*kabod*) may be at bottom physical and related to the liver (*kabed*) which was regarded as the seat of dignity, but language too has been sanctified, heightened, made into a channel of communication between Man and God. Creatureliness is involved in our very forms of speech which do not lose their connection with the organs of the body, but creatureliness itself is combined with seemingly limitless aspirations. As Job said, "in my flesh I will see God." It is an audacious claim. Job is corporeal all right, although his *corpus* is tormented with disease; but nevertheless he is going to be granted an interview with his Maker. Hobbes seized on the corporeality, but ignored the interview. That would be for him one of the mysteries of religion, which he tells us in a particularly candid passage should be "swallowed whole" like pills, rather than chewed.[37] The result is that we have in Hobbes a hebraism with all the spiritual overtones missing, all the poetry flattened out, in a word – a caricature of the Hebrew vision of Man, God and Nature.

At this point I would like to extend that thesis into the area of hermeneutics. Here too I would wish to argue that the dialectic of freedom and authority that we noted earlier in Hobbes's hermeneutic doctrine is surprisingly analogous to the pattern that emerges from rabbinic theory and practice. Here again he seems to have moved close to a Judaic way of thinking, but here again we shall note some vital differences. What we have once more is a kind of caricature version, a photographic negative of biblical and post-biblical hebraism.

I begin with the famous account given in the Mishnah[38] of the confrontation between Rabban Gamaliel II and an older teacher, R. Joshua ben Hananiah on the issue of the day on which the Day of Atonement should fall in a certain year. Gamaliel was the *Nasi* or Patriarch – the chief Jewish official in the years following the destruction of the Temple. In effect, he was the head of the government, recognized as such by the Romans, with his seat at Jabneh, where he also acted as president of the rabbinical court. The appearance of the new moon had to be reported to the court by two reliable witnesses so as to determine whether the new month should begin on the thirtieth or the thirty-first day after the beginning of the previous month. On this occasion – at the end of Ellul and the beginning of Tishri – the witnesses claimed to have seen the moon on the eve of the thirtieth day, but their testimony was ambiguous. Gamaliel accepted their word whilst Joshua disqualified them and recommended that the extra day be intercalated in the month of Ellul. The effect of R. Joshua's ruling was that for him the Day of Atonement (the tenth day of Tishri) would fall one day later than it would according to Gamaliel.

At this point the question becomes not who is right, but who is authorized to interpret the law. Gamaliel has that authority and he exercises it. The Mishnah describes how he sent to R. Joshua, and said, "I charge you that you come to me with your staff and your money on the Day of Atonement as it falls according to your reckoning." Joshua is in great distress: he is being required publicly to desecrate what he had determined in his mature judgment to be the holy day. He consults with R. Akiba who counsels submission, bringing a verse to show that "whatever Gamaliel has done is properly done." The verse reads: "These are the festivals of the Lord, holy assemblies, *which you shall proclaim* in their seasons" (Leviticus 23: 4). Akiba interprets the verse as meaning that the proclamation of the court, right or wrong, is what determines "their seasons." The sequel is touching. Joshua submits and goes to Gamaliel in Jabneh, staff and purse in hand, on the day which by his calculation should have been the Day of Atonement. When he saw him coming, "R. Gamaliel stood up and kissed him on the head and said to him: Come in peace my master and my pupil! – my master in wisdom and my pupil in that you have accepted my words." Gamaliel acknowledges here that Joshua is his master in wisdom – that is to say, above all, in the interpretation of the written and oral law. Nevertheless, on a matter of such importance for the social order as the fixing of the calendar, the interpretation of the ruler, no matter how misplaced, has final authority. In the ensuing discussion the Talmud cites another early source which declares: "Jepthah in his generation" – Jepthah being regarded as particularly weak in legal judgment – "is like Samuel in his."[39] In other words, we have to put up with the rulers who are given to us and accept their interpretations – a seemingly Hobbesian conclusion.

However, if we look more closely at this example we shall find that the decisive act of interpretation which the story records is not that of Gamaliel or Joshua, but that of Akiba. The verse in Leviticus as he reads it makes the specific decision about the proclamation of the month and thus the fixing of the dates of the festivals, a human decision and therefore subject to human error; it does not privilege the president and his court above R. Joshua as interpreters of the Torah. It simply assigns to the former the function of proclaiming the date of the new moon and relieves everyone else of that responsibility. It does not make the human ruler – in this case Rabban Gamaliel – "Gods lieutenant on earth." Far from it. There is a revealing midrashic comment on this same topic:

According to the ordinary custom of the world, if the ruler determines that the tribunal will sit to-day but the criminal says, Tomorrow, whom do we obey? Surely the ruler! But the Holy One, blessed is he, is different. When the [rabbinical] court determines that to-day is the New Year [i.e. the first day Tishri], God says to the ministering angels: set up the dais, let the defending counsel and the prosecuting counsel stand forward for my children have proclaimed today as Rosh Hashanah [when human beings are judged for their sins].[40]

Far from being the "Mortall God" of some Leviathan-like society, Gamaliel and his court are in this story seen as representing the criminals who are being graciously permitted to set the date for their own trial. Whatever date they choose, God will condescend to accept, even if they mistake a cloud for the new moon.

The true and only source of authority is God himself, the "ruler" of the above parable. But he is cautious about exercising that authority, leaving a wide space for human freedom, in particular the freedom of interpretation. Interpretation we may say is an open-ended institution – neither Gamaliel nor Akiba nor Joshua has any papal authority. They have delegated functions, but that is another matter. Is there then such a thing as an authorized interpretation, a conclusive reading of a text, privileged above others? It would seem that in principle the Jewish hermeneutic tradition is averse to such determinations of meaning. There are, of course, legal decisions, known by the term *halakha* whereby debate on a certain subject is brought to an end. Thus the long-standing debate between the house of Hillel and that of Shammai on a whole series of issues was brought to an end when a "heavenly voice" declared that the *halakha* was to be according to the House of Hillel. I will have a little to say later about the "heavenly voice" (*bat-kol*, literally, the "the daughter of a voice"). In the meantime, we may note the dialectical formula used by the "heavenly voice":

R. Abba said in the name of Samuel: for three years there was dispute between the House of Shammai and the House of Hillel; the one said, "The *halakka* accords with our position," the other said, "It accords with ours." A heavenly voice went forth and announced: "Both these and these are the words of the living God. And the *halakha* is according to the House of Hillel."[41]

It is an extraordinary juxtaposition. The judgement on almost all the matters in dispute between the two groups is in favor of the rulings of Hillel and his followers; nevertheless this does not make Hillel's reading of the text of the Torah "correct" and Shammai's "incorrect." "Both these and these are the words of the living God." Betty Roitman, discussing this same dialectic and freedom and authority in interpretation, interestingly quotes R. Akiba in another context; "All is foreseen, but freedom of choice is given," and she comments, "all is determined, and yet all is open."[42] For the purpose of laying down a standard of practice whereby a community can conduct its daily life at any particular time, the *halakha* must be finalized. But the decision-making process is problematical; authority is decentralized, distributed among a number of agencies and never without ambiguity. Sometimes decisions will be reached on the basis of a view held by a majority, but not always.[43] Sometimes an individual sage is regarded as authoritative in a certain area; thus on the many occasions when Rab and Samuel differ, Samuel's rulings on civil questions are accepted, whilst Rab's views are adopted on matters of ritual; but there are exceptions to this rule also.[44] The locus of authority is shifting, uncertain, difficult to pin down. Rabbinical courts, if they are "greater in number and wisdom" than their predecessors, can overrule earlier decisions (*Mishna, Eduyot*, 1, 5). But who determines when they are greater in wisdom? Is it popular acclaim, learned opinion, offices held, personalities, or a combination of all these? There is authority to be sure, but its location is not self-evident; sometimes it seems to be lodged in some outstanding figure like R. Akiba, or R. Meir, or R. Eliezer, or R. Judah the Prince – someone who is simply perceived by his colleagues and students as having within him the authority of the Torah. Sometimes full recognition comes only after a teacher's death; such was the case with R. Eliezer. Nor is such recognition always linked with the highest office. R. Meir in his time held the subordinate office of *hakham* whilst Simeon the son of Gamaliel was the Patriarch and R. Nathan was the head of the court (*ab bet-din*). Authority was located somewhere in the space between them, Meir's share in shaping the *halakha* being greater than Simeon's or Nathan's. Then there is *halakha* based not on an authority figure or a group of such figures but on firm traditional practice without reference even to verses of Scripture (*halakha lemoshe misinai* – "a tradition stemming from Moses at Sinai"). And then there is the "heavenly voice" or, more literally, "the daughter of a voice" mentioned earlier as having conclusively ended the debates between Hillel and Shammai and their followers. One would have thought that here we have a court of last instance, a kind of oracle. But that it seems is not so. There is a remarkable account in the Talmud of R. Joshua rejecting the supernatural authority of the *bat-kol*, and insisting instead that halakhic decisions be taken by human beings on the basis of a majority vote. The setting is a dispute between R. Eliezer – one of the most influential of the Sages – and his colleagues on a question regarding the ritual purity of a certain kind of cooking-oven. The other teachers will not accept Rabbi Eliezer's opinion on this matter, so he seeks supernatural support:

He said, "If I am right, may this carob tree move a hundred yards from its place." It did so. They said, "From a tree no proof can be brought." Then he said, "May the canal prove it." The water of the canal flowed backwards. They said, "A canal cannot prove anything." [R. Eliezer tries again by making the walls of the house cave inwards. Failing to overcome the opposition of his colleagues, he makes his last bid.] Then R. Eliezer said, "If I am right, let the heavens prove it." Then a heavenly voice [*bat-kol*] said, "What have you against R. Eliezer? The *halakha* is always in accord with his view." Then R. Joshua got up and said, "It is not in heaven..." (Deuteronomy 30: 12). What did he mean by this? R. Yirmeya said, "The Torah was given to us from Sinai: we thus pay no attention to a heavenly voice. For already from Sinai the Torah said, "By a majority you are to decide" [Exodus 23: 2 as interpreted by the Rabbis]. R. Nathan met Elijah and asked him what God did in that hour. Elijah replied: "He smiled and said, 'My children have vanquished me, my children have vanquished me.'"[45]

Here the *bat-kol*, authoritative in deciding the points at issue between Hillel and Shammai, is dismissed by R. Joshua on the grounds that the Torah is not in heaven; thus once it has been given, its interpretation belongs to human beings, not to heavenly voices. This preserves a certain openness. Authority there must be – we are not in the region of liberal democracy – but it must be of a kind that leaves room for the play of mind, for imaginative discourse and the ongoing work of interpretation. The Torah was given at Sinai both in the sense of a *datum*, something given once and for all, but also in the sense of having being handed over, given to human beings. The text has in it the authority of a commanding voice, a voice which still echoes, but it is given over to men to understand and apply to their lives.

Like Hobbes, the Rabbis saw a central, constitutive role for the interpreter. But where Hobbes saw that act of interpretation as a way of eliminating the imaginative overtones of the text, its spiritual suggestions, its ambiguities, flattening it out so as to avoid the danger of being "entangled in words as a bird in lime-twigs," the Talmudic rabbis joyfully seized upon every nuance of meaning, took words out of their context, rearranged them, proposed new vocalization for the consonantal text whenever it suited them, so as to discover new meanings buried in the letters, sought out links between passages far apart from one another thus dislodging signs from their immediate signifieds to create new semantic possibilities – the precise opposite of Hobbe's declared linguistic policy which was to make one sign have one signification "and to place it accordingly." In short, theirs was the method not of philosophy but of *midrash*.

Halakha is itself a form of *midrash*, namely, *midrash halakha*. And *midrash* is by definition non-exclusive: it implies "that other interpretations are possible."[46] We are used to this interpretive freedom in non-legal midrashic texts – known as *aggada* and consisting of fable or narrative – but it applies almost equally to legal *midrashim*. They often involve richly extravagant interpretations which clearly make no claim to be the simplest or the only way of reading the verse in question. We may take as an example the law relating to levirate marriage. Deuteronomy 25: 5 states that the brother of a man who dies without issue is to take his brother's widow for his wife. The text continues: "And it shall be that the firstborn which she bears shall succeed in the name [lit. shall rise up in the name] of his dead brother, that his name be not wiped out in Israel" (verse 6). This seemingly straightforward verse is interpreted in a remarkable fashion: according to a source cited in the Talmud to become the basis of the *halakha*, the duty of levirate marriage falls in the first instance on the oldest brother (i.e. taking the "firstborn" as referring to the firstborn of the widow's mother-in-law); "which she bears" is taken to mean that the law of levirate marriage does not apply to a brother's widow who is incapable of childbearing; "succeed in the name" is taken to mean "succeed to the inheritance," the levir acquiring the property of his dead brother; finally "that his name be not wiped out" is interpreted as exempting the widow of a castrate whose name is, so to speak, already doomed to extinction.[47]

It is clear that what we have here is a series of regulations and practices which had been handed down by tradition to those who taught and published them. Authority for them is found in a remarkably free exegesis of Deuteronomy 25: 6. The verse seems to speak of the firstborn child of the levirate marriage succeeding to his dead uncle's name. But nothing is left of this in the Talmudic reading of that verse. So much so that Raba, a later teacher, remarks that in spite of the rule that Scripture is never entirely divorced from its "literal sense" this seems to have happened in this case.

It is worth pausing to inquire what importance if any the Rabbis attached to the *peshat* or "literal sense" which later on meant so much to Hobbes and to the Protestant tradition in general. This remark of Raba in reference to Deuteronomy 25: 6 is one of four places in the Babylonian Talmud where it is said that as a general rule "Scripture does not depart from its literal sense." We should, however, be wary of supposing that the Rabbis desired to privilege the literal sense, still less the "historically original" or "plain" meaning of the text. As the most recent student of this subject has shown, at most the Rabbis meant to say that, whilst all manner of interpretation was in order, even that which violated grammar, ordinary usage, and the commonly accepted meaning of words, there was also room for the more straightforward "literal sense" and this should not be entirely lost sight of.[48] It is not true to say that for the Rabbis the *peshat* or "plain sense" was normative, still less that it was "authoritative," as Raphael Loewe has maintained.[49] It was simply one legitimate mode of interpretation which, as a general rule, should not be ignored. Here in Deuteronomy 25: 6 it is in fact expressly ignored.

At a later period, to be precise in the eleventh and twelfth centuries, *peshat*, in the broader sense in which the term is understood today, came into its own in the Bible commentaries of Rashi (Rabbi Shlomo Yizhaki), Joseph Kara and Rashi's grandson, Rashbam (Rabbi Samuel the son of Meir) and was privileged as the normal mode of interpretation for study and reading and one to be strictly differentiated from *derash*, which was appropriate for homily or for halakhic *midrash*. As Elazar Twito has shown, this development was influenced by the new rationalist emphasis which characterized the so–called "twelfth century renaissance" in Europe with its widespread demand that authority (i.e. reliance on tradition) be combined with logic.[50]

The new approach of Jewish medieval exegesis of which Rashi and Rashbam were the acknowledged masters also reflected the centrality of the *Trivium* – that is, Logic, Rhetoric and Grammar – in contemporary educational practice.[51] above all, the emphasis on *peshat* arose out of the need to provide a Jewish response to christological readings of the Hebrew Bible. This was a period of intense public debate between Jews and Christians; Jewish belief was under attack and Jewish spokesmen were required to defend their theological positions. The Christian doctors vigorously confronted "Israel of the flesh" with such doctrines as the Trinity, the Virgin Birth, the Incarnation, the Resurrection, the abrogation of the Old Covenant and its replacement by the New – all of which they claimed to find in the text of the Old Testament, often by means of allegorical and tropological interpretation, that is, Christian *midrash*. Ironically, at a much earlier period, the Church Fathers had found models for the allegorical mode in the writings of Philo the Jew.[52] But in the new polemical climate, midrashic methods of exegesis which opened the door to allegory could be an embarrassment. The *peshat* provided a much stronger line of defence.[53] For example, the literal reading of *ruah* as "wind" in the second verse of Genesis, which Hobbes later adopted, was not only a demonstrably true reading, but it also provided an effective answer to the attempt to read into that word a reference to the Holy Ghost. Rashbam reads the verse accordingly, that is, in its natural rather than its supernatural sense. This could be effective because the intellectual climate favored natural explanations, attention to the rules of grammar and logic, and scholarship based on a true knowledge of the ancient tongues. All these were part of the new style of exegesis which also emphasized the larger units and contexts of discourse in accordance with the new feeling for rhetorical structure. *Peshat* in this sense quickly established itself and Rashi became the supreme Bible commentator for Jews, with a growing reputation also among Christian Bible exegetes. Many Christians, unable to separate their theology from the work of reading and interpretation, were repelled by this Jewish literalism ("the letter killeth"), but others, including Andrew of St Victor, eagerly embraced it.[54] This was *hebraica veritas* and, in a later period, it would prove immensely serviceable to the men of the Reformation in their task of translating the Scriptures into the vernacular tongues. In fact it would become an important ingredient in the exegetical policies of the Puritans in England. William Perkins in 1592 will reject all allegories and will declare that "there is one onely sense, and the same is the literall."[55] This same literalism emerges later in Hobbes to become the basis of his revisionist reading of the Scriptures.

However, important though the *peshat* is, it is, as Frank Kermode has reminded us, no less than *derash*, a work of the interpretive imagination: "the most arduous effort to express the poetry of plain sense brings with it its own metaphors, it own distortions."[56] Moreover, we should remind ourselves that it was never intended either by the Talmudic Rabbis or by the medieval commentators to have exclusive authority. Rashi, in spite of his stated principles, reverts very often to midrashic commentary, and after his death his disciples inserted a great deal more of the same kind of material into his text, as a study of the early manuscripts of Rashi's commentary has shown.[57] Even Rashbam, a more thoroughgoing follower of the method of *peshat* than Rashi, was nevertheless far from claiming exclusive authority for that method. To the contrary, whilst insisting on the necessity for a sober and direct reading of the words of Scripture, he acknowledges that midrashic interpretation, with its hints and guesses, its parables, its pursuit of halakhic teachings in unlikely places, is ultimately, "the main thing that the Torah comes to teach us."[58]

Where then is authority hid? In the *derash* or in the *peshat*? The answer is of course, in both and neither. No single mode of interpretation has absolute authority, just as no single figure, or holder of office, or formal institution has final authority. And as we have seen, even a "heavenly voice" can be disregarded. When it is so disregarded, God merely smiles and says that his children have vanquished him. For the Torah is given to men and consequently its interpretation is fallible, many-sided, subject to the pressures of history. The Talmud relates how Moses, hearing of the extraordinary interpretative ability of R. Akiba, asks to go down from heaven to witness him in action. Receiving permission, he seats himself at the end of the eighth row of disciples in the House of Study but fails to understand the discussion. He only regains his composure when he hears one of the students asking the Master from whence he derived a certain teaching and the answer given was: "This is *halakha* given to Moses at Sinai."[59]

In other words, difficult, strange and different though Akiba's teachings may sound to Moses, there is a link, that of a continuing tradition stemming from Sinai. This is both a horizontal and a vertical bond. Horizontally, the scholars and students of the *Torah* at any one time are bound together in what Stanley Fish, in a different context, has termed an "interpretive community"[60] or what I would prefer to call a "covenantal community."[61] They are bound together by common loyalties and common purposes. Their readings, different and conflicting though they may be, are all directed to a common focus, even, we may say, a common object of love and devotion, namely the words of the Torah itself – not a dead letter, as Hobbes thought, but a commanding voice. The text through its manifest power seizes and haunts us even before it is understood. We would not be drawn to interpret it if that power were not in it. Authority is situated in the space between the covenantal community and the written text that they have received by tradition and on which they are bidden to meditate day and night. Or, as the Rabbis themselves would say, it is situated between the written and the unwritten Law (*tora shebikhtav* and *tora shebeal-pe*), between text and interpretation.

But the covenantal community is also bound vertically together through time. The bond between Moses and Akiba is problematical but it is there; it binds the generations each to each. Each person, repeating the words of the *shema*. "Hear, O Israel" from Deuteronomy 6: 4, affirms a continuity of perception, a covenantal bond with the past and future. Every reader becomes a witness to that continuity and that bond. When prophecy came to an end, the Rabbis tell us, all that was left was the *bat-kol*, "the daughter of a voice."[62] Rabbi Joshua, as we saw, would not let it interfere with the severe work of halakhic exegesis, but it will presumably go on echoing just the same, for it seems to represent the power of survival, the survival of texts and the survival of communities which interpret those texts from age to age. Prophecy is no more, but there is still the echo of its voice in the written and the unwritten word of Scripture; it survives not only within the covenantal community of Israel but for a wider circle of readers, poets and interpreters. It is heard in Milton, who well caught the dialectic of freedom and authority of which we have been speaking:

> God so commanded, and left that command
> Sole daughter of his voice; the rest, we live
> Law to ourselves, our reason is our law.
>
> (*Paradise Lost*, IX, 652–54)

Milton too is speaking of the biblical text and, like Hobbes, he too is exercised with the hermeneutic problem. But where Hobbes got it wrong, as we may now think, Milton got it right. God's commands resonate still in the book he has left us, but having bestowed on us the gift of freedom, he leaves us – a law to ourselves, free to read the writing and to make known the interpretation.

Presented at a workshop on "Institutions of Interpretation" held by the Center for Literary Studies of the Hebrew University of Jerusalem in June 1988.

NOTES

1 *Leviathan*, ed. A. R. Waller (Cambridge University Press, 1935), ch. 14, p. 87. This is a reprint of the first folio version of 1651. (Hereafter cited as *Lev.*).

2 *Ibid.*, ch. 17, p. 118.

3 *Ibid.*

4 Cf. P. Zagorin, *A History of Political Thought in the English Revolution* (London, 1954), p. 183.

5 *De Cive*, ch. 17, section 28, in *English Works*, vol. II, ed. W. Molesworth (London, 1841), p. 296.

6 *De Cive*, ch. 17, section 28, p. 296.

7 *Lev.*, ch. 4, p. 17.

8 *Lev.*, Conclusion, p. 526.

9 Job 41 : 34 as quoted by Hobbes, *Lev.*, ch. 28, p. 231.

10 *Lev.*, p. 267.

11 *Advancement of Learning*, in *Works*, ed., Spedding, Ellis and Heath, vol. II (London, 1857), pp. 396–7.

12 Cf. G. H. Wright, 'The Protestant Hobbes' (Ann Arbor, Mich.: University Microfilms, 1987), pp. 12–14; A. Funkenstein, *Theology and the Scientific Imagination from the Middle Ages to the Seventeenth Century* (Princeton, N.J., 1986), p. 334.

13 T. Sprat, *The History of the Royal Society*, 1667, 4th edition (1734), p. 113.

14 *Lev.*, ch. 36, p. 318.

15 Cf. *Behemoth*, Part I in *English Works*, VI, 190.

16 Introduction to Oakeshott's edition of *Leviathan* (Oxford: Blackwell, 1946), pp. xlvi–xlvii.

17 *De Cive*, in *English Works*, ch. 17, section 17, p. 273.

18 *Ibid.*, section 18, pp. 274–75.

19 *Ibid.*, ch. 16, pp. 245–47; *Lev.*, ch. 33, pp. 282–84; ch. 38, pp. 326–27, 331; ch. 40, p. 345.

20 F. C. Hood, *The Divine Politics of Hobbes* (Oxford University Press, 1964), pp. 201, 243–44.

21 For a more balanced view see H. G. Reventlow, *The Authority of the Bible and the Rise of the Modern World*, trans. John Bowden (London, 1984), p. 213. And see S. Shapin and S. Schaffer, *Leviathan and the Air-Pump: Hobbes, Boyle and the Experimental Life* (Princeton, N.J., 1985), p. 103.

22 *Lev.*, ch. 32, p. 270; Hood, *Divine Politics*, p. 244; Reventlow, *Authority of the Bible*, p. 220.

23 *Lev.*, ch. 38, p. 327; emphasis added.

24 *Ibid.*, p. 331.

25 See Bk. I, chs. 7 and 13.

26 W. J. Ong, "Hobbes and Talon's Ramist Rhetoric in English," in *Transactions of the Cambridge Bibliographical Society*, III (1951), 260–9.

27 Cf. Reventlow, *Authority of the Bible*, pp. 205–6.

28 *Lev.*, ch. 40, pp. 344–5; and see Reventlow, *Authority of the Bible*, pp. 209, 221–2.

29 *Jerusalem and Albion* (London, 1964), ch. 14 and especially pp. 226, 242–4.

30 *Lev.*, ch. 34, p. 287.

31 *Ibid.*, p. 289.

32 *Ibid.*, p. 294. The rational treatment of angels in the Old Testament is evidently owed to the immensely influential discussion of this topic by Maimonides (*Guide for the Perplexed*, II, chapter 6). For the importance of Maimonides in shaping the rationalizing exegesis of Spinoza and John Spencer, see Funkenstein, *Theology*, pp. 241–3.

33 "Hobbes on the Knowledge of God," in *Hobbes and Rousseau*, ed. Maurice Cranston and Richard S. Peters (New York, 1972), p. 104.

34 *Lev.*, ch. 38, pp. 330, 333–7; ch. 44, pp. 462–3.

35 *Jerusalem and Albion*, pp. 227, 233.

36 *Lev.*, ch. 40, pp. 345–6.

37 *Ibid.*, ch. 32, p. 270.

38 *Rosh Hashanah*, II, 8, 9. (See *The Mishnah*, trans. Herbert Danby (Oxford University Press, 1933), pp. 190–1.)

39 B.T., *Rosh Hashanah*, 25b.

40 J.T., *Rosh Hashanah*, ch. 1, section 3.

41 B.T., *Erubin*, 13b.

42 "Sacred Language and Open Text" in *Midrash and Literature*, ed. G. H. Hartman and S. Budick (New Haven, 1986), p.160.

43 See *Mishna, Eduyot*, I, 5 (Danby, trans., *The Mishnah*, p. 422).

44 B.T., *Bekhorot*, 49b.

45 B.T., *Baba Mezia*, 59b.

46 Max Kadushin, *The Rabbinic Mind* (New York, 1952), pp. 131–2.

47 See B.T., *Yebamoth*, 24a and Rashi *ibid.*

48 Cf. Sarah Kamin, *Rashi's Exegetical Categorization in Respect of the Distinction between Peshat and Derash* (Hebrew) (Jerusalem, 1986), pp. 37–40.

49 "The 'Plain' Meaning of Scriptures in Early Jewish Exegesis," *Papers of the Institute of Jewish Studies*, I (1964), 158.

50 "The Exegetical Method of Rashbam Viewed in Relation to the History of His Time" (Hebrew), in *Studies in Rabbinic Literature Bible and Jewish History*, ed. Y. D. Gilat, C. Levine, Z. M. Rabinowitz (Ramat-Gan, 1982), p. 59.

51 *Ibid.*, p. 61.

52 Cf. H. A. Wolfson, *Philo: Foundations of Religious Philosophy in Judaism, Christianity, and Islam*, vol. I, 3rd edition (Cambridge, Mass., 1962), pp. 158–59; Wolfson, *The Philosophy of the Church Fathers*, vol. I, 2nd edition (Cambridge, Mass., 1964), chapters 2–4; see also Beryl Smalley, *The Study of the Bible in the Middle Ages*, 2nd edition (Oxford University Press, 1952), pp. 6–7.

53 Cf. Twito, "Exegetical Method of Rashbam," pp. 51–2, 70.

54 See Smalley, *The Study of the Bible*, chapters 3 and 4.

55 "The Art of Prophecying" in *Works*, vol. II (1612), p. 651.

56 "The Plain Sense of Things" in *Midrash and Literature*, ed. Hartman and Budick, p. 181.

57 Elazar Twito, "On the Changes Made in Rashi's Commentary on the Torah" (Hebrew), *Tarbiz* (February–March, 1987), pp. 211–42.

58 Rashbam on Genesis 37: 2.

59 B.T., *Menahot*, 29b.

60 *Is There a Text in this Class?* (Cambridge, Mass., 1980), p. 11.

61 See *Poetry with a Purpose: Biblical Poetics and Interpretation* (Bloomington, Ind.,; 1988), pp. 48–50.

62 B.T., *Yoma*, 9b.

PART II

Literature and translation

Comparative Criticism 15, pp. 127–128. Cambridge University Press 1993

Winners of the 1991 BCLA Translation Competition

EC LANGUAGES PRIZE

First PRIZE

John Felstiner (Stanford), for translation from the Spanish of poems by Pablo Neruda

Second PRIZE

Lisa Sapinkopf (Cambridge, Mass.), for translation from the French of poems from *Things once without light* by Yves Bonnefoy

Commendations

Danny Price (Folkestone), for translation from the French of a portion of a novel *Le loup des brumes: Mémoires d'un sorcier* by Marieke Aucante

John Gatt-Rutter (La Trobe, Australia), for translation from the Italian of a portion of a play *Calderón* by Pier Paolo Pasolini

Bernard Hoepffner (Lyon), for translation from the French of a short story 'La Princesse Hoppy' by Jacques Roubaud

Frances Deepwell (Coventry), for translation from the German of a short story 'Manja' by Anne Gmeyner

SPECIAL PRIZES
CHINESE

First PRIZE

Richard King (Victoria, B.C.), for translation of a chapter from a novel *Chaos and all that* by Liu Sola

Second PRIZE

Jonathan Pease (Washington State), for translation of a poem 'I Dreamed of Locusts' by Wang Ling

The Special Prize for Chinese has been established by the generosity of the K.P. Tin Foundation, Hong Kong

HEBREW/YIDDISH/JEWISH THEME

First PRIZE

Marzell Kay (Tel Aviv) for translation from modern Hebrew of a short story 'A Monument to a New Life' by Yitzhak Oren

Second PRIZE

John Felstiner (Stanford), for translation from the German of poems by Paul Celan

Commendations

Kathryn Hellerstein (Philadelphia), for translation from the Yiddish of poems by Paula Moladowsky

Golda Werman (Jerusalem), for translation from the Yiddish of a short story 'Remnants' by David Bergelson

Alex Ramage (Tel Aviv), for translation from the Hebrew of a short story 'Loan' by Yonatan Shem-Ur

The Special Prize for translation from Hebrew, Yiddish, or on a Jewish theme has been established by the generosity of the Spiro Institute, London, in honour of Hannah and Jacob Lieberman.

SWEDISH

No prize awarded this year.

The Special Prize for translation from Swedish has been established by the generosity of the Anglo-Swedish Literary Foundation and the Swedish Embassy.

PERSIAN

No prize awarded this year.

The Special Prize for translation from Persian has been established by the generosity of the Foundation for Iranian Studies.

Comparative Criticism 15, pp. 129–143. Cambridge University Press 1993

"Dead Gallop" and other poems

PABLO NERUDA

TRANSLATED WITH AN INTRODUCTION BY JOHN FELSTINER

"SPEAK THROUGH MY WORDS AND MY BLOOD":
TRANSLATING NERUDA AND CELAN

Although Pablo Neruda (1904–1973) and Paul Celan (1920–1970) might have crossed paths in Paris in the spring of 1939, there seems at first glance little to link the Chilean, Communist, Nobel-Prize, Whitman-esque bard with the German-speaking, Jewish, survivor-exile kin to Kafka and Mandelshtam – the older poet born in a small town in the rainy forested south of America and dying while his nation was violently seized by military coup, the other poet born in the small Bukovina pocket of the late Austrian empire and a suicide by drowning in the Seine.

How then might Neruda and Celan, two writers so distinct in language, culture, literary tradition, geographical matrix, and historical circumstance, possibly coincide in a single translator? I think it has deeply to do with their both reaching toward a nearly obliviated people – Neruda, toward South American Indians such as the Aztec Moctezuma or the Quechua slaves who built Macchu Picchu; Celan, toward the Jewish victims of Nazi-ridden Europe.

You can feel that reach in "Cortés," when the poet says "My ruined brother...Tomorrow will rain blood," and when the verse "In Prague" arrives at "Bone-Hebrew / ground to sperm." Maybe those two histories even fuse for a moment when, at the end of "Cortés," I translate *besos traicionados* as "quisling" rather than "treasonous" kisses, since that adjective derives from the Norwegian diplomat Quisling, who collaborated with Hitler.

---

* These are ten verse translations of poems by Pablo Neruda (1904–1973), selected to represent the stylistic and chronological range of his work. The translations have not been published before, with two exceptions – but in those cases the present versions are new ones.

At the same time, what draws me (often to the verge of obsession) is the craft, the writing, the venture of making a faithful yet fresh version of lyrics so indigenous to Spanish and German. With "*El culpable*" ("Guilty"), can I find supple rhythms, natural syntax, and ordinary diction without rendering Neruda's perfectly simple *ars poetica* simplistic? With "In Egypt," does my usage of biblical speech overcharge Celan's adjustment to the strain of exile?

In *Translating Neruda: The Way to Macchu Picchu* (Stanford, 1980), I tried to generate thoroughgoing critical interpretation by tracing a double genesis – of the epic on a half-buried Incan city, and of a new verse translation. Now my forthcoming book, *Paul Celan and the Strain of Jewishness* (Yale), attempts in a sense to turn over the hourglass ("In Prague"): to retrace the dire personal and historical loss that Celan's poems register by working through – by speaking through – those poems again. As Neruda put it, "Speak through my words and my blood."

"Dead Gallop" and other poems

PABLO NERUDA

DEAD GALLOP

Like ashes, like oceans swarming,
in the sunken slowness, formlessness,
or like high on the road hearing
bellstrokes cross by crosswise,
holding that sound just free of the metal,
blurred, bearing down, reducing to dust
in the selfsame mill of forms far out of reach,
whether remembered or never seen,
and the aroma of plums rolling to earth
that rot in time, endlessly green.

All of it so quick, so livening,
immobile though, like a pulley idling on itself,
those wheels that motors have, in short.
Existing like dry stitches in the seams of trees,
silenced, encircling, in such a way,
all the planets splicing their tails.
Then from where, which way, on what shore?
The ceaseless whirl, uncertain, so still,
like lilacs around a convent,
or death as it gets to the tongue of an ox
who stumbles down unguarded, horns wanting to sound.

That's why, in what's immobile, pausing, to perceive
then, like great wingbeats, overhead,
like dead bees or numbers,
oh all that my spent heart can't embrace,
in crowds, in half-shed tears

and human toiling, turbulence,
black actions suddenly disclosed
like ice, immense disorder,
oceanwide, for me who goes in singing,
as with a sword among defenseless men.

Well then what is it made of – that spurt of doves
between night and time, like a damp ravine?
That sound so drawn out now
that drops down lining the roads with stones,
or better, when just one hour
buds up suddenly, extending endlessly.

Within the ring of summer,
once, the enormous calabashes listen,
stretching their poignant stems –
of that, of that which urging forth,
of what's full, dark with heavy drops.   (1925)

WHAT SPAIN WAS LIKE

Spain was taut and dry, diurnal
drum with an opaque tone,
prairie and eagle's nest, silence
of whiplashed weather.

Even with tears, even with my soul
I love your hard soil, your meager bread,
your meager people, even in my deep heart's
core lies the lost flower of your crumpled
villages, moveless in time,
and your mineraled fields
stretched agelong under the moon
and consumed by an empty god.

All you have built, your animal
isolation bound to intelligence,
surrounded by abstract stones of silence,
your sharp wine sweet
wine, your wild
fragile vines.

Solar stone, pure among regions
of the world, Spain pervaded
by blood and metal, blue and buoyant
worker with petals and bullets, alone
alive and somnolent and sonorous.

Huélamo, Carrascosa,
Alpedrete, Buitrago,
Palencia, Arganda, Galve,
Galapagar, Villalba.

Peñarrubia, Cedrillas,
Alcocer, Tamurejo,
Aguadulce, Pedrera,
Fuente Palmera, Colmenar, Sepúlveda.

Carcabuey, Fuencaliente,
Linares, Solana del Pino,
Carcelén, Alatox,
Mahora, Valdeganda.

Yeste, Riopar, Segorbe,
Orihuela, Montalbo,
Alcaraz, Caravaca,
Almendralejo, Castejón de Monegros.

Palma del Río, Peralta,
Granadella, Quintana
de la Serena, Atienza, Barahona,
Navalmoral, Oropesa.

Alborea, Monóvar,
Almansa, San Benito,
Moratalla, Montesa,
Torre Baja, Aldemuz.

Cevico Navero, Cevico de la Torre,
Albalate de las Nogueras,
Jabaloyas, Teruel,
Camporrobles, La Alberca.

Pozo Amargo, Candeleda,
Pedroñeras, Campillo de Altobuey,
Loranca de Tajuña, Puebla de la Mujer Muerta,
Torre la Cárcel, Játiva, Alcoy.

Puebla de Obando, Villar del Rey,
Beloraga, Brihuega,
Cetina, Villacañas, Palomas,
Navalcán, Henarejos, Albatana.

Torredonjimeno, Trasparga,
Agramón, Crevillente,
Poveda de la Sierra, Pedernoso,
Alcolea de Cinca, Matallanos.

Ventosa del Río, Alba de Tormes,
Horcajo Medianero, Piedrahita,
Minglanilla, Navamorcuende, Navalperal,
Navalcarnero, Navalmorales, Jorquera.

Argora, Torremocha, Argecilla,
Ojos Negros, Salvacañete, Utiel,
Laguna Seca, Cañamares, Salorino,
Aldea Quemada, Pesquera de Duero.

Fuenteovejuna, Alpedrete,
Torrejón, Benaguacil,
Valverde de Júcar, Vallanca,
Hiendelaencina, Robledo de Chavela.

Miñogalindo, Ossa de Montiel,
Méntrida, Valdepeñas, Titaguas,
Almodóvar, Gestaldar, Valdemoro,
Almoradiel, Orgaz.   (1937)

I EXPLAIN A FEW THINGS

You'll ask: And where are the lilacs?
And the metaphysics matted with poppies?

And the rain that kept drumming
his words, filling them
with pinholes and birds?

I'll tell you what's happening with me.

I was living in the outskirts
of Madrid, with bells,
with clocks, with trees.

From there we looked out
on Castile's lean face
like an ocean of leather.
                    My house was called
house of the flowers because everywhere
geraniums were bursting: it was
a fine house
with dogs and children.

                    Raúl, remember?

You remember, Rafael?

                    Federico, do you remember
from under the ground,
remember my house with balconies
where June light drowned flowers in your mouth?
                    Brother, my brother!

Everything
was loud voices, salted goods,
piles of palpitating bread,
market-stalls of my Argüelles quarter with its statue
like a pale inkwell amidst the hakes:
oil rose up in the spoons,
a deep pulsing
of feet and hands filled the streets,
meters, liters, keen
essence of life,
                    fish stacked up,

rooftops woven under a cold sun
that wears down the weathervane,
fine ivory delirium of potatoes,
tomatoes in waves out to the sea.

And one morning all this was blazing
and one morning bonfires
shot from the earth
burning up lives,
and since then fire,
gunpowder since then,
and since then blood.
Bandits with planes and with Moors,
bandits with finger-rings and duchesses,
bandits with black friars blessing
came out of the sky to kill children,
and in the streets the blood of the children
flowed easily, like children's blood.

Jackals the jackal would reject,
stones the dry thistle's teeth would spit out,
vipers that vipers would despise!

Against you I've seen the blood
of Spain rise up
to flood you in a single wave
of pride and knives!

Traitor
generals:
look at my dead house,
look at broken Spain:
yet from every dead house burning metal flows
instead of flowers,
from every crater in Spain
emerges Spain,
from every dead child a gun with eyes,
from every crime bullets are born
that will one day track down
your heart.

So you ask why his poems
don't tell us of dreams, and leaves,
and great volcanoes in his native land?

Come see the blood in the streets,
come see
the blood in the streets,
come see the blood
in the streets!

(1937)

THEY REACH THE GULF OF MEXICO (1493)

The deadly wind hits Veracruz.
Horses splash ashore at Veracruz.
Small boats run in, crammed with fists
and red beards from Castile.
Arias, Reyes, Rojas, Maldonados,
sons of derelict Spain,
experts at winter hunger
and the lice in the inns.

Leaning from the rail, what are they gazing at?
How much of what's ahead
and what's lost behind, the feudal
wind loose in their racking land?

They left from ports in the south
not so that common men could delve
into loot and death –
their eyes are on fresh land, freedoms,
chains broken, building to do,
and from the boat, waves dying out
on the shores of a deepset mystery.

Is it a death or new life
behind the palms in the heated air,
like some unholy oven's blast
the burning land steers toward them?
They were commonfolk, shaggy heads from Montiel,

hard chipped hands from Ocaña and Piedrahita,
ironsmiths' arms, children's eyes
staring at the fierce sun and the palms.

Hunger ancient as Europe, hunger like a dying
comet's tail manned the ship,
hunger was there, stripped clean,
a cold aimless axe, the masses'
cruel stepmother, hunger throwing dice
with the navigator, puffing the sails:
"Go on, or I'll swallow you, on,
or you're back
with your mother, your brother, the judge and priest,
with inquisitors, hell, and plague.
Go on, and on, away from the lice,
the feudal whip, the hole,
the galleys jammed with excrement."

And Núñez' and Bernales' eyes
reached toward the limitless light
for rest,
one life, another life,
the countless and punished
family of the poor of the world.   (1950)

CORTÉS

Cortés has no people, is a cold beam,
heart dead in the armor.
    Fruitful lands, my Lord and King,
    mosques that have gold encrusted
    thick by the indian's hand.

And advances burying daggers, beating
the lowlands, the pawed-up
fragrant cordilleras,
camping his troop among orchids
and crowning pines,
trampling jasmine,
up to the gates of Tlaxcala.

(My downcast brother, make no
friend of the red-flushed vulture:
I speak from the mossy earth to you, from
the roots of our realm.
Tomorrow will rain blood,
will raise tears enough
for mist and fumes and rivers
until your own eyes dissolve.)

Cortés receives a dove,
receives a pheasant, a zither
from the king's musicians,
but he wants the roomful of gold,
wants one thing more, and everything falls
in the plunderers' chests.

The king leans out from a balcony:
"This is my brother," he says. The stones
of the people fly up in answer,
and Cortés whets his daggers
on quisling kisses.

He returns to Tlaxcala, the wind bears
a muted rumor of lament.   (1950)

FLOODS

The poor live on low ground waiting for the river

to rise one night and sweep them to the sea.

I've seen small cradles floating by, the wrecks

of houses, chairs, and a great rage of ash-

pale water splaying terror through the sky:

this is all yours, poor man, for your wife and crop,

your dog and tools, so you can learn to beg.

No water laps at the homes of gentlemen

whose snowy collars flutter on the line.

It feeds on this rolling mire, these ruins winding

their idle course to the sea with your dead,

among roughcut tables and the luckless trees

that bob and tumble turning up bare root.   (1950)

RIDER IN THE RAIN

Elemental waters, walls of water, clover
and combatted oats,
cordage bound in the net of a damp
sopping night, savagely spun,
earthrending drops drummed into lament,
slant anger slashing sky.
Soaked in aroma the horses gallop
underneath water, walloping the water, their red
branchwork cleaving it, hair stone and water:
and steam like some wild milk clings to
a water ridden with fleeting doves.
No daylight is there but deep pools
in this hard tropic, this green career
and the hooves knit swift earth to swift
in the bestial aura of horse-and-rain.
Ponchos, saddles, saddlerugs massed
in russet mounds above
blazing sulfur loins that pound
the forest binding it down.
       On and on, and on, go on and on,
and on, and on, and on, and o-o-o-on,
the riders hurl down the rain, the riders
pace beneath bitter nut-trees, the rain
twists its everlasting wheat into trembling rays.
There is light from the water, a vague flash
spilled on the leaves, and the sounding gallop
spawns a flightless earth-wounded water.
Damp bridle, branched arch,
pacing on pacing, nighttime plant
of fractured stars like ice or moon, cyclone horse
spattered with arrows like an icy ghost,

bristling with new hands born in the furor,
throbbing fruit surrounded by fear
and its monarch dreadful banner. (1950)

GUILTY

I declare myself guilty of not having
made, with these hands they gave me,
a broom.

Why did I make no broom?

Why did they give me hands?

What use have they been
if all I ever did was
watch the stir of the grain,
listen up for the wind
and did not gather straws
still green in the earth
for a broom,
not set the soft stalks to dry
and bind them
in a gold bundle,
and did not lash a wooden stick
to the yellow skirt
till I had a broom for the paths?

So it goes.
How did my life
get by
without seeing, and learning,
and gathering and binding
the basic things?

It's too late to deny
I had the time,
the time,
yet the hands were lacking,
so how could I aim

for greatness
if I was never able
to make
a broom,
not one,
not even one?   (1968)

LAPIS LAZULI IN CHILE

Snowbound, shaggy, and hard,

America's harsh cordillera,

a planet:

the blue of blues lies there,

blue solitude, secret blue,

a nest of blue, lapis lazuli,

my land's blue skeleton.

A fuse burns, the shock clears

and the breast of the stone breaks up:

gentle humus above the dynamite

and under the humus blue bonework,

stone mounding ultramarine.

Cathedral of buried blues,

jolt of blue crystal,

the sea's eye sunk in snow –

again you come back from water to light,

to day, to the clear skin

of space, turning

the earth's to the sky's

blue.   (1970)

THE GREAT URINATOR

The great urinator was yellow
and the stream that came down
was bronze-colored rain
on the domes of churches,
on the roofs of cars,
on factories and cemeteries,
on the populace and their gardens.

Who was it, where was it?

It was a density, thick liquid
falling as from
a horse,
and frightened passersby
with no umbrellas
looked up skyward,
meanwhile avenues were flooding
and urine inexhaustibly flowing
underneath doors,
backing up drains, disintegrating
marble floors, carpets,
staircases.

Nothing could be detected. Where
was this peril?
What was going to happen to the world?

From on high the great urinator
was silent and urinated.

What does this signify?

I am a pale and artless poet
not here to work out riddles
or recommend special umbrellas.
Hasta la vista! I greet you and go off
to a country where they won't ask me questions.

(August 1973)

Comparative Criticism 15, pp. 145–159. Cambridge University Press 1993

Poems from *Things once without light*

YVES BONNEFOY

TRANSLATED BY LISA SAPINKOPF

THE TREES

We gazed down at our trees from the high
Terrace that we loved; the sun
Kept close to us, always,
But in retreat, a silent guest
On the threshold of the ruined house that we'd left
To its vast, blazing power.

Watch, I said to you, how it sends sliding down
The jagged, unfathomable stones that support us,
Our shoulders' mingled shadows,
Those of the nearby almond trees, and even
That of the tops of the jumbled walls –
Pierced shadow, charred boat, prow adrift
Like an overabundance of dream or smoke.

But the oak trees there are immobile,
Not even their shadows stir in the light,
They're the shores of time which flows here, where we stand,
And not one can set foot on the soil, so swift
Is the current of death's heavy hope.

We looked at the trees a whole hour.
The sun waited among the stones
And then, with compassion, threw down
Toward them in the ravine
Our lengthened shadows, which seemed to reach them
Just as one can sometimes, with arm outstretched,
Touch in the distance between two beings a moment
In the other's dream that keeps flowing onward.

THE FAREWELL

We returned to our origin.
It was once the place of evidence, now crumbled,
The windows mingled too much light,
The stairways clambered over too many stars –
Caved-in arches, rubble –
The fire seemed to be burning in another world.

And now birds fly from room to room
The shutters have fallen, the bed is strewn with stones,
The hearth, filled with the sky's debris, will burn out soon.
We used to talk there, in the evening, in whispers
Because of the vaults' rumbling echo; still,
We'd make our plans there: but a boat
Laden with red stones
Pulled relentlessly away from a shore, and forgetting
Was already leaving its ash on the dreams
We'd irrepressibly begin, as we peopled with images
The fire that burned until the last day.

It is true, my friend,
That in this language we call poetry
There is only one word to name
The morning sun and the evening sun,
Only one for the cry of joy and that of anguish,
Only one for deserted headwaters and ax blows,
Only one for the unmade bed and the stormy sky,
Only one for the new-born child and the god who died?

I believe, yes, I want to believe this – but what, then,
Are these shadows that carry the mirror in?
And look, there are brambles among the stones
Of the still overgrown path
That once showed our footsteps the way to the young trees.
It seems to be here, today, that words
Are this broken trough from which the useless
Water spills each rainy dawn.
The grass, and the water shining in the grass like a river.
All is still to be stitched back together by the world.

I know that paradise is dispersed,
And our earthly task is to spot
Its scattered flowers in the yellowed grass,
But the angel is gone now, a light
That suddenly was just a setting sun.

And like Adam and Eve we'll take
One last walk in the garden.
Like Adam the first regret and Eve
The first courage, we'll both want, and not want,
To pass through the low door ajar over there
On the far end of the tether, touched by a final
Ray with augural colors.
Is the future captured at the origin
Like the sky when it consents to a curved mirror,
Will we manage to pick with our shadowed hands
The seeds of the light that had been
The miracle of this place, for other pools
In the secrecy of other, "stone-blocked", fields?

Truly, the place to conquer, to conquer ourselves, is here.
And we are leaving this evening. Here, forever,
Like the water that keeps running from the trough.

A STONE

Summer raged through the cool rooms,
Blind, bare-flanked,
It cried out, and the cry shattered the dream
Of those who slept there in the simplicity of their day.

They stirred, their breathing changed,
Their hands set aside their cup of sleep.
Already the sky was returning to earth,
This was a summer afternoon storm in the eternal.

PASSING BY THE FIRE

I passed by the fire in the empty room
With shutters closed, lights extinguished.

And I saw it was still burning – it was even,
That instant, at the point of equilibrium
Between the forces of ash and ember
Where a flame can choose
To rage or caress in the embrace
Of the one she seduced on her bed
Of pungent grass and dead wood.
He's the bend in the branch I brought inside
Yesterday, in a sudden summer downpour,
He suggests the Hindu god who beholds,
With all the solemnity of first love,
The woman waiting for the lightning –
herald of the universe – to envelope him.

Tomorrow I'll stir
The nearly-cold flame, and no doubt
It will be a summer day such as those the sky reserves
For all rivers – the ones of this world
And those that run dark with blood.
When will the man and woman
Learn if their ardor will entwine or unravel,
What wisdom in them can foretell
In the faltering light
If their cry of joy will become one of anguish?

Morning fire,
Two sleeping beings' breath,
One's arm on the other's shoulder.

And I, who came
To open the room, to let the light in,
I sit down and behold you,
Innocence of outstretched limbs,
Time so rich with itself it has ceased to be.

THE LIGHTNING

It rained last night,
The path smells of wet grass;
Then the heat's hand

On our shoulder again, as if to say
That time will take nothing away from us.

But see, there
Where the field abuts the almond tree
A wild beast has just leapt
From yesterday into today through the foliage.

We stand motionless, outside the world,

Then I approach you,
I finish pulling you off the blackened trunk,
Branch – lightning-struck summer
From which yesterday's sap, still holy, flows.

A STONE

Come, let me whisper to you
Of a child I remember
Who kept immobile, apart
From other lives.

In the morning he'd never join
The children in the trees who played
At multiplying the universe,
Nor run across the beach
Toward a brighter light.
He kept on his way, you see,
At the base of the dunes,
The footprints are the proof
Between the thistles and the sea.

And beside them you can watch
Filling with water that mirrors the sky
The wider footprints
Of a girl, his unknown companion.

BRANCH

Branch that I gathered at the edge of the woods,
Only to abandon you at the end of the world,

Hidden among stones, in the cranny
Where the other, invisible, path begins

(For every earthly moment is a crossroads
Where, as summer wanes, our shadow
Sets off for its other country in the same trees,
And rarely, in years past, would anyone pick up again
The branch with which we'd bend the grass,
Absent-mindedly, a whole summer long),

Branch, now that it's snowing I think of you,
I see you squeezed in the senselessness
Of the gnarls in the wood, where the bark
Flakes off as your dark forces swell.

And I, a shadow on white earth, head back
Toward your sleep that haunts my memory,
I lift you out of your dream that scatters, being
Merely light-pierced water,
Then I go to the place where I know the earth
Will steal away among the trees,
I hurl you with all my might
I can hear you rebound from stone to stone.

(No – let me hold you
A moment longer. I'll walk on, I'll take
The third path, the one I saw
Disappearing in the grass, without knowing
Why I never used to enter its thickets
Truly dark and with no birdsongs in its foliage.
I walk on, and soon I'm in a house
Where I once lived, but whose path
Has been lost, just as, at life's passing,
Some words are uttered, and go unnoticed,
For the last time in the eternal.
A fire burns in one of the still-empty rooms,
I hear it searching in the ember's mirror
For the bough of light,
Like the god who believes he's about to create
Spirit and life in the night
Of endless, labyrinthine gnarls.

Then I'll place you gently on the bed of flame,
I'll watch you ignite, in your sleep,
And bending down I'll hold, much longer still,
Your hand which is childhood ending.

ON SNOW-LADEN BRANCHES

I

From one snow-covered branch to the next, from those years
That passed without any wind frightening their leaves,
Scatterings of light will appear
Now and then, as we walk on in the silence.

And the powder as it falls is only infinite,
We can no longer tell if a world still exists
Or if, in our damp hands, we've gathered
A perfect crystal of the purest reality.

Colors denser with the cold, blues and purple
That call to us from further off than the fruit,
Are you our dream so persistent
That you become our prescience, our path?

It's the sky itself that has those clouds
Whose evidence is child of the snow,
And if we turn toward the white road
The light, the peace will be the same.

II

Except, it's true, that all images in this world
Are like the flowers that pierce
The March snow before spilling, adorned,
Into our daydreamt festival.

And may one bend down there, to carry
Armfuls of their joy into our lives,
They'll be dead soon – less in their faded
Colors' shadows than in our hearts.

Beauty is arduous, an enigma almost,
Ever rebeginning the apprenticeship
Of its true meaning on the flowering meadow's flank,
Covered here and there by patches of snow.

THE SNOW

It came from further off than the roads,
It touched the meadow, the flowers' ochre
With its hand that writes in smoke,
It conquered time with silence.

There's more light this evening
Because of the snow.
It's as though leaves were burning outside the door,
And there's water in the logs we bring inside.

WHERE THE WIND BURROWS

I
They say a god once searched
On these sealed waters
Like a hawk that craves
Its distant prey

And with barren
Urgent cries
Created time: a shining
In the hollow of the wave.

Night washes over daylight
Then pulls back,
Its foam unfurls
On the stones of this place.

What is God, whose only
Work is time,
Did he mean to die,
Unable to be born?

In vain he struggled
with absence,
One tossing the net,
The other wielding the sword.

II
Yet the lightning lingers
Above the world
As though at a ford,
And seeks from stone to stone.
Was beauty
A mere dream,
The light's face,
Eyes shut?

No: for its reflection
Lives within us, it's the flame,
Nude bather
In the dead wood's water,

It's the body
That the mirror exalts
Like a fire surging up
Within a ring of stones.

Yes, the word "joy" has meaning,
In spite of death,
Where the wind burrows
In the bright embers.

III
Sufficiency of the days
That file toward dawn
In blinding flashes
In the nighttime sky.

The sword, the net,
Are now a single hand
Gently pressing
The brief nape.

And the soul, illumined,
Is like the swimmer
Plunging brusquely
Beneath the light,

Eyes closed,
Nude,
Mouth not seeking language,
Only salt.

THE DREAM'S RESTLESSNESS

I
Again the river in the dream: head-waters
Pent-up, raging, where tree-trunks
Collide and swerve; on all sides
The sterile shores enclose me,
Large birds assail me with cries
Of pain and wonder – but I step
Onto the prow of a boat, into a dawn
I've heaped up branches, someone tells me,
Smoke swirls upward
And the fire quickly catches, two twisted columns,
A portal of lightning. I rejoice
In this crackling sky, I love the smell
Of sap burning in the mist.

And later I'm stirring ashes in the hearth
Of a house where I come each night,
But they're grains of wheat now, as though the souls
Of all things consumed broke away
At their last breath from the stalk of matter,
To become the seeds of a new hope.
I pick up handfuls of the dark substance,
Which is star; I unfold
The sheets of silence and reveal
Quite far off, quite near, the nude forms

Of two beings sound asleep in dawn's
Compassionate light, so reluctant
To graze their closed lids with its finger,
And which ensures that this attic, its woodwork,
Its fading odor of yesterday's wheat
Will continue to be their place, and their joy.

I have to free myself from these images.
I awake and rise and set out. And I enter
The garden of my tenth year,
It was a mere alley, very short, between two heaps
Of densely-packed earth, where rainstorms
Would leave stubborn pools that captured
The first lights that I loved. But now it's night,
I'm alone, the beings I knew from those years
Are talking and laughing upstairs in a room
Whose light spills onto the alley, and I know
The words I uttered then, while deciding my life,
Are this dark soil.
Around me lies a maze
Of other tiny gardens, greenhouses
Torn down, hoses lying in the flower-beds
Behind gates, sheds
Whose broken furniture and frameless portraits,
Jugs, the occasional mirror on the look-out
Beneath a tarpaulin, ready to receive any passing fire,
These things also, outside time, were my first awareness
Of this world in which one is alone.
Will I be able to lift out of this hard clay
The bits of rusted iron, the shards of glass,
The lumps of coal? Kneeling down,
I separate non-existence from the infinite,
And out of it make figures
With a hand I can barely see, so violent
Is night's haste through the worlds.
And how distant is the dawn of the sign, here!
I've sketched a constellation, but everything vanishes.

II

At last I dare lift up my eyes,
I see passing before me, in the naked sky,
The boat that had revisited, with lights darkened sometimes,
So many of the dreams that shimmer in the sand
Of this night's endless shore.

I watch as the boat hesitates.
It steers as though a path
Were being drawn for it atop the swell
That traverses gently, breaking through the foam,
The star's vast shadow.

And who are they, on board? A man and a woman
Who emerge, blackened, from the smoke
Of the fire they've tended
On the prow. Whose longing
Is this fire in the maze of worlds.

III

I close my eyes again. And now,
As memory flows on, a cup of red earth
Comes into view, its flames
Spilling over onto the hand that lifts it
High above the departing boat.

And it's a child asking me
To come closer, but he's in a tree,
The reflections are tangled in the branches.
Who are you, I ask? And laughing, he replies,
Who are you, who don't know how to blow out this flame?

Who are you? See, I can blow out the world
And it will be dark, I'll no longer see you,
Do you want us to have nothing left but the light?
– But I can't answer, under a spell
That has seized me from further off than childhood.

IV

I head for the shore,
The boat, and others, has arrived.
But all is silence there, even the bright water.
The bowsprits' eyes are still closed,
On the prows of these closed-in lights.

And the oarsmen sleep, foreheads
Tucked under their arms outside the centuries.
The blood-stains on their shoulders
Still shine mournfully, in a mist
Dawn's wind cannot dispel.

A SUMMER'S NIGHT

I

You were sculpted on a prow,
Time wore you away as the foam might have done,
It closed your eyes one stormy night,
Stained with salt your half-bare breasts.

O saint, whose charred hands are recolored
By the adoration of some new flowers,
Sanctuary for the sparse, the fleeting,
At the far end of rust-sown fields,

What sleep in your arched neck,
What shade in the dry leaves on the flagstones!
One could call this our room of a year gone by,
The same bed, but the blinds drawn shut.

II

And there, among the field-flowers, the wax ones
Are no less moving, brightly painted
According to the whims of hope that still dreams
Even where memory has faded.

And the unbeliever lingering near them,
He too picks up the glass crucible,
Raises it irrepressibly before the image,
Recreating thus the miracle of fire,

Then sets it down, infinite, and continues on his way,
Having loved the sign for lack of meaning,
What will soon blacken in this flame, he wonders,
Which is the word missing from my voice?

Yet all is so luminous, as evening falls,
Why does one arch in every life
Hang lower, and the water it enthralls crash more fiercely,
Beneath the resonant vault?

III

And what an enigma, this place where things are
Evidence, almost, in spite of death!
One would think there was being here, so much
Can the light dim without ceasing to shine.

And it's like the sound of voices
Heard at evening on still water
Travelling faster than a wave made by a stone,
We can no longer tell the distant from the near.

Who's speaking there, so close to us and yet invisible?
Who's walking there, faceless in the dazzling light?
This is how the gods, long ago, would come to children
Tossing pebbles in the water as evening fell.

IV

You move on, your hand resting on the boat grazes the water.
The oarsmen are faceless now.
In the sky, the Bear has entered the bright foliage,
The Virgin's dress is torn.

Are we nothing but a tree that caught fire
In the duration unconscious of itself?
The lightning knocks now and then against the leaves
And words are embers lying dormant

In the elbow of two branches. Then the tree starts to burn,
And the one next to it perhaps. But the sky
Has its own, another, light. And the cycle
Of the stars' indifference hasn't ended.

v

You move on, and it still seems to you
That the river of moonlight on the trees is widening.
Could it be that a life quickens
In the forest's mirror where worlds are reflected?

No – it's the stars and branches commingling,
And dreams and paths. Night is a glistening stone
That blocks the river's flow,
It's four a.m. and day's already breaking.

Comparative Criticism 15, 161–181. Cambridge University Press 1993

'A monument to a new life': a story

YITZHAK OREN

TRANSLATED WITH AN INTRODUCTION BY MARZELL KAY

INTRODUCTION

Yitzhak Nadel wrote 'A monument to a new life' using Yitzhak Oren as a pen name. Born in 1917 in Siberia to Russian parents, who soon moved to Harbin in China, he acquired a Jewish education from his father, himself a Hebrew teacher and an active Zionist. In 1936 he went to what was then Palestine to read literature, history and philosophy at the Hebrew University in Jerusalem. He entered the civil service in 1944 and retired in 1978, the year he won the Prime Minister's Prize for literature. Since the 1940s he has been a frequent contributor in Hebrew to literary periodicals and literary supplements of the daily press in the country. In 1950 the first of his books appeared,[1] also in Hebrew; these were mostly original works but included translations into Hebrew of Russian classics by Gogol, Goncharov and others. In 1989 Bar Ilan University awarded him the Newman Prize for literature.

Oren/Nadel is a near-esoteric figure in Israeli literature; he differs from his contemporaries in Israeli Hebrew literature in that they are mostly native-born and raised within the newly emerging powerful local culture. The dramatic realities of a world war, the Holocaust, personal implementation of Zionist ideology, the struggles of the Mandate period and the War of Independence left little need for the imaginative in their writing. Many of the younger authors were committed to accurate, realistic and occasionally colourful descriptions of the events in our time, fully identifying with historic experience. Oren deviated from the accepted genre with his first story written in 1942;[2] it was a bombshell of surrealism, projecting the portents of the world war period out into the cosmos in a momentary meeting of reality with imagination that was to be fateful for the Jewish people and all mankind. The bombshell was a dud – it lay unpublished for eight years, and he had to wait many more years for any form of recognition from the literary establishment. Meanwhile, he continued to challenge the conventions with synoptic vision, breaching the bounds of time and place; in his creations both reader and narrator are swept off in a continuous race of the sublime against the absurd, of metaphysical purpose against everyday drudgery, of the inability to break away from the warm, the petty and the personal to satisfy the craving for what is disembodied and grand.

As *Homo Ludens* he creates a surrealistic collage of the imagination, yet maintains the tensions of a man torn between the finite of mortal reality and his feeling – that there was something within him of the infinite beyond and that in his progress through life he had to implement and verify this known truth from sources beyond consciousness.

Gershon Shaked[3] describes Oren as ahead of his time (a *progon* rather than an *epigon*) in Hebrew writing of the sixties and seventies, stating that the literature of fantasy as a mixture of inter-textual parody and the picaresque outpaced the absorptive capacity of the generation, and only social and literary change later made it acceptable. He wrote of a new crop of modernistic writers, able to communicate with a new generation of readers who merely entered a position already taken by Oren, while he himself remained in the background as long as the public was unprepared for his form of modernism.

Over the years Oren has developed a pseudo-scientific and parodic creed concerning the world and the place of the Jewish people in it; with a growing trend towards the essay it forms a central thread running through his stories. First published in 1962 in *Keshet* (vol. 15, Am ha-Sefer, Tel Aviv 1962), the avant-garde periodical of that time, and in an anthology of Hebrew writers, later also in one of his books, 'The monument' does not yet fully express this creed – thinly coated with irony, the message here is submerged within the narration. In 1988 the story also appeared in a Russian collection of his stories[4] and in a Spanish anthology of contemporary Israeli writers.[5]

In a course on 'Fantasy and Realism', the Open University of Israel has devoted a complete 100-page 'study unit'[6] to 'The monument' as an example of the fantastic story. It is subjected to rigorous literary analysis based on research by Zvetan Todorov,[7] a structural approach that distinguishes between the strange and the miraculous. Both concern an event which cannot be explained by the natural laws of material reality. The character confronting this can regard the event as strange, one which did not really take place but arose from a delusion of the senses or from the character's own imagination. An event that is miraculous has actually occurred to indicate the existence of laws which till then had been unknown to the character who lives in the world in which they operate.

Golan's analysis concludes that both solutions may apply to the present story. It leaves the reader wondering and uncertain, though it does not require a decision either way. By intellectual effort the reader may adopt the allegorical interpretation, or else prefer to surrender to a feeling of the grotesque with contradictory reactions that can range from dread to laughter. The analysis concludes by offering the reader a further option with no attempt at interpretation: enjoy the fantastic nature of the story, enter the fictional world, accept all the surprises and other experiences it has to offer and take it as it is.

Yitzhak Oren does not necessarily favour this conclusion. His pseudo-scientific creed sees the centre of creation to be not mankind itself, but rather the products of man's hands and brain: art, literature and music; thought, science and technology. Man is mortal but his work should last as long as mankind survives. This seems to be the idea Oren wished to express in the story: all that remained of the cosmic historic event is the monument rising to its full height just when the man who had been the instrument of its erection comes to the end of his life on earth – his work was done and he could go.

Oren would never insist this was the only interpretation, but would welcome all others; he has frequently expressed the opinion that the allegorical view forms an important criterion in evaluating a piece of writing; the multiplicity of interpretations it spawns is crucial to the survival and lasting influence of the work. One of his characters in fact tells his diary that 'it is the reader who must blend the essence with the waters of the mind, to his own taste, his talents and the best of his ability – after all it is the consumer and not the maker who puts the soda in the whisky and the milk in the coffee.'[8]

NOTES

1 Y. Oren (all Hebrew): *Ei-Sham*/Somewhere, 1950; *Ba-Oref* (Behind the Lines), 1953; *Massot Binyamin ha-Hamishi* (Adventures of Benjamin the Fifth) (Mordechai Newmann, Tel Aviv, 1958); *Avot va-Voser* (Fathers and Sour Grapes), 1964; *Pnei Dor Vekelev* (Portrait of the Generation as a Dog), (*Ogdan*, Jerusalem, 1968); *Konei Shamayim va-Arez* (Buyers of Heaven and Earth), 1970; *Etgarim* (Challenges), 1972; *Ha-Har ve-ha-Akhbar* (The Mountain and the Mouse), 1972; *Massa Missaviv la-Tzir* (A Voyage around the Axis), 1977; *Jabotinsky ve-Ani* (Jabotinsky

and I), 1980; *Hamesh Megilot Afot* (Five Flying Scrolls), 1985; *Mehakhel ve-ad Kaleh* (The Ultimate) (Keter Pub. House, Jerusalem, 1987).

2 Y. Oren, *Ei-Sham* (Somewhere), 1950.

3 Gershon Shaked, *Hebrew Fiction 1880–1980* (Ha-Kibbutz ha-Meukhad and Keter Publishing House, 3 vols., 1977/1988/1988 resp.).

4 Y. Oren, *My Quarry* (Aliya Pub. House, Jerusalem, 1988).

5 '*Cuentos Contemporaneos de Israel*, ed. Arna Golan (El Colegio de Mexico, Mexico D.F., 1988).

6 *Between Phantasy and Realism*, ed. Arna Golan (Everyman's University, Tel Aviv, 1984).

7 Zvetan Todorov, *The Fantastic – a Structural Approach to a Literary Genre* (Press of Case Western Reserve University, Cleveland and London, 1973).

8 Y. Orem, '*Crime and Punishment*', trans. Joseph Shachter, in *The Imaginary Number* (Y. Oren/Benmir Books, California, 1986), pp. 56–7.

'A monument to a new life': a story

YITZHAK OREN

Everything had been organized as it should be and wonderfully well planned. This was quite an achievement, particularly in view of the fact that the whole business had to be kept a secret: not a living soul beside those directly engaged in the operation knew the slightest thing about it. To this day I wonder why in fact I had been privileged to be one of the chosen few mortals informed in advance of this great event, one quite without precedent in all human history and due to take place eighteen hours from the moment I was told of it.

I am unfamiliar with the intricacies of the different sciences that claim to foretell the future. That is why I do not know whether it was observing astronomers or astrologers, physicists, statisticians, psychologists or sociologists who were the ones who predicted the Messiah was due to come on the appointed day, hour and second. All I know – and even this knowledge is no more than mere conjecture – is that someone observed and calculated, made his forecast, proposed a theory, proved it to a degree of scientific certainty and submitted it to his superiors. These superiors investigated and interpreted, organized, planned and kept it a secret until the time was right.

As for myself, I had of course no part in the forecasts or the planning – and that is really not surprising. Quite the contrary, the great surprise is that despite my being what I am, as indicated I was one of the chosen few who knew the great secret eighteen hours before it became public knowledge.

In saying that I am what I am I certainly imply nothing in any way derogatory to my own person. I am a man like any other man. I am not inferior to most of my kind. But let the truth be told: while not superior to most of my kind, it is still clear to me that I am inferior to a minority of them, that minority who succeed in everything they undertake, blessed with qualities that make their lives into one long victory parade. As I have said, I have not been blessed with these qualities and I can boast of no victories. However, just as I cannot take comfort in victories

I cannot show defeats, for in order to suffer defeat one must of necessity struggle, and never in my life have I ever struggled; not in fact and not by proxy and not in spirit.

I am not important enough to lay before you the epic of my life, if for no other reason then because the story of my life can hardly be called an epic. I will make do with describing myself the way I am; anyone interested will not find it difficult to discover the past from the present. Even this I do only to explain why I am puzzled by the fact that I suddenly find myself sharing the secrets of the great personages of my time, in this the greatest of all times.

I am just thirty years old, married and the father of two children, a boy and a girl. My son is six and my daughter is two. My wife is a practical nurse and she works in one of the hospitals. We all live in a two-room flat in one of the suburbs of the city. The flat is my own property, except that it still carries a mortgage which I am paying off in monthly instalments out of my own and my wife's salaries.

I work in one of the factories of the arms industry. I must make a confession: I have not the slightest idea what this factory manufactures. First because the end product is in the nature of a military secret, second because I have never had the slightest interest in knowing what that secret product might be.

Eight hours a day I sit alone in a narrow window-less cubicle; its only door is kept closed except for the times when I open it. I do so only four times a day: in the morning when I enter the cubicle; during the lunch break, when I go to the canteen to have a cup of tea to round off the meal of sandwiches which I bring from my home; at the end of the lunch break, when I return from the canteen to the cubicle and towards evening, when I leave it until the following day. Ventilation in my cubicle is provided artificially through concealed openings in the ceiling and the light comes from fluorescent lamps. I sit on a kind of high stool with armrests, facing a wall; mounted on this wall there is an instrument which reminds you of a large thermometer. It is a large tube made of glass (or possibly some other transparent material), which fills up with mercury (or possibly some other fluid resembling mercury). It fills up from the bottom; in other words the column of fluid starts out short and it gets longer and longer, growing taller – sometimes quickly and sometimes slowly, like the mercury in a thermometer – until it completely fills the transparent column. Then when the column is full to the top I empty it. How? In my right hand I hold the end of a rope threaded through a hole in the wall. Please note this everyone: not a lever and not a button, not a handle or a projection, but a rope. A flaxen rope, as simple as can be. As soon as I see the tube is full, I pull the rope and it empties out.

I do not know the processes involved in this job I do, just as I do not know why in this day and age I have to pull a rope to empty the tube – when every mechanism in the world is regulated automatically and every device monitors itself mechanically. It is now five years that I am living in my flat and I do not know any of the neighbours in the whole building (except those in the flat above my own). I believe this lack of curiosity is one of my most characteristic traits. In consequence of this trait I hear no news and see no newspapers, in consequence there are so few things which I know and so many I do not, and in consequence I have no formal education after elementary school. I repeat: no formal education – for until the day I married, had children and became a slave to work in the cubicle at the military factory I read extensively – without method, without order and anything I could get: detective stories and Spinoza, Jewish legends and Marcel Proust, Plato and popular science; all these in confusion served as my spiritual fare.

Except that my reading was unlike that of anyone else I know, for I do not absorb things as they are really written, but the way I imagine them, correct them and improve them in my mind. I therefore do not remember even a small fraction of the words Prince Bolkonski (we are talking of Tolstoy's *War and Peace*) whispers in the ears of his beloved Natasha but on the other hand, engraved on my heart are the words I would say to Natasha if I were to meet her one of these days, and they are words no one can erase or uproot. I believe the detective stories I have read in my lifetime must number in the hundreds, but anyone trying to ask me the way Sherlock Holmes and Poirot and Perry Mason discovered the murderers will not get a single word out of me. Nevertheless I have my own method for discovering all those criminals.

If I had only a fraction of Conan Doyle's talent, or Agatha Christie's or Stanley Gardner's I would rewrite their stories and reveal the criminals more quickly and efficiently. Even on the subject of setting up model states I have a better idea than Plato, although this idea did spring into my mind while reading Plato's *Republic*. I am prepared to make my ideas public, and do not do so only because in my heart I am convinced I would have no one to listen to me. I would go further: from books such as 'How I split the Atom', 'Electronics for the Young', 'The Stars of Heaven for Everyone', 'One, Two, Three ... Eternity' and other similar compositions I have tried to learn something about the movement of objects in space and about the component parts of the atom. I read them only once and therefore I have forgotten the main points. Even on this I have not the slightest regrets. On the contrary, in my mind I harbour a set of laws, according to which all matter in the Universe – from the electron to the Milky Way – could move through space in a way completely different from the way it moves now. I also prefer to store this set of laws within the depths of my own mind, for I know in advance that even if I were to shout it out aloud, I would only be a voice in the wilderness: in our times all men are only allowed to make laws binding on themselves, and anyone attempting to dictate laws for all creation would surely be suspected of deluding people.

I therefore sit in my cubicle and enjoy my work, and I enjoy my work because my mind is free to ponder and dream on the past of all living things, on the present of the cosmos and on the future of the human race. My eyes remain glued to the tube and my hand pulls the rope whenever the fluid reaches the top of that tube.

I have been watching the liquid for six years, pulling the rope, spending one-third of each day sunk in pleasant thoughts, in the course of which I destroy old worlds to build new and better ones.

That day someone knocked on the door of my cubicle. The time was nine forty-five.

My eyes were glued to the tube, my hand held the end of the rope, but nevertheless I remember quite clearly that the time was nine forty-five – hence I must have had time to cast a rapid glance at my watch before opening my mouth to ask loudly:

– Who's there?

– Jonah Schwartz – I heard through the door.

It was in fact the voice of Jonah Schwartz.

For the past two years Jonah Schwartz has been the only one of the workers in the factory to enter my cubicle, coming once a month to bring me my monthly pay-packet. And why only during the last two years? Because until then the salaries at the plant had been paid in cash, but two years ago they introduced payments by cheque. As long as the salaries were being paid in cash I would take myself to the cashier after working hours, queue up and wait till I got to the window. When the cheques were introduced, Jonah Schwartz would take them to all employees, myself included. I no longer had to stand in the queue and on the first of the month as soon as I got home I endorsed the cheque and gave it to my wife.

When I heard Jonah Schwartz's voice I pressed the pedal under my foot. The door opened and Jonah Schwartz came in. The security department had installed this pedal so the door could not be opened from outside unless I thought it was necessary. Only someone issued with a special key – like the key I always had with me – was able to open the door without having to wait for me to press the pedal.

I was most surprised when Jonah Schwartz came to me on a sudden visit in the middle of the month, and my surprise was even greater when he opened his mouth and addressed me as follows:

– They want you in Management. Urgent. I'll take your place.

– Me to Management?

I have never been called to the Management. I had no idea what anyone there looked like. Six years earlier, when I was engaged for work, I had been introduced to a smiling man with tender blue eyes and curly hair going grey at the temples; to that day I did not know whether this person was a member of management or not. Since then my superiors had never even once troubled me to leave my room.

– Yes, you to Management – announced Jonah Schwartz, and it seemed to me that the ends of the stubble of his greying beard stood slightly on end. (Jonah Schwartz shaved once a week, on Friday night, and that day was Tuesday.)

After the stubble of his beard had returned to its proper condition – or perhaps it only seemed to me to have returned to its proper condition – Jonah made a gesture from which I deduced that he was about to take my place in the seat which earlier I have called a form of armchair.

I got up from my seat and, as my hand released the end of the rope and my eyes watched the rising liquid in the tube, I got ready to give him a short lecture on the nature of the task. Jonah Schwartz however cast a sidelong glance at me from his yellow eyes (I am somehow convinced Jonah Schwartz in fact had brown eyes, but because he had immigrated with the Third Aliya wave and had experienced everything they had experienced, such as paving roads and digging pits, fishing in the Kinereth and guarding in Galilee, defending Jerusalem and hiking in the Negev, the colour of his eyes had faded and gone yellow in the sun) and a hint of contempt peered out of their depths. While I was trying to interpret the meaning of that look, he sat in my place, turned his eyes on the tube and took the end of my rope in his hand.

At that moment I no longer had a place in the cubicle. I left it and crossed the spacious yard on my way to the management offices.

After crossing the yard I entered a multi-storey building. I stood by the lift door and rang the bell. A pointer glowing with a yellowish light pointed upwards – indicating the lift-cage was going up.

I sat down and waited while it went wherever it was going and then came down again in response to my ring. Meanwhile a few more people had arrived and they also waited for the lift. Except that they were all impatient and therefore waited standing up, while I remained patient and waited sitting down.

When I had sat down to wait I discovered that the special key to my cubicle was still in my pocket.

At that time I had not realized that I would never return to my cubicle. On the contrary, I believed I would be back a few minutes later. It was just as well I thought so, otherwise the key would have troubled my conscience so much that I would have run to give it to Jonah Schwartz and made management wait a long time for me – something that would have endangered my future.

It became absolutely clear that the smiling man with the tender blue eyes and curly hair going grey at the temples – that is, the man who at the time had given me the job – was a member of the management, the proof of this being that it was he who sat at the head of the table in that room. The door bore the sign 'Management' and I entered without first knocking. I was certain that if I had been summoned to management I did not have to knock on the door.

Yet when I had opened the door and gone in, my confidence was a little shaken and I no longer knew whether or not I had done the right thing. Though I had come not on my own personal initiative, but instead had been asked from above to do so, it was possible nevertheless that I ought to have knocked a few times. This doubt nagging me inside caused that weakness in the knees which I felt as I walked from the door to the table. Yet on seeing the curly-haired smiler with the sad blue eyes, whose face I remembered from six years previously, I took courage: my fears dissolved and were forgotten.

The sad-eyed smiler thus sat at the head. Seated either side of him were two gentlemen whom till then I had not chanced to meet. One was lean, with a flushed face and hair trimmed short, so much so that his skull looked like a field of stubble after the harvest, while he himself was a bundle of strained nerves: sometimes he would drum on the table with his fingers, at others he distorted his face in frequent and repeated grimaces, either extending his lower lip or twitching with his left eye while screwing up the skin of his face around that eye.

This nervous character was sitting to the left of curly-hair, while sitting on the latter's right side was the total opposite: what could have been a statue or flesh and blood, bald, with eyes like rusty metal and a face frozen like an iceberg – not a move, not a twitch, not the blink of an eyelid. After Lot's wife had turned into a pillar of salt, her face probably looked like this one.

The smiler turned his tender look towards me and pointed to the chair on his left. His lips smiled even more than before.

– Sit down, Mr. Kornstein – he said leisurely.

– I am not Kornstein – I replied while still on my feet.

– Not Kornstein? – screeched the nervous one.

The frozen one did not budge.

– No. My name was Kornstein. Now I am Karni.

– When did you change your name? – asked curly-hair and, though his speech was leisurely, the echo of concealed anxiety could be detected in his voice.

– Five years ago. To tell the truth, I did not mind being called Kornstein, but my wife insisted on it.

– What did your wife insist on?

– On the change of name.

The nervous one leafed through the file lying on the table in front of him. Frozen-face angrily beetled his brow. Curly-hair produced strange humming sounds with his mouth.

I was perfectly calm. Now I became aware of the fact that I was still standing on my feet, even though a while ago they had offered me – perhaps even ordered me – to sit down. I sat down, and what is more I made myself comfortable. I no longer cared whether I was behaving properly or not.

The nervous one pushed the file towards curly-hair and showed him a particular document. Curly-hair nodded his head and whispered in the ear of frozen-face. The angry look left frozen-face and gone with the anger was the last vestige of expression of any form.

– Lot's wife in male form, after the cataclysm of Sodom and Gomorrha – was the fleeting thought which crossed my mind.

It appears I had not confined myself to inner feelings and had put them into words, for it was not likely that smiler had read my thoughts.

– Not Lot's wife, but rather the Monument of the Resurrection, and not the cataclysm of Sodom and Gomorrha but a fateful upheaval in the history of Mankind and all Creation, and not after the upheaval but before it.

While I was still trying to clarify the meaning of this verbal stew in my mind, the lips of frozen-face moved and a short, meaningful sentence issued from between his clenched teeth:

– Tomorrow before dawn, at precisely 4 a.m., the Messiah is coming.

As I have already said, to this day I wonder how I happened to have become one of the privileged few who it was thought had to be informed of the most important event to occur in the chronicles of the human race, and perhaps in the history of the universe. And yet, since frozen-face had made the pronouncement, not even a trace of surprise arose in me. I would have been far more surprised if he had said that tomorrow the alarm clock by my bed would go off at 4 in the morning, since this alarm clock of mine generally rings at 5 and not at 4.

– This is an absolute secret, an absolute secret, an absolute secret. Do you hear me? – stormed the nervous one, his left eye squinting, screwing up all the skin of his face to a distance of an inch or two around it.

Curly-haired smiler bent his head waiting for the nervous one to finish his outburst. Then he turned to me and in his usual friendly way said:

– I assume, Mr Karni, that you have heard the Coming of the Messiah is accompanied by the resurrection of the dead. It is self-evident that such an enormous addition to the number of inhabitants on the face of the earth (we estimate the number of candidates for resurrection to be many billions, and that is based on the reports of our intelligence service, who believe the resurrection order will apply to all human beings, irrespective of religion, race, nationality or beliefs – everyone who had ever been born will return to life, the righteous with the wicked) such a large additional population is liable to raise innumerable problems, particularly with food supply and housing. Therefore all appropriate measures have been taken to fly the resurrected – as soon as they emerge from their graves – to the moon, the planets and perhaps even to more remote celestial bodies. The necessary vehicles and their crews are in a state of readiness. As for secrecy, this is essential in order to avoid panic among the inhabitants of the globe. We are doing all we can to conduct the operation according to a detailed plan, without disturbing the inhabitants of Earth and insofar as is possible, even without their knowledge. With that we are determined to commemorate the event by the erection of a monument, the Monument of the Resurrection. The task of erecting it – or more precisely raising it into position – has been imposed on you.

Curly-hair took a breath. The nervous one raised the palm of his hand and rearranged his fingers for drumming with them on the table, but his hand remained suspended in the air. Frozen-face extended his arm and pointed his finger at me like someone aiming a pistol.

My lips went dry. I wanted to lick them, but did not have the courage for it. I swallowed the saliva that had gathered in my mouth and felt a sharp pain in my throat.

– The task is as simple as can be – continued the curly-haired smiler – tomorrow morning at 02:50 hours you will get up, leave your house and go to the highway leading to Ramallah. There are some who think this is Bethel, where the foot of Jacob's ladder had stood, with its head reaching into the sky. Note that you will be going on foot. When you reach the barrier at the border, turn left and go on until you see the end of a rope peeping out of the ground. Get down on the ground nearby and wait until 04:00 hours. At 04:00 hours you will hear a sound – something between the sound of a ram's horn and a hooter. You must know this is not an alarm but the sound of the Messiah's trumpet. As soon as you hear the blast, pull the rope. Make sure you do not wait until the end of the trumpet blast, you must pull it on hearing the first sounds. That is all. And now go home, lie down and rest. Rest is of the utmost importance in connection with the operation, and it must be regarded as the first step in the performance of your task. Remember: Not a word to a soul!

– Do I not go back to my cubicle? – I asked.

– No, you must rest.

– And the key?

– What key?

– The key to my cubicle. A special key – I pulled the key from my pocket. All three of them burst out laughing. Curly-hair burst into a curly trill. Frozen-face produced metallic sounds in his throat. The nervous one's shoulders were shaking.

I went outside and walked to the bus with the key in my clenched fist.

While standing on the bus that took me home, I was troubled by worries and sad thoughts were running through my brain. I was not worrying for, nor thinking of myself. In my heart I was certain I would fulfil my mission faithfully and would efficiently carry out the task which had been entrusted to me, even though objectively there was no justification for this self-confidence. I was anxious about the Messiah. I read somewhere that Napoleon was defeated at Leipzig because of a cold. I thought to myself – for instance what would happen if at the moment the Messiah put the ram's horn to his lips he was at the same time attacked by an unbearable pain in his stomach.

These and similar worries bothered me all the way home. When I reached my own front door however I stopped worrying about the Messiah and in view of the circumstances I began to worry about myself.

When I reached my own front door the time was ten fifty-five a.m. Since I had been ordered to rest I planned my day: as soon as I got in I would undress and lie down on my bed, get under the covers and go to sleep. I would sleep the sleep of the just until my son got back from school and my wife returned from work. My wife works till one o'clock and on her way home she picks up our daughter from nursery school. At one-thirty all members of my family apart from myself are at home and at two they take their lunch; as I would also be at home today we would all eat together. After lunch I will wash the dishes. This way my wife will be able to have a good rest and will return to work (from five to seven-thirty) more rested than any other day. While my wife is at work I play with my daughter and help my son with his homework ("Hello Dad", "Hello Mum", "Happy New Year" in giant letters). Since in the evening my wife will be less tired than usual, we will go out to the cinema together and ask the neighbour living on the top floor – right above us – to come down to our flat and watch the children. She also has children of her own and sometimes she needs this help for herself – and one good turn deserves another. I know the management had ordered me to rest, but a night at the cinema is the same as a rest.

At ten fifty-six this plan was fully formed in my mind. At ten fifty-seven came the first snag. Man proposes...

I stepped up to my front door with the key to my cubicle still clenched in my fist. Absent-mindedly I put it in the keyhole, or more precisely I tried to put it in, since the shape of this key is unique and there was no way it could be inserted in the keyhole of my own door. For a long time nevertheless I stubbornly shoved and pushed it until I tired of it. Only then I realized my mistake and saw my efforts had been pointless. I pulled the right key from my pocket and opened the door. While I was still at the door, from above me I heard the voice of our neighbour from the flat directly over ours, who would watch our children tonight. I raised my eyes and saw her hastily coming down the stairs with my small daughter in her arms. As she descended and came nearer, her voice got louder and louder and when she stopped in front of me the voice was a wail. The neighbour wailed but my little girl did not make a sound. She opened her eyes wide, pursed her lips and reached out to me with her arms.

I did not yet know what this meant and my heart turned over. When I found out what was happening, my heart turned over once again. It seems that morning the owner of the nursery school had brought my daughter home because the child was burning with fever. There was no doubt whatsoever – the little girl had fallen ill, perhaps even with a contagious disease. The teacher feared the other children might be infected and had hurried to bring my daughter home. She found our flat locked and bolted. She went up to the next floor and delivered the child to our neighbour. As the neighbour had three children of her own, she feared for her own children's health and refused to accept my baby; she acceded to the teacher's request only after prolonged argument. Now her anger spilled out on me, even though the words of abuse she threw at me were couched in the female gender. From all these signs of identification they were not meant for me but were intended for my wife – words like "a witch not a mother, sends a sick child to nursery school, contemptible, a fine one to be bringing up children, I wouldn't let someone like that take care of young animals", and other similar protests and condemnations that were not indicative of particularly warm feelings; until that moment I had believed that pleasant neighbourly relations existed between my spouse and her neighbours in general, with this neighbour from above us in particular.

I took my daughter from her hands, put her in the cradle and with a spoon I gave her tea to drink. She spat out the tea and burst out crying. I rocked the cradle, at first gently and then with all my strength, until the baby finally fell asleep. When she fell asleep she began to breathe heavily, producing snores and grunts from her mouth. I rushed to the grocers' and phoned the hospital where my wife worked. After getting a lot of strange and weird noises – a mixture of male and female voices – I was finally connected to the head nurse in my wife's department. The head nurse informed me that earlier that morning some one had called her in my wife's name saying that she was sick and would not come to work. I put down the receiver then picked it up again. I dialled a few times and contacted the sick fund clinic. Whoever answered my call asked what my daughter's temperature was. This I could not provide. The voice advised me to give her an aspirin and phone the following day to make an appointment. I tried to protest but the line went dead.

I returned home. My son was standing by the door. His trousers were torn and his shirt was soiled. My hand went out as though of its own will and slapped his face. This was the first slap I had given my son in all his life. He opened his mouth in astonishment and froze where he stood. I felt a twinge of pain in my heart, but since my mind was not free to dwell on my own suffering I ignored the twinge and entered the flat. My daughter was sleeping. The grunts and snores had stopped. I sat beside her cradle and touched her forehead. I let the palm of my hand rest on her forehead and was none the wiser, for I have never been able to judge a person's temperature by touch. I bent down over her and put my ear by her chest. The chest was rising and falling steadily and her breathing was regular and calm. I felt relieved. Because I felt relieved, I remembered my son. I went to the door and found it open. In my haste I had apparently forgotten to close it. I stood in the doorway and searched with my eyes for my son. I looked all around and could not see him.

I returned to my daughter's cradle, drew up a chair and sat down. I tried to think about the Messiah due at 04:00 hours and I glanced at my watch. The time was one twenty-seven p.m. – this was the time my wife usually returned from work. Even though today, as I had discovered, she had not been to work, she returned at the same precise time. When she saw me sitting by my daughter's cradle, she stopped in her tracks and looked at me in surprise. Her eyelids were red as though she had been crying.

I told her everything that had happened to me, apart from the matter of the Messiah, whose anticipated arrival at 04:00 hours I concealed from her. I also concealed the fact that I knew she had not been at work today.

She asked:

– How come you are home at this hour?

To my shame I realized I had no answer to this question, even though it was reasonable to think I would have been ready for it. The words came out of my mouth as though of their own will:

– I have lost my job.

Why those particular words came to my lips is a source of wonder for me.

Whenever I am moved or shaken by some Job's tidings which come on me suddenly, I am struck by a strong urge to lie on my bed and indulge in fantasies. As for my wife, whenever she is moved or shaken by some suddenly arrived Job's tidings she becomes excessively active.

When she heard of my supposed dismissal she leaped to the cradle, placed her lips on the baby's brow and rearranged the covers. After that she rushed into the kitchen and put a number of pans and the kettle on the gas. While these were on the stove she fetched vegetables from the refrigerator and peeled them with a special instrument, something between a knife and a saw. Quick as a flash she dumped the peeled vegetables into one of the pans and rushed out. All this she did without uttering a sound.

The baby woke up and burst into tears. Once again I tried to pacify her: I stroked her, gave her sweetened tea to drink and rocked the cradle, but this time I did not succeed. I do not know how long I spent on these futile efforts. To me they seemed to go on for hours, but by an accurate reckoning they lasted no longer than thirty minutes. When that half-hour had passed my wife reappeared; she had my son and Dr Tamir with her.

My son went off into a corner and glared at me angrily. Dr Tamir approached the cradle and stayed by it. My wife changed my son's clothes and then joined Dr Tamir.

Dr Tamir was tall and slender, fair-haired like the natives of Northern Europe.

Both of them – my wife and Dr Tamir – were busy with my daughter and I moved closer to my son, then tried to mollify him in all sorts of ways. At first he did not respond to me and all my tricks were ineffective. Finally I told him the story of the mouse that swallowed an elephant and remained as small as before. This action story captured his imagination and served as the excuse for a complete reconciliation. I had no choice but to repeat it once again.

Meanwhile Dr Tamir had completed my daughter's examination and wrote out a prescription. My wife passed me the prescription and asked me to go down to the chemist. I went to the chemist and my son went with me. On the way I told him the story of the mouse that swallowed an elephant – for the third time.

When I got back from the chemist my wife was sunk in an armchair – this was the only armchair in our flat and had come to us from my wife's parents – and standing behind the armchair was Dr Tamir. He was looking straight through me into the distance, as though I had no substance but was an empty volume of space, while my wife cast a long look towards me, beginning as a greenish flash of hatred and ending in an expression of guilt mingled with sycophancy like that of a dog that had done wrong. I knew this sharp transition from a greenish flash to the expression of a dog that had done wrong and it did not augur well.

Dr Tamir said: "One spoonful three times a day", and left.

Once more I tried to think of the Messiah and the Monument of the Resurrection. It seemed I was unable properly to direct my heart to the Day of God that was approaching like a thief in the night, but at least I managed to take my mind away from everything that was happening around me. Proof of this is the fact that I remember nothing whatsoever of what happened from the moment Dr Tamir left our home and until the moment when I woke up in my bed to the sound of sobbing from my wife lying beside me. A full moon was flooding the room with a greenish jaundice. In the light of this moon I peered at my watch. The time was twelve-o-o hours. My wife's shoulders were shaking. Her face was buried in the pillow. I have not been blessed with a good memory and never in my life have I managed to learn a single paragraph properly by heart, but on seeing my wife's shaking shoulders, at the sight of the back of her neck rising and falling (I did not see her face since it was buried in the pillow), at the sight of her hair waving with every movement of her neck, I suddenly heard playing inside me (just so, literally playing, for not only the words but also the melody was sounding inside me) one whole verse from Bialik's poem:

> and also tell him: in my bed
> I shall float at night in my tears
> and beneath my white flesh
> my pillow burns each night.

I said to her:

– You love Dr Tamir.

Her shoulders shook more than ever and she did not reply.

– And does he also love you? – I asked.

– She lifted her head, shot a look of victory at me from eyes filled with tears and said:

– Yes.

At that instant I decided to kill them both; and this decision I made was justified, since I knew very well that at 04:00 hours they would both be resurrected and would be taken to one of the planets. I might possibly have executed my plot, except that suddenly I saw before me the faces of my son and daughter. How would I sew up my son's torn trousers, when any thread in my fingers always misses the eye of the needle; how would I get a doctor for my daughter (even if it was Dr Tamir) when they cut me off the phone at the sick fund?

I said to my wife:

– I am going. Curly-hair has ordered me to leave the house at two fifty in the morning. At two fifty in the morning I will leave the house.

Luckily for me my wife only heard the last sentence. God does indeed look after the simple-minded, for if she had heard the beginning of what I had said, she would most certainly have begun to cross-examine me, demanding to know about curly-hair and bombarding me with questions; who knows if in the end I would not have succumbed and revealed a hint of what I knew about the Redemption, the Resurrection and the Monument. As she had only heard the last sentence, she raised the upper half of her body and beat the pillow with her fists:

– Not at two fifty, not at two fifty; now, you'll go now. Now, this instant – she screamed hysterically.

It was a miracle the children did not wake up at the sound of her screams.

I got up, put on my clothes and went out.

Some distance from my home there is a public garden. The saplings were still tender and the garden was still something of a hope for the future, but the benches standing in it were real benches.

I sat on one of them and waited for two fifty.

At two fifty I left the garden and went to the highway leading to Ramallah. There are some who think this is Bethel, where the foot of Jacob's ladder had stood, with its head reaching into the sky. I went on foot. When I reached the barrier at the border, I turned left and went on until I saw the end of a rope peeping out of the ground.

I saw it in the dark of night only by the light of the stars, for the moon had set and the dawn had not yet broken.

I got down on the ground near that place and waited for 04:00 hours.

The stars faded and the world began to turn blue. Dark shadows were flashing across the skyline over the mountain tops of Judaea. Some looked like tree-tops stirring in the wind and some like a detachment of soldiers standing guard and shivering in the chill of the pre-dawn dew.

At four o'clock I heard a sound – something between a trumpet call and a hooter. I knew this was not an alarm but the sound of the Messiah's horn. As soon as I heard the sound I pulled the rope. I did not wait until the end of the trumpet call. On hearing the first sounds I pulled heartily on the rope.

And as I pulled I felt I was sinking into the ground. I am sinking down and rising before me is a statue. The more I pulled the deeper I sank down and the higher the statue rose up before my eyes.

It seemed I had been pulling for quite a long while, at least until the sun had risen and lit up the land. As I was immersed in this holy task which was my work I did not see the dawn and the purple of the sunrise. I saw the sun in the full strength of its light.

And when the sun was shining at full strength, I was already buried up to my neck in the ground and only my right arm projected from the earth, its hand grasping the rope.

The statue was already almost completely erect – and if it was still inclined slightly backwards, this was no more than 5 or 6 degrees. A few more minutes and the statue would be standing before my eyes, straight up, perpendicular to the ground.

When the Indian god revealed his divine form to Arjuna, he was like a thousand suns all shining in the sky at one and the same time. He spoke out of countless mouths, saw with tens of thousands of eyes and wore the festive robes of paradise, anointed with the oil of myrrh, whose scent is the perfume of heaven. The son of Pandu was fortunate and he saw the whole of creation, with its wealth of lights and shades, embodied in the form of the god of gods.

I saw no hide or hair of him.

The Monument of Resurrection, which was rising up before me, was nothing more than the statue of a girl whose brown hair was trimmed like that of a boy, the cut of whose blue eyes were a little Mongolian, her teeth projected a little, her nose was delicate and narrow, her face glowing with a smile, in which innocence and wisdom, love and confidence were combined into a supreme completeness; her neck was inclined forward in the slightest of inclinations, her shoulders...

No. I did not manage to see her shoulders, for at the instant when she rose up vertically before me, straight and firm, the dust covered my eyes and I saw nothing more.

Ilia Murometz – or perhaps some other hero of the ancient Russian Epic – on one of his journeys came across a pouch on the highway. Ilia Murometz dismounted from his horse and tried to lift the pouch. The pouch did not budge from its place, but Ilia Murometz himself sank into the ground instead.

As God is my witness, it was not because of a pouch that I sank into the ground, it was because of the Statue of the Resurrection that I was covered by the dust. And even though the dirt covered my eyes, my ears were not blocked and the sound of the Messiah's ram's horn reached them.

My arm was still stretching out above the ground, except that my hand was paralysed and my fingers had turned to stone. I stopped pulling the rope.

When I stopped pulling the rope the voice of the Messiah's horn fell silent and a hum took its place. I knew very well that the resurrected were being flown to the celestial bodies.

And I? Now that I am buried in the ground, am I not one of them? Is my situation not like theirs?

This matter is one of doubt which requires clarification. One thing which does not require clarifying is the certainty that my wife and my children and Dr Tamir have remained upon the earth.

If it were not for the layer of dirt which was blocking my mouth and made my breathing difficult I would have burst out laughing.

Comparative Criticism 15, pp. 183–192. Cambridge University Press 1993

'Deathsfugue' and other poems

PAUL CELAN

TRANSLATED BY JOHN FELSTINER

DEATHSFUGUE

Black milk of daybreak we drink it at evening
we drink it at midday and morning we drink it at night
we drink and we drink
we shovel a grave in the air there you won't lie too cramped
A man lives in the house he plays with his vipers he writes
he writes when it grows dark to Deutschland your golden hair
    Marguerite
he writes it and steps out of doors and the stars are all sparkling
    he whistles his hounds to come close
he whistles his Jews into rows has them shovel a grave in the ground
he orders us play up for the dance

Black milk of daybreak we drink you at night
we drink you at morning and midday we drink you at evening
we drink and we drink
A man lives in the house he plays with his vipers he writes
he writes when it grows dark to Deutschland your golden hair
    Marguerite
your ashen hair Shulamith we shovel a grave in the air
    there you won't lie too cramped
He shouts jab this earth deeper you lot there you others sing up and
    play
he grabs for the rod in his belt he swings it his eyes they are blue
jab your spades deeper you lot there you others play on for the
    dancing

* These are seventeen verse translations of poems by Paul Celan (1920–1970), selected to represent the stylistic and chronological range of his work. The translations have not been published before, with two exceptions – but in those cases the present versions are new ones.

Black milk of daybreak we drink you at night
we drink you at midday and morning we drink you at evening
we drink and we drink
a man lives in the house your goldenes Haar Marguerite
your aschenes Haar Shulamith he plays with his vipers
He shouts play death more sweetly this Death is a master from
    Deutschland
he shouts scrape your strings darker then rise up as smoke to the sky
you'll have a grave then in the clouds there you won't lie too
    cramped

Black milk of daybreak we drink you at night
we drink you at midday Death is a master aus Deutschland
we drink you at evening and morning we drink and we drink
this Death is ein Meister aus Deutschland his eye it is blue
he shoots you with shot made of lead shoots you level and true
a man lives in the house your goldenes Haar Margarete
he looses his hounds on us grants us a grave in the air
he plays with his vipers and daydreams
    der Tod ist ein Meister aus Deutschland
dein goldenes Haar Margarete
dein aschenes Haar Sulamith   (1944–5)

ASPEN TREE, your leaves glint white into the dark.
My mother's hair never grew white.

Dandelion, so green is the Ukraine.
My fair haired mother did not come home.

Rain cloud, do you linger over the well?
My tender mother weeps for all.

Rounded star, you coil the golden loop.
My mother's heart was struck by lead.

Oaken door, who hove you off your hinge?
My gentle mother cannot come back.   (1947)

IN EGYPT

Thou shalt say to the eye of the woman stranger: Be the water.
Thou shalt seek in the stranger's eye those thou knowest are in
                                                         the water.
Thou shalt summon them from the water: Ruth! Naomi! Miriam!
Thou shalt adorn them when thou liest with the stranger.
Thou shalt adorn them with the stranger's cloud-hair.
Thou shalt say to Ruth and Miriam and Naomi:
Behold, I sleep with her!
Thou shalt most beautifully adorn this woman stranger near thee.
Thou shalt adorn her with sorrow for Ruth, for Miriam and Naomi.
Thou shalt say to the woman stranger:
Behold, I slept with them!   (1949)

COUNT UP the almonds,
count what was bitter and kept you waking,
count me among them:

I looked for your eye when you raised it and nobody watched,
I spun that secret thread
where the dew you mused on
slid down to pitchers
shielded by words that reached no one's heart.

There you first moved straight into the name that is yours,
you stepped toward yourself on steady feet,
hammers swung free in the belfry of your silence,
things overheard thrust through to you,
what's dead laid its arm around you too,
and the three of you walked through the evening.

Render me bitter.
Number me among the almonds.   (1952)

THE VINTAGERS

For Nani and Klaus Demus

They harvest the wine of their eyes,
they crush out everything wept, this also:
thus willed by the night,
the night, which they're leaning against, the wall,
thus forced by the stone,
the stone, over which their crook-stick speaks off
into the silence of answers –
their crook-stick, which just once,
just once in fall,
when the year swells to death, swollen grapes,
which just once will speak through muteness, down into
the mineshaft of musings.

They harvest, they crush out the wine,
they press down on time like their eyes,
they cellar the seepings, the weepings,
in a sun grave, which they ready
with night-toughened hands:
so that a mouth might thirst for this, later –
a latemouth, like to their own:
bent towards blindness and lamed –
a mouth, to which the draught from the depth foams upward,
meantime heaven descends into waxen seas, and
far off, as a candle-stub, glistens,
at last when the lip comes to moisten.   (1953)

TENEBRAE

Close by, Lord, we are
close and claspable.

Clasped already, Lord,
clawed into each other as though
each of our bodies were
your body, Lord.

Pray, Lord,
pray to us,
we are close.

Windskewed we went there,
went there, to bend
over pit and ditch.
Went to the water-trough, Lord.
It was blood, it was
what you shed, Lord.

It shined.

It cast your image into our eyes, Lord.
Eyes and mouth stand so open and void, Lord.
We have drunk, Lord.
The blood and the image that was in the blood, Lord.

Pray, Lord.
We are close.

(1957)

THERE WAS EARTH INSIDE THEM, and
they dug.

They dug and dug, so went
their day on past, their night. And they did not praise God,
who, so they heard, wanted all this,
who, so they heard, witnessed all this.

They dug and heard nothing more;
they did not grow wise, contrived no song,
devised for themselves no sort of language.
They dug.

There came a stillness, there came also a storm,
and all the oceans came.
I dig, you dig, and the worm digs too,
and the singing there says: They dig.

O one, O none, O no one, O you.
Where did it go, when it went nowhere at all?
O you dig and I dig, and I dig through to you,
and the ring on our finger awakens.   (1963)

THE SLUICE

Over all this
grief of yours: no
second heaven.

.   .   .   .

To a mouth
it was a thousandword for,
lost –
I lost a word
that was left me:
sister.

To
polygoddedness
I lost a word that sought me:
Kaddish.

Through
the sluice I had to go,
to salvage the word back into
and out of and across the salt flood:
Yizkor.   (1963)

PSALM

No one kneads us again out of earth and clay,
no one summons our dust.
No one.

Blessed art thou, No One.
In thy sight would
we bloom.
In thy
spite.

A nothing
we were, are now, and ever
shall be, blooming:
the nothing-, the
No-One's-Rose.

With
our pistil soul-bright,
our stamen heaven-waste,
our corona red
from the purpleword we sang
over, oh over
the thorn.   (1960)

GO RIGHT AHEAD and
bedeck me with snow:
whenever shoulder to shoulder I
strode through summer with the mulberry,
its latest leaf
shrieked.   (1965)

INTO RIVERS north of the future
I cast the net that
hesitant you weight
with stonewrit
shadows.   (1965)

IN PRAGUE

The death half,
suckled plump on our life,
very image of ash lay all around us –
we too
went on drinking, soul-crossed, two swords,
sewn onto heavenstones, wordblood-born
in the night bed,
plumper and plumper
we grew in and through each other, there was

no more name for
what drove us (one of the Thirty-
how many
was my living shadow
that climbed the madness-stairs up to you?),

a tower
the Half built itself into Whither,
a Hradčany
out of pure goldmaker's-No,

Bone-Hebrew,
ground to sperm,
ran through the hourglass
we swam through, two dreams now, tolling
against time, in the squares.   (1963)

JUST THINK

Just think:
the peat-bog soldier of Masada
makes a home for himself, most
unloseably
against
every barb in the wire.

Just think:
those with no eyes or shape
lead you free through the tumult, you
grow stronger and
stronger.

Just think: your
own hand
has held this
piece of habitable earth,
again suffered
up into life.

Just think:
that came toward me,
name-awake, hand-awake
for ever,
from the unburiable. (1967)

THERE STOOD
a sliver of fig on your lip,

there stood
Jerusalem around us,

there stood
the bright pine scent
above the Danish ship we thanked,

I stood
in you.   (1969)

THE TRUMPET PLACE
deep in the glowing
text-void,
at torch height,
in the timehole:

hear deep in
with your mouth. (1969)

THERE WILL BE something, soon now,
that brims full with you
and lifts up
toward a mouth

Out of a shardstrewn
craze
I rise up
and look upon my hand,
how it draws the one
and only
circle   (1970)

VINEGROWERS dig up
the darkhoured clock,
deep upon deep,

you glean,

the Invisible
summons the wind
into bounds,

you read,

the open ones carry
a stone behind the eye,
it reckons you,
come Shabbat.   (13 April 1970)

Comparative Criticism 15, pp. 193–213. Cambridge University Press 1993

Chaos and all that

LIU SOLA

TRANSLATED WITH AN INTRODUCTION BY RICHARD KING

INTRODUCTION*

Chaos and all that is the first fiction written in self-imposed English exile by the Chinese composer, rock-singer, playwright, actress and author Liu Sola. The novel has yet to appear in China, where Liu Sola is well known for popular and controversial stories written between 1985 and 1988.[1]

Liu Sola was born in 1955 to an official family in decline. Her uncle was Liu Zhidan, a general in the communist Red Army, who was killed in 1936. Sola's father Liu Jingfan had fought alongside his brother, and was honoured with high office following communist victory in 1949. However, when Liu Zhidan's former comrade Gao Gang was purged in 1955, the Liu family suffered by association, and Liu Jingfan was demoted to an insignificant but comfortable sinecure. When the Cultural Revolution erupted in 1966, the family's fortunes declined further when a fictionalized biography of Liu Zhidan by Sola's mother Li Jiantong was denounced by Communist Party chairman Mao Zedong. Li Jiantong was sent to work in a piggery, Liu Jingfan was jailed, and Sola, her brother and sister were left in the care of a loyal family retainer. Sola briefly joined the Red Guards but was thrown out because of her family's humiliation.

After the Cultural Revolution ended, Sola passed the 1977 entrance examination for the Central Conservatoire of Music, where she studied composition, producing a piano suite inspired by China's earliest poetry collection *The Book of Songs* and a symphony dedicated to her famous

---

* Parts of this introduction are derived from a paper entitled 'Haha in Z-town, Sola in London' presented to a conference on 'Travel Discourse and the Pacific Rim' at the University of British Columbia in 1991. A revised version of that paper will be included in a forthcoming conference volume.

uncle. After graduation, Sola turned her attention to pop and rock music, recording three albums of her own songs and writing music for film, theatre and television.

In England, Sola has continued to work as a writer,[2] singer, composer and dramatist: in 1990 she wrote and performed in the theatre-piece *Memories of the Middle Kingdom*, in which a pair of unsuspecting Englishmen are dragged through an absurdist version of the Cultural Revolution. The tumultuous events of Sola's early years are also the background to *Chaos and all that*. She began work on the novel in 1988, and completed a first draft in the spring of 1989. Since then, the author has made extensive revisions to her original, and a Chinese text has been released in Hong Kong.[3] The English translation remains unpublished.

In *Chaos*, a semi-autobiographical account of coming of age in Peking is framed by a second narrative set in a country far from home, and taking place as the inner novel is being composed. The protagonist Huang Haha is a young Chinese woman recently arrived in a Western city (called Z-town in the first draft but later changed to London). Numerous biographical clues link the author to her creation: their ages are the same (eleven years old in 1966); both are the daughters of high-ranking officials attacked early in the Cultural Revolution; and both are expelled from the Red Guards because of their families. Even their names are similarly eccentric: Liu is Sola as in do-re-mi-fa, while Huang is named Haha for the sound of laughter.

We learn little of London in *Chaos*; certainly nothing to compare with, say, Buchi Emechita's depiction of the immigrant experience in *Second Class Citizen* or Lao She's 1930s comedy of English and Chinese manners *The Two Mas*.[4] What is important for Sola and Haha alike is where they are not. The Peking of memory overwhelms the London of the moment: 'Her problem was that all the time she was living in the "present tense" she still imposed on it the feelings of the "past tense", which made the "present tense" feel drab and colourless.' Recollections are juxtaposed with recent experiences and conversations on such diverse topics as education, career, courtship, marriage, divorce, death and pet ownership. In one section, a country cousin gleefully describes a brutal murder in the Huang family's home village; in another, a group of educated women hold a literati-style poetry competition, composing contemporary variations on an operatic aria celebrating a paragon of marital fidelity.

The novel's language, like the narrative, involves the juxtaposition of disparate elements. There is Peking slang, amply laced with profanity and scatology (a searching test for the translator), polemic and bureaucratese, the classical and the operatic, rock lyrics from China and the United States. One illustration of the variations in stylistic level is provided by the title. 'Hundun' is an ancient term for that primordial chaos that preceded all things.[5] The word is found in the Taoist philosopher Zhuangzi's parable of innocence destroyed, in which the mythological emperor Hundun dies after being given the bodily apertures that make him human. Hundun is linked ('jia' meaning simply 'plus' or 'and') to the Peking slang term *li-ger-leng*. As the author explains it, *li-ger-leng* has three levels of meaning: (i) these are the syllables customarily used to vocalize instrumental accompaniment for operatic singing; thus, by extension, (ii) the term is used by the young to describe the speech of those so old and unhip as to like opera; leading to the definition uppermost in Sola's mind, (iii) bullshit.

What holds these disparate narrative and linguistic elements together is a comical sense of the absurd. Received truths are lampooned, values are scorned, dignity is deflated, myths are subverted, and momentous events are trivialized. It was precisely this irreverent nihilism which gained for Liu Sola a following among an alienated youth in mid-eighties China and the disapproval of authorities still hoping for a return to the optimistic and loyalist writing of the Maoist era. Addressing Sola's pre-*Chaos* stories and the writing of some of her modernist contemporaries, one Chinese critic condemned them as 'irrationalist'.[6] The qualities the critic singles out as particularly objectionable in Sola's case are ones of which the author herself would probably be proud: the futility of Albert Camus (in *The Myth of Sisyphus*) the frustration of Joseph Heller's *Catch-22*, the plotlessness of Samuel Beckett's *Waiting for Godot*, and the narrative voice of Liu Sola's favourite character in American fiction, Holden Caulfield. One expects that orthodox critics may be further outraged, and lovers of the absurd further delighted, when *Chaos* is finally unleashed on a Chinese audience.

The translation below consists of two early passages, both taken from the inner novel. By this time, the reader has been offered comic vignettes of Haha's childhood, presided over by the eccentric Auntie, and her schooldays, in which the children are trained for a life of normative thinking and mutual betrayal. Then comes 1966, and the initially liberating and euphoric chaos of the Cultural Revolution, when the young Haha decides that the time has come for activism...

NOTES

1 Stories are collected in *Ni bie wu xuanze* (You ain't got no choice) (Hong Kong: Xindi, 1988). An English translation of some of these stories by Martha Cheung will be published in 1993 by Renditions Paperbacks (Chinese University of Hong Kong Press).
2 Two recent stories are *Ren dui ren* (People piled on people) and *Yidun yuan zhi meng* (Dreams in the garden of Eden), both published in the Chinese expatriate journal *Jintian* (Today), 1 (1990) and 3 (1992) respectively.
3 Liu Sola, *Hundun jia li-ger-leng* (Hong Kong: Breakthrough, 1991), pp. 85–191.
4 Buchi Emechita, *Second Class Citizen* (London: Fontana, 1977). Lao She, *The Two Mas*, trans. Kenny K. Huang and David Finkelstein (Hong Kong: Joint Publishing, 1984).
5 See N. J. Girardot, *Myth and Meaning in Early Taoism: the Theme of Chaos (huntun)* (Berkeley: University of California Press, 1983).
6 Xiao Ying, *Jinnian fei-lixing zhuyi xiaoshuo de pipan* (Criticism of Recent Irrationalist Fiction), *Wenxue pinglun* (Literary Criticism) 5 (1990).

Chaos and all that

LIU SOLA

I

"I want to be a Red Guard too." I wanted the prestige that went with the fatigues, belt and armband.

"Piss off," said my brother.

"What's a little kid like you doing swearing?" Auntie scowled at him.

"D'you read Lu Xun?" Brother countered.

"Oh my God, I just happen to have read everything except Lu Xun!" Auntie stuck out her tongue at him.

"Didn't you read Lu Xun's essay on the swear-word 'His Mother's...'?" Brother was getting quite worked up.

Auntie and I glanced at each other, both at a loss. They hadn't told us about this one in elementary school.

"If a real authority like Lu Xun says that 'His Mother's...' is part of the National Heritage, how can you make revolution without it?" Brother's neck bulged defiantly.

Auntie didn't back off. She made a little officer suit in a delicate shade of dogshit brown for me to wear instead of fatigues with epaulettes like my brother and his crowd. I wasn't sure if it looked more like a Nationalist uniform or a Communist one, but when my brother saw it he was meaner to me than ever, well fuck you anyway big brother. I tried it on, struck some revolutionary poses in front of a mirror, and decided I was a natural to be a dancer.

I danced my way to the front door. Auntie called after me "Don't be late home!"

"Don't you fucking boss me around!" There! I'd finally managed to say it, though I didn't think I'd used the word to very good effect.

"Little brat! I should take a strap to you!" My mother appeared in the courtyard. She was wearing a mannish Mao-suit which made her waist look slimmer and showed off her breasts and hips. I fled.

197

The street was packed with Red Guards. As I stepped over the threshold of the big red gate and out into the alley, the first thing I saw was the old trishaw driver who used to scrape his tongue by the standpipe. Now he was an "Old Landlord" being beaten up by Red Guards, his nose bloody and his face bruised. The simple working man of a few days ago had suddenly been transformed into a member of the exploiting classes, in just the same way that he must have changed from landlord to trishaw-driver at some time in the past. Apparently the Red Guards had searched his house and discovered a strange chart on which was written the names of hexagrams used for divination. Some people said it was superstition, others that it was a counter-revolutionary slogan, still others that it was an old land-deed. Finally it was decided that his most heinous offence was scraping off all that yucky stuff in a deliberate attempt to turn the stomachs of the Revolutionary Masses, so that the Revolutionary Masses would be so grossed out by the sight of him at work on his tongue that they wouldn't be able to practice correct oral hygiene themselves. He was "unrepentant despite his great crimes" and the Red Guards made him eat dirt, so that his "landlord class" tongue would become physically the piece of stinking dogshit it was politically. They also gave his wife a 'yin-yang' haircut, one side left long and the other side shaved bald and shiny. When I saw him crawling along the ground licking up the dirt, his head smeared with blood and muck, his face so beaten up that he looked like a ghoul, my knees started knocking and I felt like throwing up. I'd rather have watched him scraping a pound of scum off his tongue.

I skirted unsteadily around a crowd of Red Guards about my brother's age, junior high school students and pretty tough-looking. But I still wanted to go along to school with them, to see if I could join the Red Guards too. What made a Red Guard? An old-style army uniform bleached by many washings, a webbing belt, a red armband bearing the words Red Guard in the scrawly writing of the Supreme Commander, basketball shoes and a military backpack. Even the Great Leader himself wore a red armband, and when he waved his hand at Tiananmen a million Red Guards wept their hearts out as if by some hormonal reaction. Later on we were all conditioned to burst into tears the moment He appeared on the screen. He was divine, and the revolutionary tides of the world rose and fell at His command. If even *He* wanted to be a Red Guard – their leader, that is – how could anyone, even a newborn, resist the urge to wear the red armband? Besides, I was all of eleven years old. I wasn't always going to be trailing along behind my brother and his friends selling their pamphlets or "Maintaining Revolutionary Traffic Discipline" by declaiming slogans on buses. Things like: "Make a Resolution to Fear No Hardships, Overcome Ten Thousand Difficulties and Win Final Victory." I'm not sure which genius came up with the idea of having elementary school kids bawling revolutionary songs and declaiming Directions from On High to complete strangers on the street and in the buses. We sang and shouted ourselves hoarse but no one ever applauded. Whoever's lousy idea it was, they made us look like a right bunch of idiots.

"Hey, what are you doing here?" Little Ding asked me in the schoolyard.

"I've come to join the Red Guards." I looked over to the classroom building. Classes had been suspended long ago, and the only person still around was the old commissionaire watering the flowers.

"Me too." She was chewing a toffee again, and her front teeth were black with decay. Back when we were in school she used to show off by sticking a piece of wire right through her teeth to prove how rotten they were.

"Do you know what you have to do to join?"

"People like us with good families just fill out a form..." She caught herself. "Your family's got no problems, eh?"

"Course not."

"Then you're fine." When she grinned, I could see the bits of toffee sticking to her black teeth.

I knew she'd be fine – her father was a general and her mother a doctor assigned to care for the state leaders in Zhongnanhai. Her teeth were living proof of her mother's fine quality of "Neglecting Personal Matters for the Common Good", just as my mother had got my own birth out of the way prematurely so she could get back to Serving the Revolution sooner.

Our school's only Red Guard organization was named 8-18 to commemorate August 18th, the day that the Great Leader had reviewed a Red Guard parade. The 8-18 group was headquartered in the classroom building in what had been the fifth grade classroom. As we peered around the door of the classroom, there was a crack like a whiplash. A boy with big round eyes was standing in wait for us, flicking a leather belt.

"What're you doing here?" He had one foot on the chair.

"We've come to sign up for the Red Guards" I said. Little Ding hadn't finished her toffee.

"You expect to be a Red Guard looking like that?" He glared at Little Ding's mouth. Suddenly I noticed that we were surrounded by Red Guards, boys and girls in faded military fatigues, all students from higher grades than we were.

I tried to draw myself up to my full height. The problem was that I couldn't stand up too straight, as I thought that this might make me look too much like a kid in primary school. To look like a grown-up you have to slouch a bit, but then to look like a revolutionary you have to thrust your chest forward and buttocks back. I sat down.

"Who told you you could sit down!" His eyes popped out even further. "Stand up!"

I stood up. Nothing for it, I'd just have to be a primary schoolkid. There I was, hands behind my back, chest out, buttocks back. He eyed me up and down: "How old are you?"

"Eleven."

"Eleven! A fucking eleven-year-old and she wants to be a Red Guard." His neck bulged. He can't have been more than twelve himself.

I just stood there, chest out, tummy in, buttocks back, pigeon-toed, submissive and attentive.

"Class origin?" he snapped.

"Revolutionary Cadre!" I held my head high.

"Revolutionary Military!" Little Ding's voice was louder still.

"Hm." The boy took his foot off the chair, and went over to the desk to pick up some forms. "Can you say fuck?"

Neither of us said a word. All that practice at home for nothing.

He cracked his belt on the chair again. "Got enough guts to beat the shit out of people?"

Silence again. He had us cowed.

"Dare you protect the Revolutionary Red Regime with your Life's Blood?" His eyes opened wider than ever.

Not a word. I was thinking of the old tongue-scraper.

"What's got into you? Lost your tongues?" He started to thrash the table with his belt.

"Just go home, okay? You're too young, you're no use for anything, having you tagging along would be a pain in the neck," said a fifth-form girl.

Piss off, I thought. That was what my brother had said to me.

Little Ding and I fled from the classroom. As we left, we heard them yelling and arguing inside.

"Where did we go wrong?" I asked her.

"Can't you see? It's 'cause we can't swear properly."

"So what do we do?"

"What's stopping us? Let's practice."

"How do we do that?"

"Come on." She pulled me over to the corner. "I'll say it first, then you go after me and we'll see who does best."

"Okay."

"Fuck" she said.

"Fuck" I responded. So far so good.

"Fuck you."

"Fuck you."

"Fuck your mother."

"Fuck your mother."

"Fuck your mother's eggs!"

"Fuck your mother's eggs!" Still no problem.

"Fuck your mother's bloody eggs!"

"Fuck your mother's bloody eggs!"

"Roll your mother's fucking eggs!"

"Roll your mother's fucking eggs!"

"You fucking bastard!"

"You fucking bastard!"

"Your mother's..." She checked herself in mid-flow.

"Your mother's WHAT?" I was waiting!

She tried again. "Your mother's..." She started to giggle.

"Go on, say it!"

"Your mother's..." she whispered the last word "cunt."

"Your mother's..." It was no good. I couldn't do it.

"Watch me, I can yell it to the whole schoolyard." Giggling uncontrollably, she put her legs slightly apart and braced herself like someone about to dive into a swimming pool.

I held my breath.

"Your mother...your mother's...mother's...mother's...mother's CUNT-T-T-T-T!" The final word exploded like a grenade, reverberating around the schoolyard. All the members of the 8-18 Red Guard Brigade stuck their heads out of the window and gaped at us.

The most essential qualification for being a Red Guard was that you had to be able to say to people's faces the kinds of thing you usually only find written on toilet walls. Mummy said that it was only people from the worst families with the thickest skins that would come out with things like that. When Brother heard her mention thick skin, he offered this story: There was once a man who died and went to Hell. When he reached the Nether World, he asked King Yama why he hadn't grown a beard. King Yama told him: you were actually supposed to have an inch of beard, but the skin on your face was two inches thick so the whiskers never managed to stick through. Brother obviously wasn't bothered by the prospect of not growing a beard, and didn't mind throwing in some choice vocabulary of his own. What's more important in life anyway, glory or facial hair? Auntie said: "You needn't think you're through the worst of it, there's more ahead of you yet." That was true enough: everyone seemed to be doing their best to make life difficult for us. After gym class there was walking, running, talking, pole-climbing, parallel bars, handstands, swimming, dancing, writing, arithmetic – all so that you could have a report card that said you weren't some kind of bonehead.

"Work Out till you drop!" hissed the boy as he pumped weights.

"Work Out!" shouted the captain of the Young Pioneers.

"Let's go outside and Work Out!" yelled the two boys as they squared off against each other.

All human life was reduced to one thing – "Working Out."

"Fuck!" Behind a locked door I Worked Out in front of the mirror, practicing facial expressions. As my mouth slowly opened, the eyes in the mirror grew rounder.

"*Fuck!*" Now the eyes in the mirror narrowed to slits.

"Fuck YOU!" I really worked at it this time, teeth clenched, lips thin, eyes staring more than ever. You had to practice to the point where everybody would be afraid of you as soon as you said the words. But when I said the "you" bit I noticed that I still had dimples on my cheeks.

Hey! I was getting to look like that actress, you know, what's her name! "So what's the big deal about being an actress?" Brother sneered. "They all look the same anyway." Auntie told Brother: "You need to have the Right Look to act. Haha's got it and you haven't. Go on Haha, give us your Militant Heroine again!" So I did the Revolutionary glowering at the Class Enemy, complete with bulging neck and popping eyes. Auntie clapped her hands and hooted with laughter.

"Cunt!" This was the worst word I knew. The face in the mirror blushed scarlet and looked all around. There was no one there, of course. Even the old ground-beetle on the wall didn't come out to listen.

He was a dirty great black beetle, clinging to the whitewashed toilet walls with hairy feet. Often he would work his way along the wall to a point above the toilet bowl, so that you might well see him if you looked up while you were sitting there. He never avoided people, but we all avoided him, and I got so I couldn't shit when he was around.

The house was too old and too big. I was the first generation of our family to be born there, but the beetles, rats, lizards, millipedes and ants could well have been there for hundreds of generations. Auntie told us that the human occupants of the house had changed with every change of dynasty: the previous master of the house had killed someone here and then run off to Taiwan with the Nationalists; the one before him had committed treason and got himself executed; the one before *him* had fallen out with President Yuan Shikai; the one before *him* had been an Imperial Eunuch at the court of the Dowager Empress Cixi; and the one before *that*...Daddy said it might just be that there had originally been a slaughterhouse on this site, or maybe a graveyard. Auntie told him he shouldn't say such terrible things. I said for sure the rats and beetles hadn't moved house. Brother said he wondered how bad the toilet had smelt back then.

"That's quite enough of that." Auntie ruled. "People haven't always been as picky about that sort of thing." "Come off it!" Brother complained; "The ancients wouldn't have wanted to wash and shit in the same room. Think about lovely Empress Yang emerging from the bath." "Goodness gracious me!" Auntie looked shocked; "What's a child like you know about Empress Yang in the bath?" "That," Mummy interrupted, "was the decadent lifestyle of the oppressor classes." "But we have worker-uncles looking after the boiler for us here, don't we?" I asked. "That's different," Mummy replied; "Daddy has made Great Contributions to the Revolution." Actually Daddy wasn't at all fond of washing, preferring to rub his back on a doorpost if he had an itch. I thought it was much more fun to go to the public baths with the other kids from the street. Mummy said: "How come every generation of this family acts like a bunch of peasants?"

"FUCK!" It took a lot of effort to get the word out, and I still wasn't sure when would be the right time to use it.

Ratatat! Someone was knocking at the bathroom door.

"You shitting gold bricks in there or what? Come and help me take care of your brother. His group made him Take the Lead in Destroying the Four Olds. He's burning his stamp collection."

But those stamps were brother's pride and joy! Even the rejects from his collection were exciting enough to be displayed in my school's showcases.

I dashed out.

They were already ablaze. All his sets of stamps, those lovely coloured triangles, squares and diamonds, illustrations of children's stories from all around the world, images of great men, pictures of flora and fauna, historic sites and great events of the past that might have been forgotten but for the stamps, all going up in flames, burnt to little ashes which floated up and then came down to rest on brother's white basketball shoes or his red armband. Tears were streaming down his face. Auntie began to sob in sympathy, and I could find no words of comfort.

"Fuck it!" I said suddenly. Not loudly, but I said it. Auntie's little eyes widened and she stopped crying. Brother didn't even notice.

II

I thought my brother hadn't heard me say fuck it when he was burning his stamp collection, but it turned out that he had. He rewarded me with a genuine khaki uniform.

I rolled up the sleeves and the trouser-legs, and it still fitted me like a tent.

I put on the widest leather belt I could find. It went twice round my waist and I still had to punch a whole lot of extra holes in it before I could do up the buckle.

Back straight, chest out.

The basketball shoes fitted like pontoons. My feet seemed to stick out miles in front of me.

My pigtails poked out ridiculously, and the cap fell over my eyes.

In the pockets were a bus-pass, some cash, a handkerchief, the Little Red Book and a notepad.

On the breast of the jacket was a Mao badge the size of an alarm clock.

When you do the "Rebel Dance" you need grand gestures: arms akimbo, legs apart, head facing right, you sway dramatically back and forth to the beat of the music.

I went out onto the streets to read the posters and copy them down.

Back home I reported what I'd seen to the grown-ups, but none of them could be bothered with me.

Everywhere I went I hurried.

Puffing and panting.

Full of confidence.

Was I good enough for it now?

Back I went to sign up as a Red Guard.

Shit.

Too late again.

A hero had emerged at our school with a vocabulary of obscenities a hundred times richer than my own. He had written a poster attacking our teacher which contained two hundred swearwords in the course of its two pages, without a single repetition! The crowds reading the poster blocked the road into the school. The members of the 8-18 Red Guard brigade examined the document through a telescope, and concluded that its author was just the kind of tough guy they wanted for the 8-18s.

I never actually found out what his name was, but anyway he was a hero and a tough guy. He stood proudly at the main entrance to the school, basking in the admiration of the crowd, with two long strings of snot dangling out of his nose.

This was too much for me. I was out of there. I honestly couldn't bring myself to admire someone who wouldn't wipe his nose. I just wanted to go home.

I had to walk past him on my way out. Out of the blue he asked me: "Wanna be a fucking Red Guard?"

I was speechless.

"I'm gonna start a brigade of my own so I can be the fucking leader, catch me brownnosing after the sodding 8-18s!" He snorted. The string of snot on the left disappeared back up his nose, the right-hand one got longer than ever.

"Yeah...okay." I eyed his nose dubiously. He wasn't someone I fancied "making revolution" with, but the thought of the red armband was awfully tempting.

"Got any money?" He asked straight out, the way the little boys in the schoolyard used to say "Got any sweets?"

Anyway I had. I usually did. I pulled out the five *yuan* I'd brought for my bus-pass.

"Hey, not bad!" He took the lot. "We can print up a whole fucking pile of armbands, buy a wad of fucking ID cards, and get a chop cut too. Fan-fucking-tastic!"

"Some of that's for my bus-pass. Let me have two bucks for the pass, you can keep the rest."

"Who gives a fucking shit about your lousy pass when there's a revolution on? Go get a couple more bucks from your folks. You can be the fucking 2IC." At last he wiped his nose off on his hand.

"Second In Command!" I forgave him the snot.

"Let's go get the chop cut, tomorrow we'll recruit ourselves a fucking brigade."

Which is how I got my brother's uniform in exchange for a dirty word, and a Red Guard armband and a 2IC capbadge in exchange for five *yuan*.

Supersnot turned out to be pretty smart. He got hold of everything we needed with the five *yuan*. He also jimmied open a door in the classroom building, and moved in tables, chairs, bookcases and even beds; then we swept the room and mopped the floor, cleaned the windows and put up a sign calling for volunteers. In a couple of days we had a good-sized brigade. We also recruited a teacher, who asked right away if he could be the Political Commissar, since he reckoned he could write better than us.

The Political Commissar was also a much finer talker then Supersnot. Supersnot's expertise was limited to swearing, but the Commissar would talk so earnestly that blobs of spittle would gather at the corners of his mouth and dribble down.

Within two days of its establishment, our brigade had its first assignment: to guard a "landlord's wife" who was to be "deported to her native village."

When it was time for us to take charge of her, we were having lunch at the Divine Harmony restaurant, so the old ladies in the Revolutionary Rebel Neighborhood Committee and someone from the police station hauled her along to the Divine Harmony to find us. They conferred at some length with Commander Supersnot and the Political Commissar. Then they made the "landlord's wife" sit coughing where we could all see her, and hurried off to join the queues to buy cabbages for winter storage.

The "landlord's wife" sat by our table coughing constantly. She took a pot out of her battered basket, lifted the lid and spat a lump of phlegm into it. That made me think it was phlegm that I was eating. I decided not to look up any more.

We started to chat.

"Did I ever tell you about when I was going to school and I gave my spare change to an old rag-picker woman?"

"Is that right?"

"It was *her*!"

"Didn't you know she was Landlord?"

"I thought I was doing a Good Deed like Lei Feng!"

"She picks up rags. That's Working Masses."

"Yeah, but she *used* to be Landlord. Like the kind that killed Liu Wenxue."

"It's rough to know who's what. What do you do if you suddenly discover your old man's Landlord?"

"That'd be scary. You'd have to kill yourself!"

"Couldn't you just Draw the Class Line and denounce them? D'you really have to kill yourself?"

"What I want to know is, how d'you do it without it hurting?"

"It hurts however you do it."

"What about sleeping pills?"

"I heard they make you want to puke, that's really gross."

"We could look that up somewhere."

"I can ask my mum. She's a doctor."

"What do you want to talk about it for? Got nothing better to do than think about dying?"

"Are we all prepared to die? / Yes, we're ready any time..." Little Ding giggled as she sang the Youth League chorus.

"This evening..." The Political Commissar pounded on the table and started to make a speech. He had eaten so much there was sweat pouring down his forehead onto his glasses. "...This evening there must be people standing guard at all times, and then tomorrow we deliver her to the railway station. During this time we must not allow the Class Enemy to sabotage our work, and we must Maintain our Vigilance in case she attempts Class Revenge or Flight!"

Supersnot snorted: "She's so fucking sick she can't run off anywhere, and who's she going to revenge on anyway?"

The Political Commissar scowled at him. "Platoon One keep watch tonight, Platoon Two deliver her in the morning!"

"Can the people on duty tonight go home and get their quilts?"

"Get quilts, and don't forget your Little Red Books." The Political Commissar pushed his glasses back up his nose.

"What good's the Little Red fucking Book?"

"If we haven't got the Little Red Book, how can we Unify Our Thinking, Maintain our Will to Fight and Repel All Attacks?" The Political Commissar became even more earnest, spraying the table with saliva and bits of undigested rice.

He might at least have done it into a jar.

"We Must...Firmly and Resolutely...Safeguard...Overcome Opposition...all of them!" The Political Commissar paused in anticipation of a round of applause. The "landlord's wife" started choking convulsively. We all watched as with a final splutter she dribbled a mouthful of phlegm into her jar and softly gasped for breath.

"You must behave properly. No talking or doing anything out of turn!" The Political Commissar admonished the "landlord's wife," and scowled at Supersnot again. Then he too went off to join the queue and buy cabbage for his mum.

The "landlord's wife" groaned and nodded her head, going on well after the Political Commissar was out of the restaurant.

"You got a nerve, saying Little Red fucking Book!"

"*I* said that? Did I say Little Red fucking Book, you asshole?" Supersnot slurped soup as he sniffed phlegm. Or it might have been snot he was drinking and soup he was dribbling.

"Y'talktoofingmuch!". Little Ding had a couple of big dumplings stuffed into her mouth. She hadn't said a thing so far, but *now* she did, showering bits of food in all directions.

"What's that?" Everyone watched as she chewed up the remains of the dumplings and gulped them down. When her black teeth finally came into view, she took a deep breath and repeated: "You talk too fucking much." Then she added: "The Political Commissar got so mad with you his face was black as a boot-brush."

"He's just a stinking fucking intellectual anyway, we can knock him down any time we want."

"To hell with that. We can't knock anyone down, more likely someone else will knock us down!" That was Wazi speaking. After she'd been laughed at for wanting to be an ambassador's wife, she'd gone through a period when her ambition was to drive one of the "honey-carts" that collected the contents of chamberpots. Then she'd decided to be a ballet dancer and wore practice pumps all the time. Now she'd finished eating, she had taken off her pumps and was packing cotton waste into the toes so it wouldn't hurt when she walked on her points. No one understood what she was talking about, so no one took her up on it.

Propaganda cars with loudhailers were driving up and down the streets. Our ears pricked up as they passed and then relaxed, pricked up and relaxed. People walked by.

The "landlord's wife" was still nodding.

Back home to pick up the quilts.

"If you jump down a well, you choke something awful before you drown." We were keeping watch that evening, still looking for the most painless suicide. The "landlord's wife" was locked away in a little room across the hall.

"You die pretty much straight after you breathe in the water."

"But if you can swim you won't breathe water."

"That's scary! You can't die but you're trapped down there."

"Shit, it's harder than you'd think!"

"Remember when we were in school and they used to tell us all those stories about Party members facing torture? I always used to think if I got caught I'd rather kill myself than be tortured."

"I never understood why they killed themselves."

"Cause they'd get it even worse if they didn't!"

"Our teacher said they sometimes did it to keep from giving away secrets."

"Better than getting beaten up."

"Still pretty scary though."

"My mum and the others went to special suicide classes when they were in the Party Underground."

"Wish we had that kind of class."

"Why?"

"We keep talking about suicide, but if you actually had to do it, and didn't know how, you'd mess up the suicide and land up even deeper in the shit."

"How about hanging?"

"That'd be pretty quick, eh?"

"Don't even think about it. The kids in our courtyard used to play at hanging each other. They'd fix the noose just under their chin, then kick the chair away and thrash their legs about as if they were really being hanged. One day one of the kids was playing and the noose slipped from under his chin to round his neck, so he nearly hanged himself for real. Lucky for him there was a radiator there. He managed to save himself by scrambling over to it."

"The trouble with dying that way is that your eyes bulge and your tongue sticks out, so you look like a spook."

"My granny says you die by choking, so it's bound to be really painful."

"I wouldn't want to look like that anyway."

"Sleeping pills might be best after all."

"But you might puke, remember, and you have to put all those pills in your mouth one after the other, don't you think that would just get scarier and scarier?"

"It's still the quietest, and you don't look ugly when it's over."

"I think a pistol would be the quickest way – one bang and it's all over."

"But what if you don't aim straight?"

"Let me tell you a fucking story." Supersnot sat on the floor bundled up in his padded coat, his back to the radiator. "There's this guy who breaks some fucking law or other and the magistrate sentences him to death. But they don't actually execute him, they tell him they're going to bleed him dry. So they get a couple of buggers to put a blindfold over his fucking eyes, then they stick him in the arm with a fucking needle to take the blood out. There's this bucket by him, and he has to listen to the sound of blood flowing through the needle into the bucket. So he just fucking listens, trickle, trickle, trickle..."

"Ugh!" We all groaned. We girls all curled up small in our quilts.

"Don't interrupt!" yelled the boys. We'd made a partition of tables in the classroom, and the boys lay on exercise-mats on one side of the partition, with us on more mats the other side.

"So he keeps on fucking listening. To start with it's running freely, trickle, trickle, trickle, then slower, drip, drip, drip, as the bucket fills up. His face gets whiter and whiter, he gets colder and fucking colder, and finally the bastard croaks. When he's good and dead, they take another fucking look at the bucket and it's full of water. No blood at all!"

"So how d'he die?"

"Scared the shit out of him. The magistrate had him blindfolded and made him listen, and the stupid asshole thought it was his own blood! There was some bugger pouring water into the bucket, and the needle didn't take any blood at all. You know what that is? Fucking psychology, that's what!"

"Yech!"

"I want to pee, but I don't dare go," Little Ding whimpered.

"Talking of peeing, want to hear the one about the public can?" Someone else was getting started.

"Please, *please*, not now," begged Little Ding.

"If you go to the can, there'll be spooks pulling funny faces at you!"

"Oh, no!" Little Ding pulled her coat over her head.

"So there's this girl going to the public can..."

I needed to go as well. I took Little Ding's hand and we both fled from the classroom as fast as we could so we wouldn't have to listen any more.

The window of the toilet was open, and cold air was pouring in. The lightbulb was flickering, and as we squatted down I was convinced there was a black hand about to make a grab for us. We talked to each other as loudly as we could manage, and we didn't stay in there a second longer than we had to. We were hitching up our trousers as we left, and fastening them as we hurried out of the bathroom.

As we went past the room where the "landlord's wife" was, it was pitch dark and silent. There was a padlock on the outside of the door.

Liu Wenxue was killed by the landlord while he was guarding the commune's...yams, was it? Or sweet potatoes? And how did the landlord *do* it?

Another blast of cold air blew after us through the toilet window. It gusted up our trousers and into our bottoms. We shivered as we ran to the classroom and bundled ourselves through the door, leaving the prospect of being murdered outside in the hall.

"...so all the girls that went to the can were killed and tossed in the cess-pit." That story was finished.

"Hear the one about the guy who ate human flesh?" Another was starting.

No one's killing us, so why do we have to talk about eating each other!

"Tell it with the lights out!" As if it wasn't bad enough already!

"No, leave them on!"

"This guy goes out for a midnight stroll, and he wakes up the next morning with his mouth full of blood!"

"I heard that one; he'd been eating a stiff in the night!"

"Do stiffs bleed?"

"Fresh ones do."

"How's it taste?"

"Kind of sour, they say."

"Look over there!" I screamed. "There's someone outside the window laughing at us! Help!" Everyone tried to hide under their quilts. Someone flicked the light off.

After staying quiet for a bit, we tried a few more tricks to scare each other, and when nothing would frighten us any more, we went to sleep.

In the morning there was real blood running into the classroom. When we opened our door, we saw that it was coming from the little room across the hall. Supersnot fumbled for the key and opened the door. The "landlord's wife" was lying in a pool of blood gasping for breath. He throat was slashed, and big bubbles of blood popped out of it each time she gasped. The room stank of blood. The boys called the janitor and told him to get her to hospital. Blood kept on oozing out of her neck. They found a razorblade on the floor. She must have slashed her own throat.

"She almost cut through her windpipe. If she'd done it, been the end of her right there!" said the janitor. "Just kept hacking away with her little slitter."

"Not that easy, putting yourself away." One of the other workers chipped in. "You got to know how it's done. Tough on the old lady, mind, look at all that blood."

So this was suicide. Obviously she hadn't been to classes, which was why she'd only half killed herself. If she'd been to the classes she'd be away from all this. Now here she was, just a short distance from death, but she had to travel that final stretch gasping through her punctured windpipe, or maybe with the cold air blowing straight in through the gash in her throat. She had to watch the blood oozing out of her or popping up in bubbles. She could smell the stench of it, and feel the pain. She was waiting, either for death, or for someone to patch her slashed windpipe and sew up her throat while there was still time. No matter if she lived or died, everyone would call it "suicide to escape justice." She would still be a "pile of dogshit unfit to be called human." When she died, there would be no place to lay her, if she lived... if she lived... if she lived...

"People who want to die hate you if you save them," said Wazi.

"How d'you know?" I asked.

"Read it in a book." She was practicing her ballet positions.

I'd caught a cold.

On the way home, I met my brother at the end of the alley. He sneered at me. "Just go home and stay there. Don't make any trouble." He was wearing polished leather shoes and a khaki trenchcoat. His face was deathly pale. Something was missing – his big shiny red satin armband, with the Leader's face and the words Red Guard embroidered on it in black.

I hugged my quilt and shivered. My nose was running. I wanted to go to bed.

"I want to be a Red Guard!" I protested.

"Piss off." Same as ever.

I shivered. My nose was running. I wanted to go to bed.

When I got to the house, I found that the great red front door that had survived all those dynasties now had a poster pasted on to it. On the poster were Mummy's and Daddy's names, each word slashed through with a heavy black cross.

Comparative Criticism 15, pp. 215–222. Cambridge University Press 1993

I Dreamed of Locusts

WANG LING

TRANSLATED WITH AN INTRODUCTION BY JONATHAN PEASE

INTRODUCTION

Wang Ling (1032–1059) was an orphan and a schoolteacher who lived in poverty and died aged twenty-seven. Although he wrote prolific, vigorous verse, under normal circumstances his lack of power and fame would have caused his works to vanish long ago. But as it happened, his entire collection was assembled by a careful grandson and preserved in manuscript until its first printing almost nine centuries later, in 1922.[1] His work has been anthologized occasionally, but did not influence other writers, and he has seldom been a subject of analysis, anecdotes, canonization or classification. Being poor and untravelled, he seems to have had fewer opportunities for broad reading and experience than his major poetic contemporaries had. His poetry retains a local, idiosyncratic flavour and may provide a fairly accurate picture of the writing and thinking of the earnest young intellectuals of the lower Yangtze region during the height of the Northern Sung.

Most famous of these young men was Wang An-shih (1021–1086), who eventually, as prime minister, would institute economic reforms so sweeping that for the past 900 years he has alternately been vilified for hastening the Sung's downfall, and lauded for anticipating the creation of a modern, sensible China. Wang An-shih's reputation as a writer and thinker has always been solidly immune from the vacillating assessments of his political career; the fact that he admired and befriended Wang Ling, and grieved bitterly at the younger man's death, has helped more than anything to preserve Wang Ling's name. Others in that loose circle of southern literati included the essayist Tseng Kung (1019–1083), the philosopher Sun Chüeh (1018–1090), the hermit Sun Mou (1019–1084), and the celebrated Ou-yang Hsiu (1007–1072), mentor to them all. These men took their Confucianism seriously, anticipated either doing constructive deeds as imperial officers or making powerful statements through the act of reclusion. They epitomize the curious combination of confidence and malaise that marked the Northern Sung.

This was an era whose prosperity and technology led the Eastern world, yet whose thinkers suffered constant doubts over the fact that Khitan and Tangut regimes held large parts of what had been China under the Han and T'ang. Yangtze-area literati lived at the geographical centre of Sung prosperity, an environment that seemed to allow no excuse for not pondering the true, deep sources of the poverty and injustice that remained, and inventing possible solutions for them. And they were far enough away from the barbarian-occupied northern regions that the loss of those areas may have seemed more humiliating and dangerous than it did to those who lived there. There seemed a frightening link between social injustice at home and military weakness at the borders. The nagging sense that the Sung was less glorious than the Han and T'ang, and the further thought that those dynasties' sordid downfalls showed even their glory to be hollow, caused Sung intellectuals to try to re-create a simple integrity from a more ancient past. The quest for lost ideas from that past often inspired literature and political thought of startling newness.

Wang Ling's work was part of that milieu. One notices in particular a focused, detailed anger at mediocrity, corruption and greed, and a commitment to communicate the concerns of ordinary people. Some of his most searing poems comment on droughts and other plagues, such as the locust attacks of 1054, the year he wrote this poem.[2] Using a loose, old-fashioned metre of five or seven characters per line, the poem is clearly meant to echo ancient odes; but despite a few archaic-sounding phrases, the idiom is overwhelmingly contemporary and the voice Wang's own. This was the voice of a man who claimed to have been a wild youth who terrorized his Yangchow neighbourhood at fourteen, but whose attitude soon changed when he had to go to work as a private tutor to support a widowed sister and her children.[3] He took on this burden at sixteen; the situation had changed little by 1054, when he was twenty-two. Though he had talent and needed an income, he refused to ingratiate himself with powerful men who could help him enter a mandarin's career. He frankly rejected certain kinds of aid even from people whom he professed to admire. His personal acquaintance with hardship, his vigour, and his willingness to take risks with his life all contribute to this poem's tone, including its abrupt ending and its sharp air of challenge ("Heaven's ear" – deaf to the farmers' distress – likely refers to the emperor and his court).

The poem is interesting for its view of the relationship between nature and humanity. While Wang does not blame humanity for destroying the environment (it was not an eleventh-century issue), he squarely blames human beings, especially those in power, for failing to design a system that could mitigate the effects of natural disasters. More interesting still is his indictment of the human race as the world's most rapacious, callous and irresponsible species. This view goes beyond Mencius' parable of the people who would rather live in a region infested with tigers than suffer under a tyrannical regime. Although Mencius had found human tyrants more evil than tigers, he believed human nature to be good. But Wang Ling, living in the Sung dynasty (often called a bridge between ancient and modern times), seems to question human nature itself, and perhaps to suspect that human nature has become cruelly unnatural.

NOTES

1 *Kuang-ling hsien-sheng wen-chi*, edited by Wu Yüeh (eleventh century) (Chia-yeh-t'ang ts'ung-shu edn., 1922). Punctuated, collated edition: *Wang Ling chi*, edited by Shen Wen-cho (Shanghai, 1980). Brief study of Wang Ling in Jonathan Pease, "Pei Sung Wang Ling ti 'Chu fu' ho 'Ts'ang-chih fu'" ("Wang Ling's Rhapsodies on the Bamboo and the Hidden Mushroom"), in *Wen-shih-che* (*Journal of Literature, History and Philosophy, Shantung University*) 200 (5.1990), pp. 76–80.
2 *Wang Ling chi*, 3/41–2.
3 He made efforts to ally himself with fellow idealists such as Wang An-shih and Ou-yang Hsiu, but they could not help him immediately because he was too poor to take the national examinations, although he trained students for them. To a prefect who did offer him a post, Wang wrote, "My aspiration lies in being poor and humble...Please do not try to bend that aspiration. Remember, also, that if I did not have this kind of aspiration, you should find no use for me on your staff to begin with" (letter to Shao Pi, *Wang Ling chi*, 18/314).

Opening pages of Wang Ling, *I Dreamed of Locusts, Kuang-ling hsien-sheng wen-chi*
(Collected Works of Mr Wang) (Shanghai, 1922).

A NOTE ON THE ILLUSTRATION

The illustration shows the first fifty-five lines of Wang Ling's *I Dreamed of Locusts* (the poem starts midway across the right-hand page and continues leftwards). It is taken from *Kuang-ling hsien-sheng wen-chi* (Collected Works of Mr Wang of Kuang-ling), which was published in 1922 as part of the *Chia-yeh-t'ang ts'ung-shu*, a collection of obscure works edited by Liu Ch'eng-kan and printed in Shanghai beginning in 1918. The entire production is traditional, using wooden or metal movable type that seems hand-cut, on mulberry paper. It is the earliest edition of Wang's complete works in print. (Courtesy of East Asia Library, University of Washington.)

I Dreamed of Locusts

WANG LING

No one knew how they came, the year
The Era's name was changed to "Harmony's Arrival."
  Flying
They blocked the morning sky, swallowed the sun,
Might have been ten thousand soot-shaking sieves;
And walked at dusk, chewed a thousand
Acres scarlet, criss-crossed a fathom deep –
Debarked whole trees, beheaded the bamboos –
Straw and rice vanished to the roots.
Each bore a hundred young, another month another
  swelling brood
So thick I thought they'd plug the world's Nine
  Bounds.
I dared not waste my pity on full grain or winsome
  grass
But feared the land might sink beneath the sea
And earth's million beings, starving but alive,
Limb and bone swirl into dragon's hash.

Farmers thronged to wail at Heaven,
Anointing with blood that putrid skin, their land:
Dusk-wrapt and dim, far, farther still
Did Heaven hear them? Could they tell?

O I sorrowed for those farmers then,
Both eyes abrim. Of those tears I made "A Rime
Of the Locust Plague." My anger stripped
A hundred writing brushes bald. One chanting
Of this Rime shrouded Sun's white and Heaven's blue;
Two singings – in the Nine Wellsprings ten thousand
  ghouls made moan!

219

Still privately hoping the Celestial Ear might hark,
At midnight I rose, three thousand times I read it out:

But in that silent crevice before high Heaven heard,
Suddenly I dreamed I met the locusts –
Dream-locusts, millions coming at me square,
Jaws stammering as if to speak, faces pained,
Antennae kissing – first they chirred and clicked
But once they broached their mighty theme, their talk
    became the human kind:

"Sir," they asked, "What has come upon you
"That you would make a Plague of us in Rime?
"We live our lives, you yours, no interference –
"Why do you hound us? Will you not explain?"
That made me angry, panicked as I was:
My tongue grew twigs and branches in its noise.
I said, "How dare you – fetid trash
"Come mock the human race the way you do!
"For all your clans and factions
"Our plans have long been set:
"This instant I was asking Heaven's Lord
"To lend us the River Triton's arms
"To pluck from this southeast soil each bamboo,
    spruce and pine,
"Bend iron rails to bundle them into gigantic brooms
"Then rake your kind into the sea, smother mountains
    over you,
"Let your million munching jaws sour into a single
    scum!
"Yet you dare borrow human speech
"And argue the merits of my verse?"
The locust crowd sighed as they stared at me,
"To think we'd had such hopes for you –
"Now we must tell our tale, and we shall be
"Grateful if you hold your noise:

"Though born with insect bodies, in our minds
"We share so much with you. You human beings
"Hail each other's names, quaff and sip,
"Host and guests together. Now, suppose

"Those guests can drain a hundred cauldrons dry:
"Their host does not reproach, he rolls with joy –
"Do these things happen or do they not? Please be
"So kind as to present your explanation."

"These things are true," I answered, "Among men
"This shall always be the cultured way.
"When company comes in answer to our welcome
"Of course we love to see them eat and drink."

"You say these things are true," replied the locusts,
"Then why should eating make us feel ashamed?
"Can we grow on our own?
"You hailed us here yourselves!
"You would be off the mark to curse us
"Even if we ate and drank too much.

"What's more, it has been told that among your race
"Noble rank is not the same as base:
"Your mild mandarin, talented and able,
"Wise and mighty, kindly, chivalrous
"Has flayed the skins off tigers and panthers
"So he can dress as Good King Yao or Shun,
"While awls and darts lie hid within his teeth,
"His belly packs a stuffing of grubs and worms,
"Fear or fortune ride on the opening of his jaws,
"Praise and blame devolve from his fingers and his
    cheeks;
"Four oceans answer his breathing out and in,
"All lands heed as he clenches and unclenches.
"He cuts and tears at naked children
"To drink their blood, to fatten his own skin;
"He gnaws and gulps through ranks of honest men
"In his viselike mouth that will not spit them out,
"While his organ-blowers kneel on couches ranged,
"Coiffed maidens idly lean in separated villas:
"Ten thousand feet of ridgebeams house one man,
"One thousand barns provision his single gullet,
"His boys inherit ministries and dukedoms,
"His waiting-maids' hairpins link above serried skirts,
"Rice and suet lie strewn about his kennels,

"Filigree festoons his stable doors...

"Next in rank among you human beings
"Come soldiers, constables, courtesans and players
"Who father sons but use their fathers ill,
"Take husbands, then neglect to live like wives;
"Vassals who do the errands of a lord they loathe,
"Commoners who make no homes but live in houses,
"Whose eyes cannot tell mulberry from wheat,
"Nor hands have felt the heft of plough or hoe
"Nor ever spent a day lifting a weapon,
"But hang their clubs and spears in rawhide sheaths:
"With open jaws they sit, awaiting food;
"Ten thousand silos pour out for their needs;
"They build no treasure through the generations
"But filigree with silk their coats and quilts,
"Up-end fine wine in lofty halls,
"Slice roasted ham, purée a hundred fish –
"Carved myrtle and cypress timbers buttressing
"The air in their storied manses –

"While poorer classes own no house, no hovel,
"Parents and offspring claim one mat;
"And the lowest go foodless,
"Wives and children murmur to each other...

"Yet though your base and noble are unequal,
"All of you, high and low, began the same.
"Humans eat other humans – this is a fact,
"But you have the heart to spare that from your wrath.
"Though they may call us 'Locust,' when we eat
"There are things we leave alone. But when your
    Kingdom
"Of Wu grew hungry, it could swallow Yueh;
"When Ch'i wants food, it bites off Lu and Ch'u.
"You can flee our attacks, while from your own
    marauding
"Even the dead cannot hide,
"Yet you would write a verse to cry against us!
"Might we suggest your speech be less pedantic and
    absurd?"

PART III

Essay reviews

Comparative Criticism 15, pp. 225–242. Cambridge University Press 1993

The achievements of Northrop Frye (1912–1991)

HAZARD ADAMS

Northrop Frye was one of those few people other than movie stars and politicians who were subjected to biographical scrutiny before their deaths. This has become something of a small fashion these days in the literary world, but I can think of no other critic so treated. Nor can I think of any other person primarily a critic who rose to be the most distinguished literary figure of his country or came to suffer a period of adulation by what his biographer John Ayr records as "Fryedolators" (though he hated discipleship).[1] He even endured a period of attack from Maoists and other radical groups who recognized his symbolic importance even though they did not grasp what his views really were. In his lifetime Frye was the recipient of thirty-six or more honorary degrees, the subject of several books, numerous articles, chapters, and symposia. This is all the more unusual because Frye seems to have thought of himself as, and in many ways was, an outsider. To read Ayr's biography is to discover to what extent this indeed was the case. Frye's family was poor. He spent most of his childhood and adolescence in Moncton, New Brunswick, far from an intellectual or cultural center. He remembered school as "penal servitude":

I saw children lined up and marched into a grimy brick building at nine in the morning, while a truant officer prowled the streets outside. The boys and girls were sent through sexually separate entrances: it was regarded as a matter of the highest importance that a boy should not go through a door marked "girls" even if no act of excretion was involved. They then filed into their classrooms, found their desks and sat down with their hands folded in front of them in what was referred to as "sitting position." At that point a rabble of screaming and strapping spinsters was turned loose on them, and the educational process began. The deterrent to idleness in this set up was being kept in, or having one's sentence lengthened.[2]

Frye first went to the Big City of Toronto as a participant in a

225

Northrop Frye, 1912–1991

speed-typing contest in which he won second place. He returned later for a second contest mainly as a way of obtaining train fare to attend Victoria College, to which he was admitted "on probation" with technically inadequate credentials. He was encouraged to take up study of the great outsider William Blake by another outsider Pelham Edgar, teacher of the then unpopular romantic poets and regarded among his more conventionally scholarly colleagues as rather a dilettante.

Among modern literary critics Frye was also unusual in that he was an ordained clergyman. For a short time he had endured the harsh trials of a parish in Saskatchewan which he traversed on a reluctant and later a rebellious horse. He attended Oxford and was unhappy there, found it slow getting on as a permanent faculty member in Toronto, and struggled for years with his first book, *Fearful Symmetry: A Study of William Blake*, which went through many versions and revisions before finally appearing in 1947 when he was thirty-four years old.[3]

Nor were Frye's books received with anything like universal approval. Frye himself remembered a friend telling him that when he thought of *Fearful Symmetry*'s pretensions to be a scholarly book he nearly split laughing. But Marshall McLuhan, to whom Frye became increasingly intellectually opposed, remarked that Frye had invented a new type of criticism that people would have to get used to. McLuhan was not referring to the theory of myth and archetype with which Frye is commonly associated; rather he was noting that the Blake book involved the "transmission of a poet through the entire personality of the writer."[4] The remark anticipated Frye's own desire to become in the classroom a transparent medium, to incarnate, say, Milton or Shakespeare there. (This idea pervades Frye's attitudes toward teaching in his many essays on education.) Others, however, had an entirely opposite reaction and were concerned that one could not tell where Blake left off and Frye began or vice versa.

Frye's was indeed a new sort of criticism. It was certainly not the impressionism that some of the critical reviews and later commentaries accused it of being. It was an attempt at an act of identification. In this case it was particularly intense because of Frye's certainty that Blake's religious background was not very different from his own. As a result, he thought that he knew how Blake read the Bible, and for him Blake was a "poet of the Bible."

Frye seems to have been early strongly affected by one of Blake's curious paradoxes: "The circumference is within, without is formed the selfish center." As a deliberate or perhaps fated outsider, Frye tried to show that those things seeming marginal to most critics – the long poems of Blake, Joyce's *Finnegans Wake*, and the Bible itself – were marginal only in the sense that they formed circumferences containing the whole realm of literary possibility, so that their apparent marginality was really at the center of literature. Frye moved the hitherto marginal

Blake to the centre of romanticism and thence to the center of literature
by pointing out his capacity for encyclopedic containment.

Fearful Symmetry was an enormously important book. I do not
hesitate to say that of books on single authors it was the most important
ever written. In North America, at least, it changed academic literary
fashion, particularly the status of Blake, but also that of romanticism. In
the decades before *Fearful Symmetry*, beginning with Hulme and Eliot
and culminating in the New Criticism, the romantic poets, with Shelley
the whipping-boy, were *out*, and the metaphysical poets, with John
Donne the touchstone, were *in*. Late great romantics like Yeats and
Stevens were grappled with quizzically. Blake was outside even to
embattled romanticist professors, who, unwillingly or unable to confront
him, called him "eighteenth-century," and to eighteenth-century
scholars, who regarded him as romantic and "mad." There was very
little to read on Blake in the library, and what was there was often downright misleading. Blake had, of course, attracted more than his share
of cranks, eccentrics, and occultists (as he was to do again in the sixties).
S. Foster Damon's pioneering study of Blake was turned down for the
doctorate. M. O. Percival, who wrote a learned, eccentric book on Blake
in the thirties, declared, according to my father, who was among his
students, that he wouldn't give a seminar on the subject of Blake because
none of the students knew enough even to begin it. Percival had delved
deeply into the esoteric thought that had so captured Ellis and Yeats
decades before and that had rendered the thought of Denis Saurat on
Blake theoretically suspect. Damon had tried to make Blake a traditional
practicing mystic. In all of these cases, Blake was desperately and
sometimes arbitrarily submitted by learned, intelligent autodidacts to
paradigms with which they had become intimately acquainted. Blake's
work cryptically recalls such paradigms, but he either had little or no
sympathy with them or used them to his own very special ends.

Frye's book was criticized for similar faults of imposition (and has
again recently been so criticized). He was later to argue that all really
valuable criticism must arise out of a conception of literary structure and
that the Bible was an encyclopedic work displaying that structure. His
book lacked "facts" and "sources" and had, to the horror of his
colleague Kathleen Coburn, a minimum of footnotes. Sometimes it
wasn't clear that Frye was doing a "close reading," when in fact he was,
but without mentioning line or even specific text. Frye presumed that
he read the Bible as Blake had and that his paradigm was in fact Blake's,
which was in turn a microcosm of a much larger literary symbolism on

which all texts in Western culture were inevitably grounded. This structure was given explicit treatment in *Anatomy of Criticism* ten years later, and Frye went on to treat of its implications for a reading of the Bible thirty-five years after that. In the meantime, there appeared by Frye numerous shorter studies of Shakespeare, Milton, romance, comedy, and Canadian culture.

Frye's career from the beginning can be described as having its source in a conversion or what one might call, following Yeats, an antithetical conversion. Frye described it as follows:

In early adolescence I suddenly realized, with an utter and complete conviction of which I have never lost an iota since, that the whole apparatus of afterlife in heaven and hell, unpardonable sins, and the like was a jot of junk...I think I decided very early, without realizing it at the time, that I was going to accept out of religion only what made sense to me as a human being. I was not going to worship a god whose actions, judged by human standards, were contemptible. That was where Blake helped me so much; he taught me that the lugubrious old stinker in the sky that I had heard so much about existed all right, but that his name was Satan, that his function was to promote tyranny in society and repression in the mind.[5]

Frye's work on Blake not only brought back romanticism, it also changed the study of it. For the young generation of scholars to which I belonged, its creative insights, its capacity to constitute a whole vision of a movement, invaded the way we conceived of romanticism, whether it was Blake, now at the center (circumference), or Coleridge or Wordsworth, who had been forced to share the space and in some cases were reread in the light of Blake. Certainly interest in them was renewed. The much-maligned Shelley was even reinstated as a result by works like Harold Bloom's *Shelley's Mythmaking*. Suddenly it was recognized that it was Blake, of all the romantic poets, who seemed to have had the most influence on the great modernist writers, and my own *Blake and Yeats: The Contrary Vision* followed. Among the romantics it had been mostly Coleridge who had influenced the New Critics and Keats who had best fulfilled their notion of what a poem should be. Now romanticism was *intellectually* popular, perhaps for the first time. Many of the prominent scholar–critics of a generation learned a Blake-centered romanticism from Frye.

But this enormous influence of Blake–Frye was not without dissent. Frye remained, I think, suspect even as he was respected among his own generation and among many who had been trained in the New Criticism. Frye's generation, in the United States at least, was strongly secular and suspicious of religiosity, especially if it had an evangelical tinge. Many saw more than a trace of that in Frye despite what was not so clearly seen as Frye's apostasy. Still, to many, Frye's work had the stench of the pulpit and the pew. In spite of the fact that some of the prominent New Critics were sons of clergymen, the New Criticism was secular and suspicious of belief. Ironically so was Frye, but in his own way. Clearly Frye's religiosity was different from that which might be attributed to someone ordained in the United Church of Canada, and he became more explicit about this as his career progressed. It is with respect to this point that his *Creation and Recreation* (1980) is particularly important, and I shall return to it. Further, Frye's readings were from the beginning regarded as abstract and reductive. In any case, his secular evangelism, his attempt at a sort of transparency of commentary, was diametrically opposite to the attitudes of that strange god of the New Criticism, T. S. Eliot. David Cayley aptly remarked on a CBC radio program on Frye that while Eliot was classical, royalist, and Anglo-Catholic, Frye was romantic, socialist, and Methodist.[6] Yet Frye was later to swallow the New Criticism (and almost all other types) in his *Anatomy*.

Fearful Symmetry dominated almost everything written about Blake for years and in many respects still does (though recently, in many cases, by opposition reflecting resistance to what is popularly termed "closure"). For one thing, Frye was his own kind of structuralist, though not semiotically oriented, before much was known about structuralism in North America. In recent years there has been a response to Frye influenced by deconstruction, though no deconstructive critic has managed a major treatment of Blake, possibly because Blake, though certainly obscure enough in one sense, is, as Paul de Man once remarked, "open to view."

Fearful Symmetry was not an easy book to read, and it still is not. Many readers have felt its profundity and its inspired and inspirational quality without being able to control its thought. It is worthwhile noting that Frye always produced what, following Kant, I shall call prolegomena to his major works, either as explanations after the fact or preliminary forays later expanded. (Many of his lectures, given without notes, were later written out at greater length.) Not merely a conventional critic of Blake but in a sense a Blake preacher, Frye desired to spread that gospel. Several clarifying essays followed *Fearful Symmetry*, and they could if collected have been another major Blake book. Among these, perhaps the most important are "Blake's Treatment of the Archetype," and "The Keys to the Gate." *Anatomy of Criticism* was followed by several clarifications, and *Creation and Recreation* is different only in that it preceded *The Great Code* and *Words With Power*. There are also essays that extend ideas in these books and many that have provided the initial inspiration for later work by others. "Yeats and the Language of Symbolism" was one of these for me, and "Poetry and Design in William Blake" clearly worked out that way for W. J. T. Mitchell when he wrote the excellent *Blake's Composite Art*.

It is perhaps a comfort to young scholars, or perhaps it is not, to learn that *Fearful Symmetry* gave Frye an enormous amount of trouble. The prolegomena mentioned above may have indicated his continued dissatisfaction with it. *Anatomy of Criticism* was slow in arriving, and yet some of us could see it coming in published snippets, fits and starts. It was greeted with a virtual silence in Canada and little immediate comment in the United States. When I reviewed it favorably in *The Journal of Aesthetics and Art Criticism*, Frye wrote a grateful letter indicating his disappointment at the response to that time. Like *Fearful Symmetry*, it was a gradual success, but when it was discovered it made Frye one of the most cited scholars in the world. The two books on the Bible also gave Frye difficulty, and at one time he even despaired of finishing them. This was, of course, at an age when most people don't have the energy to begin anything.

One reason it took some time for the *Anatomy* to sink in was that it was bigger than criticism as we had usually known it. In spite of its implications the New Criticism was a small criticism devoted to specific close readings. The traditional scholars, enemies often of the New Criticism, were wary of large sweeping claims of any kind. Here came a book that rewrote, among other things, Aristotle's *Poetics*, which alone loomed large enough, medieval typological hermeneutics, Sidney's *Apology*, and Wilde's "Decay of Lying." It swallowed Wordsworth, Arnold, and the New Criticism itself, for which in some quarters it was never forgiven. It incorporated Vico, Cassirer, and the tolerable parts of Eliot. It turned itself acrobatically inside out in the manner of Blake's Albion and Yeats's gyres. Perhaps most unforgivable to some was its relentless wit, often satirical at the expense of the institution of criticism itself and what passed as literary history:

The world of criticism was inhabited by a lot of people who were pretty confused about what they were doing, and didn't particularly mind that they were confused about it. I was impatient with all the semi-literate productions which I'd been compelled to read in the way of secondary sources. I was tired of a historical approach to literature that didn't know any literary history, that simply dealt with ordinary history plus a few dates of writers. It was a matter of just being fed up with a field that seemed to me to have no discipline in it.[7]

It was a bold stroke to begin the *Anatomy* with a call for criticism to become a "science." It evoked a wearying repeated critique that consistently overlooked the fact that Frye used the term in its older, more inclusive sense of disciplined thought producing knowledge. Also overlooked was the conclusion of the book, where Frye expanded his vision to speculate on the sameness as well as the difference of all symbolic structures, where criticism began to look something like an art. Frye had to be aware of the pathetic effort of Zola to scientize (I use this barabarism deliberately) literature itself and to Taine to give a scientific shape to literary history. These things were certainly not what he had in mind. But he was influenced by Spengler's effort to give system to history, which was the kind of effort that fascinated Frye.

After he'd gotten rid of the "muzzy, right-wing Teutonic, folkish mind" that was Spengler's, there was still Spengler's notion of culture, which seemed to be a form implying that the center was everywhere, the microcosm the macrocosm.[8] It is a repetition of Blake's fundamental idea, and it is the basis of all anatomies, including Frye's own, where the centre of literature is always the book you are now reading, expanding to meet the stars.

Frye's emphasis on *scientia* emphasized the need to get beyond confusing the object of study with the subject. To him every science must develop its own structure of thought, which is not the structure of the object though derived from it. The notion is not one that identifies criticism with a specialized science or with some technological trend. Rather it tries to imagine criticism as what Ernst Cassirer called a symbolic form or language with its own rules. An example is mathematics, which takes the world into itself and makes that world mathematical. It is an example that Frye himself employed in his conclusion. He had argued at the beginning that physicists study physics, not nature, which is its object. Cassirer had argued that we are the *animal symbolicum*, that we have surrounded ourselves with symbolic worlds and that this is the way we create. For Frye, criticism really had no choice but to be a symbolic structure. That was what we should study – criticism – which should be the shaper of literary nature. It is this line of reasoning that led Frye to the structures of myth and folk literature, the literature that appeals to children. Here Blake turns up once again, for Blake had said that children had always seemed to like and understand his poems. Frye thought of his own theory as explainable to the normally intelligent child.

But if all symbolic systems are different, they are also for Frye the same, and Frye's demand for science at the beginning turns all systems to art (in a much more inclusive sense than usually admitted to the term "fine art") at the end, re-establishing a dialectical effort in his writings that he never abandoned. Science and art meet precisely in their difference. Frank Kermode, a respectful dissenter, expressed the traditional English dislike of system in criticism when he described Frye's book as artistic and therefore useless. Here he perpetuated the basic mistake that English criticism in its misreading of the Kantian notion of internal purposiveness neurotically repeats. Oscar Wilde's "Decay of Lying" was a great favorite of Frye, in part because of the irony with which he declared art to be useless while proceeding to provide a ground for understanding its social value. The "autonomy" that Frye gives to criticism, science, and other symbolic forms has nothing to do with uselessness, isolation from life, or any other of the clichés that grew up around and in the critique of aestheticism. Autonomy is necessary for a symbolic form to constitute the world in its own way and thus connect to experience.

In some ways the *Anatomy* is a simple book, not a child's book but one that gives to literature that children have traditionally enjoyed a primary place. Late in life Frye said that he tended to think metaphorically to a greater extent than most critics. In referring to this kind of thinking, which Vico called "poetic logic," Frye seemed to be emphasizing once again the importance of sameness/difference and how metaphor sees both at once. Related to metaphorical thinking was Frye's diagrammatic tendency, the thing that convinced some that Frye was a wild occultist or at best a naive scientist. But Frye belongs to a long tradition of "mathesis" that includes, for example, Giordano Bruno. Mathesis is the tropological use of number and geometrical form. Bruno got into the worst trouble over it (and other things). Yeats was thought rather dippy because of it. Frye endured being called a positivist for employing it, a verbal attack among humanists the equivalent of which in Bruno's day was burning at the stake. Frye said in one of his many moments of Blakean verbal exuberance that if Yeats and Joyce had read *Fearful Symmetry* they would have saved a lot of time. But it worked the other way too. *Anatomy of Criticism* is not thinkable without *Finnegans Wake* and *A Vision*, where Yeats wrote of the wisdom of the tribe of Judwalis or diagrammatists.

But, *pace* Kermode, I return to the question of use. Few if any works other than Aristotle's *Poetics* have given so many critics things to pick up and run with: the revitalization of and interest in romance beyond that of children and medievalists, the indication of the importance of the anatomy, the idea of genres as not just categories in which to place works but also as belonging to works as characteristics, the definition of irony (in part historical) and its importance for understanding modernism, the revamping of Aristotle (including the notion of imitation), and the reworking of the literal from medieval fourfold hermeneutics. This last matter not only clarified why modernist poets and critics said a lot of what they said but also anticipated language-based postmodernism. Simply stated, Frye's "literal" is not the old medieval historical level but rather the pattern of words in itself, their interrelation or, as Saussure might have said, the *parole* of the poem. For Frye, the whole path from structuralism through to deconstruction extended emphasis on the literal level of the text, characteristic of the ironic phase that was modernism. But the literal was not the only level that for criticism was worth discussing. "Level" gave way to "circumference" as the appropriate metaphorical term in Frye's language, and the literal became the outer circumference, the boundary of poetic energy, as Blake would have put it. The other levels were inside it – until one came to the center of the text, the anagogic, where the text turned inside out. This is, of course, a mathetic metaphorical structure that ends characteristically in paradox. Frye's criticism constituted a literary "object," but had a degree of autonomy in that its laws were its own even as it contained the literary world, there being no way to know anything except by means of such structures of thought. Thus it is a severe misunderstanding to call them isolated from life.

But it is perhaps best to stop in our list of Frye's achievements in the *Anatomy* and try to reveal them further by considering specifically those things for which he has been most often criticized. Some of these have already been mentioned, and I shall not return to them: positivistic scientism and the isolation of literature from life.

Frye has frequently been charged with reducing everything to sameness. There is some reason for this charge against his practice, though less against his theory. As a theorist Frye sought to swallow all useful approaches. Thus the New Criticism is located in the ironic phase, etc. But in practice Frye is by his own admission an archetypal critic, and he locates himself in the region of his system that is sensitive to repeated motifs and thus to romance generally. Here conventions are emphasized, and Frye in practice is always pointing out relations, partly because he thought the politics of critical discourse needed this balance, tilted the other way since Wordsworth's *Preface*. But theoretically, for Frye, sameness is always also difference.

Frye kept insisting that there was a poetic use of language different from other uses. In this he was opposed to the structuralist semiotic fashion (Frye's structuralism enclosed the semiotic in the literal phase), which in spite of its emphasis on difference offered an entirely monolithic notion of language, which was always and everywhere the same. With respect to this notion, Frye was an ironic Vichian, not a believing Saussurean, that is to say, he was an apologist for those gigantic imaginations that Vico called brutes and relegated to a bygone age.

I think that Frye would have said that he didn't do in his practice what the New Critics did, and he did do what they couldn't, further that his theory included theirs, but theirs could not include his. I think that he would have said the same of deconstruction and certainly of the cultural criticism we see today, usually with an explicit ideological paradigm.

Frye has been criticized to the point of weariness for his treatment of value judgments. Yet what he said was perfectly sensible: that every value judgment that he had seen articulated was grounded on assumptions from some "language" other than the poetic and thus exhibited its own special parochialism. Criticism, he thought, couldn't explicitly judge without adopting one of these parochialisms, or "existential projections" when it put evaluation into words. Thus criticism betrayed its own structure when it did so and adopted the rules of some other structure. Today many would in their own terms say, complaining about Frye all the way, that criticism should not "close" the text.

Frye does not claim that there is no literary value, only that it can't be articulated outside literature. As a result, literature embodies value beyond ideology. This does not mean that specific works of literature do not express ideological positions; it does mean that their literary value is not locatable in the ideology. There is no question that a critic like Fredric Jameson will always be at odds with Frye on this point, since for Jameson nothing escapes the mark of ideology. For Frye the ideological grows out of mythic forms. Myth is for Frye something like Shelley's "burning fountain," where language has not been tamed to the antimetaphorical forms of discourse that characterize most symbolic structures. Thus poetic language, from any point of belief such as Jameson's Marxism has to seem totally unruly or an allegory of some belief or composed of a set of contradictions.

From Frye's point of view it would appear that deconstruction is the chasing of the ideological back into that place where it is burned up in the fire of the mythic paradox of difference as sameness.

There remains in much commentary on Frye either the suspicion that he tried to put some religious position over on us or that he was a Platonist with all the problems that creates for a poetics. Neither of these attitudes can be held without qualifications that blunt their strength. As a quotation I have already made indicates, in adolescence Frye abandoned religion as most of us think of it. His work on the Bible, as I shall later show, involves a critique of belief much more profound than that which flourished in debates by the New Critics in the forties. Frye's critique has always made Frye anathema to true believers, whether secular or religious. It caused him to be reviled by activists in the sixties and mistakenly adulated by the Fryedolators in Toronto, who for a time went around referring to him as "God."

As for the accusations of Platonism, I believe that Frye thought all poets at least unconsciously anti-Platonic simply by virtue of their commitment to metaphor. It is true that my Shelleyan metaphor of the burning fountain, itself drawn from neo–Platonism, implies some realm beyond nature that is the source of poetic ideas. But for Frye there are no poetic ideas. Ideas in the abstract Platonic sense belong to other forms of discourse. For Plato, ideas seem to have been harbored in the essence of mathematics, where the metaphor cannot intrude. Frye's myth is the Blakean contrary of that Platonic reality:

Most of my critics do not know that there is such a thing as a poetic language which is not only different from ideological language but puts up a constant fight against it in order to liberalize and individualize it. There is no such a thing as a pure myth.[9]

The concept of myth in Frye is not a form or a place but a potentiality that individual myths exploit and which becomes "twisted or skewed into ideological patterns of authority."[10] This is, one might say, an outgrowth of its poetical potentiality. Its scientific form is that of the hypothesis or necessary fiction required to carry on a discourse.

This view is implied in the *Anatomy*, but it becomes more explicit in *The Critical Path* (1971) and *Creation and Recreation* (1980). The most important thing about *The Critical Path* is Frye's invention of a dialectical relation between what he called the myth of concern and the myth of freedom. This opposition has always seemed to me both wonderfully provocative and a bit fuzzy. Or it was until I realized that the myth of freedom, which Frye originally identified with the rise of scientific thought, eventually trades places with the myth of concern, when modern life begins to worry about the threat of technology, as in Heidegger. In *The Critical Path*, Frye thought of literature as a liberating force that makes the range of concern in society not limited to those of one group or of propaganda.[11] It is positioned to do this because, not tied to belief, it can create provocative fictions. Clearly Frye's effort in this book was to show that charges against him of the isolation of literature from life were naive or themselves ideologically trapped. He referred to what he called an anxiety:

"But what about life, Professor Frye?" And I would say, "Well, literature has swallowed life. Life is inside literature. All you have to do to find out about life is read literature." Oh my. That bothered them.[12]

In the eighties Frye emphasized the tyranny of ideological belief, in part to put to rest the persistent idea that he was really an evangelical Christian preacher in disguise. Of course, in a sense, each of these three words was apt, but just as he redefined *mimesis* and the literal in the *Anatomy*, he redefined all three terms in his actions, while yet, I think, being true (in his fashion) to his own background. Like Blake and Joyce, he didn't throw things away but somehow used them in new ways. This was actually a strong principle with him: that you can never start from scratch but must use the past. Thus "recreation" was the important human imaginative activity. Frye's religious interests he recreated into literary interests, as Blake recreated his into literary and artistic interests. Most of us would call this a secularization, but Frye never did, insisting on a connection in which art purged religion entirely of its dogma and its worship of the old incompetent in the sky. Frye's Christianity, like Blake's humanized Jesus, either dispensed with the Father and the Holy Ghost or insisted on adding a fourth and renaming them all. Jesus was not important because he was an historical figure. That Jesus had become the Church. He was a figure of human imagination and aspiration. Frye's evangelism was the evangelism of the teacher's ideal transparency and disappearance into the mind of literature. As a preacher he tried to witness to the word of Blake ("Prayer is the study of art") or Milton or Joyce or whatever was being read. But literature was fiction, so that he witnessed not to belief but to a concern that was free. His work on the Bible stands antithetical to the practice and belief of all churches. This required the boldness learned from Blake and rare in the scholar. It was based on the idea that vision is a making which is always a recreation, not a discovery of some explicit external truth.

Frye's view is disturbing to many because it conflicts with received notions of what God's creation is. It repudiates an historical reading of the Bible and substitutes a redefined literal reading. Frye's argument is that although the Bible has a strongly doctrinal emphasis in its version of creation, it must be approached first "on the poetic level," which is beneath professed doctrine.[13] It appears, then, that the doctrine in a text may be subverted by the mythic structure. This is exactly what Blake thought happened in Milton, who was of the "devil's party" without knowing it, devils being representative of energy and angels of repression. For Frye, a whole community may be carried away into what he called "professed belief," which seems to be the parallel in religion to the articulation of value judgments in criticism:

It is characteristic of believing communities, anxious for their solidarity, to set up elaborate structures of faith that ask too much from their adherents in the way of professed belief, forgetting that any belief which cannot become an axiom of behavior is not merely useless but dangerous.[14]

This view leads to Frye's emphasis on fictions. Taking a page from Wilde, Frye claims, "It is only when [the Bible's] creation story is considered factually false that it can be of any conceivable use to us."[15]

Frye asserts a Christianity very much like Blake's, removing the necessity of professed belief and recognizing that religion is a life of acts of charity "in which our beliefs are what our acts show we believe." Frye's books on the Bible spin out many interesting strands from these ideas. If his position is not religious as most of us recognize religion, neither is it secular as we have become used to thinking about the secular. Always, as Blake was, he was suspicious of these binary negations and tended to bring in a third position "reprobate" enough to make some readers either uncomfortable or inspirited.

Northrop Frye was a Canadian. He had, of course, many opportunities to go to universities in the United States. Though tempted early in his career when his future was uncertain, he grew to understand the importance of place and his role in that place. Outside of Canada it is not easy to grasp the position of intellectual importance that he held. Probably no one in the United States, unless it was Emerson, ever held such a position. The nearest position England ever produced was perhaps that of Matthew Arnold. The writing that Frye did on

Canadian letters and culture was astonishing in both amount and range. In some ways he created (recreated) Canadian letters by a process of active commentary and tireless willingness to speak out.

Though many have found Frye's writings hard going, Frye thought a great deal about his audience. In his excellent introduction to Frye, Ian Balfour rightly remarks that the *Anatomy* "became a touchstone text for readers from the most advanced of theorists to the newest students of literature."[16] Frye would have been gratified at this observation. In *Creation and Recreation*, Frye states that in the eighties the center of critical theory had shifted to the reader. His essays on education, collected in *On Education* (1988) should be seen in connection with, no, as part and parcel of his achievement as a critic.[17] Here again Frye stands outside fashion. To progressivists he is a reactionary. To conservative traditionalists his suspicion of doctrinal teaching makes him appear a loose cannon. Indeed, he takes many potshots at the educational establishment. At the center of his view of education is language and the skill to read, but for him skill has nothing to do with "communication skills" or anything that today passes for the technique of teaching writing in the schools and universities. For Frye, cultivating a skill takes a lifetime, and it must be grounded in reading, which is part of the training of intellect, beginning at an early age with myths and folktales. It involves repetition in the form of habit and practice:

Reading is above all a continuous and not a fragmented experience. The written document is the focus of a community because the written document is there to be returned to. It is the basis of all the repetition, of all the habit and the practice which underlies the genuine educational process. This is why the art of reading with its stationary book which keeps patiently saying the same things no matter how often one opens it, is still the basis of all education and can never be replaced by the fragmented and temporary media, however large a part of our lives they may occupy... The basis of education therefore is the habit of reading.[18]

The rejection of discipline and authority produced in the sixties what Frye called the "Age of Hysteria." Doctrinal authority always produces what Blake railed against, the circulatory Frye named "the Orc cycle." For Frye, the university ought to be the place where the

whole notion of an opposition between freedom and authority disappears. One is free to reason only when one follows the inner law of reason; if an artist is painting a picture, what he wants to do and what he must do are the same thing. The authority of the logical argument, the repeatable experiment, the compelling imagination, is the final authority, and it is an authority that demands no submission.[19]

Frye hated "commitment without critical intelligence."[20] After reading his essays on education one comes to understand better why he remarked:

> One reason I have so little difficulty with students is that they know they have been cheated. They are very serious people and they rise to a challenge. There is also a strong self-preservative instinct in the human mind that makes them pick up the things they have been cheated of. If teachers are too dumb, too incompetent, to give their students some kind of coherent historical organization in their teaching, the students will pick it up themselves.[21]

It would perhaps be best to stop at this point, having recognized that Frye really dedicated his critical thought to the educational process. I think, however, that it is necessary to return explicitly to the theme of the outsider. Frye's notion of the outside is that it is absolutely necessary to there being an inside that is not a violent chaos. He continually offered the Blakean contrary to those destructive oppositions generated by *professed* beliefs. One illustration with respect to his relation to recent theory may suffice, though I am repeating it on the principle that anything worth saying once is worth saying twice. Frye would not have difference without the same. He would not have the same without difference. A young colleague firmly situated on one side of this Blakean negation said to me recently, "People don't read Frye anymore." They will, and he needs to.

NOTES

1 *Northrop Frye: A Biography* (Toronto, 1989), p. 204. I am in Ayr's debt for much information.
2 *Divisions on a Ground* (Toronto, 1982), pp. 139–140.
3 Princeton, 1947.
4 "The Ideas of Northrop Frye II," *Northrop Frye Newsletter* 3:2 (Spring 1991), p. 7.
5 To Roy Daniells, in Ayr, *Northrop Frye*, p. 45.
6 "The Ideas of Northrop Frye I," *Northrop Frye Newsletter* 3:1 (Winter 1990–1991), p. 5.
7 *Ibid.*, p. 9.
8 *Ibid.*, p. 6.
9 *Ibid.*, p. 13.
10 *Ibid.*
11 See *The Critical Path* (Bloomington, 1971), p. 166.
12 "The Ideas of Northrop Frye I," p. 12.
13 *Creation and Recreation* (Toronto, 1980), p. 29.
14 *Ibid.*, p. 72.
15 *Ibid.*, p. 29.

16 *Northrop Frye* (Boston, 1988), p. 18.
17 *On Education* (Ann Arbor, 1988).
18 *Ibid.*, p. 99.
19 *Ibid.*, p. 90.
20 *Ibid.*, p. 91.
21 *Ibid.*, p. 208.

BIBLIOGRAPHICAL NOTE

Northrop Frye has been well served by his recent commentators, but the earliest monographs on his work are not worth attention. Among these are Pauline Kogan's *Northrop Frye: The High Priest of Clerical Obscurantism* (Montreal, 1969) and the anonymous *Objective Idealism as Fascism: A Denunciation of Northrop Frye's "Literary Criticism," Ideological Forum* (Montreal, n.d.). As one can see from the titles, they represent some of the thinking that Frye saw too much of in the sixties. Ronald Bates's small study *Northrop Frye* (Toronto, 1971) in the Canadian Writers series was hampered, of course, by its brevity and its being able to deal only with the works that had appeared by 1968. It is of little value today.

The first extended study of Frye's work was Robert D. Denham's *Northrop Frye and Critical Method* (University Park, 1978). It was devoted, in its first four chapters, to an account of the *Anatomy*. Three chapters followed dealing with those numerous questions about Frye's position that had been worried endlessly in articles and reviews. Denham addressed these questions and the critics who asked them with clarity and care, which is much more than can be said of a number of the well-known critics and theorists in the articles and reviews he felt compelled to analyze.

In 1983, I tried to set Frye in a tradition of thinking about the symbolic from Vico through to Frye in *Philosophy of the Literary Symbolic* (Tallahassee, 1983). Also attempting a larger view, David Cook's thin *Northrop Frye: A Vision of a New World* (New York, 1985) brought some of the perspective of a political theorist to the subject in the New World Perspectives series. Cook's aim was to treat Frye as a social critic, but his effort demonstrated how centered on literature Frye's social thought is. Cook lacked an adequate sense of Frye's literary context, especially Blake, and as a result he got a good many things wrong. He argued, in behalf of his project, that he was presenting "a Frye whose features have been pulled and twisted" (p. 6). Cook was not the first to do this: one can mention Frank Lentricchia, Terry Eagleton,

and others; but he is the only one I know of to have made a virtue of
it.

The best short introductory work is Balfour's *Northrop Frye* (Boston,
1988) in the Twayne World Authors series. He begins well with Blake,
but in a book of only 110 pages he cannot do as much as is desirable with
that or any other subject. Balfour chooses five of Frye's books to discuss,
and his choices are good ones: *Fearful Symmetry*, *Anatomy of Criticism*,
The Secular Scripture, *The Critical Path*, and *The Great Code*. He also
offers a short chapter on Frye's treatments of Canadian literature and
culture.

John Ayr's *Northrop Frye: A Biography* (Toronto, 1988) has the
advantage of his having interviewed Frye himself and many people who
knew him. It is sometimes rather breezy, and it is superficial when it
comes to comments on Frye's books and ideas, but it nevertheless
succeeds in giving a new perspective on their creation.

A. C. Hamilton has produced the best book to date: *Northrop Frye:
Anatomy of His Criticism* (Toronto, 1990). Its shape is somewhat like
that of Denham's book, though, of course, it is able to consider Frye's
later work more fully. Hamilton is even better than Denham on those
issues that have kept surfacing around Frye's theories, and he shows that
many are red herrings or egregious misreadings. He understands the
importance of Blake to Frye better than any of the others; at least he
addresses it more effectively; but he doesn't do it at any sustained
length. He might have noted, incidentally, something from Blake that is
not incidental but central to Frye: the gnomic paradox involving the
expansion of center to circumference. Its ubiquity indicates that Blake's
and Frye's governing trope is synecdoche, on which their thought
always turns. Any book on Frye that steps seriously beyond Hamilton's
will have to deal at greater length with Frye's intellectual affinities.
Beyond Blake there are, of course, Spengler, Frazer, Freud, Jung, and
others. But it will also have to equal Hamilton's sensitive understanding
of Frye's religious views and their place in his work.

Students of Frye owe to Robert D. Denham a major debt, not only
for his pioneering book but also for *Northrop Frye: An Enumerative
Bibliography* (Metuchen, 1974) and his founding and editorship of the
Northrop Frye Newsletter, which contains, among essays on and by Frye
and an updating of the bibliography, a transcription of the CBC
program featuring Frye and his work. As the reader can see, I have
drawn with profit on that in the essay above.

Comparative Criticism 15, pp. 243–260. Copyright © 1993 Cambridge University Press

The creation of a prosaics: Morson and Emerson on Mikhail Bakhtin

MALCOLM V. JONES

I

Has Bakhtin's moment as one of the great thinkers of our time finally come (or come and gone)? Or are all these Bakhtin specialists mainly talking to each other? Conferences, papers, articles, new texts, translations, bibliographies, data-bases, newsletters, special numbers of journals, new books of various sizes and pretensions continue to proliferate. Is he simply a passing ship in the sea of theorrhea (as Merquior calls it)[1] or is his impact likely to be more thorough and long-lasting? Does he have a radically new theoretical approach to offer or does he do no more than reaccentuate what we already know?

One thing is not in doubt: Bakhtin, as a Russian thinker who lived most of his life (1895–1975) in the Soviet Union, developed independently of major trends in recent Western critical theory. Although often appropriated and seized on with apparent relish by its followers, he was largely innocent of Western structuralist, post-structuralist, feminist and Marxist theory; and the Freudian theory with which he was familiar was that of the 1920s. Moreover, although he first came on the scene in the West in the early 1970s, some of his work still remains untranslated into English and the interest of Western theorists came too late for him to assimilate their preoccupations, even if he had wanted to. From its origins in Saussure to its obsession with theoretical systems (even where the obsession is deconstructive) much Western theory likewise stands on the margins of Bakhtin's field of vision.

Not that Bakhtin denies the validity or usefulness of theoretical systems in their own spheres, always provided that their limits are

* G. S. Morson and C. Emerson, *Mikhail Bakhtin. Creation of a Prosaics* (Stanford, 1990).

243

understood and acknowledged. In effect, however, he sidelines them. What he questions is their capacity to account satisfactorily for the experience of everyday life, or to provide an adequate basis for understanding linguistic communication, interpersonal relations, moral choice, aesthetic judgement, literary texts or indeed any sphere of action or enquiry which takes the experience of everyday life as its chosen field. It may well be that what Bakhtin has to offer is a reorientation of theoretical priorities, a renewal and revitalization of categories (the subject, the author, reality, truth) which much of Western theory had prematurely thrown overboard.

Perhaps the most remarkable thing about Bakhtin is that, almost alone, he broke through the cultural immune system which has filtered out most Soviet critical theory[2] since the days of the Formalists and convinced many that he was offering a new paradigm capable of rescuing the human sciences from their current theoretical problems and setting them on a new course.

It seems a long time ago now that Todorov,[3] Clark and Holquist,[4] de Man,[5] Wayne Booth[6] and others were telling us in various ways that here was one of the most significant thinkers of our time who might, had he not been so unjustly and unfortunately served by history, have saved Western theorists years of misdirected and ultimately abortive activity. Tony Bennett (1979) offered the view that his book on Rabelais 'would seem fully to exemplify what a Marxist...approach to the study of literary texts should look like'.[7] Allon White (1984) even saw in Bakhtin a means of transcending both structuralism and deconstruction by revealing each to be a one-sided abstraction from the lived complexity of language.[8] It was not long before Bakhtin's name seemed to be cropping up everywhere, from anthropology to translation theory.

Yet somehow Bakhtin has never quite seemed to live up to these expectations, in spite of attempts to appropriate him (or congenial concepts such as 'dialogue', 'double-voiced discourse', 'polyphony', 'carnival', 'chronotope', 'heteroglossia') by exponents of a wide variety of theoretical positions. These have ranged from feminist theologians to neo-Marxists and to humanist critics unburdened by explicit theoretical preconceptions and happy to borrow ideas from him on a pragmatic basis. They have also ranged across the arts and social sciences. But even Holquist, writing in a recent book designed to demonstrate the catholicity of Bakhtin's appeal, appears to have toned down his earlier enthusiasms.[9] Bakhtin has, it would seem, been enormously stimulating and helpful, but has not after all brought about the Kuhnian revolution

through which some had hoped to find a way out of current
'crises'. Rather has he been welcomed aboard as a guest and ally by
those who have perceived his usefulness.

It is noticeable that Introductions to Critical/Literary Theory find it
difficult to situate him under such conventional chapter-headings as
Formalist, Structuralist, Post-structuralist, Marxist, Psychoanalytic and
Feminist and as a result marginalize him or spread him thinly in half a
dozen places. As often as not he is lined up as an alternative example of
something.[10] Dialogism/dialogics/prosaics does not merit a chapter of
its own. Is this the rearguard action of those with strong vested interests
in the old paradigms, willing to accept him as a major figure, but only
so long as he is kept at arm's length and does not radically threaten
them? Or are there incurable weaknesses in Bakhtin's own theory which
have led to a gradual disaffection?

There are, particularly among Slavists, those who come to critical
theory through Bakhtin rather than in the reverse direction. The indexes
of their books are, however, even less frequently graced by the names of
Barthes, Derrida, Foucault, Lacan and Althusser than books on these
figures are by the name of Bakhtin.[11] Freud and Marx may of course
figure, but for special reasons which have nothing to do with their
prominence in current Western theory. However, even among Slavists
Bakhtin's thought has given rise to diverse and mutually inconsistent
readings. It is almost impossible, for example, to reconcile the Bakhtin
of Holquist's *Dialogism* with that of Morson's and Emerson's *Creation
of a Prosaics* (both 1990).[12] The very titles of these books are indicative,
as they are no doubt meant to be, of a fundamental difference of
approach.

Even the widespread illusion that Bakhtin would be easy for
undergraduate students to handle ('the Model T theory') has been
frustrated, principally, it would seem, by his vagueness and inconsistency
in the use of his own key terms. As Morson and Emerson show, both
'dialogue' and 'monologue' have many different meanings in his
writings; Bakhtin never explicitly defines 'polyphony'; he never
clarifies the relation to each other of his three theories of the novel; the
term 'novel' does not have the same meaning in all his essays, even
within those of the same period; Bakhtin characteristically never offers
a concise definition of 'chronotope'; his conceptions of 'carnival' and
'carnivalization' vary from text to text.

It is easy to forgive all this, of course, on personal grounds. The
conditions under which Bakhtin laboured were not conducive to

consistency or even to the preservation of earlier manuscripts. It is also possible to defend it by pointing out that his method of working was a fitting reflection of the principles of dialogue and unfinalizability by which he sets so much store. Moreover, it is not necessary to have precise definitions of terms in order to conduct a sensible disussion about them. Yet how much inconsistency and vagueness can one get away with and still maintain a claim to intellectual coherence?

II

Against this background, Morson's and Emerson's excellent new book is both extremely welcome and a bit of a risk. Would such a comprehensive 500-page study, which usually confirms the arrival of a writer as a major figure, strengthen Bakhtin's reputation by repairing these apparent deficiencies or showing them to be unimportant, or would it undermine it by revealing them to be ultimately disabling? It is a risk, incidentally, which Holquist in his new book declines to take. Like other commentators on Bakhtin he is inclined to ascribe his own strong version of 'dialogism' to Bakhtin where his master appears to falter, often drafting in intellectual giants, by way of contrast or reinforcing analogy, on the principle that you know a man by the company he keeps. The Marburg neo-Kantians conveniently play this role for the early period. Others, ranging from Einstein to Saussure and George Herbert Mead, are marshalled later.

Morson and Emerson would no doubt want to claim, with justification, that their account of Bakhtin is the most balanced, exhaustive and plausible available. To which they would probably want to add that it is also the one most likely to have been agreeable to Bakhtin himself. As a comprehensive, scholarly discussion of Bakhtin's entire *œuvre*, Morson's and Emerson's is therefore a much-needed book. And it has no rival. While its approach is basically sympathetic, it recognizes problems, addresses them and takes a clear line. Moreover, the authors feel no compulsion to demonstrate either Bakhtin's compatibility with Western theory or with their own political credentials. The context in which Bakhtin is placed is predominantly that of Russian thought.

Rather as Bakhtin himself does in his book on Dostoevsky, Morson and Emerson begin by identifying a number of wrong readings of Bakhtin, thus clearly setting out their own stall. One of these is the superimposition of one of Bakhtin's works on the others. The most common example is his Rabelais book with its concepts of carnival and carnivalization. As it turns out, Morson and Emerson think that Bakhtin's views on the carnival have been greatly overrated, which makes this particular misreading doubly regrettable. The second type of misreading is hagiography, to which Russian admirers are particularly prone and which sees Bakhtin as an example of the clowns and jesters he celebrates in some of his works, and gives undue weight to the personal recollections of those who had the good fortune to know him. A third type of misreading is to use his mistrust of closed systems as an excuse for incoherent judgements of Bakhtin on the grounds that reason, clarity and precision would be inappropriate in relation to a thinker of his kind.

More seriously, they identify a structuralist approach (e.g. Todorov) which sees a writer's life and *œuvre* as surface transformations of a single deep structure – leading Todorov to disappointment when he fails to find the deep structure he is looking for. Or the embryonic approach, which sees his work as variations on an initial idea or problem (e.g. Clark and Holquist in relation to 'Art and Answerability'). Or the teleological approach, in which his *œuvre* is seen as tending towards a final outcome. Finally, and recognizably, there are those works which use his key concepts on the level of cliché.

Morson and Emerson are of the view that his intellectual development cannot be easily integrated or accurately described in terms of a single overriding concern. 'Indeed, in a career spanning some sixty years, he experienced both dramatic and gradual changes in his thinking, returned to abandoned insights that he then developed in unexpected ways, and worked through new ideas only loosely related to his earlier concerns.'[13]

In addition to rejecting what they consider to be mistaken readings and writing an account which avoids them, Morson's and Emerson's book is itself characterized by a number of distinctive lines of interpretation.

One of those, as I have hinted above, is a downgrading of the Rabelais book. A second is the rejection of the case (enthusiastically canvassed by Clark and Holquist) for Bakhtin's authorship of the books bearing the names of Medvedev and Voloshinov. In his most recent book Holquist intimates that he believes the debate will continue to be fiercely fought.[14] No doubt he is right, but it seems to me that the ultimate victors in this particular American mixed-doubles are no longer in doubt. Morson and Emerson are surely right in claiming that the onus is on those who believe Bakhtin is the author to prove their case, not the other way round. But when all is said and done, an account which holds that the Medvedev and Voloshinov books were the product of long discussions with Bakhtin, who so impressed them that they undertook attempts (characteristic of the late twenties) to reconcile Bakhtin with a Marxist outlook, is highly plausible. It does not rule out the possibility of collaboration, of their farming out different projects in which they had a common interest and on which they held similar views. It does not rule out the possibility that Mrs Bakhtin copied out some of the texts by hand. Even if her husband did not write them they were evidently works in which he took a close interest. And there is no limit to the possible explanations of why Bakhtin in his old age was unwilling to say yea or nay when asked if he was the author. Justified or unjustified guilt feelings about the fate under Stalin of friends with whom he had so closely worked, could, in the context of his own survival, easily account for reluctance of this kind.

One reason why all this is important is that it threatens Marxist claims to ownership of Bakhtin. The most conclusive argument in favour of Morson's and Emerson's reading is that they show by careful exposition and juxtaposition just how far the Medvedev and Voloshinov texts exemplify that theoretism against which Bakhtin so vigorously and in this case consistently campaigned. Even the contemporaneous Dostoevsky book can be seen as having an implicit anti-Marxist agenda.[15] Separating Bakhtin from Voloshinov and Medvedev was, say Morson and Emerson, probably the most difficult part of writing their book, because they too had tended to identify them in the past. Still, they do it very effectively, only occasionally talking of the influence of Medvedev and Voloshinov on Bakhtin almost as if he became familiar with them only in print.[16]

Morson's and Emerson's downgrading of the ideas of carnival and carnivalization also puts a question mark against the easy appropriation of Bakhtin by those deconstructionists who have assumed him to be a kindred spirit on the strength of the Rabelais text.

A third characteristic of Morson's and Emerson's approach is the relative downgrading of the early (neo-Kantian, Bergsonian) work which has recently, with the publication of much of it in English, been receiving a great deal of attention. They neither neglect it nor fail to recognize points of continuity, but they regard it rightly as immature and representative of a period before Bakhtin found his own voice. In the light of this view, their periodization of Bakhtin's work is extremely helpful.

In the first period (1919–24) ethics dominated and the 'act' was the central category of his thought, not yet the 'word'.

In the second period (1924–30) Bakhtin redefined language as uttered dialogic discourse. Speaking becomes the most privileged human act. He began his quest for the possibility of a 'non-material' aesthetics to which *Problems of Dostoevsky's Art* is an answer.

From 1930 to the early 1950s marks the third phase, in which two lines of thought issue from the Dostoevsky book. The first line (which Morson and Emerson call IIIa) is marked by the expansion of the idea of 'novelness'. Double-voiced discourse and dialogized language are generalized into desirable qualities of consciousness; heteroglossia (the diversity of speech types in a language) is seen as the necessary condition for the development of the novel, which exemplified it better than any other genre. Polyphony (the position of the author in relation to the voices in the text) was not, however, extended to all novels. Bakhtin speculated on 'novelistic consciousness' in terms of the chronotope and the way that discourse works in novels. In phase IIIb he succumbed, according to Morson and Emerson, to exaggerating and idealizing 'novelization' in a line of thought which reached its peak in the 1930s and 1940s in the ideas of carnival and carnivalization. In Morson's and Emerson's view, however, this was a cul-de-sac. Bakhtin was much more interested in the constraints and responsibilities of everyday living than in millenarian fantasies and holy foolishness.

The fourth period (from the early 1950s to 1975) was a time of recapitulation and 'professionalization' when he became an established academic and eventually a cult figure. In this period he attempted to reconcile ideas of different periods, a task for which he had previously lacked the time and perhaps the motivation.

Bakhtin's true voice, for Morson and Emerson, is the one we hear in his book(s) on Dostoevsky, in 'Discourse in the Novel' and in *Speech Genres*.[17]

III

Morson's and Emerson's own approach to Bakhtin is to identify three basic 'global' concepts in his work. These are 'prosaics', 'unfinalizability' and 'dialogue'. The order is interesting, as is the coinage of a term ('prosaics'). This term does not appear as a noun in Bakhtin himself, whereas 'poetics', the term to which they oppose it, most certainly does, notably in the title of the revised (1963) edition of the Dostoevsky book. No one is going to quarrel about the fundamental role of dialogue in Bakhtin's thought, though there is room for dispute about the merits of the term 'dialogism' favoured by Holquist and many other theorists. (Is not any kind of '-ism' alien to Bakhtin's style of thinking?) But Morson and Emerson put their coinage first. This is important because it situates Bakhtin's field of interest. Prosaics encompasses two concepts. First, it is a theory of literature which privileges prose in general and the novel in particular and rejects the claims of poetics, rhetoric or narratology to do justice to the novel. Secondly it is a form of thinking (or style of enquiry) that presumes the overriding importance of the everyday, the prosaic, in language as in experience in general. It is easy enough to see what Bakhtin does not like in the human sciences: theoretism, finalization, dogmatism, monologism, the authoritative word (to use his own terms), 'semiotic totalitarianism' (to use Morson's and Emerson's expression), procrusteanism of all kinds, all attempts to sum up the individual in terms of closed, abstract concepts or systems. 'To resist the theoretical and the abstract is the major philosophical challenge of our time.'[18] Not to reject or overturn, note, but to resist. In this he is not only cousin to existentialists, but also grandchild to the Slavophils and some kind of relative to Tolstoy and Dostoevsky, who agree on this point. His theoretical objections are embodied, characteristically, in his commentary on a literary text, Dostoevsky's 'Notes from the Underground'.[19]

This, of course, brings us to 'unfinalizability'. What Bakhtin does like are notions such as unfinalizability, indeterminacy, openness, multivoicedness (though not relativism) or, as Morson and Emerson put it, the messiness of life. Later, Morson and Emerson tell us that throughout his career Bakhtin explored the 'proper ratio' of unfinalizability to finalization,[20] of the centripetal to the centrifugal, and he sought it not principally in abstract formulations but by careful attention to actual literary texts. The 'proper ratio' must vary from case to case, but unfinalizability must be given relative priority in the value-laden discourse of everyday life.

Dialogue, double-voiced discourse, the dialogic utterance and so on were the key concepts which enabled Bakhtin to focus the search for this ratio and to place it in a context which promised positive results not only in the field of literary studies, but also in the fields of linguistics, psychology and history. Holquist rightly points out that anthropologists and social theorists have found stimulation in Bakhtin. For Bakhtin saw 'dialogue' as the key to psychological development and also to a proper understanding of human communication and human relations in general.

I am not sure that Morson and Emerson help us much by talking variously of 'a dialogic sense/conception of *truth*' (though they are only following Bakhtin), even less of dialogue being conceived as 'a model of the *world*'.[21] I do not think that Bakhtin conceived of the world as dialogic. In fact it is far from clear what such a proposition would mean. But he certainly conceived of the process by which we come to consciousness of the world as dialogic and he held that any theory of the human sciences that loses sight of this is of limited value and may become oppressive and stultifying. Indeed, Bakhtin's elaboration of the idea has important philosophical as well as psychological consequences. His concepts of 'surplus' and 'discourse with a loophole' are definitive in this respect. What I can see about you which you cannot see about yourself constitutes my surplus with regard to you (which is not the same as environment which may include things I cannot see).[22] 'Discourse with a loophole' is the term by which Bakhtin designates 'the retention for oneself of the possibility of altering the ultimate, final meaning of one's words'.[23] Stewart Sutherland has shown, by juxtaposing Bakhtin's analysis of Dostoevsky's treatment of determinism and freedom with discussions by Strawson and McKay, how this discovery opens the door to a coherent doctrine of indeterminacy.[24] A prediction made by one human being about another, even if we could assume a complete knowledge of the agent's brain state, is logically different from such a prediction about inorganic matter. In the latter case the prediction is true for all language-users and can be made public. In the former case neither of these things is true because as soon as the observer makes his prediction public he invalidates the assumption upon which it is made, namely that he possesses all the relevant information. This, says Sutherland, is precisely the point Bakhtin notes in Dostoevsky.

Moreover, as Dostoevsky shows, and Bakhtin follows him here too, 'the notion of a human action which is based on an "objective" view of human beings, and which ignores the web of social and reactive attitudes to which we belong, verges on incoherence. The point here is not one of psychological but of logical impossibility.'[25] A similar point is made by Strawson in his lecture on 'Freedom and Resentment'.[26] Bakhtin puts it this way.

In real life...we very keenly and subtly hear all these nuances in the speech of people surrounding us, and we ourselves work very skillfully with all these colors on the verbal palette. We very sensitively catch the smallest shift in intonation, the slightest interruption of voices in anything of importance to us in another person's practical, everyday discourse...All the more astonishing, then, that up to now all this has found no precise theoretical cognizance, nor the assessment it deserves![27]

What is needed is a new model which builds in openness (unfinalizability), and Bakhtin claims that this should be sought in the ordinary processes of everyday life. Apart from everyday experience itself, it is the novel which most adequately embodies these processes.

Bakhtin therefore proposes a new approach to theorizing, and the concept with which he arms himself is the 'dialogic utterance'.

Morson and Emerson rightly give due prominence to the concept of the utterance, recognizing its centrality in Bakhtin's thought. They not only cover well-trodden ground in stressing the difference between the utterance as Bakhtin sees it and the sentence as, according to Bakhtin, it is seen by linguisticians (the utterance is addressed to someone, echoes the already-spoken and anticipates the not-yet-spoken; the utterance may be of any length, from a grunt to *War and Peace*; each utterance is by its very nature unrepeatable), but also its ethical dimension. When we treat something as an utterance, we necessarily posit an author with a personality and a voice. An utterance always evaluates; every utterance has ethical import. Value systems interact: they interanimate each other as they come into dialogue.

A vital extension on the level of social interaction is the role assigned to dialogized heteroglossia and speech genres in everyday life. There is an astonishing variety of actual languages, languages within languages, languages overlapping, languages of small social groups as well as large, languages with staying power and others which quickly pass. Each academic institution, each class in school, may have its own language.[28]

No reader of Bakhtin needs to be reminded of the extraordinarily rich analyses of Dickens, Dostoevsky and others, which these insights and elaborations of them have produced in Bakhtin's mature writings. Nevertheless, Morson's and Emerson's critical analysis is much to be welcomed.

Morson and Emerson are also good on the psychological dimension, insisting rightly on its close links to the theory of the utterance. And this is important, because if Bakhtin's theory can ever claim any kind of scientific validity it will in all probability be in this field that it will have to establish its credentials. Of course, as Morson and Emerson point out, Bakhtin was not an experimental scientist (though he knew perfectly well what science is and tried at times to make theoretical distinctions between the natural and the human sciences), but his contemporary, Lev Vygotsky, undoubtedly was and there are significant parallels between their views of the development of individual consciousness which Morson and Emerson begin to draw out. Here, I think, the introduction of a figure with a reputation in an established discipline does more than simply shore up a weak area in Bakhtin.

Morson and Emerson provide persuasive analyses of Bakhtin's genre theory, of his theories of the novel, of the great books on Rabelais and Dostoevsky and of such concepts as carnival and chronotope. Like D. H. Lawrence (whose view of Dostoevsky is strikingly different from Bakhtin's) Bakhtin believed that the novel was the supreme achievement of Western thought, greater than any other genre or academic discipline. In particular it had produced, notably in Dostoevsky, the polyphonic novel, with its peculiar sensitivity to dialogue and heteroglossia. It is here that Bakhtin (and Morson and Emerson) come closest to a satisfactory account of the 'dialogic conception of truth', understood in the sense of a phenomenological account of experience. 'It is quite possible to imagine and postulate a unified truth that requires a plurality of consciousnesses, one that cannot in principle be fitted into the bounds of a single consciousness',[29] writes Bakhtin, and he finds such a conception in Dostoevsky's novels where several consciousnesses, including that of the author, meet as equals and engage in a dialogue that is in principle unfinalizable because it has several distinct and irreducible centres.

Bakhtin's weakness in both his treatment of Dostoevsky and of Rabelais is undoubtedly his blindness to the negative potential of dialogue (or carnival), the point at which it does not contribute to mutual enrichment but becomes destructive, even consciously so. Stallybrass and White have noted that carnival pillories not only stronger groups but also weaker groups (a point which evidently eluded Bakhtin).[30] Likewise, Morson and Emerson point out that Bakhtin overlooks the mystical and apocalyptic in Dostoevsky and interprets some of Dostoevsky's most pathological characters and situations as benevolent and open-ended.[31] Bakhtin also misses the destructive potential of dialogue in human relationships, in part at least, because of his unwillingness to recognize those forces which Freud assigned to the id.[32] Of course, Bakhtin understood quite well the role of what he calls 'authoritative discourse', which ranges from Holy Writ to fashionable cult, any word which cannot be questioned and demands obedience.[33] It is a partner to the inwardly persuasive word which is the key to mature development through dialogue. Others have protested that, in spite of any misconceptions which may have arisen from references to revolution in Holquist's introduction to the translation of the Rabelais book,[34] Bakhtin regrettably stops short of discussion of carnival's potential (if any) for development in the direction of political revolution. What all this points to is a conception of dialogue which is rather too comfortable, even utopian.

With respect to the book on Dostoevsky, Morson and Emerson point to a bias which has undoubtedly caused legitimate dissatisfaction with the Bakhtinian reading of Dostoevsky in spite of its undoubted power, and this is an important corrective. It is not so clear that they are right in relegating the Rabelais book to a place outside the canon, almost wishing, it seems to me, that it had borne the name of another author so that they could claim it was not by Bakhtin at all. They are no doubt justified in regretting its uncharacteristic mix of the turgidity of the post-graduate thesis and the effervescence of a mind liberated by new and exciting discoveries. But there is more to it than that. Morson and Emerson claim that in it Bakhtin celebrates pure unfinalizability as a utopian ideal.[35] I am less convinced by this argument.

There is a good deal that is unclear in this book as elsewhere in Bakhtin on matters of vital importance. The combination of this lack of clarity with a style whose sense of discovery (what Belknap calls novosimilitude)[36] is infectious no doubt explains the variety of current readings. In fact, however, Bakhtin does make it fairly clear that carnival is ambivalent in respect of unfinalizability. To a significant degree carnival is bound to the principle of *temporary reversal* of hierarchical structures rather than their abolition.[37] To this extent it depends on the persistence of inflexible structures for its very occurrence. Moreover, and this is the point to which Morson and Emerson seem not to give due attention, carnival is *holiday*, not a prescription for a real-world utopia. It is possible to see this book as a carnival holiday in Bakhtin's own *œuvre* in which the impulse to kick over the traces is given freer rein than elsewhere, both in terms of subject-matter and presentation. Yet in both spheres centripetal forces remain an essential part of the equation.

That is not to dispute their central point that carnival is one of Bakhtin's weaker theoretical formulations. It is intensely irritating to those who know better to encounter the still wide-spread view that Bakhtin is a man of one idea: carnivalization. It is even more annoying to discover that his worth as a thinker is being measured in terms of a concept which is marginal to his thought and one of his weaker formulations. Yet here again we discover a typically Bakhtinian paradox. Weak or not (theoretically) the concept has (practically) proved an extremely productive heuristic principle which has fired the imagination of many specialists in the humanities who might otherwise have written much less interestingly.

IV

In pointing out that Bakhtin failed to take cognizance of some of the philosophical and still more the political implications of carnival, Morson and Emerson echo a discussion which was given momentum by an article by Ken Hirschkop in 1986 and is reflected in several of the contributions to essays edited by Hirschkop and Shepherd under the title *Bakhtin and Cultural Theory* (1989).[38]

This recent collection contains some admirable contributions, most of them clearly set out, on a variety of topics. Several of the essays attempt to draw Bakhtin into dialogue with leading figures, movements and issues in Western critical theory. The same year saw Morson's and Emerson's *Rethinking Bakhtin*,[39] while 1990 saw a special number of *Social Discourses* edited by Barsky and Holquist under the title *Bakhtin and Otherness*.[40] With greater or lesser success various contributors to these collections have attempted to create links and ask fundamental questions about Bakhtin's theoretical viability. Many juxtapose and discuss the relative positions on key issues of Bakhtin and other leading theorists.[41] Some of the most interesting, in my view, are those which take some of Bakhtin's perceived weaknesses as their starting-points and proceed to show how these can be repaired and his position strengthened.[42] The sub-title of *Rethinking Bakhtin*, *Extensions and Challenges* seems to strike exactly the right note. It acknowledges the irresistible power of the master to provoke and stimulate important new lines of thought while at the same time recognizing their unfinalizedness. If Bakhtin is indeed one of the major thinkers of the twentieth century it may not be because of any implicit claim to have solved our intellectual problems. It may be because he has done sufficient to persuade us of the value of setting off in new directions, because he has reformulated questions of genuine interest to the arts and the human sciences. And this may not be such a mean achievement in a world where theories characterized by exceptionally strong emotional, intellectual and institutional investments hold sway.

It is also worthy of note that most of these responses to Bakhtin are remarkably free of that addiction to problem-solving by concept-juggling which mars certain types of fashionable critical theory today. The most memorable passages in Bakhtin's own work are probably his close readings of literary texts, in which he seems to develop his theory as he goes and the most lasting of these are his readings of Dostoevsky. Even where his concepts themselves seem unclear (e.g. polyphony) he gives so many examples that the reader cannot fail to be impressed by his case. With Bakhtin we are never left feeling, like Levin in Tolstoy's *Anna Karenina*,[43] that the theory sounds plausible enough until you try to apply it to 'real life'. If anything, Bakhtin seems to have the opposite effect. It works incredibly well in practice. It is when you look at the theory that you begin to wonder.

Morson and Emerson perform an impressive feat: they never conceal inconsistencies, confusion and vagueness, but they nevertheless succeed in demonstrating that some of these do not matter very much, that others can be clarified and reconciled. In other cases they demonstrate that a careful reading of Bakhtin shows important subtleties which Bakhtin himself, by avoiding definitions, blurs. Elsewhere (as in the false equation between heteroglossia and polyphony) they show that the confusion lies with the reader. Moreover, the result is a very plausible attempt to establish the 'non-monologic unity' of Bakhtin's thought, by analogy, they claim, to the notion of 'aggregate' as used by general systems theorists rather than system in the normally accepted sense.[44] They could have claimed, though if they do I did not notice it, that a lack of precise definition and variability of usage is an invitation to the reader to establish meaning in relation to context, an invitation entirely consistent with Bakhtin's view of the utterance and an additional deterrent to any attempt to turn Bakhtin into an abstract system. Graham Pechey refers to the 'circulation' or *migration* of concepts in Bakhtin and of their emigration into other texts.[45] In itself this term does no more than give an otherwise disquieting phenomenon a reassuring label, but it does prompt reflection on the compatibility of Bakhtin's method with his theory. There will undoubtedly be readers who will quarrel with some of Morson's and Emerson's conclusions, regard some criticisms as too strong, others as too weak. And there will be some who are put off Bakhtin by an opening 100 pages of an introductory kind which constantly refer the reader forward and appear to dodge the awkward theoretical questions. But this is an attempt, within the limitations of an analytic technique which suggests an application of Bakhtin's concept of *vzhivanie*, to present Bakhtin with all his imperfections. There is no doubt that our understanding of him is much enhanced.

Bakhtin makes no attempt to finalize his own thought. It would seem to follow, theoretically as well as pragmatically, that different readings and responses are to be both expected and welcomed. In that case one would expect that any attempt to elucidate such a body of thought would provoke alternative readings. That this is so is an empirically verifiable fact. However, Morson and Emerson have gone a long way towards demonstrating that while this is a natural consequence, we are not condemned to a full-blown relativism. There are more or less implausible readings of Bakhtin; there are indefensible ones too; there are areas of genuine uncertainty; there are strong and weak aspects to his thought. Morson and Emerson have staked a good claim to have discovered that balance between finalization and unfinalizability of which Bakhtin would have approved. And they have achieved this by and large by means of well-established methods of scholarship rather than by reconstructing him in their own or someone else's image. It is the scholarly intonation of the book which must be one of its chief attractions.

The book, interestingly, has no conclusion, no overall evaluation. It ends almost with a whimper at the end of a critique of Bakhtin at his most explosive, on carnival. Just a single sentence, like a vague afterthought hedged about with reservations, returns us to the book's opening gambit,

Bakhtin's global concepts do not completely cohere, to be sure, but in the larger perspective of his life they appear to have subjected each other to unexpected critiques and form-shaping insights.[46]

Is this a sign of exhaustion, or a signal to the reader that it does not matter where one ends? The important thing, according to this view, is that readers continue the work for themselves.

As undoubtedly they will. Bakhtin claims that great works often echo previous discoveries not through the conscious knowledge or intention of their authors, but because the author has absorbed the unspoken conventions of the 'genre' to which they belong. Dostoevsky did not even have to have heard of the Mennipaean satire to absorb its conventions. Similarly they may unconsciously anticipate future readings. It is most certainly the fate of Bakhtin, whatever criticism may be levelled at him, to have intuitively anticipated future developments in Western thought, not in the sense of coincidence (neither his biography nor his 'conception of dialogic truth' would lead one to expect this) but in such a way as to awaken echoes in later writers who may or may not even have heard of him.

I look forward, for example, to some future discussion of Bakhtin and Robert Pirsig's Metaphysics of Quality, perhaps by Michael Holquist who perceives in Bakhtin the possibility of 'an epistemology that would be recognizably valid in a physics laboratory in MIT and which would yet have a place in the Yale University library on the 8th floor of Bingham Tower...'[47]

There is one other extensive area of enquiry which is worth mentioning in relation to Bakhtin's fortunes. This is his impact on theory in his own country. While he became a cult figure during his own lifetime, he died too early for the official ideology to have anything but an inhibiting effect on his full assimilation. However, because few critical theorists in the West know Russian, and because the post-war development of theory in the Soviet Union lies outside the sphere of interest of most of them, there is a significant field here waiting to be opened up, especially now that the Soviet Union has ceased to exist and the official ideology has ceased to have its inhibiting effect. In this respect it is pleasant to close by noting the appearance in Russia of a new journal devoted to Bakhtin and a continuing lively debate about his heritage.[48] It is incidentally, unlikely that Russian Bakhtinians will wring their hands about his alleged failure adequately to theorize political revolution. The signs are that they are more likely to welcome his contribution to a theoretical understanding of those forms of parliamentary democracy for which history seems to have left them so ill equipped but on which, for the time being, they have staked their future.

NOTES

1 J. G. Merquior, *From Prague to Paris* (London, 1986), p. 253.
2 Another partial exception is, of course, Uspensky; and an even more partial exception is Lotman, who, although extensively translated into English, seems to have attracted little interest outside Slavist circles.
3 T. Todorov, *Mikhail Bakhtin. The Dialogical Principle* (Manchester University Press, 1984).
4 K. Clark and M. Holquist, *Mikhail Bakhtin* (Cambridge, Mass., and London, 1984).

5 P. de Man, 'Dialogue and Dialogism', *Poetics Today*, 4, 1, (1983) 99–107, reprinted in G. S. Morson and C. Emerson, eds., *Rethinking Bakhtin, Extensions and Challenges* (Evanston, Ill., 1989), pp. 105–14.

6 W. Booth, Introduction to *Problems of Dostoevsky's Poetics* (Minnesota and Manchester, 1984), pp. xiii–xxvii.

7 T. Bennett, *Formalism and Marxism* (London, 1979), p. 95.

8 A. White, 'Bakhtin, Sociolinguistics and Deconstruction', in F. Gloversmith, ed., *The Theory of Reading* (Sussex and New Jersey, 1984), p. 141.

9 M. Holquist, 'Dialogue: Conversation between Robert F. Barsky and Michael Holquist, Saturday–Sunday August 18–19, 1990', in R. F. Barsky and M. Holquist, *Bakhtin and Otherness, Discours social/Social Discourse*, 3, 1 and 2 (Spring–Summer 1990), 1–22, p. 5.

10 An exception is D. Tallack, ed., *Literary Theory at Work*, London 1987.

11 I note that the index to G. S. Morson and C. Emerson, *Mikhail Bakhtin. Creation of a Prosaics* (Stanford, 1990) records none of these names. M. Holquist, *Dialogism. Bakhtin and His World* (London and New York, 1990) has one mention each of Derrida and Lacan. This reticence is not true, of course, of books which make a special point of making links, though even Morson and Emerson, *Rethinking Bakhtin*, has only one reference each to Barthes, Derrida and Foucault. Holquist and Barsky, *Bakhtin and Otherness*, has no index. However, K. Hirschkop and D. Shepherd, eds., *Bakhtin and Cultural Theory* (Manchester and New York, 1989) has 20 references to Barthes, some of them covering several pages, 14 to Derrida, 3 to Foucault, 5 to Lacan and 1 to Althusser.

12 See note 11.

13 Morson and Emerson, *Prosaics*, p. 1.

14 Holquist, *Dialogism*. The point is not explicitly made, but he holds to his view that 'Bakhtin is, in his own charged sense of the word, primarily responsible for the texts in question' (p. 8). And his book is 'synoptic in style', treating all of Bakhtin's texts including the disputed texts of Kanaev, Medvedev and Voloshinov as 'a single body of work' (p. 11).

15 Morson and Emerson, *Prosaics*, p. 267.

16 *Ibid.*, p. 271.

17 *Ibid.*, pp. 123ff.

18 *Ibid.*, p. 69.

19 See the discussion by Stewart R. Sutherland in M. V. Jones and G. M. Terry, *New Essays on Dostoyevsky* (Cambridge University Press 1983), pp. 169–85.

20 Morson and Emerson, *Prosaics*, p. 91.

21 *Ibid.*, p. 49.

22 *Ibid.*, p. 185.

23 *Ibid.*, p. 160.

24 Sutherland in Jones and Terry, eds., *New Essays*.

25 *Ibid.*, p. 183.

26 P. F. Strawson, *Freedom and Resentment and Other Essays* (London, 1974), p. 5.

27 M. Bakhtin, *Problems of Dostoevsky's Poetics* (Manchester, 1984), p. 201. See Morson and Emerson, *Prosaics*, p. 34.

28 Morson and Emerson, *Prosaics*, p. 142.

29 Bakhtin, *Dostoevsky's Poetics*, p. 81; Morson and Emerson, *Prosaics*, p. 236.

30 P. Stallybrass and A. White, *The Politics and Poetics of Transgression* (London, 1986), p. 19.

31 Morson and Emerson, *Prosaics*, p. 198.

32 *Ibid.*, p. 198. D. K. Danow's recent book, *The Thought of Mikhail Bakhtin* (London, 1991), ends with a plea along the same lines. It is also the theme of an article by Aaron Fogel, 'Coerced Speech and the Oedipus Dialogue Complex', in Morson and Emerson, eds., *Rethinking Bakhtin*, pp. 173–96.

33 M. Bakhtin, 'Discourse in the Novel', in M. Holquist, ed., *The Dialogic Imagination* (Austin, 1981), pp. 259–422, pp. 342ff.

34 M. Holquist, Prologue to M. Bakhtin, *Rabelais and His World* (Bloomington, 1984), pp. xiii–xxiii, p. xviii.

35 Morson and Emerson, *Prosaics*, p. 89ff.

36 R. Belknap, *The Genesis of 'The Brothers Karamazov'* (Evanston, Ill., 1990), p. 10.

37 Bakhtin, *Dostoevsky's Poetics*, pp. 409ff.

38 See note 11.

39 See note 5.

40 See note 9.

41 For example, Piaget, Freud, Nietzsche, Schopenhauer, Sartre, Barthes, Derrida, Kristeva, Irigaray, Cixous, Jauss, Benjamin, Lukács.

42 Some of the essays in Morson and Emerson, *Rethinking Bakhtin*, fall into this category. It is also the underlying ambition of my own *Dostoevsky after Bakhtin* (Cambridge University Press, 1990).

43 L. N. Tolstoy, *Anna Karenina*, Part 8, chapter 9.

44 Morson and Emerson, *Prosaics*, p. 45.

45 G. Pechey, 'On the Borders of Bakhtin: Dialogisation, Decolonisation', in Hirschkop and Shepherd, *Bakhtin and Cultural Theory*, pp. 39–67, pp. 40–1.

46 Morson and Emerson, *Prosaics*, p. 470.

47 Barsky and Holquist, *Bakhtin and Otherness*, p. 5. I have in mind the philosophical positions expressed in Robert Pirsig's novel *Lila, An Inquiry into Morals* (London and New York), 1991.

48 *Bakhtinskiy sbornik*, 1 (Moscow, 1990). On Russian responses to Bakhtin see C. Emerson, Review Essay in Barsky and Holquist, *Bakhtin and Otherness*, pp. 351–6.

Comparative Criticism 15, pp. 261–269. Cambridge University Press 1993

Research or criticism? A note on the canon debate

DOUWE FOKKEMA

With very few exceptions the present canon debate is a critical debate: opinions are set against opinions, evaluative positions against other evaluative positions. The polemics may touch on educational curricula, policies of publishing houses, aesthetics, ethics, history, philosophy, economics and politics, in fact any subject. Moreover, no one is excluded from the debate, which in recent years has attracted the attention of journalists and government circles. Touching on almost everything, the debate has been confused and inconclusive, notably in the United States where internal developments in literary studies as well as external pressures called for radical changes. So far, research has played a minor role in the debate. The appearance of Gorak's book as well as *The Hospitable Canon*, which also contains several contributions reporting on research, is therefore particularly welcome.

Gorak observes that 'what has been lost in the flurry of contemporary argument is a sense of the historical dimensions of that debate' (p. 6). Therefore he offers a history of canon formation since Greek antiquity, discussing early Christian canons, Renaissance and Enlightenment canons, up until twentieth-century attempts at revising what is believed to be the traditional canon. Finally, Gorak devotes separate chapters to three critics, Northrop Frye, Frank Kermode and Edward Said, and one art historian, Ernst Gombrich. Gorak concludes with a chapter in which he comments on the present canon debate, both in North America and the United Kingdom. Although this last chapter, too, is analytic and informative, Gorak's own commonsensical position, which is close to that of Kermode's, becomes clear as well.

---

* Review of Jan Gorak, *The Making of the Modern Canon: Genesis and Crisis of a Literary Idea* (London & Atlantic Highlands, NJ: Athlone, 1991), and Virgil Nemoianu and Robert Royal, eds. *The Hospitable Canon: Essays on Literary Play, Scholarly Choice, and Popular Pressures* (Philadelphia/Amsterdam: John Benjamins, 1991).

In *The Hospitable Canon* it is the contributions of Glen M. Johnson and Yves Chevrel which focus on manifestations of canonization such as changes in successive editions of anthologies, including the *Norton Anthology of American Literature* (Johnson), and titles of examination topics in France (Chrevel). Other contributions are useful and informative as well, like Nemoianu's, which distinguishes between curriculum and canon. Charles Altieri, however, seems to have said everything he wanted to say in his seminal article 'An Idea and Ideal of a Literary Canon,' reprinted in Robert von Hallberg, ed., *Canons* (Chicago: University of Chicago Press, 1984). I am giving the full bibliographical details as a counterpoint to the fact that Altieri does not do this in his essay opening *The Hospitable Canon*. His polemics against Barbara Herrnstein Smith, Annette Kolodny, and others, without ever mentioning where we can find what they have written, is at odds with scholarly practice.

As mentioned, much of Gorak's book and part of *The Hospitable Canon* are based on research. Although I will incidentally report on the evaluative positions which are expressed as well in these publications, my major purpose is to indicate what kind of research could provide the canon debate with a firmer basis. My assumption is that there are unmistakable results in research about literary communication and that participants (including opponents) in the canon debate cannot ignore these. I have in mind research concerning the question of how readers distinguish between literary and non-literary texts and how we can know whether an author or a text belongs to a particular canon. Finally, I will discuss the relation between parliamentary democracy and cultural democracy, and its consequences for canon formation.

In the last two or more decades, in particular following a quasi-experiment by Stanley Fish (1980), the idea has come up that *any* text can be interpreted as being a literary text and that there is no way of deciding on the basis of textual properties alone whether a text should be read as a literary text or not. I believe that this idea, as phrased here, is correct, but it calls for some further discussion.

The words '*can* be interpreted' point to a possibility which any thoughtful person acquainted with the genre of *poèmes trouvés* would like to keep open.

The phrasing 'on the basis of textual properties *alone*' introduces a limitation which serious researchers should reject as unnecessarily restrictive. If textual properties alone are not enough to decide whether a text should be interpreted as literature or not, we should examine other factors: expectations and knowledge of the readers of that text, cultural context, etcetera.

Finally, the words '*should* be read' point to the implied but mistaken supposition that one may think in terms of obligatory ways of reading. In principle, however, interpretation is free. Indeed, the question of whether a text should be considered a literary text cannot be answered in the abstract. On the other hand, it is quite possible to establish whether a particular text *has been* read by particular readers as a literary text.

The idea that there are interpretive communities (Fish 1980) which decide on the literariness of texts is not very disquieting. These interpretive communities nowadays overlap each other in one way or another; even international or religious differences rarely divide all aspects of life. Therefore, interpretive communities do not necessarily correspond to social communities. The supposition, criticized by Christopher Clausen, that 'literary works have value and meaning only for the period, culture, class, sex, or ethnic group that produces them' (*The Hospitable Canon*, p. 200), can easily be refuted. This position was not maintained even by Marx or Engels, only by some short-lived radical groups in the history of Marxist ideology.

Indeed, there is no way of deciding in the abstract whether a text is to be considered a literary text or not. This means that we must try to be a little more concrete. As researchers we are able to find out which texts in various cultures have been interpreted by readers as literary texts, that is, texts with a metaphorical significance which do not refer to one particular social-historical reality only. Other conceptions of the notion 'literary' may supplement my brief explanation, but it seems crucial to me that literary texts also function outside the historical context in which they were shaped – the *Iliad* still being read and appreciated long after the social conditions under which it was written had disappeared, as Marx had to admit (Marx and Engels, 1967: I, 125), and as was elaborated by Clausen (*The Hospitable Canon*, pp. 201–3).

In other words, granted that all texts have been written in view of a particular readership and in a particular context, certain texts were amenable to being interpreted in other contexts as well, sometimes contexts at great geographical, historical and cultural distance. If we accept this criterion for distinguishing literary texts, it is possible to establish through historical research which those texts are. (In fact, the criterion mentioned does not distinguish clearly between literary, religious and philosophical writings, but that is a less relevant problem within the framework of this paper.)

Those who are opposed to distinguishing between literary and non-literary ways of reading perhaps do not deny that this metaphorical way of reading has been practised, but they may wish to point out that it is merely a convention, similar to the aesthetic convention as phrased by S. J. Schmidt (1980). They may consider it not only a convention, but also a wrong one, which should be replaced by a more political way of reading. I agree that like most if not all cultural phenomena, the literary way of reading as defined above is based on a convention. I also concede that the notion of convention, as explained by David Lewis (1969), implies that there is no compelling logic or biological necessity to maintain it. In theory, it is possible to do away with the literary or aesthetic way of reading if we can find enough people to join that effort. I doubt, however, whether the latter condition will ever be met. I do not known of any culture with a script that does not have this possibility of a literary or metaphorical way of reading texts. In Maoist China several attempts were made to abolish the aesthetic convention, but although some politicians succeeded in reducing the realm of aesthetic appreciation considerably for a limited period of time, in the long run they did not succeed at all (Fokkema 1991).

Why should people abolish a particular way of reading which for a long time has co-existed with more pragmatic and directly instructive and informative modes of reading as applied to scientific texts, technical manuals, recipes for cooking and newspapers? After all, the re-reading and re-using of older texts, sometimes several thousand years old, seems a rational thing to do, both from an economic and an ecological point of view. In contemporary literature, too, a particular kind of information is stored which can be used and re-used in different contexts. As such, writing literature is an activity which can be defended on economic grounds. Discarding the possibility of literary encoding and decoding would be like cutting off one limb on the assumption that with three we will be able to function better than with four.

Research alone, however, cannot decide the question of whether we should maintain the aesthetic convention of reading, and whether we should continue to teach it to the next generation of students.

In the final instance, the value judgement must be made as to whether we believe it is more profitable to maintain, develop and teach various reading competences (or comprehension control systems) or only one, for instance, the political reading competence. By analogy with the desirability of biological diversity, we may decide in favour of maintaining and developing a variety of reading competences, but the decision will have an evaluative aspect. Research can be helpful, however, by showing that the mind of educated adults is equipped with a literary comprehension control system (Zwaan 1991) and that certain texts are more likely to be read in a literary way than others (Hoffstaedter 1986). Historical research has shown that in the past, and not only in the European and American traditions, numerous texts have been read in accord with the aesthetic convention. More research, of course, can be done in order to explain *why* particular texts time and again were subjected to literary ways of reading, with the exclusion of others. This is Clausen's problem in *The Hospitable Canon*, which he courageously tries to answer by referring to thematic contents.

How do we recognize a canon when we believe we see one? This is the second field where research has been done that may be helpful in the canon debate. Gorak points out that it is not easy to determine which texts belong to a particular canon and which not. Critics often have been more explicit about an assumed canon they wished to reject than about a canon they preferred. Gorak notes the 'tendency to narrow the cultural and historical diversity of *canons* into one reactionary *canon*' (p. 248). His own historical research has shown to what extent canons can be different in size, scope (national/international), and rigidity. Indeed, a distinction must be made, as Nemoianu has done, between the canon of the critics (or different groups of critics) and the school canon (the curriculum). The latter can be differentiated again with respect to language and level. The canon of English literature at high school may well be different from that at the university, and at different universities there may be different school canons or reading lists (Kaat 1987). Perhaps we should also distinguish a canon of the literary historians, which generally will be wider than that of the critics.

Glen Johnson has found a way to study a school canon, that is, the canon of English literature at universities in North America, by comparing various editions of anthologies designed for teaching. However, the anthologies offer a rather wide net, which from the publisher's point of view seems the profitable thing to do. Rosa Penna investigated the personal canon of Jorge Luis Borges, which he used in teaching English at university level in Buenos Aires (*The Hospitable Canon*, pp. 97–110).

Karl Erik Rosengren (1968), who remains unmentioned in the two books under review, developed a method for studying the canons of critics. He suggested counting the number of times particular authors (or texts) have been mentioned in criticism focusing on another author. This method derives from the idea that a canon of significant authors and texts serves as a frame of reference to a critic, as well as to his or her readers. Only writers who are well known can be referred to for reasons of comparison or explanation. Rosengren has been quite successful in putting his operational definition of canon into practice, and although it can be improved by distinguishing between long and short, negative and positive mentions (Dijkstra 1989), his method can also be applied to literary-historical publications.

Instead of speculating that Homer, Sophocles, Dante and Shakespeare (Altieri in *The Hospitable Canon*, p. 2) belong to the canon (whose canon?), it is possible now to examine more precisely which authors belong to the canon of a particular critic or group of critics, or to the canon of a particular literary historian or group of literary historians. Moreover, we are now able to study fluctuations in the composition of these various canons in the course of time, and we may detect the hurdles which an author (or text) has to take before he or she is admitted to the rather stable canon of the literary historians, who, like the editors of anthologies, prefer to add rather than to delete, expressing their personal emphasis mainly by allotting more or less space.

This sort of research cannot liberate university teachers and others from their own responsibility of selecting a canon, but by observing that canons have changed in the past and by trying to explain why this has happened, they may see their own active intervention in cannon formation in a historical perspective. If canon formation can indeed be conceived of as a way of providing a framework to solving certain personal, intellectual and social problems (see Fokkema 1986), then perhaps the definition of current problems may guide us when proposing to amend a canon. Almost everyone seems to agree – Gorak as well as Nemoianu, Johnson, Clausen and other contributors to *The Hospitable Canon* – that changing a school canon is not a strictly literary affair. Didactic and sometimes political goals can be expected to appear in the discussion. If that happens, it is helpful if those goals are explicitly phrased in order that they can be criticized or can lead to rival proposals. If intellectual pluralism is an ideal of political democracy, then indeed we should be suspicious of any attempts to draw up a monolithic school canon. We cannot be sure that the existing selections of reading materials are the best that could be made, nor should we believe that alternative selections will definitely be better.

Are these selections of texts really necessary? Cannot we do without canon formation? We may speculate that we can, but research into what has happened in different cultures until the present moment has yielded the fact that in some way or another selections of texts have always been made. In teaching this seems rather evident. Every teacher may, of course, make a selection of his or her own; this has been practised in a number of schools in Germany (Bohn 1982) and also in the Netherlands, and it has been found rather impracticable because the knowledge acquired by the students appeared difficult to compare. Even within one generation of students the situation that E. D. Hirsch (1987) had proposed to combat nationwide had occurred: students from different schools appeared to have different frames of reference, since they had read different texts. Teachers in Germany have expressed their dissatisfaction with such a situation.

Critics, too, appear to be guided by the silent understanding that they as well as their readers need a relatively small number of authors' names and book titles which, as almost everyone should know, signal certain clusters of experience and values. A canon, then, is indeed a frame of reference, or, to use Altieri's metaphor, a 'historical grammar of forms and themes' or 'cultural grammar' (*The Hospitable Canon*, pp. ix, 9, 29). Research has shown that a relatively small number of names are being frequently mentioned. Some people may dislike this, but it would surprise me if they were able to change this economical way of carrying on our cultural discourse. The only practicable way to intervene seems to consist of proposing additions to or deletions from the current selective frames of reference.

Political democracy came to its full development only in this century. Whereas ten years ago we still may have believed that our century will be primarily known for a struggle between ideologies, or for the end of colonization, or for major technological discoveries, nowadays we may well argue that it will be remembered first of all as the age of political, including parliamentary, democracy. In principle, this includes cultural democracy as well. But just as political democracy has not put an end to all aspects of hierarchization, cultural democracy – which in principle means that every minority group or indeed each person may express its cultural preferences and act accordingly – will not lead to an anarchy of values. Some values are and will be defended with more emphasis than others. Some values are and will be protected by law. There seem to be social conditions which make it plausible to expect that some hierarchization of cultural values will occur also in future times.

Research by Bourdieu (1979) and other sociologists (e.g. Knulst
1993; Ultee *et al.* 1993) seems to warrant this expectation, but their
sociological research does not predict which values will be at the top of
the hierarchy, nor does it predict that it will necessarily be the
intellectual values of the well-educated elite which will prevail. Yet their
research has yielded results which are pertinent to the canon debate. We
should hope that knowledge of research into the continuously changing
composition of the various literary canons as well as sociological research
into the reasons for these changes will enable us to continue the canon
debate at a higher level – a debate in which, as I see it, primarily critics
and educators are to participate.

REFERENCES

Bohn, Volker. 1982. 'In dieser Problematik denken können'. *Diskussion Deutsch* 13:
    165–8.
Bourdieu, Pierre. 1979. *La Distinction. Critique sociale du jugement*. Paris: Minuit.
Dijkstra, Katinka. 1989. 'Canonvorming in de literaire communicatie: Indicatoren voor
    de analyse van de literair-kritische canon'. *Spektator* 18: 159–68.
Fish, Stanley. 1980. *Is there a Text in this Class? The Authority of Interpretive
    Communities*. Cambridge, MA: Harvard University Press.
Fokkema, Douwe. 1986. 'The Canon as an Instrument for Problem Solving', in *Sensus
    Communis: Contemporary Trends in Comparative Literature*. Festschrift for Henry
    Remak, ed. János Riesz, Peter Boerner and Bernhard Scholz. Tübingen: Gunter
    Narr.
    1991. 'Creativity and Politics', in Denis Twitchett and John K. Fairbank, eds. *The
    Cambridge History of China*. Vol XV. Cambridge University Press: 594–618.
Hallberg, Robert von, ed. 1984. *Canons*. University of Chicago Press.
Hirsch, Jr, E. D. 1987. *Cultural Literacy: What Every American Needs to Know*. New
    York: Vintage Books, 1988.
Hoffstaedter, Petra. 1986. *Poetizität aus der Sicht des Lesers: Eine empirische Untersuchung
    der Rolle von Text-, Leser- und Kontexteigenschaften bei der poetischen Verarbeitung
    von Texten*. Hamburg: Buske.
Kaat, Jacques. 1987. 'The Reception of Dutch Fictional Prose in Great Britain'. Ph.D.
    Thesis, University of Hull.
Knulst, Wim. 1993. 'The Gentrification of a Rearguard: An Attempt to Explain
    Changes in the Extent and Composition of the Arts Public in the Age of
    Television', in Rigney and Fokkema 1993 (forthcoming).
Lewis, David K. 1969. *Convention: A Philosophical Study*. Cambridge, MA: Harvard
    University Press.
Marx, Karl, and Friedrich Engels. 1967–68. *Über Kunst und Literatur*. 2 vols. Berlin:
    Dietz.
Rigney, Ann, and Douwe Fokkema, eds. 1993. *Cultural Participation: Trends since the
    Middle Ages*. Amsterdam and Philadelphia: Benjamins (forthcoming).

Rosengren, Karl Erik. 1968. *Sociological Aspects of the Literary System*. Lund: Natur och Kultur.

Schmidt, Siegfried J. 1980. *Grundriss der empirischen Literaturwissenschaft*, I: *Der gesellschaftliche Handlungsbereich Literatur*. Braunschweig and Wiesbaden: Vieweg.

Ultee, Wout C., Ronald Batenburg, and Harry Ganzeboom. 1993. 'Cultural Inequalities in Cross-National Perspective: A Secondary Analysis of Survey Data for the 1980s', in Rigney and Fokkema 1993 (forthcoming).

Zwaan, Rolf A. 1991. 'Some Parameters of Literary and News Comprehension: Effects of Discourse-Type on Reading Rate and Surface-Structure Representation'. *Poetics* 20: 139–56.

Comparative Criticism 15, pp. 271–278. Copyright © 1993 Cambridge University Press

'*Scribo, ergo sum*': Strindberg in letters

INGA-STINA EWBANK

'*Scribo, ergo sum*': when Strindberg penned this Cartesian dictum in a somewhat frantic letter to Edvard Brandes on 28 May 1887, he might be said to have articulated, with unusual succinctness, the subtext of his entire corpus and not least of his vast output of letters. Among the many forms in which he chose to write, that of the letter is of peculiar importance. As Michael Robinson points out in the admirably cogent Preface to his translation of this selection of letters, and as he had already demonstrated in his seminal study of *Strindberg and Auto-biography* (Norvik Press, 1986), letter-writing fulfilled for Strindberg vital and complex needs for self-expression, self-fashioning and self-definition. Strindberg wanted his letters to be published and read as an integral part of his works, but until now only those to Harriet Bosse[1] have been available in English translation. The publication of these two volumes is a major event in Strindberg studies, opening up to readers with Swedish a series of key documents for the understanding of his work.

'Available' is the operative word for these volumes, for their elegance and user-friendliness may not at first sight reveal the hard and scholarly labour which must have gone into their preparation. The sheer volume of Strindberg's correspondence – some 10,000 letters extant and many lost – has meant that the Swedish edition of *Strindbergs Brev* which began to appear in 1948, edited first by Torsten Eklund and then by Björn Meidal, has now reached its seventeenth volume, taking us up to April 1909, and that four more volumes are planned, which will include letters that have come to light after the chronologically relevant volume was published. From printed and manuscript sources Michael Robinson has selected for translation 679 letters spanning fifty years of life and work, from the letter in which the young August informs his brother

* *Strindberg's Letters*, vol. I, 1862–1892, vol. II, 1892–1912, selected, edited and translated by Michael Robinson (University of Chicago Press, Chicago, and The Athlone Press, London, 1992).

271

Oscar of the death of their mother in 1862, to the letter Strindberg wrote less than three weeks before his death in 1912, thanking the staff of *Social-Demokraten*, a paper to which he had been contributing, for their flowers: 'I still had a great deal to say in the paper when the pen fell from my hand.'

The principle of selection has been to present 'as even-handedly as possible' each period of Strindberg's life, each kind of letter he wrote, and each facet of a career which is only partially known outside Scandinavia and which included work as 'historian, painter, novelist, story-teller, scientist, alchemist, linguist and photographer'. Swedish readers might regret the loss of favourite letters, but to complain about this overall-judicious selection would be nit-picking. And to complain, as Michael Meyer has done in the *New York Review of Books* (a review also published in Swedish translation in *Dagens Nyheter*), that some of the letters concern themselves with authors and texts of interest only to scholars of Swedish literature, who could read them in the original language anyway, is to miss one of the chief virtues of Robinson's selection: that it not only puts Strindberg in his context as a man rooted in Swedish culture, however much he inveighed against it over the years, but also provides, through economically packed head- and end-notes, an introduction to the history of Scandinavian culture, art and literature in the nineteenth and early twentieth centuries. Such complaints perpetuate just that Anglo-Saxon parochialism which Robinson is combating, and which sets Strindberg down, once and for all, as the author of a handful of important plays and an armful of rubbish in various genres.[2] Strindberg's whole career, the letters show, was a fight against cultural parochialism: to be a Scandinavian must not be, as he writes to Edvard Brandes in June 1885, 'to be buried alive as we now are with three dead languages and two and a half royal houses'. But in the same month he writes to Oscar Levertin to praise his stories because they have 'something so splendidly universal, tellurian, European, un-Swedish about them that I blush to the roots of my ears at the thought of all those models in genuine Uppland clay that I've baked so far'. No doubt he can afford to be so generous because he does not really believe it – because he knows his sources of strength are in that clay and in the Swedish language which he treats as so much clay.

In effect, rather than being a second-best for non-Scandinavians, these two volumes make a contribution all their own. Whereas no one would sit down to read right through the (eventually) twenty-one volumes of the complete Swedish edition of the letters, it is just possible to do so with Robinson's selection, and the result is first-hand illumination of Strindberg's whole achievement from a source far less biassed and more informative than any existing biography or critical study. I use 'first-hand' advisedly, although we are dealing with a translation, for Michael Robinson is sensitive to Strindberg's style as it varies with time, mood, subject and correspondent. He is not afraid to reproduce the liberties (usually creative ones) which Strindberg takes with the vocabulary, syntax and punctuation of the Swedish (and sometimes French or German) language. As a translator he achieves the important – but not always appreciated – quality of transparency.

The experience of reading this distillment of fifty years of letters has a wholeness which, paradoxically, lies in the constant exposure to variety. At the heart of it – and prompting intertextual comparisons with the autobiographical and the more explicitly fictive works – is the sense of a fragmented self, one made up of contradictory impulses, and one where life and art, authenticity and role-playing, are inextricably woven together. In one of several 'last will' letters, this one envisaging for himself either madness or suicide, Strindberg writes the often-quoted words about his life and writing having 'got all jumbled up. I don't know if *The Father* is a work of literature, or if my life has been' (12 November 1887). Much less well known are such Keatsian declarations of negative capability as this postscript in a letter to Emil Schering, his German translator and impresario, in March 1901: 'I am a Dramatist, have no constant "opinions" (like Shakespeare) but incarnate the characters I portray.' But lest we think in terms of a steady development towards such resolutions of the 'jumble', six years later and in the midst of composing the Chamber Plays (between *The Ghost Sonata* and *The Pelican*) he writes to Schering that his whole life often seems to him 'as if it had been staged for me, so that I might both suffer and portray it'. And to stave off demonstrations in connection with his sixtieth birthday, in 1909, he can claim: 'My incarnations are as numerous as the cast list of a play, and in such disarray that I don't know who people wish to celebrate'. If there is one stance that arrests, because it contains, all this flux, it is that presented in an 1890 letter to one of the editors of *Nordisk familjebok*, the great Swedish encyclopedia, where Strindberg was anxious to have his story rightly told to posterity: 'Popularly speaking, I think one could call me a Seeker, who experiments with points of view'.

This experimenting with viewpoints means that the letters can be used both to prove and to disprove almost any attempt to define any one

'Strindbergian' attitude. If there are plenty of outrageous statements from the years of *Getting Married* and the break-up of his first marriage, to confirm received ideas of his misogyny, there are also counter-statements like this, from just before the formal dissolution of the marriage: 'I love women and adore children; though divorced, I commend marriage as the only form of intercourse between the sexes.' And after he has been agonisingly divorced from Harriet Bosse, his third wife, he can write to her, in language evoking a Victorian Angel in the House, that 'a woman's presence elevates a man who then not only appears a better person but is one! In fact it is everyman's dream to seek salvation through a woman, salvation from what is low and coarse.' Again, Strindberg is also able to put his finger on the root cause of these apparent contradictions, when he wonders whether it is not simply his own 'projections' that he sees in woman: 'whether She isn't simply a *tabula rasa* on which I write with my best blood-ink' (23 November 1903). Such a *tabula* was Tekla, in *Creditors*, whom Gustaf says he found like an empty 'slate' on which he 'wrote new texts, of my own making'.

If writing creates identity, then the letters project similarly contradictory identities of Strindberg the writer. Was he a dramatist primarily? Or even a writer of fiction in any form? In the process of completing *Son of a Servant* he writes to his publisher 'The deliberate conjuring up of hallucinations at one's desk seems to me like masturbation. The novel and the theatre are just right for women'; but shortly he was again committed to both genres, and within six months he had 'conjured up' *The Father*. The years of scientific and alchemical experimentation in the 1890s were followed by a second great outflow of narrative and dramatic writing. As the 'Inferno' crisis released itself into *To Damascus I* he could feel that 'The Stage is after all my own art' (26 December 1898), but by April 1906 this has become 'The novel tempts me most. I loathe the theatre.' Yet, a year later, completing the Chamber Plays and with the prospect of a stage for his own plays in August Falck's Intimate Theatre, he sees 'the secret of all my novels, stories and tales: they are plays.'

The real secret, the letters suggest, was that Strindberg was forever changing and developing, that in his case it is useless to speak of formative years, because he was being formed all the time – and often using the letters to form himself. This is not simply vacillation but an ultimately purposeful moving with the times, being what he call in a letter of 1904 'my own contemporary'. He explains this more fully in the *Julius Caesar* pamphlet of the *Open Letters to the Intimate Theatre*: 'To be "your own contemporary" is the aim of the artist who is ever growing, ever renewing himself.'[3]

This in turn means that, read sequentially, Michael Robinson's selection of letters amounts to a literary biography of Strindberg, and not least because the letters so vividly reflect Strindberg's voracious reading and its impact on him. 'I've read too much lately: psychology, ethics, psychiatry, sociology and economics, so that my head is like pulp', he writes to Edvard Brandes in April 1886. Two years later he comes under the influence of Nietzsche who is 'blinding' him; his brain is 'like a wound', but 'the incredible self-esteem in his books has induced a similar feeling in me'. In Strindberg's language 'influence' is not an ethereal fluid flowing from the stars but a violent sexual transmission: 'the uterus of my mental world has received a tremendous ejaculation of sperm from Friedrich Nietzsche, so that I feel like a bitch with a full belly' (4 September 1888). Thus in the days when he has finished *Comrades* and is conceiving *The Father* he has to keep away from the influence of Georg Brandes: 'I am afraid, afraid of him as of all fertilizing spirits, afraid as I was of Zola, Bjørnson, Ibsen, of becoming pregnant with other men's seed and bearing the offspring of other men' (3 January 1887). Strindberg's language leaps between the sexes and between the literal and metaphorical, in an obsession with paternity that also adumbrates the subject of the play he was about to write. But even Ibsen, normally so non-committal in his letters and throughout his career so suspicious of 'influence' as a threat to the integrity of the self, had been moved to use the same metaphor for Georg Brandes' power over other minds. Writing to Brandes to thank him for a copy of *Main Currents* – the lectures which marked the 'modern break-through' in Scandinavian literature – he admitted that 'a more dangerous book could not fall into the hands of a "*frugtsommelig*" [i.e. ready-to-conceive] writer'.[4] Clearly Brandes was a challenge to those concerned for the paternity of their offspring, literary or otherwise.

Not that Strindberg is afraid of influence as such. Early and late it comes natural to him to refer to his own work in terms of 'models'. For an early play, which he burned, 'my model is Oehlenschläger'; *The Father* was composed, he claims in a famous letter to Zola, 'with a view to the experimental formula' of *Le naturalisme au théâtre*; in the late 1890s he returns to writing history plays 'with Shakespeare as a teacher';[5] *Advent* is both 'a serious fairy-tale play in the style of Andersen's *Stories*' and a 'Mystery in the style of Swedenborg'; and

The Crown Bride, like *Swanwhite*, is 'an attempt to enter into Maeterlinck's wonderful world of beauty'. The list of models he claims for his fictive and semi-fictive narrative works reads like an outline history of European literature; and in his cultural criticism he can claim to be 'only a disciple of the masters – Rousseau, Edv. v. Hartmann, Haeckel, Tolstoy' (23 March 1888). On the other hand he is fiercely protective of his own intellectual property and position as an innovator, and ready to counter mistaken attributions of influence. The similarity between Huysmans' *En route* and his own *Inferno*, he must insist, is a 'coincidence of two human fates developing in a parallel direction...What I have recounted in *Inferno* is lived, hence my property.' For discipleship does not mean plagiarism but being part of the same intellectual and artistic movement. Thus he writes to George Brandes in April 1890: 'When I found the whole movement formulated in Nietzsche, whom I partly anticipated, I adopted his standpoint, and intend henceforth to experiment with that point of view, to see where it leads.' And, four year later, Nietzsche 'has never buggered my soul' (4? August 1894). Increasingly, from the late 1880s, his discourse of such relationships is not so much of seeing others as models as of finding himself in others. 'Read *Bête humaine* and had my own experiences and observations confirmed by Zola' (12 April 1890). Reading Balzac leads to 'having all my conjectures about life and people confirmed' (1 October 1890). He is vastly excited to discover that many of his own works are 'Poe before Poe', and this is no anxiety of influence but an assurance of being both with and ahead of his own time: 'The next age will belong to E[dgar Allan]. P[oe]...And how far in advance of its time *Creditors* is! When he *produces* the epilepsy! I didn't know how right I was – but I do now!' (3 January 1889).

What feeds this assurance is not only reading others as confirmations of himself but also the influence from himself which, rightly or wrongly, he perceives in others. In particular, this becomes his way of asserting himself against Ibsen, 'the Nora Man', whose achievement he is forever attempting to minimise, but whose *Rosmersholm* he had acknowledged, in his essay on 'Soul Murder', as seminal for his own thinking on the power of one mind over another. *Hedda Gabler* gives him the chance to get his own back: all the 'ingredients' in that play, he insists, can be traced back to him, and the heroine herself is 'a bastardess of Laura in *The Father* and Tekla in *Creditors*'. The joy of thinking that he has turned Ibsen's 'brain pan' into a 'uterus' for his own 'seed' expresses itself in Nietzschean vocabulary: 'It is *Wille zur Macht*, and the pleasure I derive from setting other people's brains in molecular movement!' (8 and 10 March 1891). No wonder that Strindberg was anxious to 'prove' his influence on Ibsen, who had taken two months to thank the publisher of *The Father* for his complimentary copy and then, in the briefest of comments, felt obliged, while recognising the pull of 'the author's violent strength', to point out that 'Strindberg's observations and experiences in the area with which *The Father* is most concerned do not correspond with mine'. But writing also comes to mean the exercise of power on a much wider scale. When *Creditors* was playing in Paris, where it had opened at the Théâtre de l'Oeuvre on 21 June 1894, he wrote to Leopold Littmansson, the particular *confidant* of this period, of his 'happiness, this feeling of power... knowing that right now, in Paris, in the intellectual headquarters of the world, 500 people are sitting like mice in an auditorium and foolishly exposing their brains to my suggestions. Some revolt, but many leave there with my spores in their grey matter; they go home pregnant with the seed of my mind, and then spawn my brood. In six months, I'll read a French book, a French paper, and recognize my offspring!'

Strindberg's will to power is no more (or less) a political creed than is his *scribo, ergo sum* – of which it is an inextricable part. It is the will to grow out of parochialism, to grow with the time, to find language and forms for fragmented selves in a transitional time. It was for these reasons, I think, that Thomas Mann regarded Strindberg's works as 'ein unerlässliches Bildungszubehör zur Zeit meiner Jugend': 'an indispensable element of the *Bildung* – culture and education – of my youth'.[6] Michael Robinson's two volumes, for much the same reasons, are *unerlässlich*, not only for students of Strindberg but for anyone interested in European literature in the nineteenth and twentieth centuries.

NOTES

1 In a translation by Arvid Paulson (New York, 1959).

2 See the collection of essays, *Strindberg and Genre*, edited by Michael Robinson (Proceedings of the Tenth International Strindberg Conference) (Norvik Press, 1991), for a concerted effort to correct this attitude.

3 *Samlade Skrifter av August Strindberg*, ed. John Landquist, vol. L (Stockholm, 1921), p. 137.

4 Henrik Ibsen, *Samlede verker* (*Hundreårsutgave*), vol. XVII (Oslo, 1946), p. 31.

5 This comment is made by Strindberg in his 'Preface to the history plays', first published in 1903, in the second German edition of his *Queen Christina*, and then

included in the last of the *Open letters to the Intimate Theatre* (1909). (*Samlade Skrifter*, vol. L, p. 240.)

6 *Gesammelte Werke*, x (Frankfurt, 1960), p. 371.

Comparative Criticism 15, pp. 279–283. Copyright © 1993 Cambridge University Press

Romantic irony: the comparative history of European literature

GARY HANDWERK

This volume, sixth in the series of comparatist studies coordinated by the International Comparative Literature Association, takes as its task a retracing of the tracks of Romantic irony in European literature. Trying to obtain a comprehensive overview of so elusive and intermittent a phenomenon as Romantic irony is a project that lends itself to certain ironies of execution, ones not unnoticed by the editor and certain contributors. For the traces of Romantic irony are often obscure, even nonexistent, in considerable stretches of literary history. Indeed, the coherence of the concept itself can seem hard to ascertain in the sometimes furious debate between its detractors and its advocates.

The essays in this collection fall into three distinct sections, emphasizing in turn the genealogy of Romantic irony, its presence in various national literatures, and more synthetic perspectives. The two initial essays examine the influence exerted upon Romantic writers by Cervantes and Sterne, the most prominent precursors for many attitudes and techniques characteristic of Romantic irony. The second section, by far the most extensive, contains thirteen essays, each of which focuses largely on a single European literature; they begin with pieces by Ernst Behler and Raymond Immerwahr on the German scene, but spread out in a genuinely comprehensive way to embrace Romance, Scandinavian, Slavic, Dutch and English literatures as well. The final section, 'Syntheses,' contains several essays that deal with the relationship of Romantic irony to issues in narrative theory, in music and in drama, and in relation to the grotesque.

For all their diversity of approaches and emphases, these essays exhibit surprising unanimity about certain features that seem essential for a given instance of irony to be distinctively Romantic. First, such

---

* Frederick Garber, ed., *Romantic Irony* (Budapest: Akadémiai Kiadó, 1988)

irony must manifest a particular sense of human subjectivity. As neatly defined by Frederick Garber in his essay on Sterne, 'Romantic irony is the product of a self-consciousness aware of both the proximity of chaos and the strength of artifice' (p. 38). Key theorists of irony such as Friedrich Schlegel and Solger began with a conviction (nurtured by their study of Kant) that the world was and would remain paradoxical and contrary, at least to our human senses, and that irremediable tensions – between aspiration and insight, between ideal and real – were therefore embedded in the structure of human consciousness itself. An ironic awareness would thus take all human creation (and preeminently the work of art) as just that – humanly created, hence always in some measure arbitrary and capricious, but likewise always impermanent and refashionable. Secondly, Romantic irony as a literary strategy involves actively manifesting this epistemological principle in every aspect of aesthetic production, using devices such as the shattering of aesthetic illusion, narratorial intervention, or incongruous juxtapositions of tone, with the specific aim of 'making the critical consciousness of a work's literary creation explicit in the work itself' (Maria de Lourdes Ferraz and Jacinto do Prado Coehlo, p. 121).

In some crucial ways, the volume admirably fulfils both the general aims of the ICLA project and its own, more specific goals. The scope of these essays profitably underscores how complex and diverse the currents within Romanticism were, and they bring to our attention numerous works that have been excluded from the traditional canons of Romantic literature or may be little known outside their national context. Articles such as Vera Calin's study of narrative tonalities in the Romanian poet Eminescu or Mihaly Szegedy-Maszak's analysis of totalizing irony in the *Phantom Visions* of the Hungarian novelist, Kemeny, illuminate intriguing byways of European literary history. Other essays, such as Ferraz's and Coelho's on Portuguese literature or George Bisztray's on Scandinavian literature, provide useful commentary for non-specialists about national variations in the spread of Romanticism. Still others, including Roman Struc's on Russian literature and G. R. Thompson's on American literature, do particularly fine work in exploring and expanding traditional categories of Romanticism by reconsidering writers such as Pushkin or Poe in terms of ironic disjunctions within their works.

Yet, in some part thanks to the success of these essays in honing our understanding of Romantic irony, certain historical and conceptual instabilities hover insistently in the background. Apart from Germany, there has never been much convergence among theoretical formulations, literary manifestations, and critical recognition of Romantic irony. Rarely have even those writers whose texts might be said to exhibit Romantic irony invoked it explicitly, nor has literary history given it a very prominent place outside of German Romanticism (despite some recent treatments of it in England and France). So the critic's task here becomes a matter of locating literary works to which the label 'Romantic irony' might plausibly be applied or, in the most extreme cases, explaining the absence of such works in certain national contexts. Those contributors confronting the latter problem have a particularly daunting problem, but even where candidates for ironic canonization do exist, this project involves an exercise in historical revisionism. Its success requires an exceptionally alert critical consciousness, one that sees the need to explain what we gain for interpretation by realigning literary history in this way and choosing to view Romanticism through an ironic lens, or how this act of recategorizing can enrich and extend our interpretive understanding of particular texts and their reception. Without such theoretical framing, we can all too easily find ourselves simply relabelling isolated literary works.

So the most provocative pieces here are those where testing the label, 'irony,' becomes an occasion for reflecting upon the coherence and conditions of Romantic thought. Behler's essay, for instance, extends his earlier work on Romantic irony in striking ways, suggesting affinities of its dialectical structures even to so surprising a figure as Karl Marx. The three-stage development that he describes for Romantic irony, from its Socratic and Fichtean origins in Friedrich Schlegel, through its association with tragedy in Solger, modulating finally into the historical irony of Hegel or Nietzsche, provides a way of making historical sense out of the wilfully divergent tones to which irony has been attuned. With similar historical scope and power, Gerald Gillespie explores the links between irony and its shadowy double, the grotesque, and highlights numerous correspondences between Romanticism and the baroque. Anthony Thorlby's study of Romantic irony within the English tradition makes a careful and compelling comparison of the modes of intellectual synthesis entailed by irony and by the Romantic imagination (although he rather too readily attributes to the English Romantics an ethical integrity toward reality which he denies to their German counterparts). And Frederick Garber's coda, quite sensibly resisting any urge to sum up the volume, provides a beautifully resonant pairing of individual writers (Byron and Heine, Shelley and Hölderlin) that both explicates and embodies his treatment of Romantic irony as a counterpoint to Romantic ideas about metaphor and organicism.

At another level, though, even this volume seems unable to extricate Romantic irony from its own critical past, where it has been burdened by a tendency to blur into other conceptual categories (Jean Paul's humor, for instance) and by an inability to disentangle itself from charges of abetting a narcissistic aestheticism. The lineage of Romantic irony is dual and contradictory, a duality manifesting itself here in the recurrent resurfacing of Søren Kierkegaard, whose bitter critiques of Romantic irony, even more than Friedrich Schlegel's formulations, have dominated our reception and understanding of this concept. Thus, Calin's ironist exhibits a 'frantic exaltation of the ego' (p. 189), Thorlby's pursues a 'total freedom from the cares of actuality' (p. 148), and for Lillian Furst the fullest irony tends toward an 'overwrought subjectivity' (p. 305), its metaphoric equivalent 'a disease that may long be present in isolated cases and that may then under special circumstances become epidemic' (p. 307) – all versions of Kierkegaard's insistence that Romantic irony perpetually moves toward sceptical relativism and a moral indifference at odds with Romantic empathy. Schlegel's irony would resist the absorption into Hegelianism such teleologies imply, as it would resist the existential stability to which Kierkegaard condemns it.

Romantic irony does indeed broach the problem of modern subjectivity in a particularly telling way, as Kierkegaard perceived. Yet one need not follow Kierkegaard, as so many critics do, in seeing such irony inevitably breeding a capricious aestheticism. Schlegel's 'clear consciousness' can as easily betoken a provisional and instrumental stance as a rigid existential attitude; his ironist by no means exempts himself from the paradoxes and indeterminacies he perceives in history, either by his emotional detachment from them or intellectual superiority over them. The essays here do nearly always understand Romantic irony as more than the deployment of metafictional devices, as entailing a determinable range of specific ethical attitudes. Yet a great deal depends, for artist and critic alike, on precisely how one delimits that range, on taking up the profound quarrel between Kierkegaard and Schlegel in a more explicit way than these analyses tend to do. Even those critics, like Furst, who do rigorously trace the lines between ironic literary strategies and an ironic ethos, tend implicitly to adopt Kierkegaard's view that Romantic irony terminates in self-indulgent subjectivity, as if that subjectivity might not yet again turn itself inside out – out toward others, toward commitment, toward history.

Indeed, the very logic of Romantic irony would entail a multiplicity of modulations and connections beyond what even this volume can suggest. These essays bring us considerably farther in assessing what and where Romantic irony is, and is not, but what it means lies still wide open to debate. In that regard, one might have wished this volume to be itself a bit more ironic: not explicitly playful, necessarily, but more consciously attentive throughout to the potential in the material it unearths for intensely fertile juxtapositions (of the sort embodied in Garber's coda or Immerwahr's overview of the shadings taken on by Germanic irony) – more in dialogue, that is, with itself.

Comparative Criticism 15, pp. 285–291. Cambridge University Press 1993

Books and periodicals received

COMPILED BY HUGH STEVENS

The inclusion of a book in this list does not preclude a review in a later volume of *Comparative Criticism*.

BOOKS

Aspley, Keith and Peter France, eds. *Poetry in France: Metamorphoses of a Muse*. Edinburgh: Edinburgh University Press, 1992

Attebury, Brian. *Strategies of Fantasy*. Bloomington and Indianapolis: Indiana University Press, 1992

Barratt, Alexandra, ed. *Women's Writing in Middle English*. Longman Annotated Texts. London and New York: Longman, 1992

Bergeron, Katherine and Philip V. Bohlman, eds. *Disciplining Music: Musicology and Its Canons*. Chicago and London: The University of Chicago Press, 1992

Berkowitz, Gerald M. *American Drama of the Twentieth Century*. Longman Literature in English Series. London and New York: Longman, 1992

Bersani, Leo. *The Culture of Redemption*. Cambridge, MA and London: Harvard University Press, 1990

Bjornson, Richard. *The African Quest for Freedom and Identity: Cameroonian Writing and the National Experience*. Bloomington and Indianapolis: Indiana University Press, 1991

Bodmer, Beatriz Pastir. *The Armature of Conquest: Spanish Accounts of the Discovery of America, 1492–1589*. Translated by Lydia Longstreth Hunt. Stanford, CA: Stanford University Press, 1992

Bolt, Sydney. *A Preface to James Joyce*. First edition: Longman, 1991. London and New York: Longman, 1992

Bové, Paul. *In the Wake of Theory*. Hanover and London: Wesleyan University Press, 1992

Bowden, Betsy, ed. *Eighteenth-Century Modernizations from the Canterbury Tales*. Chaucer Studies XVI. Rochester, NY and Woodbridge, Suffolk: D. S. Brewer, 1991

Bowlby, Rachel, ed. *Virginia Woolf*. Longman Critical Readers. London and New York: Longman, 1992

Bradford, Richard. *Silence and Sound: Theories of Poetics from the Eighteenth Century*. London and Toronto: Associated University Presses, 1992

   Paradise Lost. Open Guides to Literature. Buckingham and Philadelphia: Open University Press, 1992

Brant, Clare and Diane Purkiss, eds. *Women, Texts and Histories 1575–1760*. London and New York: Routledge, 1992

Bremmer, Rolf H., Jr. *A Bibliographical Guide to Old Frisian Studies*. North-Western European Language Evolution, Supplement Vol. 6. Odense: Odense University Press, 1992

Brennan, Teresa. *The Interpretation of the Flesh: Freud and Femininity*. London and New York: Routledge, 1992

Britton, Celia. *The Nouveau Roman: Fiction, Theory and Politics*. London: Macmillan; New York: St Martin's Press, 1992

Brooker, Peter, ed. *Modernism/Postmodernism*. Longman Critical Readers. London and New York: Longman, 1992

Brown, Andrew. *Roland Barthes: The Figures of Writing*. Oxford: Clarendon Press, 1992

Burwick, Frederick and Paul Douglass, eds. *The Crisis in Modernism: Bergson and the Vitalist Controversy*. Cambridge University Press, 1992

Caron, Jacques. *Angoisse et Communication chez S. Kierkegaard*. Odense University Studies in Scandinavian Languages and Literatures Vol. 26. Odense University Press, 1992

Carter, William C. *The Proustian Quest*. New York and London: New York University Press, 1992

Cavendish, Margaret. *The Description of a New World Called The Blazing World and Other Writings*. Ed. Kate Lilley. London: William Pickering, 1992

Cendrars, Blaise. *Complete Poems*. Translated by Ron Padgett and introduced by Jay Bochner. Berkeley, Los Angeles, and Oxford: University of California Press, 1992

Cixous, Hélène. Coming to Writing *and Other Essays*. Edited by Deborah Jenson with an introductory essay by Susan Rubin Suleiman. Cambridge, MA and London: Harvard University Press, 1991

Clark, Suzanne. *Sentimental Modernism: Women Writers and the Revolution of the Word*. Bloomington and Indianapolis: Indiana University Press, 1991

Clark, Timothy. *Derrida, Heidegger, Blanchot: Sources of Derrida's Notion and Practice of Literature*. Cambridge University Press, 1992

Colman, Fran, ed. *Evidence for Old English: Material and Theoretical Bases for Reconstruction*. Edinburgh Studies in the English Language 2. Edinburgh: John Donald Publishers Ltd, 1992

Conley, Tom. *The Graphic Unconscious in Early Modern French Writing*. Cambridge University Press, 1992

Corngold, Stanley and Irene Giersing. *Borrowed Lives*. Albany, NY: State University of New York Press, 1991

Cornwell, Neil, ed. *Daniel Kharms and the Poetics of the Absurd: Essays and Materials*. Studies in Russia and East Europe. Basingstoke and London: Macmillan, 1991

Crawford, Robert. *Devolving English Literature*. Oxford: Clarendon Press, 1992

Derwin, Susan. *The Ambivalence of Form: Lukács, Freud, and the Novel*. Baltimore and London: Johns Hopkins University Press, 1992

Dunn, Francis M. and Thomas Cole. *Beginnings in Classical Literature*. Cambridge University Press, 1992

Duyfhuizen, Bernard. *Narratives of Transmission*. London and Toronto: Associated University Presses, 1992

Eco, Umberto, Richard Rorty, Jonathan Culler and Christine Brooke-Rose.

Interpretation and Overinterpretation. Ed. Stefan Collini. Cambridge University Press, 1992

Ellis, Steve. *The English Eliot: Design, Language and Landscape in 'Four Quartets'*. London and New York: Routledge, 1991

Felman, Shoshana and Dori Laub, eds. *Testimony: Crises of Witnessing in Literature, Psychoanalysis, and History*. New York and London: Routledge, 1992

Ferguson, Gary. *Mirroring Belief: Marguerite de Navarre's Devotional Poetry*. Edinburgh: Edinburgh University Press, 1992

Finnegan, Ruth. *Oral Poetry: Its Nature, Significance and Social Context*. Bloomington and Indianapolis: Indiana University Press, 1992

Forsås-Scott, Helena. *Textual Liberation: European Feminist Writing in the Twentieth Century*. London and New York: Routledge, 1991

Fowler, Edward. *The Rhetoric of Confession: Shishosetsu in Early Twentieth-Century Japanese Fiction*. Berkeley, Los Angeles and Oxford: University of California Press, 1992 (first edn 1988)

France, Peter. *Politeness and its Discontents: Problems in French Classical Literature*. Cambridge University Press, 1992

France, Peter and Duncan Glen, eds. *European Poetry in Scotland: An Anthology of Translations*. Edinburgh: Edinburgh University Press, 1989

Friedman, Michael. *Kant and the Exact Sciences*. Cambridge, MA and London: Harvard University Press, 1992

Furst, Lilian R., ed. *Realism*. Modern Literatures in Perspective. London and New York: Longman, 1992

Fusso, Susanne and Priscilla Meyer, eds. *Essays on Gogol: Logos and the Russian Word*. Evanston, IL: Northwestern University Press, 1992

Gallop, Jane. *Around 1981: Academic Feminist Literary Theory*. New York and London: Routledge, 1992

Gaskill, Howard, ed. *Ossian Revisited*. Edinburgh: Edinburgh University Press, 1991

Giddings, Robert. *The Author, The Book and the Reader*. London: Greenwich Exchange, 1991

Gillespie, Gerald, ed. *German Theater Before 1750*. With a foreword by Martin Esslin. New York: Continuum, 1992

Goldhill, Simon. *Aeschylus: The Oresteia*. Landmarks of World Literature. Cambridge University Press, 1992

Greenblatt, Stephen. *Marvelous Possessions: The Wonder of the New World*. The Clarendon Lectures and the Carpenter Lectures 1988. Oxford: Clarendon Press, 1991

Guibert, Herve. *The Gangsters*. Translated by Iain White. London: Serpent's Tail, 1991. First published in Paris: Les Editions de Minuit, 1988

Gunn, Edward. *Rewriting Chinese: Style and Innovation in Twentieth-Century Chinese Prose*. Stanford, CA: Stanford University Press, 1991

Hall, David Lynn. *The Arimaspian Eye*. Albany, NY: State University of New York Press, 1992

Harpham, Geoffrey Galt. *Getting it Right: Language, Literature, and Ethics*. Chicago and London: University of Chicago Press, 1992

Hilfer, Tony. *American Fiction Since 1940*. Longman Literature in English Series. London and New York: Longman, 1992

Hollahan, Eugene. *Crisis-Consciousness and the Novel*. London and Toronto: Associated University Presses, 1992

Holub, Robert C. *Jürgen Habermas: Critic in the Public Sphere*. London and New York: Routledge, 1991

Hulme, Peter and Neil L. Whitehead. *Wild Majesty: Encounters with Caribs from Columbus to the Present Day. An Anthology*. Oxford: Clarendon Press, 1992

Hume, Kathryn. *Calvino's Fictions: Cogito and Cosmos*. Oxford: Clarendon Press, 1992

Hunt, Peter, ed. *Literature for Children: Contemporary Criticism*. London and New York: Routledge, 1992

Hutcheon, Linda. *The Politics of Postmodernism*. New Accents. London and New York: Routledge, 1989

Ibsch, Elrud, Dick Schram and Gerard Steen, eds. *Empirical Studies of Literature: Proceedings of the Second IGEL-Conference, Amsterdam 1989*. Amsterdam and Atlanta, GA: Rodopi, 1991

Ito, Ken K. *Visions of Desire: Tanizaki's Fictional Worlds*. Stanford, CA: Stanford University Press, 1991

Jacoff, Rachel and Jeffrey T. Schnapp, eds. *The Poetry of Allusion: Virgil and Ovid in Dante's 'Commedia'*. Stanford, CA: Stanford University Press, 1991

Jones, Gwyn. *'Background to Dylan Thomas' and Other Explorations*. Oxford and New York: Oxford University Press, 1992

Josipovici, Gabriel. *Text and Voice: Essays 1981–1991*. Manchester: Carcanet, and New York: St Martin's Press, 1992

Lawler, James. *Rimbaud's Theatre of the Self*. Cambridge, MA and London: Harvard University Press, 1992

Lawrence, D. H. *Sons and Lovers*. The Cambridge edition, established from the original sources. Ed. Helen Baron and Carl Baron. Cambridge University Press, 1992

Livingston, Paisley. *Literature and Rationality: Ideas of Agency in Theory and Fiction*. Cambridge University Press, 1991

Longxi, Zhang. *The Tao and the Logos: Literary Hermeneutics, East and West*. Durham, NC and London: Duke University Press, 1992

Mailloux, Steven and Hershel Parker. *Checklist of Melville Reviews*. Revised by Kevin J. Hayes and Hershel Parker. Evanston, IL: Northwestern University Press, 1991

Majeed, Javed. *Ungoverned Imaginings: James Mill's 'The History of British India' and Orientalism*. Oxford: Clarendon Press, 1992

Malraux, André. *The Conquerors*. Translated by Stephen Becker, with a new foreword by Herbert R. Lottman. Chicago and London: University of Chicago Press, 1992. First published as *Les Conquérants*, Bernard Grasset, 1928

The Temptation of the West. Translated with an introduction by Robert Hollander, with a new preface by Jonathan D. Spence. Chicago and London: University of Chicago Press, 1992. First published as *La Tentation de L'Occident*, Bernard Grasset, 1926

The Walnut Trees of Alternburg. Translated by A. W. Fielding, with a new foreword by Cornor Cruise O'Brien. Chicago and London: University of Chicago Press, 1992. First published as *Les Noyers de l'Altenburg*, Gallimard, 1948

Manuel, Frank E. *The Broken Staff: Judaism Through Christian Eyes*. Cambridge, MA and London: Harvard University Press, 1992

Meese, Elizabeth A. (*Sem*)*Erotics: Theorizing Lesbian Writing*. New York and London: New York University Press, 1992

Mendelssohn, Moses, trans. *Dis Psalmen*. Edited by Walter Pape, with an afterword by Walter Pape and Gideon Toury. Berlin: Henssel, 1991

Mikhail, Mona N. *Studies in the Short Fiction of Mahfouz and Idris*. New York University Studies in Near Eastern Civilization 16. New York and London: New York University Press, 1992

Minahan, John A. *Word Like a Bell: John Keats, Music and the Romantic Poet*. Kent, Ohio and London: Kent State University Press, 1992

Monteith, Moira and Robert Miles, eds. *Teaching Creative Writing: Theory and Practice*. Buckingham and Philadelphia, Open University Press, 1992

Münch, Marc-Mathieu. *Le pluriel de beau: genèse du relativisme esthétique en littérature: du singulier au pluriel*. Metz: Centre de recherche littérature et spiritualité, 1991

Naddaff, Sandra. *Arabesque: Narrative Structure and the Aesthetics of Repetition in the '1001 Nights'*. Evanston, IL: Northwestern University Press, 1991

Nelson, Brian. *Naturalism in the European Novel: New Critical Perspectives*. Berg European Studies Series. New York and Oxford: Berg, 1992

Nelson, Cary. *Repression and Recovery: Modern American Poetry and the Politics of Cultural Memory, 1910–1945*. Madison, Wisconsin and London: University of Wisconsin Press, 1989

Ohly, Friedrich. *The Damned and the Elect: Guilt in Western Culture*. Translated from the German by Linda Archibald. Cambridge University Press, 1992

Okada, H. Richard. *Figures of Resistance: Language, Poetry and Narrating in The Tale of Genji and Other Mid-Heian Texts*. Durham, NC and London: Duke University Press, 1991

Olender, Maurice. *The Language of Paradise: Race, Religion and Philology in the Nineteenth Century*. Translated by Arthur Goldhammer. Cambridge, MA and London: Harvard University Press, 1992

Olrik, Axel. *Principles for Oral Narrative Research*. Translated by Kirsten Wolf and Jody Jensen. Bloomington and Indianapolis: Indiana University Press, 1992

Orr, Leonard. *A Dictionary of Critical Theory*. New York, Westport, Connecticut and London: Greenwood Press, 1991

Ousby, Ian, ed. *The Cambridge Guide to Literature in English*. With a foreword by Margaret Atwood. Rev. edn. Cambridge University Press, 1992

Pardes, Ilana. *Countertraditions in the Bible: A Feminist Approach*. Cambridge, MA and London: Harvard University Press, 1992

Parry, Ann. *The Poetry of Rudyard Kipling: Rousing the Nation*. Buckingham and Philadelphia: Open University Press, 1992

Perkins, David, ed. *Theoretical Issues in Literary History*. Cambridge, MA and London: Harvard University Press, 1991

Pinget, Robert. *The Enemy*. Translated by Barbara Wright. New York: Red Dust, 1987. First published as *L'Ennemi*, Paris: Editions de Minuit, 1987

Rainey, Lawrence S. *Ezra Pound and the Monument of Culture: Text, History and the Malatesta Cantos*. Chicago and London: University of Chicago Press, 1991

Rajchman, John. *Truth and Eros: Foucault, Lacan, and the Question of Ethics*. New York and London: Routledge, 1991

Richardson, J. A. *Falling Towers: The Trojan Imagination in 'The Waste Land', 'The*

Dunciad', and 'Speke Parott'. Newark, NJ: University of Delaware Press. London and Toronto: Associated University Presses, 1992

Rignall, John. *Realist Fiction and the Strolling Spectator.* London and New York: Routledge, 1992

Roberts, David and Philip Thomson. *The Modern German Historical Novel: Paradigms, Problems, Perspectives.* Berg European Studies Series. New York and Oxford: Berg, 1991

Roberts, Gareth. *The Faerie Queene.* Buckingham and Philadelphia: Open University Press, 1992

Rose, Margaret A. *The Post-modern and the Post-industrial: A Critical analysis.* Cambridge University Press, 1991

Ryan, Marie-Laure. *Possible Worlds, Artificial Intelligence, and Narrative Theory.* Bloomington and Indianapolis: Indiana University Press, 1991

Segal, Naomi. *The Adulteress's Child: Authorship and Desire in the Nineteenth-Century Novel.* Cambridge: Polity, 1992

Shakespeare, William. *King Henry V.* Ed. Andrew Gurr. The New Cambridge Shakespeare. Cambridge University Press, 1992

Shaughnessy, Robert. *Three Socialist Plays: Lear, Roots, Sergeant Musgrave's Dance.* Buckingham and Philadelphia: Open University Press, 1992

Sinfield, Alan. *Faultlines: Cultural Materialism and the Politics of Dissident Reading.* Oxford: Clarendon Press, 1992

Smith, Iain Crichton. *Critical Essays.* Ed. Colin Nicholson. Edinburgh: Edinburgh University Press, 1992

Smith, Paul Julian. *Laws of Desire: Questions of Homosexuality in Spanish Writing and Film 1960–1990.* Oxford: Clarendon Press, 1992

Stafford, Barbara. *Body Criticism: Imaging the Unseen in Enlightenment Art and Medicine.* Cambridge, MA and London: MIT Press, 1991

Sten, Christopher, ed. *Savage Eye: Melville and the Visual Arts.* Kent, Ohio and London: Kent State University Press, 1991

Still, Arthur and Irving Velody, eds. *Rewriting the History of Madness: Studies in Foucault's 'Histoire de la folie'.* London and New York: Routledge, 1992

Strindberg, August. *Strindberg's Letters.* In two volumes. Selected, edited and translated by Michael Robinson. London: Athlone Press, 1992

Sturgess, Philip J. M. *Narrativity: Theory and Practice.* Oxford: Clarendon Press, 1992

Sugano, Marian Zwerling. *The Poetics of the Occasion: Mallarmé and the Poetry of Circumstance.* Stanford, CA: Stanford University Press, 1992

Sumida, Stephen H. *And the View from the Shore: Literary Traditions of Hawaii.* Seattle and London: University of Washington Press, 1991

Taylor, Charles. *The Ethics of Authenticity.* Cambridge, MA and London: Harvard University Press, 1992

Turton, Glyn. *Turgenev and the Context of English Literature 1850–1900.* London and New York: Routledge, 1992

Van Dyke, Annette. *The Search for a Woman-Centered Spirituality.* New York and London: New York University Press, 1992

Van Erven, Eugene. *The Playful Revolution: Theatre and Liberation in Asia.* Bloomington and Indianapolis: Indiana University Press, 1992

Vines, Lois Davis, *Valéry and Poe: A Literary Legacy*. New York and London: New York University Press, 1992

Von Mücke, Dorothea E. *Virtue and the Veil of Illusion: Generic Innovation and the Pedagogical Project in Eighteenth-Century Literature*. Stanford, CA: Stanford University Press, 1991

Wallace, Robert K. *Melville and Turner: Spheres of Love and Fright*. Atlanta, GA: University of Georgia Press, 1992

Wang, David Der-wei. *Fictional Realism in Twentieth-Century China: Mao Dun, Lao She, Shen Congwen*. New York: Columbia University Press, 1992

Wang, Jing. *The Story of Stone: Intertextuality, Ancient Chinese Stone Lore, and the Stone Symbolism in 'Dream of the Red Chamber', 'Water Margin', and 'The Journey to the West'*. Durham, NC and London: Duke University Press, 1992

Watson, J. R. *English Poetry of the Romantic Period 1789–1830*. First edition Longman, 1985. London and New York: London, 1992

Wees, William C. *Light Moving in Time: Studies in the Visual Aesthetics of Avant-Garde Film*. Berkeley, Los Angeles and Oxford: University of California Press, 1992

Whitlark, James and Wendell Aycock. *The Literature of Emigration and Exile*. Studies in Comparative Literature 23. Lubbock, Texas: Texas Technical University Press, 1992

Widdowson, Peter, ed. and intr. *D. H. Lawrence*. Longman Critical Readers. London and New York: Longman, 1992

Wilentz, Gay. *Binding Cultures: Black Women Writers in Africa and the Diaspora*. Bloomington and Indianapolis: Indiana University Press, 1992

Wilson, Richard and Richard Dutton, eds. *New Historicism and Renaissance Drama*. London and New York: Longman, 1992

Witte, Bernd. *Walter Benjamin: An Intellectual Biography*. Translated by James Rolleston. Detroit: Wayne State University Press, 1991. First published as *Walter Benjamin: rowohlts monographien*, Rowohlt Taschenbuch Verlag, 1985

Yarrow, Ralph, ed. *European Theatre 1960–1990: Cross-cultural Perspectives*. London and New York: Routledge, 1992

PERIODICALS

AUMLA 74 (1990). Special issue: *Narratives Issues*. Ed. John Hay and Marie Maclean

Books from Finland 25.3 (1991) and 26.3 (1992)

British Journal for Eighteenth-Century Studies 14.2 (1991), 15.1 (1992) and 15.2 (1992)

Canadian Review of Comparative Literature 19.1/2 (1992)

Chung-Wai Literary Monthly 20 (1991)

Comparative Literature 44.1 (1992)

Critical Studies 2.1/2 (1990)

Dedalus 1 (1991)

German Life and Letters 45.3 (1992). Special number for J. M. Ritchie

Iichiko 4 (1992)

Kris 36/37 (1988) and 38 (1989)

Literary Research/Recherche littéraire 18 (1992)

Littérature comparée/Littérature mondiale. Actes due XIème Congrès de l'Association Internationale de Littérature Comparée 5 (1985)

Modern Poetry in Translation 1 (NS, 1992)
New Comparison: A Journal of Comparative and General Literary Studies 13 (1992)
Parataxis: Modernism and Modern Writing 1 (1991)
P N Review 18.5 (1992) and 19.2 (1992)
Science as Culture 2.4 (1991)
Svet a Divadio 6, 9 and 10 (1991)
Synthesis 18 (1991)
Zeitschrift für Semiotik 14.1/2 (1992)

Comparative Criticism 15, pp. 293–313. Cambridge University Press 1993

Bibliography of comparative literature in Britain and Ireland, 1971–1974

COMPILED BY JOSEPH TH. LEERSSEN

The headings used are those of the full annual bibliography, discontinued in 1971, in the *Yearbook of Comparative and General Literature* (Chapel Hill, NC, 1950); entries are arranged chronologically by year of publication under each heading, and alphabetically by author within each year. The year of publication is omitted in the individual entries, as is the place of publication in the case of university presses; with other publishers, the place of publication is London unless otherwise stated.

I. COMPARATIVE, WORLD AND GENERAL LITERATURE AND CRITICISM

1971

Bateson, F. W. *Essays in Critical Dissent*. Longman, 153 pp.

Culler, Jonathan. 'Jakobson and the Linguistic Attributes of Literary Texts', *Language and Style*, 5, 53–66.

Daiches, David. 'Politics and the Literary Imagination', in *Liberations: New Essays on the Humanities in Revolution*, edited by Ihab Hassan (Wesleyan University Press), pp. 103–19.

Dickson, Keith. 'In Defence of "Comparative" Criticism', *German Life and Letters*, 25, 327–34.

Dixon, Peter. *Rhetoric*. Methuen, viii + 88 pp. (The Critical Idiom, 19)

Forrest-Thomson, Veronica. 'Irrationality and Artifice: A Problem in Recent Poetics', *British Journal of Aesthetics*, 11, 123–33.

Fowler, Roger. 'Literature and Linguistics: 1950–1970', *Dutch Quarterly Review of Anglo-American Letters*, 2, 65–81.

Gilman, E. 'Literary and Moral Values', *Essays in Criticism*, 21, 180–94.

Grimsley, Ronald. 'Two Philosophical Views of the Literary Imagination: Sartre and Bachelard', *Comparative Literature Studies*, 8, 42–57.

Kolnai, Aurel. 'Contrasting the Ethical with the Aesthetical', *British Journal of Aesthetics*, 11, 178–88; 12 (1972), 331–43.

Margolis, Joseph. 'Critics and Literature', *British Journal of Aesthetics*, 11, 368–84.

Maskell, Duke. 'In Praise of the Contemporary Critic', *Cambridge Quarterly*, 5, 327–34.

Mason, H. A. 'The Young Critic', *Cambridge Quarterly*, 5, 311–26.

Mew, Peter. 'Metaphor and Truth', *British Journal of Aesthetics*, 11, 189–95. See also Kipp, below (1973).

Newton, J. M. 'Literary Criticism, Universities, Murder', *Cambridge Quarterly*, 5, 335–54. Originally read at the Institute of Contemporary Arts, London, in a course of several lectures, by different people, on 'Literary Criticism as Discipline and Language'.

'The Poetics of Cultural Criticism', *Times Literary Supplement*, 17 December, 1565–6.

Steiner, George. *In Bluebeard's Castle. Some Notes towards the Re-Definition of Culture.* Faber and Faber, 111 pp.

Extraterrestrial: Papers on Literature and the Language Revolution. Faber and Faber, xiii + 211 pp.

Witte, W. 'The Literary Uses of Obscenity', *German Life and Letters*, 28, 360–73.

                                    1972

Aitken, A. J. 'The Literary Uses of the Computer', *Times Literary Supplement*, 21 April, 456–7.

Bateson, F. W. *The Scholar-Critic: An Introduction to Literary Research.* Routledge and Kegan Paul, xi + 202 pp.

Berry, Francis. 'Commentary' (on the contributions in this issue of *NLH*, on 'The Language of Literature'), *New Literary History*, 4, 167–80.

Bradbrook, M. C. *Literature in Action. Studies in Continental and Commonwealth Society.* Chatto and Windus, 200 pp.

Cohen, Gillian. 'The Psychology of Reading', *New Literary History*, 4, 75–90.

Dyson, Anthony Edward. *Between Two Worlds: Aspects of Literary Form.* Macmillan, ix + 157 pp.

Eaton, Marcia. 'The Truth Value of Literary Statements', *British Journal of Aesthetics*, 12, 163–74.

Forrest-Thomson, Veronica. 'Levels in Poetic Convention', *Journal of European Studies*, 2, 35–51.

Hawkes, Terence. *Metaphor.* Methuen, 102 pp. (The Critical Idiom, 25)

Hoggart, Richard. *Only Connect. On Culture and Communication.* Chatto and Windus, 111 pp.

Laurenson, Diana and Alan Swingewood. *The Sociology of Literature.* MacGibbon and Kee, 281 pp.

Leavis, F. R. *Nor Shall My Sword. Discourses on Pluralism, Compassion and Social Hope.* Chatto and Windus, 232 pp.

Lodge, David, ed. *Twentieth Century Literary Criticism.* Longman, xx + 683 pp.

Peacock, Ronald. *Criticism and Personal Taste.* Clarendon, 142 pp.

Reiss, Hans. 'Problems of Demarcation in the Study of Literature: Some Reflections', *Deutsche Vierteljahrsschrift für Literaturwissenschaft und Geistesgeschichte*, 46, 189–212.

Righter, William. 'Myth and Interpretation', *New Literary History*, 3, 319–44.

Rogers, Pat. 'Shaftesbury and the Aesthetics of Rhapsody', *British Journal of Aesthetics*, 12, 244–57.

Rycroft, Charles. 'The Artist as Patient', *Times Literary Supplement*, 22 September, 1089–90.

Scott, Clive. 'Poetics and Critics', *Journal of European Studies*, 2, 52–64.

Skinner, Quentin. 'Motives, Intentions, and the Interpretation of Texts', *New Literary History*, 3, 393–408.

'The State of English', *Times Literary Supplement*, various issues, pp. 147–8, 183–4, 215–16, 251–2, 269–70, 331–2, 389–90, 411–12.

Steiner, George. 'Whorf, Chomsky and the Student of Literature', *New Literary History*, 4, 15–34.

Thomson, Philip. *The Grotesque*. Methuen, viii + 76 pp. (The Critical Idiom, 24)

Wain, John. 'The New Puritanism, the New Academicism, the New, the New...', *Critical Quarterly*, 14, 7–18.

Walsh, Dorothy. 'Literary Art and Linguistic Meaning', *British Journal of Aesthetics*, 12, 321–30.

Young, Kenneth. 'The Literature of Politics', *Essays by Divers Hands*, 37, 134–52.

1973

Bann, Stephen and John E. Bowlt, eds. *Russian Formalism*. Scottish Academic Press, 177 pp.

Bergonzi, Bernard. 'Critical Situations: From the Fifties to the Seventies', *Critical Quarterly*, 15, 59–73.

Burns, Elizabeth and Tom Burns. *The Sociology of Literature and Drama*. Penguin, 506 pp.

Butler, Christopher. 'What Is a Literary Work?', *New Literary History*, 5, 17–30.

Chapman, Raymond. *Linguistics and Literature: An Introduction to Literary Stylistics*. Edward Arnold, viii + 119 pp.

Craig, David. *The Real Foundations: Literature and Social Change*. Chatto and Windus, 318 pp.

Dickie, George. 'Psychical Distance: In a Fog at Sea', *British Journal of Aesthetics*, 13, 17–29.

Dutton, Denis. 'Criticism and Method', *British Journal of Aesthetics*, 13, 232–42.

Enright, D. J. *Man is an Onion: Reviews and Essays*. Chatto and Windus, 222 pp.

Fowler, Alastair. *Readers of Literature*. University of Edinburgh, 21 pp.

Gill, Roma. 'As We Read the Living?', *Essays in Criticism*, 23, 167–75. With a reply by F. W. Bateson, pp. 175–8.

Gurr, Andrew and Pio Zirimu, eds. *Black Aesthetics: Papers from a Colloquium Held at the University of Nairobi, June 1971*. Nairobi, Kampala & Dar es Salaam, East African Literary Bureau, 216 pp.

Hawthorn, Jeremy. *Identity and Relationship: A Contribution to Marxist Theory of Literary Criticism*. Lawrence & Wishart, xi + 195 pp.

Kermode, Frank. 'The Use of Codes', in *Approaches to Poetics: Selected Papers from the English Institute*, edited by S. Chatman (Columbia University Press), pp. 51–79.

Kipp, David. 'Metaphor, Truth and Mew on Elliott', *British Journal of Aesthetics*, 13, 30–40. See also Mew, above (1971).

Olsen, Stein Haugom. 'Authorial Intention', *British Journal of Aesthetics*, 13, 219–231.

Parekh, Bhikhu and R. N. Berki. 'The History of Politicial Ideas: A Critique of Q. Skinner's Methodology', *Journal of the History of Ideas*, 34, 163–84.

Robson, Vincent. 'Literary Criticism and the Academic Canon', *Linguistica et litteraria*, 2, no. 1, 30–53.

Selden, Raman. 'Objectivity and Theory in Literary Criticism', *Essays in Criticism*, 23, 283–97.

Short, M. H. 'Linguistic Criticism and Baudelaire's "Les Chats"', *Journal of Literary Semantics*, 2, 79–93.

Steiner, George. 'Beyond the Parish Pump', *Times Literary Supplement*, 25 May, 581–2. 'The Way to Silence', *Semiotica*, 8, 94–6.

Stern, J. P. 'Occlusions, Disclosures, Conclusions', *New Literary History*, 5, 149–68.

Swingewood, Alan. 'Literature and *Praxis*: A Sociological Commentary', *New Literary History*, 5, 169–76.

Wain, John. 'The Single Mind: A Review of Lionel Trilling, *Sincerity and Authenticity*', *Critical Quarterly*, 15, 173–9.

Warner, Martin. 'Black's Metaphors', *British Journal of Aesthetics*, 13, 367–72.

1974

Brewer, D. S. 'Some Observations on the Development of Liberalism and Verbal Criticism', *Poetics* (Tokyo), 1, 71–95.

Culler, Jonathan. 'Commentary' (on the contributions in this issue of *NLH*, on 'Metaphor'), *New Literary History*, 6, 219–29.

Donoghue, Denis. 'Between Value and Fact', *Times Literary Supplement*, 6 December, 1358.
  Imagination. Glasgow University Press, 40 pp. (W. P. Ker Memorial Lecture)
  'Some Versions of Empson', *Times Literary Supplement*, 7 June, 589–90.

Edge, David. 'Technological Metaphor and Social Control', *New Literary History*, 6, 135–48.

Ellis, A. J. 'Intention and Interpretation in Literature', *British Journal of Aesthetics*, 14, 315–25.

Grigson, Geoffrey. *The Contrary View: Glimpses of Fudge and Gold*. Macmillan, xi + 243 pp.

Heath, Stephen. *Le vertige du déplacement*. Paris: Fayard, 214 pp.

Jones, Robert Maynard. *Tafod y llenor: Gwersi ar theori llenyddiaeth*. Gwasg Prifysgol Cymru, 310 pp.

King, Bruce, ed. *Literatures of the World in English*. Routledge and Kegan Paul, 225 pp.

Norris, Christopher. '*Les plaisirs des clercs*: Barthes's Latest Writing', *British Journal of Aesthetics*, 14, 250–7.

Nuttall, A. D. *A Common Sky: Philosophy and the Literary Imagination*. Chatto and Windus for Sussex University Press, 298 pp.

Prawer, S. S. *Comparative Literary Studies: An Introduction*. Duckworth, xi + 180 pp.

Rockwell, Joan. *Fact in Fiction: The Use of Literature in the Systematic Study of Society*. Routledge and Kegan Paul, x + 211 pp.

Steiner, George. Review of Michel Foucault's *The Order of Things*, *New York Times Book Review*, 28 February. Also, *Diacritics*, 1, no. 1 (Fall), 57–60; no. 2 (Winter), 59–60.

Webster, Richard. 'Frank Kermode's *The Sense of an Ending*', *Critical Quarterly*, 16, 311–24.

Wetherill, Peter Michael. *The Literary Text: An Examination of Critical Methods.* Oxford: Basil Blackwell, xx + 331 pp. (Language and Style, 15)

Williams, Raymond. 'The English Language and the English Tripos', *Times Literary Supplement*, 15 November, 1293–4.

II. THEMES AND MOTIFS

1971

Deane, Seamus F. 'John Bull and Voltaire: The Emergence of a Cultural Cliché', *Revue de littérature comparée*, 45, 581–94.

Rees, Christine. 'The Metamorphosis of Daphne in Sixteenth- and Seventeenth-Century English Poetry', *Modern Language Review*, 66, 252–63.

Sayce, Olive. 'Chaucer's "Retractions": The Conclusion of the *Canterbury Tales* and its Place in Literary Tradition', *Medium Aevum*, 40, 230–48.

Selden, Raman. 'Roughness in Satire from Horace to Dryden', *Modern Language Review*, 66, 264–72.

Wells, D. A. 'Source and Tradition in the *Moriaen*', in *European Context* (see King and Vincent, section VI below), pp. 30–51.

1972

Dove, Mary. 'Gawain and the *Blasme des Femmes* Tradition', *Medium Aevum*, 41, 20–6.

Harbert, Bruce. 'The Myth of Tereus in Ovid and Gower', *Medium Aevum*, 41, 208–14.

Owen, D. D. R. *The Vision of Hell. Infernal Journeys in Medieval French Literature.* Scottish Academic Press, 322 pp.

Rivers, Isabel. *The Poetry of Conservatism, 1600–1745. A Study of Poets and Public Affairs, from Jonson to Pope.* Cambridge: Rivers Press, 279 pp.

Salaman, Esther. *The Great Confession. From Aksakov and De Quincey to Tolstoy and Proust.* Allen Lane, 312 pp.

Shackleton, Robert. 'The Greatest Happiness of the Greatest Number: The History of Bentham's Phrase', *Studies on Voltaire and the Eighteenth Century*, 90 (*Transactions of the Third Congress on the Enlightenment*, 4), 1461–82.

Short, Ian. 'A Study in Carolingian Legend and its Persistence in Latin Historiography (XII–XVI Centuries)', *Mittellateinisches Jahrbuch*, 7, 127–32.

Wagner, Geoffrey. *Five for Freedom: A Study of Feminism in Fiction.* George Allen and Unwin, 234 pp.

Waley, Pamela. 'The Nurse in Boccaccio's *Fiammetta*: Source and Invention', *Neophilologus*, 56, 164–74.

1973

Bennett, P. E. 'The Literary Source of Béroul's Godoïne', *Medium Aevum*, 42, 133–40.

Cave, Terence. 'Mythes de l'abondance et de la privation chez Ronsard', *Cahiers de l'Association internationale des études françaises*, 25, 247–60.

Flavell, M. K., '"Arkadisch frei sei unser Glück": The Myth of the Golden Age in Eighteenth-Century Germany', *Publications of the English Goethe Society*, 43, 1-27.

'Goethe, Rousseau, and the "Hyp"', *Oxford German Studies*, 7, 5-23.

Lyle, E. B. '*Sir Landevale* and the Fairy-Mistress Theme in *Thomas of Erceldoune*', *Medium Aevum*, 42, 244-50.

Williams, Raymond, *The Country and the City*. Chatto and Windus, 335 pp.

1974

Bance, A. F. 'The Kaspar Hauser Legend and its Literary Survival', *German Life and Letters*, 28, 199-210.

Currie, Robert. *Genius: An Ideology in Literature*. Chatto and Windus, 222 pp.

Fowler, Frank M. 'Hebbel, Jeanne d'Arc und *Die Jungfrau von Orleans*', *Hebbel-Jahrbuch*, 1974, 126-38.

Hardwick, Elizabeth. *Seduction and Betrayal: Women and Literature*. Weidenfeld and Nicolson, 208 pp.

Jackson, W. H. 'Ulrich von Zatzikhoven's *Lanzelet* and the Theme of Resistance to Royal Power', *German Life and Letters*, 28, 285-97.

Lester, G. A. 'The Caedmon Story and its Analogues', *Neophilologus*, 58, 225-37.

Mendel, Sydney. *Roads to Consciousness*. Allen and Unwin, 276 pp.

Moore, Gerald. 'Reintegration with the Lost Self: A Theme in Contemporary African Literature', *Revue de littérature comparée*, 48, 488-503.

Morrison, Mary. 'Some Aspects of the Treatment of the Theme of Antony and Cleopatra in Tragedies of the Sixteenth Century', *Journal of European Studies*, 4, 113-25.

Murdoch, Brian. 'Transformations of the Holocaust: Auschwitz in Modern Lyric Poetry', *Comparative Literature Studies*, 11, 123-50.

Nuttall, A. D. 'Fishes in the Trees', *Essays in Criticism*, 24, 20-38.

Pearsall, Derek and Elizabeth Salter. *Landscapes and Seasons of the Medieval World*. Elek, xvi + 252 pp.

Pickering, F. P. 'The Western Image of Byzantium in the Late Middle Ages', *German Life and Letters*, 28, 326-40.

Sage, Lorna. 'The Case of the Active Victim', *Times Literary Supplement*, 26 July, 803-4.

West, Rebecca. 'And They All Lived Unhappily Ever After', *Times Literary Supplement*, 26 July, 779.

III. LITERARY GENRES, TYPES AND FORMS

1971

Bragg, Melvyn. 'Class and the Novel', *Times Literary Supplement*, 15 October, 1261-3.

Daly, Peter M. 'Emblematic Poetry of Occasional Meditation', *German Life and Letters*, 25, 126-39.

Draper, R. P. 'Concrete Poetry', *New Literary History*, 2, 329-40.

Edwards, Michael. 'Racinian Tragedy', *Critical Quarterly*, 13, 329–48.

Ellmann, Richard. *Literary Biography*. Clarendon Press, 19 pp.

Fowler, Alastair. 'The Life and Death of Literary Forms', *New Literary History*, 2, 199–216.

Josipovici, Gabriel. *The World and the Book: A Study of Modern Fiction*. Macmillan, xviii + 318 pp.

Killham, John. 'A Novel's Relevance to Life', *British Journal of Aesthetics*, 11, 63–73.

McInnes, Edward. 'Drama as Protest and Prophecy: The Historical Drama of the Jungdeutsche', *Maske und Kothurn*, 17, 190–202.

Maskell, D. W. 'The Transformation of History into Epic: the *Stuartide* (1611) of Jean de Schelandre', *Modern Language Review*, 66, 53–65.

Merchant, Paul. *The Epic*. Methuen, viii + 103 pp. (The Critical Idiom, 17)

'New Frontiers in the Theory of Fiction', *Times Literary Supplement*, 3 September, 1005–6.

Press, John. *The Lengthening Shadows*. Oxford University Press, ix + 191 pp.

Skelton, Robin. *The Practice of Poetry*. Heinemann, vii + 184 pp.

1972

Berry, Francis. *Thoughts on Poetic Time*. Abingdon, Abbey Press, 23 pp.

Butler (Lord). 'The Prevalence of Indirect Biography', *Essays by Divers Hands*, 37, 17–30.

Edwards, Michael. *La tragédie racinienne*. Paris, La pensée universelle, 379 pp.

Fuller, John. *The Sonnet*. Methuen, 58 pp. (The Critical Idiom, 26)

Heath, Stephen. *The Nouveau Roman: A Study in the Practice of Writing*. Elek, 252 pp.

Hepburn, Ronald. 'Poetry and "Concrete Imagination": Problems of Truth and Illusion', *British Journal of Aesthetics*, 12, 3–18.

Hewitt, Douglas. *The Approach to Fiction: Good and Bad Readings of Novels*. Longman, 198 pp.

Holbrook, David. 'Pornography and Death', *Critical Quarterly*, 14, 29–41.

Jenkins, Ray. 'The Development of Modern Political Biography, 1945–70', *Essays by Divers Hands*, 37, 63–74.

Jump, John D. *Burlesque*. Methuen, x + 77 pp. (The Critical Idiom, 22)

Kermode, Frank. *Novel and Narrative*. University of Glasgow, 28 pp.

Lerner, Laurence. *The Uses of Nostalgia: Studies in Pastoral Poetry*. Chatto & Windus, 248 pp.

Lodge, David. 'Onions and Apricots; or, Was the Rise of the Novel a Fall from Grace? Serious Reflections on Gabriel Josipovici's *The World and the Book*', *Critical Quarterly*, 14, 171–85.

McInnes, Edward. 'Strategies of Inwardness: Gutzkow's Domestic Plays and the Liberal Drama of the 1840's', *Maske und Kothurn*, 18, 219–33.

Merchant, W. Moelwyn. *Comedy*. Methuen, x + 92 pp. (The Critical Idiom, 21)

Moore, W. G. 'Raison et structure dans la comédie de Molière', *Revue d'histoire littéraire de la France*, 72, 800–5.

Radford, Colin. 'Theatre within the Theatre', *Nottingham French Studies*, 11, 76–90.

Shergold, Norman D., ed. *Studies in the Spanish and Portuguese Ballad*. Tamesis, vii + 176 pp.

Symons, Julian. *Bloody Murder: From the Detective Story to the Crime Novel*. Faber and Faber, 254 pp.

1973

Aldiss, Brian. *Billion Year Spree: The History of Science Fiction*. Weidenfeld and Nicolson, 339 pp.

Bradbrook, M. C. 'The Nature of Theatrical Experience in Ben Jonson, with Special Reference to the Masques', in *Expression, Communication and Experience in Literature and Language. Proceedings of the XIIth Congress of the International Federation for Modern Languages and Literatures, Held at Cambridge University, 20 to 26 August 1972*, edited by R. G. Popperwell (Modern Humanities Research Association), pp. 103–17.

Bradbury, Malcolm. *Possibilities*. Clarendon, 197 pp.

Bullock-Davies, Constance. 'The Form of the Breton Lay', *Medium Aevum*, 42, 18–31.

Denny, Neville, ed. *Medieval Drama*. Edward Arnold, 254 pp. (Stratford-upon-Avon Studies, 16)

Gable, A. T. 'Tragic Lament and Tragic Action', *Journal of European Studies*, 3, 59–69.

Griffin, Nigel. 'Miguel Venegas and the Sixteenth-Century Jesuit School Drama', *Modern Language Review*, 68, 796–806.

Haggis, D. R. 'Scott, Balzac, and the Historical Novel as Social and Political Analysis: *Waverley* and *Les Chouans*', *Modern Language Review*, 68, 50–68.

McClelland, John. 'Sonnet ou quatorzain? Marot et le choix d'une forme poétique', *Revue d'histoire littéraire de la France*, 73, 591–607.

McInnes, Edward. 'Lessing's *Hamburgische Dramaturgie* and the Theory of the Drama in the Nineteenth Century', *Orbis Litterarum*, 28, 294–318.

Mitchell, Julian. *Truth and Fiction*. Covent Garden Press, 25 pp.

Paton, Margaret. 'Hume on Tragedy', *British Journal of Aesthetics*, 13, 121–32.

Renault, Mary. 'History in Fiction', *Times Literary Supplement*, 23 March, 315–16. See also Taylor, below.

Roddy, Kevin. 'Epic Qualities in the Cycle Plays', in *Medieval Drama* (see Denny, above), pp. 154–71.

Shepard, Leslie. *The History of Street Literature: The Story of Broadside Ballads, Chapbooks, Proclamations, Election Bills, Tracts, Pamphlets, Cocks, Catchpennies, and Other Ephemera*. Newton Abbot: David and Charles, 238 pp.

Smith, James L. *Melodrama*. Methuen, viii + 96 pp. (The Critical Idiom, 28)

Stevens, John. *Medieval Romance*. Hutchinson, 255 pp.

Swift, Bernard. 'The Hypothesis of the French Symbolist Novel', *Modern Language Review*, 68, 776–87.

Taylor, A. J. P. 'Fiction in History', *Times Literary Supplement*, 23 March, 327–8. See also Renault, above.

Williams, Arnold. 'The Comic in the Cycles', in *Medieval Drama* (see Denny, above), pp. 108–23.

1974

Axton, Richard. *European Drama of the Early Middle Ages*. Hutchinson, 227 pp.

Bond, Martyn. 'Das Hörspiel: Epic, Lyric or Dramatic? The Critical Debate about a Literary Form', *German Life and Letters*, 28, 45–58.

Brissenden, Robert Francis. *Virtue in Distress: Studies in the Novel of Sentiment from Richardson to Sade*. Macmillan, xiii + 306 pp.

Charlton, William. 'Is Philosophy a Form of Literature?', *British Journal of Aesthetics*, 14, 3–16.

Cross, J. E. 'The Poem in Transmitted Text – Editor and Critic', *Essays and Studies*, 27, 84–97.

Denny, Neville. 'Aspects of the Staging of Mankind', *Medium Aevum*, 43, 252–63.

Donoghue, Denis. 'A Reply to Frank Kermode', *Critical Inquiry*, 1, 447–52. See Kermode, below.

Ellis, John M. *Narration in the German Novelle: Theory and Interpretation*. Cambridge University Press, 219 pp.

Fletcher, J. 'The Difficult Dialogue: Conflicting Attitudes to the Contemporary Novel', *Journal of European Studies*, 4, 274–86.

Green, D. H. 'The *Alexanderlied* and the Emergence of the Romance', *German Life and Letters*, 28, 246–62.

Haining, Peter, ed. *The Penny Dreadful*. Gollancz, 382 pp.

Hall, Kathleen M. 'How to Get the Corpse Off the Stage', *French Studies*, 28, 282–93.

Halperin, John, ed. *The Theory of the Novel: New Essays*. Oxford University Press, xi + 396 pp.

Jump, John D. *The Ode*. Methuen, ix + 67 pp. (The Critical Idiom, 30)

Kermode, Frank. 'Novels: Recognition and Deception', *Critical Inquiry*, 1, no. 1, 103–21. Replied to by Denis Donoghue (see above).

Theobald, D. W. 'Philosophy and Fiction: The Novel as Eloquent Philosophy', *British Journal of Aesthetics*, 14, 17–25.

Whitbourn, Christine Janet, ed. *Knaves and Swindlers: Essays on the Picaresque Novel in Europe*. Oxford University Press for the University of Hull, xix + 145 pp.

IV. EPOCHS, CURRENTS AND MOVEMENTS

1971

Bradbury, Malcolm. 'Style of Life, Style of Art and the American Novelist in the Nineteen Twenties', in *The American Novel in the Nineteen Twenties* (Edward Arnold, 269 pp.; Stratford-upon-Avon Studies, edited by M. Bradbury and D. Palmer, 13), pp. 10–35.

Chadwick, Charles. *Symbolism*. Methuen, viii + 71 pp. (The Critical Idiom, 16)

Furst, Lilian R. and Peter N. Skrine. *Naturalism*. Methuen, vi + 81 pp. (The Critical Idiom, 18)

Krailsheimer, A. J., ed. *The Continental Renaissance, 1500–1600*. Penguin, 575 pp. (Pelican guides to European literature)

Lucas, John, ed. *Literature and Politics in the Nineteenth Century*. Methuen, 283 pp.

Mann, Nicholas. 'Humanisme et patriotisme en France au XVe siècle', *Cahiers de l'Association internationale des études françaises*, 23, 51–66.

Menhennet, A. 'Between Baroque and Rococo: The "Galant Style" of Christian Hölmann', *Modern Language Review*, 66, 343–52.

Mottram, Eric. 'The Hostile Environment and the Survival Artist: A Note on the Twenties', in *The American Novel and the Nineteen Twenties* (see Bradbury, above), pp. 232–62.

West, Thomas G. 'Schopenhauer, Huysmans and French Naturalism', *Journal of European Studies*, 1, 313–24.

Wilson, Jean. 'The "Nineties" Movement in Poetry: Myth or Reality?', *Yearbook of English Studies*, 1, 160–74.

1972

Armstrong, Isobel. *Victorian Scrutinies: Reviews of Poetry, 1830–1870*. Athlone, x + 344 pp.

Bell, Michael. *Primitivism*. Methuen, ix + 93 pp. (The Critical Idiom, 20)

Bigsby, C. W. E. *Dada and Surrealism*. Methuen, viii + 91 pp. (The Critical Idiom, 23)

Dashwood, Julie R. 'Futurism and Fascism', *Italian Studies*, 27, 91–103.

Gent, Victoria. '"To Flinch from Modern Varnish": The Appeal of the Past to the Victorian Imagination', in *Victorian Poetry* (Edward Arnold, 304 pp.; Stratford-upon-Avon Studies, edited by M. Bradbury and D. Palmer, 15), pp. 10–35.

Lerner, Michael. 'The *Revue Contemporaine* and Fin de Siècle Cosmopolitanism', *Arcadia*, 7, 281–4.

Menhennet, A. 'Order and Freedom in Haller's "Lehrgedichte": On the Limitations and Achievements of Strict Rationalism within the "Aufklärung"', *Neophilologus*, 56, 180–7.

Small, I. C. 'Plato and Pater: Fin-de-siècle Aesthetics', *British Journal of Aesthetics*, 12, 369–83.

Stern, J. P. 'Reflections on Realism', *Journal of European Studies*, 1, 1–31.
On Realism. Routledge and Kegan Paul, 199 pp.

1973

Bowlt, J. E. 'Russian Symbolism and the "Blue Rose" Movement', *Slavonic and East European Review*, 51, 161–81.

Daiches, David and Anthony Thorlby, eds. *The Mediaeval World*. Aldus, 725 pp. (Literature and Western Civilization, 2)

Forrest-Thomson, Veronica. 'Necessary Artifice: Form and Theory in the Poetry of *Tel Quel*', *Language and Style*, 6, 3–26.

Furness, R. S. *Expressionism*. Methuen, vi + 105 pp. (The Critical Idiom, 29)

Furst, Lilian R. 'The Structure of Romantic Agony', *Comparative Literature Studies*, 10, 125–38.

Gaskill, P. H. 'Hölderlin's Medievalism', *Neophilologus*, 57, 353–69.

Gibbons, Tom. 'Modernism in Poetry: The Debt to Arthur Symons', *British Journal of Aesthetics*, 13, 47–60.

Hunt, Tony. 'The Structure of Medieval Narrative', *Journal of European Studies*, 3, 295–328.

Martin, Angus. 'Baculard d'Arnaud et la vogue des séries de nouvelles en France au XVIIIe siècle', *Revue d'histoire littéraire de la France*, 73, 982–92.

Secretan, Dominique. *Classicism*. Methuen, viii + 85 pp. (The Critical Idiom, 27)

Southall, Raymond. *Literature and the Rise of Capitalism. Critical Essays Mainly on the Sixteenth and Seventeenth Centuries*. Lawrence and Wishart, 175 pp.

Weightman, John. *The Concept of the Avant-Garde: Explorations in Modernism*. Alcove, 323 pp.

West, J. D. 'Neo-Romanticism in the Russian Symbolist Aesthetic', *Slavonic and East European Review*, 51, 413–27.

1974

Chapman, Raymond. 'Words and Sounds: Auditory Experience in the Poetry of the 1914–18 War', *Poetics* (Tokyo), 1, 46–62.

Daiches, David and Anthony Thorlby, eds. *The Old World: Discovery and Rebirth*. Aldus, 624 pp. (Literature and Western Civilization, 3)

Gaskell, P. H. 'Hölderlin's Contact with Pietism', *Modern Language Review*, 69, 805–20.

Hemmings, F. W. J., ed. *The Age of Realism*. Penguin, 415 pp. (Pelican guides to European literature)

Murdoch, John. 'English Realism: George Eliot and the Pre-Raphaelites', *Journal of the Warburg and Courtauld Institutes*, 37, 313–29.

Reed, T. J. 'An Alternative Germany', *Times Literary Supplement*, 25 October, 1199–201.

Rogers, Pat. *The Augustan Vision*. Weidenfeld and Nicolson, 318 pp.

Vicinus, Martha. *The Industrial Muse. A Study of Nineteenth-Century British Working Class Literature*. Croom Helm, 357 pp.

White, J. J. 'Signs of Disturbance: The Semiological Import of Some Recent Fiction by Michel Tournier and Peter Handke', *Journal of European Studies*, 4, 233–54.

V. THE BIBLE, CLASSICAL ANTIQUITY

1971

Barr, James. 'The Book of Job and its Modern Interpreters', *Bulletin of the John Rylands University Library of Manchester*, 54, no. 1, 28–46.

Bolgar, R. R., ed. *Classical Influences on European Culture, AD 500–1500: Proceedings of an International Conference Held at King's College, Cambridge, April 1971*. Cambridge University Press, xvi + 320 pp.

Cooper, B. 'Pushkin and the Anacreonta', *Slavonic and East European Review*, 52, 182–7.

'Epistula ad Pisones and the Poetry of Antiquity', *Times Literary Supplement*, 14 May, 549–50.

Evans, S. 'Odyssean Echoes in Propertius IV.8', *Greece & Rome*, 18, 51–3.

Gulley, Norman. *Aristotle on the Purposes of Literature*. University of Wales Press, 18 pp.

Huxley, George. 'Crete in Aristotle's *Politics*', *Greek, Roman and Byzantine Studies*, 12, 505–16.

King, Christine M. 'Seneca's *Hercules Oetaeus*: A Stoic Interpretation of the Greek Myth', *Greece & Rome*, 18, 215–22.

McFarlane, I. D. 'Notes on the Composition and Reception of George Buchanan's Psalm Paraphrases', *Forum for Modern Language Studies*, 7, 319–60.

Thomson, George. 'The Continuity of Hellenism', *Greece & Rome*, 18, 18–29.

'The Unity of Greek', *Times Literary Supplement*, 29 October, 1363–5.

1972

Bowra, C. M. *Homer*. Duckworth, 191 pp.

Daiches, David and Anthony Thorlby, eds. *The Classical World*. Aldus, 557 pp. (Literature and Western Civilization, 1)

Lebans, W. M. 'The Influence of the Classics in Donne's *Epicedes and Obsequies*', *Review of English Studies*, 23, 127–37.

Mason, H. A. *To Homer through Pope. An Introduction to Homer's 'Iliad' and Pope's Translation*. Chatto and Windus, vii + 216 pp.

Rees, B. R. '*Pathos* in the *Poetics* of Aristotle', *Greece & Rome*, 19, 1–11.

Shields, Hugh. 'Bishop Turpin and the Source of *Nicodemus Gospell*', *English Studies*, 53, 497–502.

Trendall, A. D. and T. B. L. Webster. *Illustrations of Greek Drama*. Phaidon, x + 159 pp.

Tucker, Susie. 'Biblical Translation in the Eighteenth Century', *Essays and Studies*, 25, 106–20.

1973

Andrew, Malcolm. 'Jonah and Christ in *Patience*', *Modern Philology*, 70, 230–3.

Barr, James. 'Reading the Bible as Literature', *Bulletin of the John Rylands University Library of Manchester*, 56, no. 1, 10–33.

Fowler, Rowena. 'Ernest Dowson and the Classics', *Yearbook of English Studies*, 3, 243–52.

Hammond, Gerald. 'English Bible Translation', *Critical Quarterly*, 15, 361–70.

Mason, H. A. 'Books on Catullus', *Cambridge Quarterly*, 6, 152–77.

Murdoch, Brian. 'An Early Irish Adam and Eve: *Saltair na Rann* and the Traditions of the Fall', *Medieval Studies*, 35, 146–77.

Selden, Raman. 'Juvenal and Restoration Modes of Translation', *Modern Language Review*, 68, 481–93.

Shiel, James. 'The Latin Aristotle', *Medium Aevum*, 42, 147–52.

Steiner, George. 'The Writer as Remembrancer: A Note on *Poetics*, 9', *Yearbook of Comparative and General Literature*, 22, 51–7.

Vickers, Brian. *Towards Greek Tragedy*. Longman, 658 pp.

West, M. L. 'Greek Poetry 2000–700 BC', *Classical Quarterly*, 23, 179–92.

1974

Bawcutt, Priscilla. 'Douglas and Surrey: Translators of Virgil', *Essays and Studies*, 27, 52–67.

Hopkins, D. W. 'Two Hitherto Unrecorded Sources for Dryden's Ovid Translations', *Notes & Queries*, 219, 419–21.

Horsfall, Nicholas. 'Classical Studies in England, 1810–1825', *Greek, Roman and Byzantine Studies*, 15, 449–77.

Huxley, George. 'Aristotle's Interest in Biography', *Greek, Roman and Byzantine Studies*, 15, 203–13.

Kermode, Frank. 'A Modern Way with the Classic', *New Literary History*, 5, 415–34.

Macleod, C. W. 'A Use of Myth in Ancient Poetry', *Classical Quarterly*, 24, 82–93.

Silk, M. S. *Introduction to Poetic Imagery: With Special Reference to Early Greek Poetry.* Cambridge University Press, 263 pp.

Stopp, F. J. 'Latin Plays at the Academy of Altdorf, 1577–1626', *Journal of European Studies*, 4, 189–213.

VI. INDIVIDUAL COUNTRIES OR REGIONS

1971

Bradbury, Malcolm. *The Social Context of Modern English Literature.* Oxford, Blackwell, 277 pp.

Brathwaite, Edward. 'Rehabilitations', *Critical Quarterly*, 13, 175–83.

Cross, A. G. 'An Oxford Don in Catherine the Great's Russia', *Journal of European Studies*, 1, 166–74.

Daiches, David, ed. *Britain and the Commonwealth.* Allen Lane and Penguin, 575 pp. (Penguine companion to literature, 1)

Dudley, D. R. and D. M. Lang, eds. *Classical and Byzantine; Oriental and African.* Allen Lane and Penguin, 359 pp. (Penguin companion to literature, 4)

Furst, Lilian R. 'Lessing and Mme de Staël vis-à-vis the Literature of the Mediterranean', *Journal of European Studies*, 1, 161–5.

Hatto, A. T. *Shamanism and Epic Poetry in Northern Asia.* School of Oriental and African Studies, University of London, 19 pp.

Jones, R. O., general ed. *A Literary History of Spain.* 8 vols., Ernest Benn, 1971–73; 1: A. D. Deyermond, *The Middle Ages* (xix + 244 pp.); 2: R. O. Jones, *The Golden Age: Prose and Poetry. The Sixteenth and Seventeenth Centuries* (xvii + 233 pp.); 3: E. M. Wilson and D. Moir, *The Golden Age: Drama, 1492–1700* (xviii + 171 pp.); 4: N. Glendinning, *The Eighteenth Century* (1972, xv + 160 pp.); 5: D. L. Shaw, *The Nineteenth Century* (1972, xxii + 200 pp.); 6: G. G. Brown, *The Twentieth Century* (1972, xv + 176 pp.); 7: J. Franco, *Spanish American Literature since Independence* (1973, xiv + 306 pp.); 8: A. Terry, *Catalan Literature* (1972, xix + 136 pp.).

King, Jonathan H. 'Philosophy and Experience: French Intellectuals and the Second World War', *Journal of European Studies*, 1, 198–212.

King, P. K. and P. F. Vincent, eds. *European Context. Studies in the History and Literature of the Netherlands Presented to Theodoor Weevers.* Cambridge, Modern Humanities Research Association, xiv + 415 pp.

Mainland, William F. 'In Pursuit of Flemish: Escape or the Homeward Journey?', in *European Context* (see King and Vincent, above), pp. 386–99.

Mottram, Eric, Malcolm Bradbury and Jean Franco, eds. *USA and Latin America*. Allen Lane and Penguin, 384 pp. (Penguin companion to literature, 3)

Sagarra, Eda. *Tradition and Revolution: German Literature and Society 1830–1890*. Weidenfeld and Nicolson, 348 pp.

Stern, J. P. *Idylls and Realities. Studies in Nineteenth-Century German Literature*. Methuen, 232 pp.

Thorlby, Anthony, ed. *Europe*. Allen Lane and Penguin, 907 pp. (Penguin companion to literature, 2)

Ambrose, Mary E. '*La Donna del Lago*: The First Italian Translators of Scott', *Modern Language Review*, 67, 74–82.

Brotherston, Gordon. 'Ubirajara, Hiawatha, Cumandá: National Virtue from American Indian Literature', *Comparative Literature Studies*, 9, 243–52.

Buxton, John. 'A Second Supplement to Toynbee's *Dante in English Literature*', *Italian Studies*, 27, 41–3.

Freeborn, Richard. *The Rise of the Russian Novel*. Cambridge University Press, 289 pp.

Grigson, Geoffrey. 'The Writer and his Territory', *Times Literary Supplement*, 28 July, 859–60.

Heald, David. 'Grillparzer and the Germans', *Oxford German Studies*, 6, 61–73.

Hutchinson, Peter. '"Conditioned against us…"': The East German View of the Federal Republic', *Forum for Modern Language Studies*, 8, 40–51.

Jack, R. D. S. *The Italian Influence on Scottish Literature*. Edinburgh University Press, 256 pp.

Jones, Gwyn. 'Writing for Wales and the Welsh', *Times Literary Supplement*, 28 July, 869–70.

Morgan, Edwin. 'The Resources of Scotland', *Times Literary Supplement*, 28 July, 885–6.

Morris, C. B. *Surrealism and Spain*. Cambridge University Press, 291 pp.

Palmer, Eustace. *An Introduction to the African Novel*. Heinemann, 176 pp.

Tierney, William. 'Irish Writers and the Spanish Civil War', *Éire – Ireland*, 7, 36–55.

1973

Auty, Robert. 'The Role of Poetry in the Early Nineteenth-Century Slavonic Language Revivals', in *Expression, Communication and Experience* (see Bradbrook, section III above), pp. 229–30.

Boa, Elizabeth and J. H. Reid. *Critical Strategies: German Fiction in the Twentieth Century*. Edward Arnold, 206 pp.

Ellis, D. G. 'Romans français dans la prude Angleterre (1830–1870)', *Revue de littérature comparée*, 47, 306–15.

Fraser, J. H. 'German Exile Publishing: The Malik-Aurora Verlag of Wieland Herzfeld', *German Life and Letters*, 27, 115–24.

Harding, F. W. J. 'Notes on Aesthetic Theory in France in the Nineteenth Century', *British Journal of Aesthetics*, 13, 251–70.

Keller, R. E. 'Diglossia in German-Speaking Switzerland', *Bulletin of the John Rylands University Library of Manchester*, 56, no. 1, 130–49.

Larry, N. M. *Dostoevsky and Dickens: A Study of Literary Influence.* Routledge and Kegan Paul, 172 pp.

Ritchie, J. M. 'Translations of the German Expressionists in Eugène Jolas's Journal *Transition*', *Oxford German Studies*, 8, 149–58.

Robson-Scott, W. D., ed. *Essays in German and Dutch Literature.* Institute of Germanic Studies, University of London, vii + 191 pp.

Smith, G. S. 'The Contribution of Glück and Paus to the Development of Russian Versification: The Evidence of Rhyme and Stanza Forms', *Slavonic and East European Review*, 51, 22–35.

Walsh, William. *Commonwealth Literature.* Oxford University Press, 150 pp.

1974

Binns, J. W. *The Latin Poetry of English Poets.* Routledge and Kegan Paul, x + 198 pp.

Bruford, W. H. 'Some Early Cambridge Links with German Scholarship and Literature', in *Erfahrung und Überlieferung. Festschrift for C. P. Magill* (University of Wales Press, 1974); continued in *German Life and Letters*, 28, 233–45.

Foster, John Wilson. *Forces and Themes in Ulster Fiction.* Dublin, Gill and Macmillan, 299 pp.

Hall, J. B. 'Tablante de Ricamonte and Other Castilian Versions of Arthurian Romances', *Revue de littérature comparée*, 48, 177–89.

Lyons, F. S. L. 'Two Traditions in One', *Times Literary Supplement*, 19 July, 763.

McFarlane, I. D. *Renaissance France, 1470–1589.* Benn, xxiv + 557 pp. (A literary history of France)

Magill, C. P. *German Literature.* Oxford University Press, 190 pp.

Ridley, H. 'Germany in the Mirror of its Colonial Literature', *German Life and Letters*, 28, 375–86.

Smith, Michael. 'English Translations and Imitations of Italian Madrigal Verse', *Journal of European Studies*, 4, 164–77.

Spender, Stephen. *Love–Hate Relations*, Hamish Hamilton, 246 pp.

Stanley, Eric Gerald. 'The Oldest English Poetry Now Extant', *Poetics* (Tokyo), 1, 1–24.

Williams, C. E. *The Broken Eagle. The Politics of Austrian Literature from Empire to Anschluss.* Elek, 281 pp.

VII. INDIVIDUAL AUTHORS

1971

Bawcutt, N. W. '*Don Quixote*, Part I, and *The Duchess of Malfi*', *Modern Language Review*, 66, 488–91.

Bradbury, Malcolm. '*Fanny Hill* and the Comic Novel', *Critical Quarterly*, 13, 263–75.

Coleman, Dorothy. 'Rabelais and *The Water-Babies*', *Modern Language Review*, 66, 511–21.

Downs, B. W. 'Three Seventeenth-Century Hamlets', in *European Context* (see King and Vincent, section VI above), pp. 151–63.

308   Bibliography 1971–1974

Eland, Rosamund G. 'Problems in the Middle Style: La Fontaine in Eighteenth-Century England', *Modern Language Review*, 66, 731–7.

Forster, Leonard. 'Charles Utenhove and Germany', in *European Context* (see King and Vincent, section VI above), pp. 60–80.

Gillies, A. 'John Osborn, FRS and Goethe', *Modern Language Review*, 66, 353–4.

Grover, P. R. 'Two Modes of Possessing – Conquest and Appreciation: *The Princess Casamassima* and *L'éducation sentimentale*', *Modern Language Review*, 66, 760–71.

Guest, Tanis M. 'Hadewych and Minne', in *European Context* (see King and Vincent, section VI above), pp. 14–29.

Humble, M. E. 'Early British Interest in Nietzsche', *German Life and Letters*, 24, 327–35.

Jones, Malcolm. 'Some Echoes of Hegel in Dostoyevsky', *Slavonic and East European Review*, 49, 500–20.

Mouret, François. 'Le voyage d'André Gide en littérature anglaise', *Romanistisches Jahrbuch*, 22, 162–77.

Newton de Molina, David. 'Sceptical Library Historicism: A Fictional Analogue in Jorge Luis Borges', *Essays in Criticism*, 21, 57–73.

Parry, Idris. 'Margiad Evans and Tendencies in European Literature', *Transactions of the Honourable Society of Cymmrodorion*, 1971 session, 224–36.

Saz, Sara M. 'Güiraldes and Kipling: A Possible Influence', *Neophilologus*, 55, 270–84.

Sheppard, R. 'Two Liberals: A Comparison of the Humanism of Matthew Arnold and Wilhelm von Humboldt', *German Life and Letters*, 24, 219–34.

Snowden, J. A. 'Sean O'Casey and Naturalism', *Essays and Studies*, 24, 56–68.

Tompkins, J. M. S. 'Kipling and Nordic Myth and Saga', *English Studies*, 52, 147–57.

Vincent, P. F. 'Menno ter Braak's Anglo-Saxon Attitudes', in *European Context* (see King and Vincent, section VI above), pp. 362–85.

'Sir Edmund Gosse and Frederik van Eeden: Some Reflections on an Unpublished Correspondence', *Modern Language Review*, 66, 125–38.

Waddington, Patrick. 'Turgenev and George Eliot: A Literary Friendship', *Modern Language Review*, 66, 751–9.

Walshe, M. O'C. '*Der Ackermann aus Böhmen* and *Elkerlijc*', in *European Context* (see King and Vincent, section VI above), pp. 52–9.

Watson, George. 'Orwell and the Spectrum of European Politics', *Journal of European Studies*, 1, 191–7.

Weatherby, H. L. 'Newman and Victorian Literature: A Study in the Failure of Influence', *Critical Quarterly*, 13, 205–14.

White, J. J. 'Goethe in the Machine: Georges Perec's Computer-Based Exercises with the Repertoire of "Über allen Gipfeln"', *Publications of the English Goethe Society*, 41, 103–20.

1972

Bann, Stephen. 'L'anti-histoire de Henry Esmond', *Poétique*, 9, 61–79.

Barnes, Christopher J. 'Boris Pasternak and Rainer Maria Rilke: Some Missing Links', *Forum for Modern Language Studies*, 8, 61–8.

Bickerton, David. 'A Scientific and Literary Periodical, the *Bibliothèque britannique*

(1796–1815). Its Foundation and Early Development', *Revue de littérature comparée*, 46, 527–47.

Bird, Alan. 'Rahel Varnhagen von Ense and Some English Assessments of her Character', *German Life and Letters*, 26, 183–92.

Blackman, Maurice. 'Gérard de Nerval et Thomas Moore: Note sur "Stances élégiaques"', *Revue d'histoire littéraire de la France*, 72, 428–31.

Bridgwater, Patrick. *Nietzsche in Anglosaxony: A Study of Nietzsche's Impact on English and American Literature*. Leicester University Press, 236 pp.

Briggs, A. D. 'Alexander Pushkin: A Possible Influence on Henry James', *Forum for Modern Language Studies*, 8, 52–60.

'Someone Else's Sledge: Further Notes on Turgenev's *Virgin Soil* and Henry James's *The Princess Casamassima*', *Oxford Slavonic Papers*, 5, 52–60.

Brooks, Harold. 'Dryden's *Aureng-Zebe*: Debts to Corneille and Racine', *Revue de littérature comparée*, 46, 5–34.

Brotherston, Gordon. 'How Aesop Fared in Nahuatl', *Arcadia*, 7, 37–42.

Bullen, J. B. 'Browning's "Pictor Ignotus" and Vasari's Life of Fra Bartolommeo di San Marco', *Review of English Studies*, 23, 313–19.

Close, A. J. '*Don Quixote* and the "Intentionalist Fallacy"', *British Journal of Aesthetics*, 12, 19–39.

Davies, Laurence. 'Cunninghame Graham's South American Sketches', *Comparative Literature Studies*, 9, 253–65.

Davies, Norman. 'Izaak Babel's *Konarmiya* Stories, and the Polish-Soviet War', *Modern Language Review*, 67, 845–57.

Day, W. G. 'Sterne and Ozell', *English Studies*, 53, 434–6.

Fowler, Rowena. ''Η "Ερημη Χώρα: Seferis' Translation of *The Waste Land*', *Comparative Literature Studies*, 9, 443–54.

Garson, Ronald. 'The English Aristophanes', *Revue de littérature comparée*, 46, 177–93.

Gent, C. L. '*Measure for Measure* and the Fourth Book of Castiglione's *Il Cortegiano*', *Modern Language Review*, 67, 252–6.

Hall, Kathleen M. 'A Defence of Jean de la Taille as a Translator of Ariosto', *Modern Language Review*, 67, 537–42.

Hemmings, F. W. J. 'Emile Zola devant l'Exposition universelle de 1878', *Cahiers de l'Association internationale des études françaises*, 24, 131–53.

Henry, P. L. 'The Land of Cockaygne: Cultures in Contact in Medieval Ireland', *Studia Hibernica*, 12, 120–41.

Hutchinson, Peter. 'Franz Fühmann's *Böhmen am Meer*: A Socialist Version of *The Winter's Tale*', *Modern Language Review*, 67, 579–89.

Jones, G. L. 'The Mulde's "Half-Prodigal Son": Paul Fleming, Germany and the Thirty Years' War', *German Life and Letters*, 26, 125–36.

Kuna, F. M. 'Art as Direct Vision: Kafka and Sacher-Masoch', *Journal of European Studies*, 2, 237–46.

Limentani, U. 'Foscolo and the Wells Family', *Italian Studies*, 27, 64–84; 28 (1973), 50–1.

Lofmark, Carl. 'Wolfram's Source References in *Parzival*', *Modern Language Review*, 67, 820–44.

Lyle, E. B. 'Two Parallels in *Macbeth* to Seneca's *Hercules Oetaeus*', *English Studies*, 53, 109–12.

Mainzer, Conrad. 'John Gower's Use of the "Mediaeval Ovid" in the *Confessio Amantis*', *Medium Aevum*, 41, 215–29.

Mistry, F. 'Hofmannsthal's Response to China in his Unpublished "Über chinesische Gedichte"', *German Life and Letters*, 26, 306–14.

Morris, J. A. 'T. S. Eliot and Antisemitism', *Journal of European Studies*, 2, 173–82.

Rogers, Pat. 'Freedom and Fidelity in Augustan Translation: An Adapted Version of Bouhours', *Revue de littérature comparée*, 46, 360–75.

Smith, James. 'Notes on the Criticism of T. S. Eliot', *Essays in Criticism*, 22, 333–61.

Thomson, Patricia. 'George Sand and English Reviewers: The First Twenty Years', *Modern Language Review*, 67, 501–16.

1973

Auty, Robert. 'Prešeren's German Poems', *Oxford Slavonic Papers*, 6, 1–11.

Barnes, Annie. 'Proust et Goethe', *Oxford German Studies*, 8, 128–48.

Batchelor, R. 'The Presence of Nietzsche in André Malraux', *Journal of European Studies*, 3, 218–29.

Bryan-Kinns, Merrick. 'Philippe Habert's *Temple de la Mort*: Probable Source of a German Baroque Allegory', *Arcadia*, 8, 296–9.

Cain, Tom. 'Tolstoy's Use of *David Copperfield*', *Critical Quarterly*, 15, 237–46.

Donaghey, B. S. 'Another English Manuscript of an Old French Translation of Boethius', *Medium Aevum*, 42, 38–43.

Duncan, Alistair B. 'Claude Simon and William Faulkner', *Forum for Modern Language Studies*, 9, 235–52.

Foote, I. P. '*Otechestvennye Zapiski* and English Literature, 1868–84', *Oxford Slavonic Papers*, 6, 28–47.

Green, R. J. 'Oscar Wilde's *Intentions*: An Early Modernist Manifesto', *British Journal of Aesthetics*, 13, 397–404.

Greenwood, E. B. 'Eikhenbaum, Formalism, and Tolstoy', *Essays in Criticism*, 23, 372–87.

Hibberd, John. 'Gessner in England', *Revue de littérature comparée*, 47, 296–306.

Honderich, Pauline. 'John Calvin and Doctor Faustus', *Modern Language Review*, 68, 1–13.

Jephcott, E. F. N. *Proust and Rilke*. Chatto and Windus, 315 pp.

Jones, Michael R. 'Censorship as an Obstacle to the Production of Shakespeare on the Stage of the Burgtheater in the Nineteenth Century', *German Life and Letters*, 27, 187–94.

Lewis, Hanna B. 'Hofmannsthal, Shelley, and Keats', *German Life and Letters*, 27, 220–34.

Makin, Peter. 'Ezra Pound and Scotus Erigena', *Comparative Literature Studies*, 10, 60–83.

McVay, Gordon. 'Sergey Esenin in America', *Oxford Slavonic Papers*, 6, 82–91.

Moloney, Brian. 'Svevo as a Jewish Writer', *Italian Studies*, 28, 52–63.

Ó Tuama, Seán. 'Seán Ó Ríordáin agus an nuafhilíocht', *Studia Hibernica*, 13, 100–67.

Parkin, John. 'Machiavellism in Etienne Pasquier's *Pourparler du prince*', *Modern Language Review*, 68, 530–44.

Reynolds, Lorna. 'Collective Intellect: Yeats, Synge and Nietzsche', *Essays and Studies*, 26, 83–98.

Ridley, Hugh. 'The Colonial Imagination: A Comparison of Kipling with French and German Colonial Writers', *Revue de littérature comparée*, 47, 574–85.
'Hans Grimm and Rudyard Kipling', *Modern Language Review*, 68, 863–9.

Roe, G. M. W. 'Paul Valéry as a Literary Critic: Theory and Practice', *Nottingham French Studies*, 13, 23–32; 73–84.

Thomson, Patricia. '*Wuthering Heights* and *Mauprat*', *Review of English Studies*, 24, 26–37.

Thorlby, Ant[h]ony. 'Liberty and Self-Development: Goethe and John Stuart Mill', *Neohelicon*, 1, no. 3–4, 91–110.

Turner, C. J. G. 'A Slavonic Version of John Cantecuzenus's *Against Islam*', *Slavonic and East European Review*, 51, 113–17.

Wells, Margaret Brady. 'Du Bellay and Fracastoro', *Modern Language Review*, 68, 756–61.

Whitfield, J. H. 'Machiavelli Guicciardini Montaigne', *Italian Studies*, 28, 31–47.

Williams, C. E. 'Not an Inn, but a Hospital. *The Magic Mountain* and *Cancer Ward*', *Forum for Modern Language Studies*, 9, 311–32.

1974

Close, Anthony. 'Don Quixote as a Burlesque Hero: A Re-Constructed Eighteenth-Century View', *Forum for Modern Language Studies*, 10, 365–78.

Doherty, F. 'Boyle and *Tristram Shandy*: "Stage-Loads of Chymical Nostrums and Peripatetic Lumber"', *Neophilologus*, 58, 339–48.

Fiddian, R. W. 'Unamuno – Bergson: A Reconsideration', *Modern Language Review*, 69, 787–95.

Furst, Lilian R. 'Stefan George's *Die Blumen des Bösen*: A Problem of Translation', *Revue de littérature comparée*, 48, 203–17.

Grover, P. R. 'French Literature and James's Early Criticism, 1864–1874', *Forum for Modern Language Studies*, 10, 300–12.

Haggis, D. R. 'Fiction and Historical Change: *La Cousine Bette* and the Lesson of Walter Scott', *Forum for Modern Language Studies*, 10, 323–33.
'*Clotilde de Lusignan, Ivanhoe*, and the Development of Scott's Influence on Balzac', *French Studies*, 28, 159–68.

Hough, Graham. 'Dante and Eliot', *Critical Quarterly*, 16, 293–306.

Jacoby, E. G. 'Thomas Hobbes in Europe', *Journal of European Studies*, 4, 57–65.

Knowles, Dorothy. 'Eugène Ionesco's Rhinoceroses: Their Romanian Origin and their Western Fortunes', *French Studies*, 28, 294–307.

Low, Donald A. 'Byron and Europe', *Journal of European Studies*, 4, 364–7.

McGurk, P. 'Computus Helperici: Its Transmission in England in the Eleventh and Twelfth Centuries', *Medium Aevum*, 43, 1–5.

Mulryne, J. R. 'The French Source for the Sub-plot of Middleton's *Women Beware Women*', *Review of English Studies*, 25, 439–45.

Philip Grover, *Henry James and the French Novel*. Elek, 221 pp.

Ringrose, C. X. 'F. R. Leavis and Yvor Winters on G. M. Hopkins', *English Studies*, 55, 32–42.

Shields, Hugh. 'A Text of Nicole Bozon's "Proverbes de bon enseignement" in Irish Transmission', *Modern Language Review*, 69, 274–8.
Stang, Maurice. 'The German Original of a George Eliot Poem', *Notes & Queries*, 219, 15.
Williams, David. 'Observations on an English Translation of Voltaire's Commentary on Corneille', *Studies on Voltaire and the Eighteenth Century*, 124, 143–8.
Woodman, A. J. 'Sleepless Poets: Catullus and Keats', *Greece & Rome*, 21, 51–3.

VIII. LITERATURE AND THE OTHER ARTS

1971

Ettinghausen, Henry. 'Neo-Stoicism in Pictures: Lipsius and the Engraved Title-Page and Portrait in Quevedo's *Epicteto y Phocilides*', *Modern Language Review*, 66, 94–100.
Gordon, Catherine. 'The Illustration of Sir Walter Scott. Nineteenth-Century Enthusiasm and Adaptation', *Journal of the Warburg and Courtauld Institutes*, 34, 297–317.
Holcomb, Adèle M. 'Turner and Scott', *Journal of the Warburg and Courtauld Institutes*, 34, 386–97.
Kelley, D. J. 'Delacroix, Ingres and Poe: Valeurs picturales et valeurs littéraires dans l'œuvre critique de Baudelaire', *Revue d'histoire littéraire de la France*, 71, 606–14.
Little, Roger. 'Saint-John Perse and Music', *French Studies*, 25, 305–13.
Robson-Scott, W. D. 'Goethe and the Art of the Netherlands', in *European Context* (see King and Vincent, section VI above), pp. 194–208.
Sparkes, B. A. 'The Trojan Horse in Classical Art', *Greece & Rome*, 18, 54–70.
Thompson, C. W. 'John Martin et l'image de la ville moderne chez Vigny et Lamartine', *Revue de littérature comparée*, 45, 5–17.

1972

Brodsley, Laurel. 'Butler's Character of Hudibras and Contemporary Graphic Satire', *Journal of the Warburg and Courtauld Institutes*, 35, 401–4.
Falaschi, Enid T. 'Giotto: The Literary Legend', *Italian Studies*, 27, 1–27.
Finley, Gerald E. 'J. M. W. Turner and Sir Walter Scott: Iconography of a Tour', *Journal of the Warburg and Courtauld Institutes*, 35, 359–85.
Fowler, Alastair. 'Periodization and Interart Analogies', *New Literary History*, 3, 487–510.
Murdoch, J. D. W. 'Scott, Pictures, and Pointers', *Modern Language Review*, 67, 31–43.
Prickett, Stephen. 'Dante, Beatrice and M. C. Escher: Disconfirmation as a Metaphor', *Journal of European Studies*, 2, 333–54.
Rolfe, C. D. *Saint-Amant and the Theory of 'Ut pictura poesis'*. Modern Humanities Research Association, 113 pp.
Rothenberg, J. 'Music in the Theatre of Jean Anouilh', *Forum for Modern Language Studies*, 8, 345–53.

Sayce, Richard. 'Littérature et architecture au XVIIe siècle', *Cahiers de l'Association internationale des études françaises*, 24, 233–50.

Thompson, C. W. 'Mérimée and Pictorial Inspiration: The Sources of *Les Ames du Purgatoire*', *Modern Language Review*, 67, 62–73.

1973

Cardinal, Roger. 'Image and Word in Schizophrenic Creation', *Forum for Modern Language Studies*, 9, 103–20.

Driscoll, Irene Joan. 'Visual Allusion in the Work of Théophile Gautier', *French Studies*, 27, 418–28.

Findlay, Charles. 'The Opera and Operatic Elements in the Fragmentary Biography of Johannes Kreisler', *German Life and Letters*, 27, 22–34.

Higgins, Ian. 'Towards a Poetic Theatre: Poetry and the Plastic Arts in Verhaeren's Aesthetics', *Forum for Modern Language Studies*, 9, 1–23. Higgins edited seven essays from this issue of *Forum for Modern Language Studies* (entered separately) under the title *Literature and the Plastic Arts, 1880–1930* (Scottish Academic Press, x + 123 pp.).

Meech, Peter. 'The Frog and the Star: The Role of Music in the Dramatic and Visual Works of Ernst Barlach', *Forum for Modern Language Studies*, 9, 24–34.

Noszlopy, George T. 'Apollinaire, Allegorical Imagery and the Visual Arts', *Forum for Modern Language Studies*, 9, 49–74.

Bell, Quentin. 'Art and the Elite', *Critical Inquiry*, 1, no. 1, 33–46.

Gifford, D. J. 'Iconographical Notes towards a Definition of the Medieval Fool', *Journal of the Warburg and Courtauld Institutes*, 37, 336–42.

Meyers, Jeffrey. 'Greuze and Lampedusa's *Il Gattopardo*', *Modern Language Review*, 69, 308–15.

Mitchells, K. '"Nur nicht lesen! Immer singen!" Goethe's "Lieder" into Schubert Lieder', *Publications of the English Goethe Society*, 44, 63–82.

Comparative Criticism 15, p. 314. Copyright © 1993 Cambridge University Press

Errata

'*Playback*: A play for radio' by Gabriel Josipovici, *Comparative Criticism*, volume 14, pp. 155–70.

The last line on page 169 should have read MARY (*over*): Another cup of tea Daddy?

'Extracts from Mikhail Bulgakov, *The White Guard/The Days of the Turbins*', translated by Patrick Miles, *Comparative Criticism*, volume 14, pp. 247–57.

The publisher very much regrets that no translator's proof corrections were incorporated in the publication of this translation, and it thus included a number of errors and misprints (numbers refer to page and line numbers):

247, l. 19   'But didn't you see...' should have read 'But don't you see...'

248, l. 3   '*Bandit in a nobleman's peaked hat*' should have read '*Bandit in a Nobleman's Peaked Hat*'

248, l. 24   'Tfuui' should have read 'Tfui'

248, l. 40   'so to have more' should have read 'so as to have more'

249, l. 21   'And Nikolka.' should have read 'And Nikolka?'

249, l. 30   'Look what's happened...' should have read 'Look what's happening...'

250, l. 20   '*Uragen*' should have read '*Uragan*'

250, l. 42   'Keep your hands up!' should have read 'Keep your hand up!'

250, l. 44   'he doesn't feed his own wife' should have read 'he doesn't feed his own wife.'

251, l. 22   'concealing property than belongs...' should have read 'concealing property that belongs...'

252, l. 18   'We're here on order...' should have read 'We're here on orders...'

252, l. 41   'Don't worry:' should have read 'Don't worry, don't worry:'

254, l. 28   '*Myshlaeyevsky*' should have read '*Myshlayevsky*'

257, l. 9   'by bark.' should have read 'my bark.'

The translation of the extract from Act IV, Finale on page 257 should have been attributed to Lesley Milne, author of 'Unbowdlerizing Bulgakov', the article which the translation accompanied.

Lightning Source UK Ltd.
Milton Keynes UK
12 July 2010

156832UK00001BA/9/P